HOW YOUR
HORSE WANTS
YOU TO RIDE

T0266501

Also by Gincy Self Bucklin:

What Your Horse Wants You to Know: What Horses' "Bad" Behavior Means, and How to Correct It

HOW YOUR HORSE WANTS YOU TO RIDE

Starting Out ∾ Starting Over

GINCY SELF BUCKLIN

HOWELL
BOOK
HOUSE

Howell Book House
Published by Wiley Publishing, Inc., Hoboken, NJ
Published simultaneously in Canada

For general information about our other products and services, please contact our Customer Care Department within the United States at (800) 762-2974, outside the United States at (317) 572-3993 or fax (317) 572-4002.

Wiley also publishes its books in a variety of electronic formats. Some content that appears in print may not be available in electronic books. For more information about Wiley products, visit our web site at www.wiley.com.

Library of Congress Cataloging-in-Publication data is available from the publisher upon request.

ISBN: 0-7645-7099-4

Printed in the United States of America

10 9 8 7 6 5 4 3 2 1

To Harris Howard Bucklin Jr., finest of horsemen and best of husbands, this book is lovingly dedicated.

"There is only one kind of mistake, that is, the fundamental mistake. Regardless of how advanced the exercise, if the performance is defective, one can directly trace that fault to a lack in the fundamental training of either the horse or the rider."

—Erik Herbermann

Contents

Acknowledgments

This book represents a lifetime of help from my teachers, my students and my horses, but it owes its existence as a manuscript to Brigit van Loggem, who encouraged me to write it and helped me through the early years of its creation. It owes its existence as an actual published book to my agent, Pat Snell, who made me write and rewrite the proposal more times than either of us wants to remember, and to my daughter, Karen Hayes, who encouraged and nagged as needed to keep me going. My editor, Beth Adelman, has been invaluable in supporting me when I get discouraged, helping me work to deadline and answering all my questions about the publishing business. My thanks also especially to George Morris and Jane Savoie for taking the time during their busy Florida season to write the kind remarks on the back of this book. And finally, I want to thank again the members and contributors to my Riding With Confidence e-group, who constantly challenge me on the one hand, and on the other, bring new thoughts and concepts to me every day.

And thank you to publisher J. A. Allen & Co., Ltd., and Mr. Herbermann himself, for allowing me to include the quote on page vi from Erik Herbermann's 1999 book *Dressage Formula,* Third Edition.

Photo acknowledgments: For their generous contributions of time and their patience, I am most grateful to the following:

Photographers: Terri Miller for the cover; Ron Whittemore, to whom special thanks are due for the many hours he spent in ice-cold indoor arenas in New England in February; also Josh Sprague, Karen Hayes, Douglas Murray and Paul Coupland.

Models, Humans: Kelly Shine and Liz Anderson (cover), Peg Megan, Douglas Murray, Katy Murray, Heather Holloway, Jackey Davies. Equine (and their owners): Fox Robin and Honey (cover), Sammy and Edie Johnson, Prince William (Wills) and Maggie Clarke, Colette Star and Judy Truesdale, Miss Kitty Coker and Kathy Bowser.

Locations: Clouds Hill Farm, Cherry Croft Farm, Glen Farm, Castlefield Farm.

Introduction

How It All Began
30 Years of Revelations

When my husband and I retired from actively running a large stable and riding program, I naturally had time on my hands. I started exploring the Internet and stumbled across the horsey newsgroups. Eventually I found my way to the Horseman Off-Topic group, and discovered the joys of talking to like-minded fellow horse people all over the world. With my extensive experience as a professional, I could often help others with problem solving. When Brigit, one of my correspondents from the Netherlands and an editor by trade, suggested I should write a book, I agreed to try. As a result of her invaluable assistance—and constant nagging—over a period of several years, this book was written.

Why did I accept her challenge? Why does any one write a book? Because they have something to say that they think is important, and they want the message to reach a large group of people. Also, it must be a message that is too complex to be transmitted in a few words, or even pictures. My message is twofold: **I believe anyone who really wants to can ride well, I think people who love horses should have the pleasure of enjoying riding them, and, most important of all, I think the horses should enjoy it too.** This book starts you on the way to accomplishing those goals.

The next question might be, what qualifies me to make that statement? As the daughter of Margaret Cabell Self, a well-known instructor and author of horse books, I grew up with a solid background in teaching, which, as of this writing, I have been doing for nearly 60 years. Growing up in an area with many top show stables and Olympic riders also exposed me to the best there was in riding. For many years I followed the traditional methods of how to teach riding.

Then, about 30 years ago, I was teaching in Connecticut at a moderate-sized stable, one that I also comanaged. We had the usual mix of students and schedules, but it happened that I had two classes, back to back, of teenagers in the 14- to 16-year range. The first class, a group of advanced beginners riding less than a year, were walking, trotting and learning basic control. The second, my most advanced group, had been riding six years or more and were showing over fences and training their own horses.

For weeks I taught the two lessons, one right after the other. Then one day I suddenly realized that I was repeating myself! Even though each group was training at a completely different level, I was giving the advanced riders the *same* corrections as the beginners. That is, there were basic skills they had started working on when *they* were beginners that they *still* hadn't mastered! I would find myself saying, "Look up," "Get your weight back," or "Heels down," just as often to the advanced class as I did to the beginners.

I pondered this for some time, then came to the conclusion that I hadn't spent enough time making sure the beginners had *mastered* each skill before I moved them on to the next. This meant that when they tried to learn a new skill, they would lose some of the old one, since they couldn't think about both at the same time. Then, since each skill was built on the preceding ones, as they advanced the students became in many ways *less* competent, not *more*. And of course, by permitting them to do things the wrong way, I allowed their faults to develop into habits they couldn't break.

At about the same time, a group of mothers of my younger students decided they would like to learn to ride as well. They all talked about how frightened they were, how concerned they were about having an accident, which, of course, none of them could afford.

In those days the usual first lesson was to quickly introduce the student to the horse, put her on and give her the reins and stirrups. After some walking, unless she was terribly awkward or nervous, she would try to trot. Her trotting would be dangerously tense and clumsy, but of course that was the way beginners trotted!

Thinking about how my advanced students hadn't learned their basic skills made me realize that having a student trot in her first lesson was about the equivalent of having a beginning driver travel at 40 mph on a major thoroughfare the first time out. So as I planned the first lesson for my nervous mothers, I decided to give them a fairly extensive introduction to the horse on the ground, followed by having each rider sit on her horse briefly and walk a few steps as correctly as possible.

When I suggested this change in routine to my partners, they were horrified. The students would hate it! They would be bored to death and never return. But I managed to prevail and the lesson went as planned. To the astonishment of my partners, and even a little to me, my students loved it! Instead of being tense and fearful, they talked about how secure they felt. Several of them said they would feel more comfortable if their children were started the same way. **This made me see that having new students spend time getting to know the horse before trying to ride him was an important addition to the learning process.**

With this encouragement, I began to develop a totally different way to teach riding. **My goal was to design a program that would build—and maintain—correct skills from the very beginning.** I began taking my new students much more slowly, spending more time on each step. We played lots of slow games, went for trail walks with hand leaders and did other things that would entertain the students' minds while their bodies learned how to ride.

After a year or two of this, I was delighted to see that my students were indeed learning to ride more correctly sooner, with better balance and less tension. But I also noticed something else that I hadn't expected.

It is common practice on most school horses for the rider to carry a stick, which sometimes needs to be used with a bit of firmness. Novice riders, especially timid ones, are notoriously reluctant to use the stick, partly because the horse may respond with a sudden movement, and partly, I suspect, because they don't want to make him angry. But my new students didn't have this problem. Even the most timid ones, when told to use the stick, were quite willing to do so. I don't mean that they became aggressive, simply that the new, slower way of teaching seemed to have made them more *confident*.

This marked the beginning of my interest in the problem of dealing with fear. I saw that most riders who lack confidence do so because they tried to do too much too soon. Therefore, I could help fearful riders by taking them back and starting them again slowly; **by rebuilding their physical skills, I could rebuild their confidence at the same time.**

This, in turn, led to a new discovery: **Because the riders weren't trying to do things that they weren't ready for, the horses weren't being abused as beginner school horses usually are, so they were far less "disobedient." This, in turn, increased the riders' confidence, so they were more relaxed; the horses were more relaxed as well, and enjoyed their work much more.**

Over the next 30 years I worked with many different people of all abilities and ages on all sorts of horses. I took clinics with instructors I admired, to increase my own skills and knowledge. With the help of my students, my horses, and the instructors under my tutelage, I gradually fine-tuned the program so that **almost anyone can use it to learn to ride correctly, safely, and confidently, and keep the horse happy and comfortable throughout the learning process as well.** The *goals*—relaxation, balance, understanding—do not differ appreciably from those of any riding program, but the *method* for reaching those goals is far more detailed, with much more time spent on the *basic concepts*. Because I have taught so many riders over such a long period, I am familiar with nearly all the problems that students run into while learning, so I am able to incorporate solutions for these problems into the book. Thus the problems can be addressed or avoided before they lead to more and more serious difficulties.

When I try to explain to a new student the reasoning behind my methods, which are so different from those of typical instructors, I often liken them to finishing a piece of furniture. One way, the so-called easy way, is to do a minimum of preparation, then slap on a couple of coats of varnish and consider it done. The furniture may, from a distance, look fine. But when you put it to use, the finish is rough, it starts to chip, and before long it has to be refinished. Again, you have a choice of throwing on a couple more coats of varnish, but the same problems will quickly reoccur. If you want to fix it right, you have to remove all the old coats and start over. *Very* time-consuming and tedious.

The *right* way—which appears at first glance to be the harder, longer way— is to spend the necessary time in preparation—what artisans call the prep work. You carefully sand each piece, first with coarse, then gradually finer and finer grades of sandpaper, followed by a thin coat of varnish, then more sanding, another coat and so on until you have built up a solid foundation that is impervious to damage.

When you do the work this way, there is a long period where nothing much seems to be accomplished; but when you are finished, it's for good! In the same way, when you build a solid foundation for riding by proceeding slowly and carefully, you seem to spend a long time at a very "beginnery" level, but you actually reach a level of *true* competence—and confidence—far sooner.

HOW TO USE THIS BOOK

If you are an experienced rider who wants to improve, you can work directly from the book without outside help. You should start in a safe space, such as a round pen or small arena, so you can concentrate on your body without worrying about controlling the horse. If you are a beginning student, you must start out with help from an experienced person. The horse, carefully chosen for his quiet temperament, is held or led by a ground person during all the early lessons, whether you are on or off the horse. Gradually, over a period of weeks, the instructor or assistant should allow you more freedom, in a limited space, not to control the horse but to discover that you don't *have* to control him. At this stage you only want the horse to walk or jog quietly as best he can under your unbalanced body, so the horse has no need to be "disobedient." Later on, as you grow in competence and knowledge, you can begin to ask the horse to listen to you and accept your guidance.

For either level of student, eventually it becomes simply a matter of adding the basic skills—developing balance at the different gaits, both sitting and standing in the stirrups; managing the reins; learning to use your aids without losing your position, and *only then* learning to use them to communicate with the horse. **Once you have fully mastered these skills, you can do anything on a horse that the horse is able and willing to do.**

One of the reasons you may not spend enough time working on your basic skills is the feeling that you aren't getting anywhere. Just like the person refinishing the furniture. Therefore, I have included an arrangement for keeping track of your progress. One of the things that impressed me about the Parelli training method is that it makes the "prep work" interesting. What Parelli has done, and what I have tried to do in this book, is to divide your progress into different stages.

Pat Parelli calls his stages Levels. I have chosen to call mine Plateaus because riders tend to think of reaching a plateau as a negative. "I seem to be at a plateau, and I'm not getting anywhere," is a familiar complaint. But being on a plateau really means that your mind and body have taken in an enormous amount of information, and now they have to process it. What you should observe when you are on a plateau is not that you are constantly learning new stuff, which is what you are doing as you are "climbing" to the plateau. Instead, you are now focused on improving the skills you learned on the climb. Rather than thinking, "Oh, I'm still working on shortening my reins," you should find yourself thinking, "Wow, I can shorten my reins so much more easily than I could a month ago." When you are on a plateau, your body is storing information in muscle memory. You find yourself, for example, shortening and lengthening your reins *without thinking about it* when your horse shortens or lengthens his neck. When he spooks a little, you *immediately* grow, breathe, center and ground, instead of curling up in a ball and hauling on his mouth! The plateaus, and the steps that lead to each one, are covered in Appendix B.

Using this book to help you in the learning process, you have the option of following it pretty much in the sequence in which it is written, or of skipping around. You may want to work on one concept for a while, then go on to another and come back to the first one later on. This is often a good thing to do if you find you are stuck. By following the flow chart in Appendix C, you can determine where to go next, and what to go back to if you get in over your head. This will be another gauge of your progress, and will add variety to your learning. Remember, it should be fun! Just be careful not to get so hung up on "progress" that you don't spend enough time just consolidating what you have learned until you truly know it.

Especially for novices, as indicated in the Plateaus, the work on the ground should be interwoven with actual riding. Generally speaking, I don't believe that the novice should be asked to control the horse *in any way* until she feels really comfortable with him. This means that tacking and leading, which are often taught in the first lesson, should be left until a good deal later on. Other than that, if you are more experienced and have a particular hang-up, you may want to work on that right away and skip some earlier chapters. Throughout the book, if there is something you need to know from another chapter there will be a reference.

There are some chapters that you *should* read first (besides this one!) They are the first two chapters, and Chapter 7. Chapters 2 and 7, The Seven Steps, Parts I and II, are especially important, and there are constant references to them throughout the book. **They are the foundation on which all your riding skills will be built.**

I would like to thank Mary Wanless for the writing concept of referring to all riders as "she" and all horses as "he," which simplifies explanations enormously. I refuse to refer to the horse as "it" as though he were an inanimate object, which thinking lies at the bottom of a great deal of abuse. I apologize to any male humans or female horses who may be offended by this convention.

Finally, I would ask you to consider something else about working from a book—about working from *any* book. Even when you read a thing carefully, if it is complex it is rare for you to understand it completely the first time. You have to try bits of it, then *come back and read some more*, and other pieces will start to make sense. It's a little like putting together a disassembled piece of furniture from the directions. They always tell you to read all the directions first, and you start to, but you find yourself completely confused after the first few paragraphs. So you say, "The heck with it," and you find part A and start fitting it together with part B. As you work along, not only does the piece of furniture start to make sense, but so do the directions. This book is arranged so that fitting part A to part B is fairly easy. I hope you enjoy it and find it useful, which is to say I hope it helps you to enjoy your horse and your riding to the fullest.

Part I

Getting Started or Starting Over

Success Is Easier Than You Think

1

Looking into Your Future
A Confident Rider on a Confident Horse

I have always been interested in learning more about my trade. There is so much to know that you never learn it all, but the more sources you investigate, the more tools you have to work with. As a result of this, I was watching a videotape about a well-recognized ground training system. The trainer was working with a horse who was obviously very tense and difficult, and it was fascinating to watch how much the horse improved in both comfort and attitude under the trainer's guidance. Then, as the tape approached its end, the owner got back on the horse to see how he had improved. Well! The owner was an absolutely appalling rider—unbalanced, rough, and clumsy! The poor horse struggled to apply his new lessons, but his owner's incompetence interfered with all of his efforts. I suspect the trainer must have felt a degree of frustration, as well. I know I would cheerfully have slaughtered the owner, had it been me!

This is the one argument I have with ground training systems. There tends to be a certain implication that if you develop a good relationship with your horse, you don't have to bother with anything else. **Nothing could be more wrong, or more unfair to your horse.** If you've ever carried anyone piggyback, even for a few minutes, you know how much their movements affect your ability to balance and move easily.

As I said in the Introduction, learning to ride correctly first means developing a good foundation, and this takes time—more time than many students are willing to take or their instructors to give. Unless they are very lucky, nearly all of these students—and their horses—eventually end up in difficulties.

∽

Full of enthusiasm and courage, Darcy was in her early 20s when she came to ride with me. She loved horses and was eager to pick up again the riding career she had begun as a child. However, because her life was now teeming with other activities as well, she could only ride once a week. Other, more experienced riders were cantering, jumping, and showing. Darcy was eager to do the same, instead of working on perfecting basic skills. She seemed to listen patiently to explanations that she wasn't ready, that trying the "fun stuff" too soon could be dangerous and result in bad habits. More importantly, her lack of riding skills would interfere with the horse, making him uncomfortable or even scaring him—hardly fair to the horse. But she knew there were other stables in the area that would allow her to do what she wanted, so after a few months she left.

Continuing to take lessons in the area, Darcy soon bought her own horse. In a very short time she was showing at a moderately advanced level. But there she stuck. She had achieved just enough skill to perform adequately, but was never willing to do the necessary work to overcome the bad habits she had developed in her hurry to move up. Periodically she would change stables and work with a new instructor, and often change horses as well, but since she lacked the proper foundation, she was never able to progress beyond mediocrity.

Darcy loved horses and riding, yet was unlikely to reach her full potential as a happy, competent rider. Only if she was willing to change her thinking, or even start again, would she be likely to eventually ride with both skill and confidence and provide her horse with the comfort he needed.

☙

One of the most difficult tasks facing any instructor is teaching the student the necessity of learning slowly. Some of my best pupils have been those who have had traumatic experiences with horses. Caught between their fears and their love of horses, the only way they could cope was to be very, very cautious. The result was the **necessary willingness to go slowly, and spend the time on the basics that every rider needs** if she is to learn to ride correctly.

Let's put it right up front: This book is about learning to ride correctly, so it contains a lot about *equitation*! But, you say, I'm not *interested* in equitation. I'm never going to show, and you only need to know about equitation if you're going to show, right? Wrong! Equitation is what it's *all* about. But read on.

Webster defines "equitation" as "the art of riding," and defines "art" as "a skill" or "system of rules." Nope, you say, I'm still not interested. I don't want to fool around with a lot of rules, I just want to have fun. Well, I go along with that, but how much fun would you have playing golf if you couldn't hit the ball most of the time, or skiing if you fell down every 50 feet? **Every skill has a system of rules, and the purpose of those rules is to help you to be successful.** That's what equitation is—a system of rules that enables you to ride successfully. Which, in turn, makes the horse more comfortable and more obedient, so when you go out to have fun on the trail you don't get run off with, and the horse goes where and as fast or slow as *you* want to go. And you both have fun.

One more thing. There is *nothing* in equitation that does not have a valid purpose that is important for both you and the horse!

Now let's talk a little more specifically about what's in the book. This is a book that can teach you how to ride *well* much faster than any other method you've tried. But let's make sure that you understand my definition of riding well. Many people's definition of a good rider is someone who jumps high jumps, or rides in advanced dressage tests or reining classes. It is true that many of those people *are* good riders, but it is perfectly possible to engage in those endeavors because you are brave, or possibly a little stupid, or rich enough to afford a horse and a trainer who can get you to the big leagues, whatever your skills.

My definition of a good rider is someone who can ride in a way that always gets the best out of a particular horse at a particular moment and in such a way that the horse feels successful as well, and whose horses continue to improve over time. A good rider is safe, comfortable on the horse, and able to get him to do what she wants through willing cooperation rather than fear.

If you are reading this book seriously, it's because you want to become a better rider. You probably agree, at least in part, with the definition I've just given. And what are the necessary qualifications for becoming a good rider? Many people think it's having the "right build": slender, long-legged, elegant. Certainly it is easier to learn the physical skills of riding with a good build, but I have known many top riders who didn't fit that mold at all.

Perhaps it's being a good athlete? But no, many people ride successfully well into old age when they can't even walk very well anymore, and many people who are severely disabled are still able to ride well. Or perhaps you have to be "born on a horse," that is, start riding when you are very young and ride a lot thereafter. I can tell you from personal experience that doesn't necessarily work. I could ride before I could walk, but by the time I was 20 I had developed so many bad habits that I had to learn all over again.

The answer is very simple: **Anybody can learn to be a good rider who really wants to!** No great talent, as you would need to become even an adequate musician. No great athletic skills, such as you would need to compete successfully in any other athletic endeavor. Just the willingness to *learn*, and the patience to spend the time it takes to *know* and *understand*. And I can safely say that becoming a *good* rider and becoming a *confident rider on a comfortable horse* are virtually synonymous!

LEARNING, KNOWING, AND UNDERSTANDING

I am standing out by the parking lot talking to a client when a car drives in. A man gets out and asks, "Do you rent horses?" "No," I reply, "we only offer lessons." Immediately he comes back with, "Oh, I don't need any lessons. I *know* how to ride!"

I have experienced this many times, as I'm sure everyone has who manages a riding establishment open to the public. It usually turns out this person either rode a little as a child or has rented horses from a hack stable before and survived the experience. It is very difficult to get some of them to take no for an answer. This is a perfect example of someone who doesn't know the difference between learning, knowing, and understanding. He has, at some time *learned* a bit about riding, but has not had enough experience to find out what he doesn't *know*, far less what he doesn't *understand*.

Let's explore the difference between learning and knowing. Using arithmetic as an example, when you are learning to add, you *learn* by repetition. To *know* your addition tables, you must practice them over and over until, when someone asks, "What's eight and nine?" the correct answer, 17, comes out of your mouth without any conscious thought. *It has become a reflex.*

When you practice a physical activity until you know it in the same way, it is sometimes called "putting it into your muscle memory." This simply means that your muscles now know how to do it without any input from your conscious mind. When you are building a skill, it is essential that each step be worked on and practiced until it is in your muscle memory before you start to concentrate on the next step. Why? Because you can only think of—that is, focus on—one thing at a time. If you have to *think* about staying on your horse, and keeping your feet in the stirrups, and posting, and holding your reins correctly, and steering, and paying attention to where the horse is going, you are going to do *all* of them badly.

It is this need to practice each step at some length that is probably at the root of most of the problems people have learning to ride well and confidently.

Arranging practice time is not easy for the novice, who, for safety reasons should not try to ride on her own. A good instructor will allow practice time during each lesson. Games and controlled trail rides on a safe horse are other ways to gain the necessary "mileage." Unfortunately, the average amateur rider spends only one or two hours a week on a horse; therefore, the time it takes to build a good foundation is spread out over months and years. It is not always easy for a busy, active person to be patient. However, this is by far the fastest way to become an accomplished rider, because once the foundation is solid, the more advanced skills come easily.

There is another aspect of the learning process that is often overlooked. Besides the time spent riding, it seems to take a certain amount of *elapsed* time for a new skill to sink in. I have observed that while a student learns faster taking two lessons a week than taking one, she doesn't learn *twice* as fast. Apparently, there is a law of diminishing returns involved, because any student can only absorb just so much new information at once.

Sometimes it is months or even years before a piece of information learned earlier finally fits into place and begins to make sense. This is where the

---

Tidbits & Supplements

One learning aid that you may find useful is to review your ride—whether taught or not—on the way home, perhaps even keeping a diary. It is surprising how often you will come up with a new approach to a problem just by thinking about it quietly. A friend of mind keeps a running record on an appointment calendar. She makes brief notes of what she did each day, whether riding or groundwork, and what they accomplished. In the process, she finds herself reviewing the ride and rethinking it. Looking back over past months gives her a sense of how her riding is progressing over the long term, as well.

---

understanding part comes in. You *learn* to shorten and lengthen your reins early in your riding career. You practice shortening and lengthening them until the actions are automatic, and you no longer have to think about them because you *know* how to do it. But it may be much later in your riding career before you fully *understand* how shortening and lengthening your reins affects your and your horse's balance and grounding.

ESPECIALLY FOR BEGINNERS, OR THOSE WITH SERIOUS FEARS

Rider fear is the cause of probably 75 percent of the problems riders have with their horses. The tensions created, both physical and emotional, make the horse tense as well, so his responses to the aids are delayed, awkward or incorrect. Fear causes the rider's body to react in ways that often hurt the horse, who then behaves in a "disobedient" manner, frightening the rider still further. And of course, if you're frightened, you're probably not having much fun.

If you have had a bad experience from which you are trying to recover, you must make a commitment to *patience*. To many riders this sounds like a commitment to boredom. Not so! By understanding and accepting the need to deal with your fear, and committing yourself to giving it the necessary time, you relieve yourself of much of the pressure. You also become more deeply involved in the total learning process and riding starts to be fun again.

Almost everyone has at least some fear when they first start to ride. Whether or not this becomes a serious problem or quietly disappears depends on the innate courage of the individual, but even more on what happens to her in her early lessons. One of the most common causes of serious fear is insufficient time spent on early skills, so that the rider is unprepared to deal with the problems she meets. Novices—and often their instructors as well—make the mistake of thinking that the way to be safe is to learn to "control" the horse, but no living thing is absolutely controllable. Instead, the rider needs to learn such skills as good balance, emergency dismounts, and how to recognize and, most important, avoid potentially dangerous situations.

The two major fears for most riders are fear of falling and fear of losing control of the horse. This book is about dealing with those problems in very concrete ways. But there is a third, very common fear: fear of what others may think, or of what you think of yourself. Many riders constantly push themselves into frightening situations because they think they "should be able to do it." What these riders don't realize is that fear originates in our innermost, reflex brain. Our outer, rational brain has no direct connection with this inner creature, so telling yourself to relax when your insecure, terrified body is telling your reflex brain that danger is imminent is an exercise in futility. What does work is to treat your body like a separate, frightened animal that needs lots of support, careful direction and successful experience to regain its confidence.

It is especially important for people with fear problems to take lessons, and from the right instructor. Research has shown that the greatest barrier to learning any new skill is fear. Therefore, before signing up for lessons, watch a lesson at the level at which you expect to be riding. Look for relaxation and confidence in both horses and riders. Beginners should not look extremely insecure, which would indicate they are being faced with more than they can handle. Ground helpers should be available so that students can focus on position first. Talk at length with the instructor or manager and find out their teaching philosophy. Are they in a hurry to get you to shows, or are they more interested in developing good skills and having you enjoy your riding and be safe? If you know yourself to be naturally timid and are starting from the very beginning, talk with a prospective instructor about her attitude toward fear. Be sure she is willing to take you as slowly as you need to go.

Circumstances often determine who your instructor will be, and each one has her own technique, which may not fit in with your needs. However, by being aware yourself of what your needs are, you can sometimes discuss them with your instructor and find she is willing to work with you. This is something that must, of course, be handled with tact and discretion, but a riding experience that leaves you confused and unsure is almost worse than nothing. And surprisingly often the instructor is open to new approaches to teaching. It can be very hard to come up with a bright, fresh approach to the same horses and pupils working on the same basic skills. And, by the way, just what *are* "the basics?"

THE BASICS: MORE THAN "HEELS DOWN"

The definition of "basics" or "fundamentals" varies somewhat from instructor to instructor, but usually is taken to mean certain essentials of position; things like "sit up straight" and "heels down." These are, of course, very important but they are not the basics. They are things that occur as a *result* of correct basics.

The real basics, if I may put it that way, are:

- A good relationship with the horse, so that you trust one another

- The ability to work around the horse on the ground and sit on him at all gaits, in a way that does not disturb either horse or rider

- Understanding the language; knowing how to communicate with the horse and understanding what he is telling you

Let's have a closer look at these basics, one by one.

A Good Relationship

The first and most important basic is a good attitude toward the horse. I know many of us were taught that we must "master" the horse, and be the boss, but while I don't believe in spoiling horses, I do feel that this kind of thinking is as outdated as women automatically being submissive to men, or children being seen and not heard. The results of allowing the horse to tell you when you are wrong (as long as he doesn't tell you in an aggressive way) are astounding and rewarding for everyone. The horse is far less frustrated and irritable—therefore safer—and you really learn what works best for the horse and what doesn't. And what's best for the horse ultimately will always be best for you.

When I still had school horses, if a rider learning to trot on one of my horses got off balance, her horse would stop. Not nasty, he just stopped to let her get organized, then he would go on again. As she improved, his performance improved, so the student was taught *by the horse* what was correct *for the horse* and became a better rider sooner as a result.

Relationship issues should always be worked out on the ground. You wouldn't get into a taxi if you felt the driver was untrustworthy and wouldn't take directions. You wouldn't want to commit your personal safety to such a person. No more should you do so with a horse.

Fortunately, there are a number of relationship-building ground systems, with clinics, books, videos, and support all in place. They all have much to offer, and any serious rider should investigate them. The best known are clicker training (positive reinforcement training), Parelli Natural Horse-Man-Ship

---

Tidbits & Supplements

I was once giving a sitting trot lesson on the longe to Robin, a new pupil who had had a lot of previous experience. The horse, O'Malley, kept stopping, and Robin got quite upset with me, maintaining that she couldn't possibly learn to sit if I didn't keep O'Malley going. Immediately after her lesson another pupil, Eleanor, who had been with me for a while, also rode O'Malley. Robin was still nearby when Eleanor started her sitting trot work. Without any help from me or apparent effort on Eleanor's part, O'Malley trotted steadily and quietly for as long as she wanted. Robin, being a nice person, promptly underwent an attitude change, and her riding improved rapidly.

(PNH), round pen training, and Tellington-Jones Equine Awareness Method (TTeam). It is not necessary to own your own horse to benefit from these methods, since they help your understanding of any horse you work with. My book *What Your Horse Wants You to Know* will give you an overview of these systems, along with their use for many common problems. For more detailed information about resources, see Appendix D.

Establishing a Balance of Power

Although we hear a lot about the need to "control" the horse, the horse is always in physical charge of his own body, simply because it is his brain and muscles and reflexes that control his body. The rider is generally in charge of what the horse should be doing with his body, because usually horses are operating in a world in which humans have made the rules. For example, when a horse and rider go for a trail ride it is probably the human who knows the best way to go, therefore the human should expect to be in charge of which trail they take. However, it is the horse who knows whether or not he can negotiate difficult terrain at a particular pace, and the rider should expect to give the horse some choice when riding over trappy ground.

So a successful horse–rider relationship becomes a partnership that works, not because the two are always equal, but because each one is able to either take or relinquish leadership as necessary for the most successful functioning of the partnership.

When you think about working with your horse, think about how you feel about the different things you do; how hard you work at things that are "fun" and how cranky you get when you feel threatened. Listen to your horse if you want him to listen to you! Tell him about it when he is good, try again a different way when he fails, but don't punish or humiliate him. If he doesn't do what you want, let him show you what *he* wants. Then, keeping that in mind, show him how what you want is a better solution . . . *if* it is! That's how he finds out that you have his welfare at heart. Once he knows that, he becomes part of the solution rather than part of the problem.

This does not mean that we permit the horse total freedom right from the start. It is important that the horse learn the same sort of rules for social behavior that we expect from anyone with whom we interact. People who allow their horses too much leeway are really treating them very unfairly. If a horse is constantly doing things that make you tense, even though you don't show it outwardly the horse will be aware of it and will feel uncomfortable without knowing why—which makes for a very nervous animal. Further, if a horse has no manners and he has to interact with people other than his owner, they may not be as patient. He will be constantly offending and may even find himself being punished in a way that seems unreasonable to him. Ordinary good manners are useful for everybody, and should be quietly insisted upon until they become a habit. And of course, you need to set the example.

A Working Relationship

If you work a horse to the point where he isn't enjoying it anymore, he will stop wanting to work for you because he will really be frightened of the lessons. If, instead, you let the horse tell you when he's had enough and reward him for what he has done, gradually his willingness to work will increase. Note that this does not "spoil" the horse. The horse realizes that you are being considerate of his needs and will reciprocate, if necessary. One of the horses I work with used to be very cranky about work. Once we made it fun for him, he learned to love it. However, sometimes he gets tired toward the end of a lesson and wants to quit. If I need to do a little bit more, I can just make it plain, in a nonaggressive way, that it is important to me to continue a little longer, and he settles down and goes back to work. In return, when we finish I make a point of thanking him for the extra effort.

Horses understand consideration and fairness far more than we realize. I want my horse to pay attention to me because he has learned that I have useful messages to give him that help him to function better, and because he enjoys working with me. I have found that horses on the whole enjoy the challenge of working with us, provided we treat them fairly. So any sort of riding where you have specific but fair and sensible goals for the horse can and should be as interesting to him as our riding lessons are for us.

Perhaps the most difficult situation of all to deal with is one in which a rider has become frightened of her own horse but still cares enough about him to want to keep him. This situation tends to be self-perpetuating, because the rider's fear is passed to the horse as tension, and he then tends to react in just the way that she feared. A lot of the skills in this book will give you physical tools to deal with your fears in this situation, but your attitude toward your horse and his toward you are a big part of the cure. If you treat your horse fairly, kindly and lovingly, once he understands which actions of his are frightening to you he will try very hard not to repeat them.

Freedom and Balance

The second basic, to be able to sit on and work with the horse in a way that does not disturb either horse or rider, is divided into two parts: freedom from tension, and physical balance. The two are mutually dependent, because you can't be balanced as long as you're tense and you can't be free from tension if you are unbalanced.

Freedom from physical tension is often the most difficult to achieve and maintain. If you are a beginner, just getting past your body's innate fear of the horse, his height and his movement may take several months. You may need to be careful that your instructor doesn't put you in situations that create tension. I am not just talking about overmounting you, but about such things as having you trot before you have had sufficient experience at the walk or expecting you to keep your horse out on the rail and away from the other horses before your position is pretty well-established—things that most beginner instructors consider far easier than they are.

More experienced riders have often developed many bad habits that result in overall body tensions that they may not even be aware of. People who complain of stiffness or muscle soreness after riding are feeling the results of this kind of tension. You may have some bad responses that have become reflexes, and reflexes are not easy to change. Reflexes do not involve conscious thought, so you can't change them by thinking about them. You change them by practicing the correct reflex until the body learns *that* as new behavior. Probably one reason many people keep riding with the same bad habits, or give up in disgust, is that they don't realize how long it takes to change a reflex. But it sure is worth the effort!

Emotional stress creates physical tensions as a side effect. An all too common kind of tension is that which you bring with you from your "other life," the workplace or home. Rushing to your horse after a bad day at work and a long commute can make for a very unsuccessful ride. Using relaxation techniques such as TTeam for both you and your horse before riding can be very helpful and a real time-saver in the long run.

A source of tension that is often overlooked is nutritional. Caffeine is the big offender, but sugar and in some cases allergens can be problems as well. Low blood sugar is also a common problem; if you ride after school or work, you should have a healthy snack first.

True phobia—overpowering, mind-warping fear that bears little relationship to what is actually happening—is a whole different thing, and usually needs some sort of professional help, either from conventional or alternative medicine practitioners.

Physical balance is the second requirement. If you aren't balanced, your body (whether you want it to

---

Tidbits & Supplements

Accidents can happen, of course, just as they can with your car. All you can do in either case is to learn the best techniques, use common sense and good judgment, and then have a little faith.

---

or not!) is going to hang on, either obviously with your hands and reins, or less obviously with your buttocks and legs. It is not possible to develop correct use of the aids without true balance. You must learn to balance yourself without any tension, especially in those parts of your body that directly affect the horse—that is, your arms, hands, and legs. You must be able to balance both in full seat (sitting) and in half seat (standing in the stirrups), eventually at all gaits.

Finally, **correct position**, which is both the cause and the result of good balance and freedom from tension, is essential. Good position is not just about looking pretty on your horse; good position is about being on the horse in a manner that does not interfere with either his or your optimal functioning. What does "optimal functioning" mean? That neither of you should *ever* feel nervous or unsure of your ability to cope physically with whatever comes up! It's about staying out of the horse's way while he does his job. And the great thing about correct position is that it makes riding *much* easier. Our motto is not "No pain, no gain," but "If it isn't easy, it's wrong!"

If your position is really correct, it is perfectly possible for you to feel just about as comfortable and secure on a horse at any gait or speed, including over fences and up and down hill, as you do standing still! The main part of this book is devoted to teaching you correct position. If you are able to follow the directions, and are willing to give yourself enough time to learn, you will eventually reach this degree of security. Probably sooner than you think.

Learning to Communicate

The third basic is the ability to communicate. This involves, first of all, learning how to use your tools—your aids—correctly and effectively. To shorten and lengthen the reins quickly and easily. To use your body so that the pressure on the reins doesn't become tense. To use your legs so that your thighs and seat stay soft. To be able to carry a whip, apply it, change it from one hand to the other. Having these skills in your muscle memory enables you to use your aids effortlessly.

However, having these skills is not the same as having "control." **Control of the horse comes from the horse himself. At best, it is a gift he gives us because we have a good relationship. At worst, it is a grudging result of fear, liable to be withdrawn at any time, out of either anger or panic.** Webster defines communication as "the *exchange* of information or opinions." By focusing on the communication aspect of the aids, rather than control, we have a greater chance of maintaining the good relationship we need. That is, if we listen to the horse, he is far more likely to listen to us.

Contrary to what is often thought, the aids do not differ greatly from discipline to discipline. If they did, a dressage rider could not ride a reining horse, and vice versa, but the fact is that any expert rider in any discipline can ride a horse who has been trained in a different discipline and have no trouble with the basic aids. She might not be able to get the horse to do things that are related only to that discipline—for example, a saddle seat rider who has never jumped would probably have difficulty getting a hunter around a course, and a Western rider might have difficulty getting a gaited horse to rack. But the basic aids are the same for all horses.

These basic aids that you will find described in this book are, for the most part, not "tricks" that the horse has to be taught. They work because they affect the horse physically in some way, and result in a physical response. For that reason, the horse finds them very easy to understand. Naturally, a horse's responses to the aids will always improve along with his coordination, musculature, and willingness to please.

Learning to ride well is not something you will accomplish in a couple of months, or a couple of years. Riding is undoubtedly the most difficult of sports to do well, because there are so few constants. Every horse is an individual, and every day is a new one. On the plus side, as long as you retain even a modicum of physical and mental health, you can ride for your entire life. Lots of people ride well into their 80s and even 90s and never stop learning.

You can look at this concept and say, "Well, I just don't want to have to spend my whole life learning," or you can say, "Hey, this is great, I can be learning something new all the time for my whole life. I'm *never* going to be bored!" It's all in how you look at it.

SAFETY ISSUES

Anyone who writes about riding has, in my mind, an obligation to at least mention safety. Horses, because of their sheer size, strength, and quick reactions, have a potential for danger even when their intentions are the best. When you factor in the possibility of the horse having been abused or having an unsuspected phobia, the possibility of danger is greatly increased. I remember an incident that occurred with an old pony named Johnny whom I had owned for years. This was the bomb-proof one whom I always used for my most timid pupils. I was using him to sit on while I directed my class, who were learning a musical ride. At one point I forgot what the next pattern was supposed to be, so I reached into my pocket, pulled out a paper copy of the ride and unfolded it. The pony absolutely panicked and almost bolted out from underneath me. Talk about totally unexpected! And yet I constantly hear people say, "Oh, I can trust old Mike absolutely. He would *never* hurt me." On purpose, no, probably not, but if you accidentally trigger a reflex that you didn't even know the horse had, as I did with Johnny, you can get in trouble.

I hope riders at all levels of skill will use this book, so there may be places where the more experienced rider-reader will say, "Yes, yes, I know all that." I hope she will consider that others less experienced may not have thought of an aspect of horse handling or riding that is second nature to her.

It would be impossible to list every scenario that might be dangerous, but it is possible to list a dozen simple, general rules that will keep you safe in most instances.

Safety Rules

1. Begin your riding career by taking lessons from a mature, experienced professional. Visit the stable beforehand and look for calm horses and riders and a neat, well-kept facility. Ask if they teach ground handling techniques *in depth* as well as riding. Avoid instructors who are aggressive with their horses—horses who are expecting to get hurt tend to kick first and ask questions afterward. Hard hats should be a requirement. Keep taking lessons as long as you can on some regular basis, and for at least 200 hours.

2. Don't buy a horse until you are pretty comfortable, and keep him with a professional for the first few months at least. Better yet, lease a horse to make sure you have the time and the desire to work by yourself. Learn about your and the horse's equipment. Know how it should fit and how to use it, and keep it in good shape.

3. Spend time making friends with any horse you ride, even if you are only going to ride him once. The safest horse is the one who is not afraid of what you might do to him, and who knows enough about you to care at least a little what happens to you. Learn how your horse (or the horse you ride) shows tension, discomfort, and aggression. Watch his eyes, his ears, his tail, his body position.

4. When you are working on the ground with a horse, always stay in the area around his shoulder whenever possible. You are the least likely to get hurt there.

5. *Never* touch a horse on his hindquarters on first approach. Always go to his head, then work your way back.

6. Never approach a loose, unknown horse in a field without some sort of defensive instrument, even a lead rope, in your hand.

7. Always be especially cautious when more than one horse is involved. Never assume just because two horses have met that they won't do anything aggressive. Horses often play games with each other that can be extremely dangerous to nearby humans, and they don't realize that you can't get out of the way as fast as they can.

8. When you try *anything* with a horse that you have not done before *yourself*, be a little careful until you're sure he's okay with it.

9. Listen to what *your* body tells you. If you feel really nervous about something, don't do it if you can possibly avoid it. Walking home on your own two feet is better than being carried home on a stretcher.

10. Try not to ride alone. If you must, make sure that someone knows you're out and will check to make sure you are safely home.

11. Wear a hard hat, even if you think they're stupid and uncomfortable. You can get used to anything except a smashed skull! I have personally known three people who died of head injuries received as a result of falls from horses. They were all riding their own horses and none of them were jumping. In two of the instances the horses were walking quietly immediately before the accident; in the third instance a piece of new equipment failed.

12. Bear in mind that horses are living creatures, and therefore by definition unpredictable. Just as people can never be counted on to show exactly the same behavior under a certain set of circumstances, neither can horses. Pay attention to the state of mind of the particular horse you are on, and to the relationship between you. General principles apply to all, but evaluating each horse as you ride has a lot to do with a safe and successful experience.

2

Building the Foundation

The Seven Steps, Part One

Kitty had ridden for many years, but had recently suffered a very serious fall from a horse. She was anxious to get back into riding again, and wanted to deal with her new and severe fear problem. When she came for her first lesson I brought a horse out for her to groom right away, assuming that with her lengthy experience there would be no difficulties at this level. Much to my astonishment, she was extremely tense working around the horse on the ground. She stood very awkwardly, with her feet placed far away from the horse. This forced her to lean forward, out of balance, to use the grooming tools. As a result, her moves were clumsy and disturbing to the horse, thus making him feel tense as well.

I realized I would have to correct her body at this level before we even could think about riding. Although neither she nor the horse wanted to hurt the other, the subconscious messages they were exchanging were very threatening to both, and could only result in trouble.

Though she may not be conscious of it herself, almost every new rider is dealing with a certain amount of fear. The standard practice of giving the beginning rider far too many challenges—stirrups, reins, posting—and not giving her enough time to develop a feeling of security on the horse allows that fear to grow and solidify, creating a monster that may take years to tame. Without the secure position that can only be built on a careful foundation, there can be no real confidence and relaxation.

While it is not a concept that leaps to mind when you think of riding, it is obvious that in order to ride well your body must function well. If it is full of tensions, or is unresponsive or unbalanced, the horse will be affected and you won't get the results you want or expect. In this chapter and in Chapter 7 you will be introduced to some basic ways to improve your body, release tensions and find balance.

Tidbits & Supplements

What is covered in this and the related chapters is just the tip of the iceberg. If you really want to reach your full potential as a rider, you should explore such things as Centered Riding, Alexander Technique, yoga, and tai chi. There are also many individual practitioners who have developed useful variations of the standard techniques.

In trying to solve these problems over the years, and with much help from my pupils and especially from Sally Swift, the creator of Centered Riding, I worked out Seven Steps that I found could overcome the initial fear and make almost anyone comfortable on a horse in a comparatively short time. Eventually, I could put an absolute beginner on a horse for the first time after half an hour on the ground during which she had learned the first five steps, and at the end of the hour, using all seven steps, have her walking (hand led) and looking correct as well as comfortable.

GROUNDING: WHAT IT'S ALL ABOUT

The Seven Steps can be described as the tools the rider needs to achieve the second of my basics; that is, to be able to sit on the horse in a way that is not disturbing to either horse or rider. Another name for this concept is "grounding." **Grounding is probably the single most important factor for the success of any athletic endeavor.** When I look at a new student, her ability to ground, or lack thereof, is what I see first. When I start to work with her, that is where I begin. I suspect that experienced instructors in any sport see and work with their students in exactly the same way. The diver who must balance on the board, the golfer who must have a firm stance, a batter, a quarterback, a bowler—all these must be firmly grounded in order to perform even adequately. Grounding is what we see when we look at a rider and say, "She has a wonderful seat on a horse!"

Grounding begins with allowing your body to truly *connect to the ground.* If you envision standing on a solid floor in sneakers, as opposed to standing on a patch of ice in slick-soled shoes, you can envision how the lack of ability to connect with the ground deprives you of security if you have to make a sudden move.

When you are securely connected with the ground, which, when you are mounted, means the stirrups or the saddle seat, your body can relax and center over your base—that is, your feet or your seatbones. This enables you to react effortlessly in any situation. By focusing on grounding as you move around the horse on the ground, you teach your body to stand and move in a way that imparts confidence to both you and the horse, as you will see more clearly as we work through this section.

When you have completed the work laid out in this chapter, you will have "learned" the first five of the Seven Steps. That is, you will have read and applied the exercises, and felt how they worked. When you ride, you will take these, and the two additional steps explained in Chapter 7, and apply them to sitting on the horse. Over time you will find that the Seven Steps have become established in your muscle memory, so that you *immediately notice* when your body is wrong and are able to correct the error promptly, and even without conscious thought. At that stage, they have become an integrated whole. You will *know* them.

You can and should practice the unmounted exercises at home. In addition, you can begin to apply the techniques of the exercises to any situation in your life where you feel tense. Driving in traffic or preparing for a difficult interview are some examples that come to mind. And the more you practice the exercises in situations where you are not tense, the easier it will be to produce them when you need them.

The majority of these exercises originate in the Chinese martial art of tai chi and similar sources—I just put them together in a way that I found works the best

---

Tidbits & Supplements

One of my students, who is a fairly advanced rider, was having some trouble handling her horse on the ground. She tends to be a quiet, nonaggressive person and the horse is rather a macho gelding. As we were working with the horse, I put a strong emphasis on my student carrying her body correctly and keeping herself firmly grounded. The horse responded very well to the work, and she had no more trouble. As we were talking over the lesson afterward, I realized that she actually appeared taller, and something about her facial expression made me ask her if she felt more confident in a general way. After a moment's thought she replied in a somewhat surprised voice that she did, indeed, feel more self-confidence.

for people starting out, which is something I discovered by experimenting. For example, I tried starting with breathing, and found that most people were so scrunched up, they couldn't breathe. So I tried starting with other aspects and in different sequences, and found that this Seven Step plan worked. But of course, not for everyone, so you can do them in a different order if you like.

When working with these exercises on the ground, stand with your feet comfortably apart and your hip and knee joints unlocked but not bent.

1. GROWING

Growing is part of the loosening process. Muscles need to be stretched and lengthened to become soft and flexible. For the body to bend easily, while the muscles on the outside of the bend are lengthening, the inside muscles must compress without tension. To achieve this, they must first be stretched to make them relaxed and soft. Growing assists this process. For nearly everyone, the left side is stiffer than the right, so it is *always* stretched first.

1. First, think about your feet. Imagine them growing both longer and wider. Let your heels grow out the back of your feet, and your toes grow out in front. Let your toes spread out like duck's feet. Now, starting from the ankles and working up, release the tension in your hips and legs and let your whole body rest on your feet, so you feel connected to the ground.

2. Drop your left arm by your side, then bend your elbow and bring your left hand up in front of your face, thumb toward you. Your face should be vertical when seen from the side. For many of us, that means dropping the chin just a little, as though you were looking straight ahead over a pair of "granny glasses."

3. Imagine a string pulling the hand up over your head, and allow your head to tilt gently back to watch the hand going up. If you like, imagine the string is attached to a large helium balloon, which is pulling your arm up (but not too hard).

4. When the arm is straight up (vertical) from the shoulder, bring your eyes and head back level, then reach up a little higher until you feel a stretch at the waist as though your shirt is pulling out of your waistband. Remain in that position for a short time, as long as it is comfortable, then bring the arm slowly down in front of you and back to your side.

5. Repeat with your right arm, but this time bring your hand down to the top of your head, to the point where a line drawn from one ear to the other would intersect a line drawn straight back from your nose. Tap that place, as though you were attaching the string, then bring your hand down to your side.

Peg growing her right side. Notice how
much longer the whole growing side is,
and how well grounded Peg's right foot is.

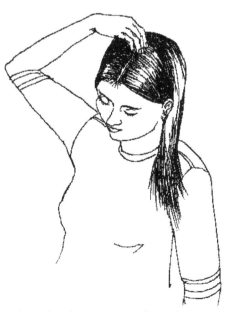

Locating the exact top of your head.

6. Now imagine yourself floating along in the sky, hanging by the top of your head from the string of the balloon. Your body will feel very straight and tall, but not stiff or straining.

7. Finish by thinking about your feet again and letting your weight rest firmly on them.

Standing (or sitting) up straight is a concept that is often misunderstood and incorrectly taught. An upright posture results from *releasing* the tension, primarily in the front muscles, not *increasing* the tension in the back muscles. The body naturally wants to balance itself, and allowing the front muscles to relax will accomplish this without effort.

An optional method of growing
and grounding.

Tidbits & Supplements

I recently came across another good way to grow and ground. You can't do it on a horse, but at least it's quick.

Stand against a wall. Keeping the back of your head against the wall and your neck and body straight, walk your feet out from the wall about six or eight inches. Allow your feet to ground, and allow your arms to dangle straight down. Hold this position for 30 seconds, then walk your feet back to the wall and step away. Your whole body will feel very tall, straight and yet relaxed. The photo on page 22 illustrates this method.

2. SHAKE-OUT

Shake-out helps rid your body of little tensions deep inside the muscles that you may not even be aware are there.

1. Starting with your left hand dangling at your side, begin shaking your fingers as though you had water on them and were trying to shake it off. This is a very loose, floppy, uncontrolled movement. Then shake your hand, followed by your wrist, forearm, elbow, and upper arm.

2. Repeat with your right hand. When you finish the right side, let your arms drop and shiver your shoulders as though you were cold.

3. Do the same exercise lifting your left leg, starting with your foot and ending at your thigh, then your right leg.

4. Then allow your upper body to fall forward so that your arms are dangling. Now shake out your whole body, especially the hips. You should feel all the muscles in your limbs become very loose and soft. Straighten up slowly and check to make sure you haven't lost your growing or your grounding.

The shake-out, even a partial one, is a particularly useful exercise before competition or any potentially stressful situation. You often see swimmers and tennis players shaking out just before starting.

Ready for the final shake-out.

3. BREATHING

Breathing is always the first thing to check if you notice yourself or your horse tensing up. Short, rapid inhalations with the chest, or holding the breath, will always *create* tension. Long, slow breaths with long exhales from the diaphragm will *release* tension.

1. Place one hand on your diaphragm/stomach and take a deep breath (through your nose, if possible), pushing your hand out with your diaphragm. Feel your lower ribs expand, not only in front but on the sides and in back as well, and try not to let your upper chest move until the very end of the inhalation. Your shoulders should not move appreciably.

2. Without any break between inhale and exhale, breathe out slowly through your mouth, trying to make the exhale last about twice as long as the inhale. Feel your upper chest, then your lower chest and finally, your diaphragm, going in. Feel as though your belly button was going to touch your spine. Try not to let your shoulders collapse.

Tidbits & Supplements

Many people have difficulty learning to breathe from the diaphragm. A good way to learn is to lie on your stomach on a carpeted floor (see the photo below). Place your elbows on the floor directly under your shoulders, and turn your forearms so that they are side by side, with the fingers of each hand by the opposite elbow. With your shoulders elevated in this way, begin to take some fairly deep breaths. Your shoulders will be held still by the position, and you will be able to easily feel your diaphragm expanding against the carpet. If you practice this regularly for a few days, correct breathing will begin to feel more natural.

---

3. Repeat several times. You can also try holding your breath to see how tense you become throughout your body. Shake out again afterward, if necessary.

Breathing is probably the single most important exercise. It is used by many other disciplines to induce relaxation and can be practiced at any time. Needless to say, I am referring to conscious breathing exercises. Not breathing at all except when you thought about it would not improve your riding! But a surprising number of people do just that when they are tense.

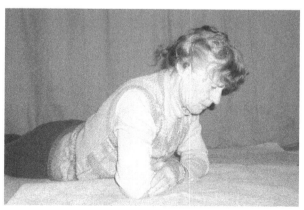

The correct position for practicing diaphragm breathing.

4. SOFT EYES

Soft eyes, as described here, are desirable for several reasons. Because they enable you to see all around, you can be much more aware of yourself in relation to your surroundings. They also help you to be aware of yourself in relation to your horse. If the horse makes a sudden move when you are standing near him, you are far more likely to notice it in time and respond appropriately.

1. Without dropping your head, choose a point directly in front of you and not too far away, perhaps 10 feet (3 meters), and focus on it intensely. Try to block out everything else. This is called *hard eyes*. It is one of the things we do (incorrectly!) when the horse does something sudden and violent.

2. Now, still looking at the point, allow your eyes to become a little less focused, so that you can see other things around you. Notice what you can see *without moving your head or your eyes*. Sky, ground, fences, buildings are all easily seen at once. Also notice that you can see quite far behind you. If you have someone to help, have her walk slowly past you from front to back. Do not move your head or eyes. When you can no longer see her, say "stop." Then turn your head and notice that she is well behind you. Your range of vision is much greater than you realize. This unfocused way of looking is called *soft eyes*.

Soft eyes are tied in to your right brain. Your left brain helps you learn things step-by-step (like these numbered directions). Your right brain helps you put the whole thing together so you begin to *feel* it instead of having to think about it step-by-step. *By consciously turning on your soft eyes, you can turn on your right brain at any time* to help you do things holistically and thus more naturally. Interestingly, a horse who is working and concentrating, but relaxed, nearly always seems to have a soft eye. An experienced trainer will often point this out.

5. TEETER-TOTTER (LONGITUDINAL CENTERING)

This exercise helps you find the longitudinal (forward and back) centered position. Your physical center is located a little below and behind your navel. Your goal is to line up your center and your base.

1. Stand with your feet quite close together, toes pointed straight ahead, arms by your sides. Closing your eyes may increase your awareness. Bending only at the ankles, allow your body to sway slowly forward until you start to lose your balance and have to take a step. Observe how, as you start to go out of balance forward, your toes curl up and tension runs all the way up your body, especially into your thighs.

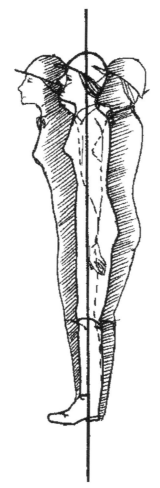

The teeter-totter; notice that only the ankle
joints open and close.

2. Next, sway backward the same way. When you start to go out of balance backward your toes come up and tension appears in your lower back and buttocks.

3. Repeat the swaying back and forth several times, finishing in the too-far-back position. Then come forward slowly until the tension leaves your back and the weight feels even on your feet. Allow yourself to ground.

If your center is directly over your base, there will be very little tension, since you will be perfectly balanced and will not require any noticeable muscular effort to stay in that position.

Tidbits & Supplements

Betsy, a friend of my new pupil Joanie, was watching Joanie learning the first five steps. I invited Betsy to join us, and explained that I felt these exercises would help Joanie's rather nervous mare to feel more relaxed. Sure enough, as we went through the steps the mare's head came down and she gave a relaxed sigh. Joanie and I continued the lesson while Betsy went to look after her own horse. This horse was the buddy of Joanie's horse, and always became very upset when Joanie's horse was out. Usually Betsy, a novice horsewoman, was unable to deal with this at all, but this time she decided to try the five steps. Within a few minutes the horse had settled down and allowed Betsy to groom her and pick out the stall without incident. When Joanie and I returned with her mare, instead of hearing whinnying and stamping of feet, we were met with silence and a calm expression. What a relief to all concerned!

Notice also what part of your foot leaves the ground just as you lose your balance either forward or back. This point, which is at the back of the ball of your foot, behind your second toe, is an important element in grounding. It's called your "bubbling spring," and we'll talk more about it later in Chapter 12.

This is the last of the exercises that can be done standing still. If you are able, review them several times before you begin with your actual riding. Always finish by grounding onto your feet. Later on in this book we will see how these exercises transfer to mounted work, and will add two more so they are truly the Seven Steps to a Secure Position.

Besides restoring your body to a safe, grounded position, and thus building your confidence, having the Seven Steps as a specific routine to follow gives you something concrete to do when a scary situation arises. This helps prevent the sort of panic you get into when your mind focuses on the problem instead of the solution. With practice, your reactions can become so quick and automatic that you rarely lose your grounding at all. Your physical security will also help your horse's confidence, thus making him safer to work around.

Even though the Seven Steps should be taught to a rider from the first time she approaches a horse, they must never be thought of as "beginner" exercises. They are the tools you will use throughout your riding career to tell your body how to return to its optimum position whenever that position is disturbed. In fact, the more advanced the work you are doing, the greater your need for them will be.

3

Meeting and Greeting

*Good First Impressions Create a
Positive Relationship*

Jane was 17 when she went on her first and only horseback ride. She and a group of young friends were visiting Florida and decided it would be fun to rent horses. At the stable, horses were brought out and the riders were immediately mounted. With no further instruction than being briefly shown how to hold and use the reins and their legs, off they went. They had been out just a short time when something happened to scare Jane's horse. He took off at a gallop between the other horses, bucking and swerving until she fell off. Frightened but unhurt, she was coaxed into remounting and continuing the ride, which finished uneventfully. She dismounted, breathed a sigh of relief, and for 10 years never went near a horse.

Long after that event, she realized that she had developed a serious phobia about horses. Wanting to get past her fear, she called us. We described our program, and she came for a lesson. She spent the customary half-hour on the ground getting acquainted with her mount, a gentle pony. Once she seemed comfortable, the time came to mount. She swung her leg over, sat down and froze. **Her body still remembered her past experience!** Fortunately, the kindly little mare stood like a stone for the 10 minutes it took the instructor to gently persuade Jane's body that it could give up its fear. Jane continued to ride for several months, until she accomplished her goal and became reasonably comfortable around horses.

Jane's Florida experience was her first contact with a horse, and because it was so traumatic, it nearly became her last. Only because she found a stable that would reintroduce her to horses slowly and safely was she able to begin her recovery.

One of the most important moments in any relationship is that very first moment when you meet each other. If each has a favorable impression, then the chances are the relationship will continue to develop successfully, at least for a while. If one party is rude or clumsy, so that the other one feels annoyed or threatened, a wall is erected that then has to be dealt with before the relationship can develop. This is even more true when the two don't speak the same language.

The introduction to the horse should be looked at both from the point of view of the horse and from the point of view of the rider. I have met many horses who were fearful of meeting new people, and I have met even more riders who were fearful of meeting an unfamiliar horse.

Introductions between horse and beginning rider need to be handled especially carefully. First impressions of a different species are really important. I remember a mistake I made that I didn't even realize was a mistake for many years. It is my practice to exercise school horses before riding by turning them loose in the arena and encouraging them to loosen up by running and bucking, so that they don't feel the need for such activities with a rider on their backs. I usually turn out at least two horses together so that they encourage one another, and I don't have to work so hard to keep them going. One day I was doing this while waiting for some new students to arrive. They did so while the horses were having a good run, and I thought nothing of it until I saw their expressions. They were petrified! What I perceived as a couple of old schoolies having a good time together, they saw as large, violent animals hurling themselves about. It took me quite a long time to persuade my new students that what the horses did on their own time was not related to what they were going to do in the lesson ring. But I had been letting horses run free for years with beginning students looking on and it had never occurred to me that this was threatening to an inexperienced horse person.

The major part of this chapter is different from the others in this book because it is mostly a description of the way I personally introduce a total beginner to a horse for the first time. I cannot know which parts apply to you, or how you will use this chapter. The introduction described is the least threatening not only to the (novice) rider, but also to the horse, so advanced riders can adapt it to working with new horses. Although many of the moves described here may seem like overkill to an experienced horseman, I have found that the best rule is to assume the worst and take every safety precaution possible in a new relationship with a horse. Once you and the horse have gotten to know each other, you will know what corners you can safely cut.

I should also mention that I have *always* used a version of this with every new rider who takes lessons with me, no matter how experienced, and have rarely failed at least once during the lesson to get a reaction of either "Nobody ever told me that before," or "I never thought of it quite that way."

We begin with some basic instruction in handling your own body in what many perceive as a threatening situation.

THE APPROACH

I begin with my new student standing outside of the stall of the horse I have chosen to work with. If possible, this horse should not be too large and should not be the sort of horse who fidgets while being groomed or standing on the floor. One who behaves rather like a large boulder is kind of what I look for. If it is fly season, the horse should be well fly-sprayed so that he is not constantly twitching and stamping his feet.

Before bringing the student into the stable, I have asked her not to do *anything* to the horse unless I tell her to do so. The first thing I explain to her is that safety is always a consideration when working around a horse. However, it is *not* because the horse is aggressive. The average horse in a well-managed stable is no more likely to bite or kick you for no reason than the average person you meet in a nice part of town is liable to haul off and slug you. What makes horses dangerous is not their attitude but their size.

In our everyday life, we deal with another large, potentially dangerous object—the automobile. If you are crossing the street and a car comes along, it is extremely unlikely to run over you on purpose. However, if you habitually cross the street carelessly, without using ordinary good sense, eventually you will probably get hurt by a car. The same is true of horses. Ordinary common sense and knowledge of safety practices should keep you safe from all except the fluke accident, and those are rare. The few times I have been actually hurt by a horse on the ground were invariably the result of my own carelessness.

Getting the Horse's Attention

As we stand in front of the horse's stall, I explain that approaching a horse has to be done the right way, for two reasons. One is that the horse, in the general scheme of things, has the potential to become some predator's lunch, so aggressiveness in one's approach can be perceived as threatening. The second is that, while horses do sleep lying down with their eyes closed, they are quite capable of nodding off while standing up with their eyes open. After all, if we can sleep with our ears "open," why shouldn't the horse be able to sleep with his eyes open? And horses sleep as much as 20 hours a day.

If you walk up quietly to a horse who is standing there with his eyes open but not doing much and you put your hand on him, if he was asleep he's going to jump right out of his skin! And in the process he may take you with him. Of course, I also explain that running, shouting or any loud noises or sudden moves can startle even a horse who is awake, and thereby endanger anyone who happens to be standing nearby.

Your first action, then, is to get the horse's attention so that you know that he knows you're there. How can you tell if you have his attention? The same way you can tell if you try to attract the attention of a person who is some distance away: She turns and looks at you. The horse will look at you, too. However, because he can see very nearly 360 degrees around himself, if his tail is more or less toward you he may not turn his body around; he may not even turn his head, even though he is looking at you. Luckily, it's easy to tell which way he is looking because he always turns his ears in the direction he wants to focus on. Essentially, his ears and eyes work together, so if his ears are turned toward you, you know his eyes are as well.

The following little story illustrates the importance of getting the horse's attention before approaching him, even if you know the horse very well. I had a horse in my barn who, although he didn't belong to me, had lived there for many years. He was in a stall with a Dutch door to the outside, so when the top section was open he could put his head out and look around. One day I went to go into his stall from the door that opened into the barn aisle, while his head was outside. The latch on the aisle door was very noisy, and usually was more than enough to catch a horse's attention when the stall was entered. As I walked in and spoke he didn't turn around, but I thought nothing of it because he knew me well. And since he was standing with his side to me, I didn't feel in danger from his heels. I couldn't approach his head directly because it was outside the outer door, though fully in my view (and I in his). But, to be on the safe side, I went to what I considered a safe position, a little in front of his shoulder, before I spoke to him again and put my hand on his shoulder.

He lashed out instantly with a cow kick, and only the fact that he realized even as he kicked that it was me and stopped the kick in mid-delivery saved me from serious injury. As it was, I had a bruise that lasted several weeks!

What went wrong? Unbeknownst to me or anyone else, the horse had gradually been growing deaf. He was probably napping with his head in the sun, and never heard either the stall bolt or my voice. By taking for granted that because I made the right moves I was safe, rather than paying attention to the horse's response, I nearly had a bad accident.

Entering the Horse's Space

Whenever possible, the horse should be approached from the front at a slight angle. The location of his eyes (on the sides of his head so that he can see a predator coming from any direction) leaves him with a small blind spot directly in front of his face. Politeness also indicates that you should address him at the head first, just as you would a person.

The approach to be avoided is from any point behind the front leg, and especially from directly to the rear, where the horse has an even larger blind spot. However, sometimes when you are walking into the stall, the horse will

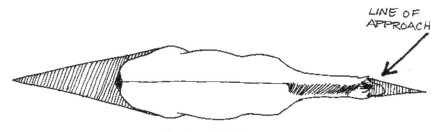

The horse's blind spots.

have his tail toward you, perhaps because his hay is in a far corner. Also, some horses are kept in standing stalls, which are stalls in which the horse can't turn around but stands with his head toward the front of the stall so that his tail is toward anyone entering the stall. (Incidentally, the name doesn't mean the horse can't lie down!)

Many people are taught that in these circumstances they should touch the horse on the hindquarters first, so that he knows you're there. But if you have approached him properly, clucking or speaking and looking for a response, he already knows you're there. If he feels threatened by your touch for any reason, since he has no place to run to in the stall, he may kick at you. If you walk quietly past his hindquarters and up to his head before touching him, if he feels threatened he will simply turn away.

As with so many things, I was taught this by a pony. At one time we bought a stable and the horses with it. The previous owner was not especially considerate of his animals, so many of them had bad habits. One pony in particular was kept in a standing stall. The method I had always used to enter a standing stall was to stand off to one side outside the stall and tap the horse on the rump to get him to move over before entering the stall. No matter what we did, Taters would always put his ears back and lift his hind leg, threatening to kick. Naturally, we never let anyone but members of the staff into his stall. Then one day, one of the younger children who was very fond of Taters mentioned that she never had any trouble going into the stall with him. I asked her to show me how she did it. She simply walked up to the stall and stood to one side, then called the pony's name and clucked to him without touching him at all. He immediately stepped over and she walked in and gave him a big hug. And I got a big lesson.

Because being enclosed in any stall with a large and unfamiliar animal is very threatening to the novice, for the early lessons I always have the horse brought out of the stall to be groomed. Later, as the student gains experience she learns first to bring the horse back into the stall after the lesson, and eventually to groom and tack up in the stall if aisle space is at a premium.

THE GREETING

Before approaching the horse for the first time, the student is taken quickly through the first five of the Seven Steps (see Chapter 2). Almost every novice feels some tension the first time she meets a horse close-up, even if she is unaware of it. However, once the student knows the Seven Steps the instructor can quickly remind her to breathe or grow or whatever may be necessary to release any tension that occurs.

Introductions between humans follow a fairly consistent pattern. First you stand a little outside of the other person's space and hold out an empty hand to show peaceful intentions. Then some sort of verbal greeting is followed by verbal identification and perhaps a grasping of hands to complete the connection. Animal introductions are different in that the animals lack hands or words. Therefore, they depend more on smells and body language and perhaps even telepathy to give them information about the other creature. So in introducing yourself to a horse, you need to combine a little of each technique.

Personal Space

The concept of personal space is often not considered, but invading what an individual considers his personal space without invitation is very threatening. Protection of personal space is what causes many horses to act in a menacing fashion if someone comes close to their stall. It also is often the cause of horses pulling back when tied.

For this reason, I begin the introduction, if possible, with the horse in his stall and the student outside. Each then feels protected from the other. Asking the student to stand back from the door, I open the door and put up the breast chain so that the horse can hang his head out but not come closer. I explain a little about the nature of the horse, while he and I greet each other and I tell the student his name. One of the things I feel is very important is to always include the horse in the conversation as though he were another person, not an object. The horse notices and appreciates this, and the student learns by example.

Introducing Yourself

I next mention that while people introduce themselves by speaking their names, this is meaningless to the horse, who identifies others by smell. I also point out that the horse's eyes are on the side of his head, so that objects directly in front of him are hard to see. Thus horses touch noses to sniff each other from the side, while dogs, for example, whose eyes are in front, touch noses directly facing each other. Because smell is such an important part of identifying new objects, horses use their muzzles in the same way that we use our hands—to touch and explore. For this reason, the muzzle is not part of the horse's immediate personal space, meaning that he is more comfortable approaching strange things with his muzzle, just as we are with our hands. However, beginning from just above the muzzle and extending back to the base of the neck at the shoulder, this area is all considered immediate personal space by the horse, just as your face and neck are your personal space. You would be very uncomfortable if a stranger came up and patted you on your face, and horses usually feel the same way, though many of them learn to accept having their faces touched.

Demonstrating with my own hand, I explain that the horse places different interpretations on your actions, depending on how you hold your hand. Hand horizontal and palm up means food, and if there is no food the horse may grab a finger accidentally. Hand vertical with fingers up and palm facing the horse can mean a slap, and is threatening. The safest and least threatening way to offer your hand to the horse is palm down, with fingers lightly curled.

I then ask the student to quickly run through the five of the Seven Steps that she has learned, and then walk over so that she is standing to my left. (I am standing to the horse's left, and very slightly behind his head.) I have her hold out her right hand, and I take it in mine so that my hand is covering hers, between her and the horse's muzzle. If I feel tension in her arm and hand, I may ask her to rebalance herself, breathe and shake out again, until her arm is as it would be if she were shaking hands with a person. This will also help later when she begins leading.

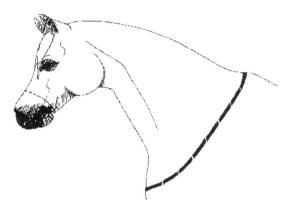

The horse's personal space lies between the dotted lines on the neck and muzzle. As you approach the face and ear areas, a nervous horse feels the most threatened.

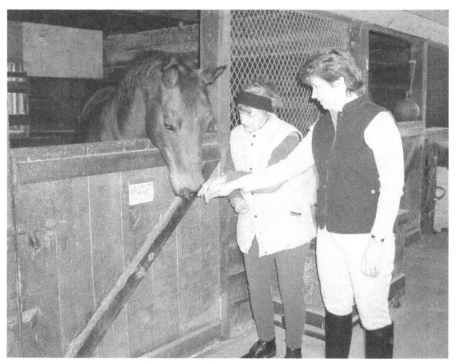

I introduce Peg and Sammy to each another.

When her arm relaxes, I bring it over to a point two or three inches from the horse's muzzle while explaining that, just as you would not grab the other person's hand before he offered it, so you don't shove your hand into the horse's muzzle, but offer it to him and allow him to reach out and make the introductory sniff on his own. I then allow the horse to sniff her hand *through* mine, which helps to overcome the tendency of the novice to jerk her hand back when she feels the horse's muzzle. I find that most beginners are quite surprised at how thoroughly the horse sniffs their hand. Again, this is important to help the student realize that the horse is just as concerned about the relationship as she is.

If the student seems comfortable, I remove my hand and suggest that she rub the horse a little just behind the nostril with her knuckle. On most horses this is a very soft place, so it feels good to the student as well as to the horse. Being on the muzzle, it is noninvasive.

GETTING UP-CLOSE AND PERSONAL

Once the horse has had a good sniff, I ask the student to step out of the way, and I bring the horse out of his stall and cross or ground tie him so that he stays still. I position myself facing the horse's side just behind his left shoulder and invite the student to come and stand beside me on my left. I then ask her to again go through the five steps, so that she feels comfortable. I use the shoulder area because it is out of the horse's immediate personal space and also away from the danger area within range of his hind legs. I explain to her that if at any time she feels uncomfortable, she is free to step away from the horse.

To confirm this, I suggest that she step toward the horse, thinking about staying centered over her feet, and then step away again. I have her repeat this a couple of times. I find that novices have a tendency when close to the horse to stand with their feet as far away as possible and lean toward the horse. This, of course, puts them off balance, and if they need to move quickly it will be difficult. Their lack of centering also is transmitted to the horse as tension. I point this out to my student, and also mention that the way to keep from being stepped on, which is a fear many people have, is simply to step back away from the horse if he picks up the foot nearest her.

When she is comfortable standing close to the horse, I ask her to stretch out her hand and lay it softly on the horse's shoulder, just below the withers. I tell her not to pat or rub the horse with her hand, but simply let it lie there quietly. This says to the horse that she will be touching him and invading his space as she grooms and eventually rides him, but that her touch is as noninvasive and nonthreatening as possible. Even patting or rubbing is invasive when done by a stranger. Think of how you would respond if a stranger started patting you, as opposed to simply putting his hand on your shoulder or arm. Placing her hand on his shoulder also tells a more experienced person a great deal about the horse, because a horse who has been mishandled, or not handled at all, will move away from the touch or even jump back.

Next, I look for a place the horse likes to have scratched, usually in the hollow around the withers or on the neck near the shoulder, and I scratch him in whatever way seems to please. Many horses will go into wonderful and amusing contortions of neck and lips, which contribute greatly to the novice's accepting the horse as an individual with character and personality, rather than merely a large vehicle. It is the beginning of establishing a relationship, which is essential for the enjoyment of both horse and rider.

Tidbits & Supplements

If, as a more experienced rider, you are working with a new horse who is nervous about being touched, it is important to spend the necessary time to help him overcome this, using one of the ground relationship disciplines (see the Resources in Appendix D). Otherwise grooming, tacking, and in fact all contact will create tension that you neither want nor need.

Mock Grooming

Mock grooming introduces the student to grooming safety skills without worrying about handling the tools themselves. Safety when working close to the horse has a great deal to do with positioning your body correctly relative to the horse.

I remind the student about the horse's personal space, and then have her use the flat of her hand to stroke the horse firmly with the grain of the hair, as though she were dusting him off. I show her how the grain runs differently in different places, and have her start "grooming." She stands at the horse's left shoulder facing forward, places her right hand on his withers or shoulder, and grooms with her left hand, beginning on the front of the shoulder and moving up his neck a little at a time.

By standing at his shoulder, she is out of reach of the horse's hind legs and tail and can see what he is doing with his head and ears. Thus, if the horse has any tendency to nip she can avoid it. Keeping her other hand on his body seems to help maintain a connection between them, as well as helping her balance as she leans over to groom. At the same time, by moving gradually up his neck, she can observe immediately if the horse has any nervousness about his head or ears and treat him accordingly. I tell her to watch his ears and eyes, and show her the difference between the horse turning his ear toward her and laying it back in anger. I explain that if the horse is fidgety, it indicates tension or discomfort. I also explain that the horse cannot kick back with a front leg, but can kick forward with it (called "striking"), so the area to be avoided is directly in front of the front leg. I do not have her work on the legs quite yet, since many students find this threatening.

Next the student turns around so that she is facing the rear of the horse. I tell her that if she has any fears about the horse's hindquarters, not to go any farther back than she feels comfortable. I explain that the horse has to lift his hind leg and bring it forward to kick, but that the force of a kick with the hind leg is directed back. She now places her left hand on the horse's withers and grooms with her right. The reason for this position is that, first, she can see the horse's hind leg, so if it seems restless she can move away; and second, if the horse kicks, if she were facing forward the kick would be more likely to cause severe damage to the front of her leg than to the back of her leg, as would happen if she is facing the rear. With any luck, the horse we have chosen will be standing as though he would never dream of lifting a leg voluntarily for any reason!

I also point out the horse's flank area and mention that some horses are very sensitive here, so that grooming in this area should be approached carefully.

As long as the student is standing up, she usually feels pretty confident, since she is fairly tall relative to the horse. But bending down so that the horse is towering above her can be a bit threatening. I prefer not to try to teach brand-new beginners how to pick up the horse's feet, because they have so many other concerns that they are invariably clumsy and tend to create bad habits in the horse. So at this point I merely show them how to stand when working around the legs and under the belly. If either horse or student seems tense, I leave this part of the lesson to another time.

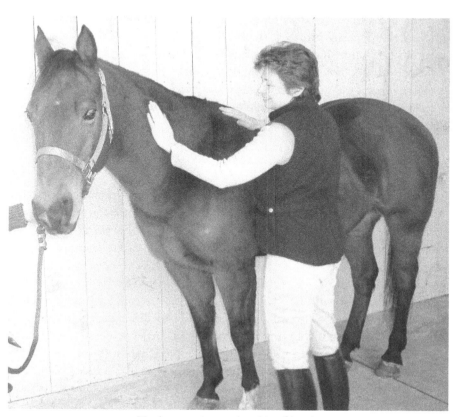

Mock grooming and making friends.

The concern here is primarily with how the student stands as she reaches down. For reaching under the horse's belly, the important thing is to have the student standing close to the horse's front leg with her nearer hand resting on the horse's back or side, keeping an eye on the hind leg while she reaches underneath with her outside hand. I also caution her that this is another potentially sensitive area, and suggest that she watch for rapid tail swishing, which could be a sign of discomfort or of flies, either of which might lead to a kick.

As she brushes the front leg, she first stands facing the rear to do the back of the leg, then facing the front to do the front. I also have her reach across to do the inside of the opposite leg. I caution her not to bring her head across in front of the horse's leg, because if he happens to pick it up he will crack her on the face with his knee. As she goes farther down the leg, she may have the option of bending her knees and squatting to work on the lower leg, but I caution her never to actually kneel, because if the horse moves suddenly, she won't be able to get out of his way fast enough to avoid being stepped on.

For brushing the hind leg, I have her face the rear while doing the back of the leg, but face the front when doing the front of the leg, since her hand on the front of the horse's leg will discourage him from bringing it forward, which he must do in order to kick. Similarly, when she reaches through to do the inside of the opposite hind leg, she should reach in *front* of the nearer leg, as her arm will then be blocking that leg from coming forward.

Since at this point we are pointing out a number of possible dangers, it is just as well to remind the student that almost any potentially dangerous action would be most unlikely in a mature, well-trained horse. At this point you are merely trying to help her develop safe habits to help her in her future riding career.

Changing Sides

After we have finished "grooming" the left side, it is time to move over to the other side of the horse. I explain that you always walk in front of the horse if at all possible, so that he can see you and so that if he isn't tied, he isn't tempted to walk away. If the horse is crosstied, I explain that you must be careful not to pull on the horse if you lift the crosstie when you duck under.

Once on the other side of the horse, I have the student "hand groom" him on that side as well, with her hand positions reversed from left-side grooming.

Next she learns how to walk around the horse's hindquarters to reach the other side, unless she is very timid about that area, in which case it is left for a later lesson. (Since I want the student to develop the habit of going around the front of the horse anyway, this can be left for later with all students, but in that case it may be overlooked.) I tell the student that for the moment she should only walk around behind the horse if she can't walk in front of him—if he is standing with his head in the corner of the stall, for example. I explain that the horse cannot see directly behind him, and also that he sees separately out of each eye. Therefore, when you walk into his blind spot you disappear for a moment and then suddenly reappear on the other side as a different image. A nervous horse may be threatened by this.

There are two safe ways to walk around a horse's hindquarters. The safer way, if there is plenty of space, is to walk about a horse's length away from the animal all the way around. The horse's kicking range is far greater than most people realize, and some horses will even hurl themselves backward with their front legs to increase their range. If you had to get around a horse while carrying something that he found really threatening, or perhaps leading a horse that he didn't like, you would want to leave at least this distance for safety.

For ordinary purposes, and especially when grooming and tacking, the safest way is to walk as close to the horse as possible as you walk around him. I have the student watch me while I start at the horse's withers, facing the rear, with the hand closest to the horse resting on his back. I then walk around him at a steady pace, keeping my hand on him until I am on the other side, then lifting it so as not to rub the hair the wrong way as I continue up to his shoulder before beginning to work on the new side. Next, I return to a position directly behind the horse and point out that I am so close to him that it would be difficult for him to kick me really hard even if he wanted to. I point out that the worst place to be is about a step away, and I show how some people walk around the horse with their hand on his quarters, but walking as far away as they can reach, which is right in the danger area. This is a good time, if the horse likes it, to scratch him above the tail to demonstrate that the back end of a horse is pretty cute too!

Next I have the student follow me around the horse's quarters, placing her hand as I do mine. By leading her, I give her a little extra confidence. We walk from one side to the other several times.

MOVING THE HORSE OVER

This is another lesson that may be saved for later, since it asks the student to assume some control of the horse. However, this is a good time to introduce the concept that the horse moves himself—the person merely gives directions—so strength must never be used in the sense of trying to push the horse one way or another.

I begin by pointing out that in asking the horse to do something, you must also make it *possible* for him to do it if you are to get a result. I explain that for the horse to move over, he has to be able to pick up his foot and keep his balance. I then ask the student to stand with her feet together, and I stand beside her and push on her shoulder, pushing her sideways. She takes a step sideways and I continue pushing as she steps. She immediately feels how she is being pushed off balance. I point out that a horse under the same conditions will push back, which can be disconcerting, not to say scary, if you happen to be between him and the wall.

I then repeat the pushing, but this time as the student lifts her foot to step over, I stop pushing, so she feels how the release actually helps her to move. I ask for another step or two so she feels how the push and release gets the number of steps I want. Then I have her try with the horse, asking him to move his hindquarters over by pressing with her hand against the side of his hindquarter, and releasing as she feels him shift his weight.

This is a good time to teach the Parelli concept of four levels of pressure, and the clicker concept of positive reinforcement. If he doesn't move right away, I suggest using a cluck, but I try to use a horse who moves easily. If necessary, I move him a step or so myself to remind him of his job.

To move his forehand, I demonstrate using the halter and lead rope to bring his head to the side we want him to step to, again applying pressure until the horse starts to step, then releasing to allow the step.

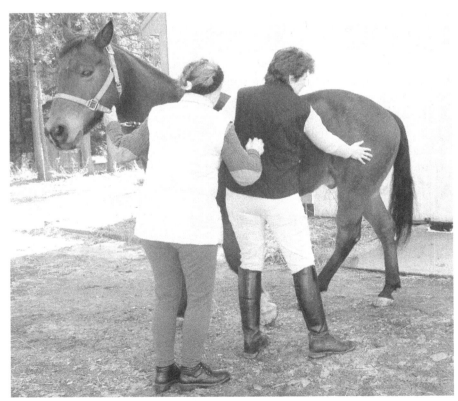

Peg is learning to move Sammy's hindquarters. I'm holding him a little tight, so he's tense in the neck, but he's crossing over nicely behind.

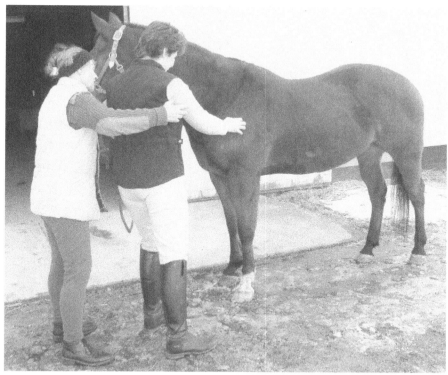

Moving Sammy's forehand to the right. His left front foot is just starting to come off the ground and will cross in front of the right foot, as it should.

HOLDING THE HORSE

If the student is part of a group, she may need to be able to hold her horse while she is waiting her turn. The important concept to introduce here is that she shouldn't worry if she cannot stop the horse if he chooses to move, and that controlling the horse in any way is not expected of her until she has had more experience. It is my belief that many riders are made either aggressive or timid by being asked to control a horse before they have either the confidence or the essential basics from which controlling skills are derived. In addition, I would certainly never give a beginner a horse to hold under circumstances that would tempt him to move, such as near grass or when other horses are leaving; nor would I leave her if I felt she was at all insecure. It is my practice in beginner lessons always to have a ground person for each horse, or at least for every two horses.

After the horse has been tacked I choose a place where the horse will probably stand quietly, perhaps still in the stable. I leave the reins on the horse's neck on the theory that if the beginner should have to let go of the horse, he will be less likely to break the reins before I catch him.

Peg is holding Sammy on her own. She isn't really a novice, so holding him outside the stable is okay. Notice the loose line, and how she is keeping his attention by facing him and rubbing his muzzle.

Having explained that I do not expect her to hold the horse still, I then show her that if she stands fairly close to the horse's head in a "conversational" position and talks to him or perhaps scratches him, he will probably be perfectly content to stand there. I pull the rein around so that there is slack on the left side, then, after having her check her five steps again, I have her hold the rein about a foot (30 cm) from the bit. I make sure that her arm is relaxed from the shoulder to the fingers and, taking the rein in my hand, pull it back and forth through her hand a little to make sure it slides freely. I then take the horse's head and turn it away and back, telling her to keep her arm relaxed and allow this to happen. I also tell her that if the horse started to walk away, she should call me immediately and not try to stop him by herself. If she feels comfortable walking beside him until I get there, she may do so; otherwise, she should let him go and get out of the way.

This might sound like asking for trouble, but to begin with it is my responsibility as instructor to choose the horse and the situation so that a horse doesn't try to take advantage. And if the student tries to stop the horse and fails, it leaves her with an unfortunate feeling that she can't control the horse, which in turn leads to loss of confidence. Whereas if she doesn't make the attempt, she hasn't failed. This is another important part of developing the relationship between rider and horse, which is what the introduction is about.

By the time the introduction is complete, the student should be quite comfortable with the horse she is working with. Since the next step is for her to be sitting on the horse and trusting him with her safety, her level of comfort needs to be quite high. And since her first experience with something new has a tremendous effect on her whole future in the field, spending the extra half-hour developing a comfortable relationship with the horse may well affect her entire riding career.

4

Grooming, Tack, and Tacking
Talking to Your Horse in Different Ways

I attended a clinic with a woman who worked for me, where we rode the hosts' horses. Because they had a school program, our horse assignments changed each day. The first day, we noticed one horse who was very difficult to control under tack. He was obviously extremely tense and had to be restrained all the time.

On the third day, my friend was assigned this horse for the afternoon session. She was then not a terribly experienced rider and was concerned that she wouldn't be able to handle the horse. Having observed the horse for several days, I had seen no signs of aggressiveness, just fear. We swallowed our lunch quickly and went to the horse's stall to get him ready for the session. Every one else was tacking up rapidly, bringing their horses out and warming them up, to get to know them. Instead, we stayed in the stall with our horse for quite a while, using TTeam to get him to relax and accept us, which he wasn't prepared to do at first.

Gradually he settled down and we tacked him up slowly, pausing to reassure him at each step. Eventually we brought him out and immediately he tensed up again. So that he wouldn't transfer his tension to my friend, I took him and led him around quietly for a few minutes. By now he was beginning to realize we weren't going to ask too much of him, since we had spent so much time with him in the stall, so he quickly settled down. He had one more little panic attack when she mounted, so I led him around again until he was calm.

Later, during my teaching session, I looked down to watch my friend and the tense horse. He was going like a reasonable animal. Occasionally he would start to tense up a little, and she would just pat him and tell him it was all right, and he believed her! He went better for her than for anyone else who rode him, not because she was a better rider but because we used the grooming time to develop trust, which was all he wanted.

If you are into techniques that emphasize groundwork, I don't have to tell you the importance of groundwork in building a good relationship with your horse. However, not everyone has worked with these techniques or has the time or desire to do so. But everyone grooms and tacks up, and these necessary jobs can be made to do double duty. Grooming involves all kinds of communication, one of the most important of which is the way you use your voice.

TALKING TO YOUR HORSE

Talking to others is such a natural thing that we tend not to think about it at all. Sometimes this is good, sometimes not so good. You need to recognize right from the start how the horse responds to your voice and the different ways you can use it, because many people talk to their horse almost as much as they talk to other people. And he responds, though not in ways you are accustomed to. I have read that conversation is to people as mutual grooming is to animals— a way to establish and strengthen relationships. If this is so, then talking to your horse may be something he can understand on an emotional level even when the words are meaningless.

How much can the horse understand of what you say? Most older horses have quite a large vocabulary of words they know the meaning of. Any horse who shows on the flat very much, and any experienced lesson horse, knows the basic commands walk, trot, canter, halt, line up, and often responds more quickly than the rider. And virtually all horses with any experience at all understand the cluck that means move and the whoa that means slow down or stop.

In addition, most horses can interpret some of what you are saying by the way you say it, and they seem to have some faculty for reading either your thoughts or your body language and putting that together with your words. Just the other day I was riding a horse I work with who is having trouble with his canter. As he started off he started to crowhop a little to release the tension in his back. That was okay, but then he started to crowhop a bit harder, so it was starting to be more like a buck. I said to him, "Hey, not *too* rough, please," and he immediately eased up and started to go forward more and straighten out. I can do the same thing with my cat when he wants to grab my hand and play with it.

Of course, I was not at all disturbed by the little crowhopping, so my voice and attitude were calm and without fear. If I had been frightened or angry and shouted at him with the same words, he might well have reacted differently. But under similar circumstances so would another human, wouldn't she?

In any case, your voice is an important tool and one you will be using quite a bit, so let's discuss some of the things you should know.

Voice Commands

Voice commands are the specific words or sounds you use to get a specific action; words the horse either knows or can easily learn. Most trainers agree commands should be only one or two syllables long so the horse can understand them clearly.

The following are the most common commands horses understand, but some horses have a much larger vocabulary.

The Cluck

The cluck isn't a word, and it doesn't even really sound like a cluck. In fact, when I was young we used the term "click," which I think describes the sound more accurately. It is made with your tongue in the side of your mouth and your cheek muscles. There is a very clear description of it in Alexandra Kurland's book *Clicker Training for Your Horse*. Most people learn it just from hearing other people use it and watching. Some people are unable to learn it at all, just as some people are unable to curl up their tongues.

The cluck simply asks the horse to move, or to move faster, or to keep moving, depending on circumstances. Accompanying body movements make it clear to him which direction you want. For instance, if you are standing at his side facing his barrel and you tap him on the quarters and cluck, he understands that you want him to step sideways away from you, whereas if you are standing near his head facing forward holding his lead line and you start forward and cluck, he understands that you want him to follow you.

The cluck can be used both for ground training and riding. You do have to be a little careful using it when riding with others, because some horses will react to it no matter who is doing it. Many trainers, especially, have a very authoritative cluck that they use when a horse is considering being disobedient with a student. Horses who are accustomed to this will often react in an "Uh-oh, now what have I done?" kind of way when they hear it, which can be disconcerting for their riders.

Whoa

Again, the word we use in print isn't necessarily the word we use. Often we shorten it to "ho." If it is short and sharp when you're working with the horse on the ground, it means "stand still and stop fidgeting," or if the horse is moving around either loose or under tack, it means "stop now." If it is drawn out and sort of sung, it means either "slow down" or "It's okay, relax, nothing's going to hurt you."

Many trainers believe the whoa command is a very important safety device and teach the horse very thoroughly *always* to stop when he hears it. They also insist—rightfully—that it never be used unless you want the horse to stop.

However, I have observed that if the horse is really frightened, either by the rider or by circumstances, he may not respond to just a voice command even if he's well trained.

The whoa command is very useful, though, and you should make a point of listening to the way experienced horsemen use it and how their voices sound, since you will be using it a lot.

Walk, Trot, Canter

Horses are often trained to respond to these commands, coming either from the trainer or instructor or from the rider. They can be used both when riding and when working the horse from the ground.

When you are asking the horse to *increase* the gait—say, from the halt to the walk—the word "walk" (or sometimes "walk on") is spoken with a rising inflection, and the word is kept short. Very often it is combined with a cluck. When you are asking the horse to *decrease* the gait—say, from the trot to the walk—your inflection drops at the end of the word and the word is dragged out. The addition of the whoa is also often added, as in "hooooo, waaaalk" (long o sound, long *aw* sound).

Some trainers believe that during training you should first use the cluck or the whoa plus whatever other aids are appropriate to get the gait you want, and then use the word *as* the horse breaks into that gait, so he makes the association between the word and the gait.

Sounds and Feelings

As we said, to a great extent the horse is influenced by the *sound* of the words, not just the words themselves. Thus, a rising inflection tells the horse to move on and a falling inflection tells him to slow down. In addition, the emotions behind the words have a strong influence. We have all met people whose words were very polite but who carried a great deal of anger inside, so that no matter what they *said*, they made their hearers very uncomfortable. Horses are even more consciously aware of the emotions behind our words than we are, since most of the time the words are fairly meaningless unless they are commands the horse knows.

Periodically, horsemen will debate whether a rider should talk to her horse all the time, with both sides of the question defended very actively. I think there are several kinds of people who talk to their horses all the time while riding. One is a very secure, supportive person who finds that talking verbalizes her thinking and sends good, clear messages to the horse: "That's it. Steady. Very good. Careful. Okay!" Another kind is the person who is extremely insecure and nervous and just happens to be the sort of person who talks when she's nervous. It is really more babbling than talking, and makes everyone around her nervous and irritable as well. Neither of these is the same as the person who simply talks to her horse as she would to a human friend.

Shouting, whether in fear or in anger, is rarely a good thing to do, especially if you are inexperienced. There are times when it is appropriate for an experienced horseman for example, if she sees that one horse is about to attack another, either in the field or during a lesson, shouting at him to stop will very often make him back off long enough to get them separated. Most horses know perfectly well what behavior is unacceptable. However, if the horse expects to be punished, shouting may make him panic and run to avoid it—not very desirable if a beginner is sitting on him. Some people can raise their voices without disturbing the horses, others seem to create fear instantly, which is probably a function of their underlying emotions.

When you see horses who appear to be very confident, calm, and well trained, make a point of listening to how their trainer uses her voice, both with horses and with people. The voice can be a very effective aid when used correctly, but it takes some study both of the technique and of yourself!

Now that you know something about how to relate to the horse in your language, it's time to learn how to relate to him in his.

GROOMING: HORSE AND RIDER MAKING FRIENDS

There are lots and lots of books about grooming, and a saddlery catalog will provide you with a choice of grooming tools to suit any horse and pocketbook. It is not the goal of this book to teach you how to retrain a horse with a problem. Therefore, we are going to assume the horse you are working with is accustomed to being groomed and tacked and has no difficulty accepting them. Instead, my goal is to teach you how to work with the horse without *creating* a problem.

There is far more to grooming than just scrubbing a dirty horse. Grooming is a time when human and horse can really build a relationship. Mutual grooming is one of the main actions all mammals use to create trust and express love. It is done every time the horse is ridden, so the rider has a constantly recurring opportunity to become closer emotionally to her horse. I think people who never groom their own horses are missing out on a major aspect of the relationship.

Some of the less sentimental might say, "I'm not interested in a close relationship with my horse. I just want him to get the job done." Fine. But if you are the one *doing* the job, will you not put out a far greater effort for a person you really want to please, a person you feel cares about you, than you will for someone who treats you as just another cog in the machine?

One of my students and her horse wanted to jump. At least, the student wanted to jump. The horse was not very sound and not very talented over fences. The rider was also no great shakes at that point. However, they had a very close relationship. The girl just adored that horse and spent hours grooming and playing with him on the ground. And the horse would jump for her. He wouldn't jump for other, better riders, but would consistently jump for her!

If you get into a tight corner, will you be willing to endanger your own perceived safety to protect a person who doesn't care about you? I had a horse of whom I was extremely fond, who had a hind leg injury that needed treatment. It was a hot summer day and I was squatting pretty much underneath him to reach the wound. I heard a buzzing sound and realized one of those enormous horseflies who seem to have a bite like a wolf had landed on my horse's sensitive midline. Rather than lashing out at the fly with his foot, which would certainly have knocked me down at the very least, my horse lifted his hind foot and very slowly and carefully *scraped* the fly off his belly! I recently heard from a woman in a similar situation with a horse she didn't know very well, who was kicked in the face. The kick was unintentional, but also indicated a lack of concern on the part of the horse!

So developing a warm, caring relationship with your horse can pay big dividends, and grooming is the place to start. We groom a horse for four reasons. The first is to get him clean, not only for appearances but also to prevent skin inflammations and chafing sores on dirty hide. The second is to look for injuries that might have occurred in the stall or field. The third is for massage and increased circulation—especially important with stallbound horses or during cold weather. But the fourth and most important is the relationship.

Unfortunately, very often the first reason is overemphasized at the cost of the last one. Many times I have been in show stables where a professional groom seemed to be attacking the horse with grooming tools. At least the horse thought so, and he would have his ears back, his tail would be lashing and he would be pawing or stomping back and forth on the crossties while the groom yelled at him to stand still. I have to really feel sorry for the rider who was expected to get on this tense and angry animal in a few minutes.

Part of this treatment is based on the assumption that somehow all horses are alike, so what one horse will accept every other horse should also accept. I'm not quite sure how people reconcile that with the different ways horses respond to training! There is no question that some horses are more sensitive physically than others, that some like being curried vigorously while others hate it, that some horses love having their faces and ears brushed while others don't.

So what are we talking about? Listening to your horse. Paying attention to his responses. This will accomplish at least two things. It will help your horse stand pleasantly for grooming and it will teach you a lot about how horses express themselves. A contented, relaxed horse stands still, with his tail still and his head low, unless you hit a really special spot, in which case his head usually goes up and his nose out, accompanied by a wriggling upper lip. This is a reflexive response—when he is being scratched the right way he wants to return the favor and scratch you back. Occasionally, if someone is standing by the horse's head talking to you as you groom, they suddenly find themselves the recipient of a free back scratch!

If your horse is not happy with what you are doing, he may show it subtly at first: fidgeting, swishing his tail quickly (as opposed to the slow, leisurely swing to keep flies away), raising his head. As you ignore him, the signals will become stronger. Fidgeting becomes pawing, the tail begins to swish continuously, the ears go back. Raising the hind leg to kick or snapping the teeth comes next. The horse is by now "shouting" at you. Why aren't you listening?

Choosing and Using Grooming Tools

The two factors that affect how your horse responds to grooming are the tools you choose and the way you use them. Horse owners often end up with a large collection of grooming tools, many of which are unused because the horse rejects them.

The basic tools are the curry comb and the brush. Avoid metal or plastic curry combs and stick to the flexible rubber ones, in a size that fits your hand. The Grooma brand groomer has big, soft, flexible teeth that many horses love. The grooming mitten is a rubber mitten with little pimples, good for sensitive skin! Most horses like curry combs, but only if used with discretion, especially in cold weather when skin and muscles are more sensitive. If your horse can't abide even the softest curry comb, try a hot, damp piece of an old towel. Curry combs are used across or against the hair about the way you would scrub a pot. You don't use them on bony places such as the lower leg, except very carefully if necessary to loosen caked dirt. They bring all the dust to the surface, and when you're finished currying, the horse looks like a large dust bunny.

After currying comes brushing. Brushes come in a number of different stiffnesses and two basic shapes. The long-bristled, long, oval dandy brush acts rather like a broom, sweeping the dust down the horse and off. Usually you have two or three of these—one of moderate stiffness to sweep, then a very soft finishing brush to polish and a stiffer mud brush to use on the longer hair (if you're not into clipping) on the backs of the lower legs. Some horses will accept only the softest finishing brush on their bodies.

Many horses like the body brush, especially if you spring for a really good, expensive one. This acts more like a vacuum cleaner, picking up the dust and holding it until you clean it by scrubbing across it with the curry comb, which you then bang on the floor (not the varnished wall!) to clear it of dust. Some of them have an outer row or two of slightly stiffer bristles that push the dust

> ### *Tidbits & Supplements*
>
> Clicker training is very effective for working with horses who are phobic about grooming. It helps them find out that they can stand still for grooming and you aren't going to hurt them.

along, with soft bristles in the middle that collect the dust and polish at the same time. Their only fault is that they are quite large and therefore difficult for people with small hands.

Manes can be a source of difficulty. Many horses have had their manes pulled roughly (if it doesn't hurt, why is he throwing himself over backward?). The best tool for every day is an ordinary human hairbrush, fairly stiff. Always brush manes and tails from the bottom up, that is, brush out the bottom two or three inches, then move up and brush out the bottom six inches, and so on. You don't pull out as much hair, which keeps the mane from hurting and the tail skirt from getting too thin.

I have found that some horses who don't like brushes and curry combs don't mind a horse vacuum cleaner, perhaps because it doesn't have the same associations. And you can get the horse very clean. However, in cold climates using the vacuum in a cold barn on a cold day is the same as having an icy wind blowing right over the skin, so again, you have to listen to the horse.

PICKING HOOVES

Picking feet is something that often scares the handler more than the horse. If you are a novice, you should be pretty comfortable with the horse on the ground before you start picking out feet, especially the hind ones. The best hoofpicks do *not* fold and have a point like a screwdriver blade. An attached stiff brush is also handy, though I haven't seen one accompanying the screwdriver point.

You pick up the foot by standing facing the horse's tail, running the nearer hand down the back of the horse's leg and pinching either just below the knee or just above the fetlock. With most horses, if you don't grab their hoof as soon as they pick it up, they put it right back down.

Once you have the foot up, start at a back corner and clean with the pick around the outside, which is the sole and is fairly impervious to pain. Work your way in toward the frog, with its cleft and comasures. These should be cleaned thoroughly but carefully, since if the horse has thrush—the equine equivalent of athlete's foot—they can be quite sensitive. Finish by using a brush to remove loose scrapings.

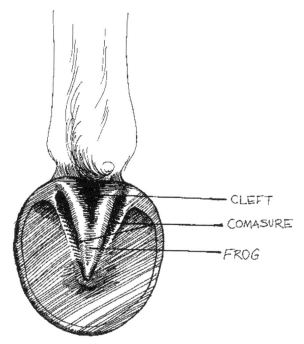

CLEFT

COMASURE

FROG

The bottom of a healthy hoof. The large area is the sole, and the lower edge of the wall is around the outside. If thrush is present, the cleft and comasures will be much deeper, and the frog may be eroded and deformed.

Things to be conscious of include:

• Make sure the horse is standing squarely so he can balance on three legs. If you move him around until he picks up the foot you want, then puts it down quietly and stands, he will be ready to pick it up and hold it for you.

• Pick the foot straight up and place your near leg *under* the horse. *Do not* pull his leg out to the side (this is the part novices have trouble with!).

• When working with the hind foot for any length of time, place the hoof so it rests inside your knee. This is much less tiring and it is not possible for the horse to kick you, since he has to move you out of the way first.

• Hold the *hoof*, not the pastern, with one hand as you pick with the other, so you don't bend his pastern joint backward as you dig in.

• Avoid using painful treatments for thrush or digging too hard with the pick if the horse's foot is sensitive. If the horse says it hurts, believe him!

Running around in sand scours out a foot pretty effectively if the horse has a problem and won't allow you to work with his feet. This can give you a chance to retrain him slowly without having to force the issue for health reasons.

TACKING UP: HALTERS AND BRIDLES

The halter gives you your first tool for directing the movement of the horse's head, and thus the beginning of directing the horse himself. Putting on the halter is the introduction to working around the horse's head, and especially learning to handle his ears. Many horses are extremely sensitive about their heads and ears, either through lack of training or through actual mishandling. Because the ears project up and out from the head, they are easily grabbed by a predator or other enemy, so the horse instinctively rejects having them handled. (The reason horses—and other animals—put their ears back when they're angry is to keep them out of harm's way in case of a fight.)

The best way to *learn* to put on the halter is to have the horse you are going to learn on standing on crossties with an extra halter already on him, but around his neck instead of on his head. If this is not possible, he should be in a stall. If it is necessary to work with the horse outside, unless the horse is exceptionally calm and obedient you should have an experienced person help you until you become comfortable with the skill. This is because the horse will sense your lack of confidence, which may make him tense and unwilling to stand long enough for you to get the halter on—and if he is loose it can be very difficult to keep his attention.

The Halter

The most common type of halter, made of either leather, nylon or rope, has a long crown strap that goes over the horse's head just behind the ears and fastens with a buckle or clasp on the left side just behind and above the horse's eye. There is sometimes a buckle on the other side as well, which is usually used only for adjustments. The buckle(s) are attached, in some cases by rings, to short cheek straps, which hold up the nose band on the sides. A third strap under the jaw holds up the back of the nose band. This jaw strap hangs from a throat strap, which may have a snap on the left side, fastened to the ring at the top of the cheek strap.

Putting the Halter On
The most important part of putting the halter on is how you approach the horse and where you stand. Unless you know the horse well, if you walk straight toward his face from the front holding the halter in front of you, his instinct not to get caught (and eaten) may take over and he will turn his back and

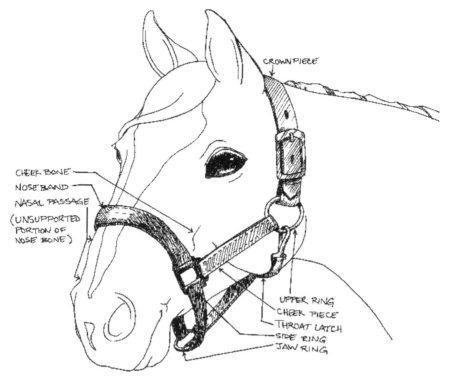

Parts of the halter. This halter is nicely fitted, but if your horse likes to remove his,
it could be safely adjusted a little higher on his throat.

leave. Instead, keep the halter by your side or even a little behind you while
you approach the horse and allow him to sniff. If hand feeding is allowed, you
can also feed him a little treat.

Once he has accepted your presence, step around until you are standing
quite close to him, right behind his head, facing forward. With your body in
this position, you make it just a little awkward for him to either step forward or
back up, and yet you are not threatening him at all. If you like (and he likes it),
before you start putting the halter on you can reach back and scratch his withers. This is a good thing to do psychologically, because it helps him think of you
as a companion rather than a predator, and thus improves the chances of his
allowing you to approach when he is not restricted by a stall.

There are two ways to put an ordinary halter on an ordinary horse. The first
way is the same as bridling, except for the bit, and therefore is the most practical for the novice to learn. The second way is used for halters that do not unfasten at the throat strap, or for horses who are sensitive about their ears.

Preparing to put on the halter. So that I
have some control, the lead rope is around
his neck, just behind my arm.

For the first method, the crown strap of the halter should be fastened and the throat strap unfastened.

1. Hold the crown strap in your right hand with the halter facing forward and your fingers on top. With your left hand, hold the nose band of the halter just about at the side ring.

2. If you are tall enough, slide your right arm gently over the horse's left ear so your forearm is resting lightly on top of his head and your hand is in front of him just about between his eyes. If you can't reach that high easily, instead bring your arm across below his left ear and above his eye until your hand—holding the halter—is in the center of his face. Be careful not to drag the halter across his eye. At the same time (this is what takes practice), guide the rest of the halter with your left hand so the nose band goes around his nose.

3. Pull the halter up smoothly until the nose band is snug, but *do not attempt to pull it back over both the horse's ears at once*. This cramps his ears

---

Tidbits & Supplements

Here is a little trick that helps if the horse puts his head up when you start to put the halter on. If you tilt *your* head back to look up at him, that will encourage him to raise his head even more. Instead, keep your head level and look up with just your eyes.

---

uncomfortably and leads to resistance. Instead, bring your left hand up and take the crown strap in your left hand. With your right hand, gently guide the horse's left ear forward. Notice that the ear does not go straight forward, but out and forward in a little half circle. Feel how the ear moves most easily and let it follow the path of least resistance.

4. Lift the crown strap over the ear and place it behind, being careful not to drag the halter across the horse's eye. If it will not go easily, do not force it, but check the halter again to make sure it's not twisted somewhere or caught on the horse's face.

5. If you can reach the other ear easily over the top of the horse's head, also point it forward and bring the crown strap over in the same way. If you cannot reach it, walk quietly around to the other side of the horse's head, keeping a hand lightly on the halter (the halter will stay on by one ear for the moment), and use your *left* hand to guide the right ear forward, then bring the crown strap into place with your right hand.

6. Finally, return to the horse's left side and fasten up the throat strap. If it seems tight, make sure the jaw strap is in the center, not pulled off to one side.

Now check the fit of the halter. The nose band should rest just below the horse's cheekbones, and if it's adjustable it should not be tight, but should not be so loose that he could get a foot through it. The throat latch should be at the top of the horse's jaw but not digging into his throat. While adjusting the halter is not as delicate as adjusting the bridle, if the halter is too loose it can be dangerous because of the greater possibility of getting caught on something, and if it's too tight it is uncomfortable for the horse, especially if it's left on for long periods.

Putting on the halter. Step one, with my arm over Sammy's poll.

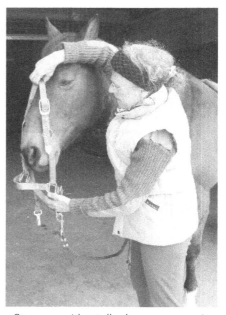

Step one with a taller horse; my arm is over his temple instead.

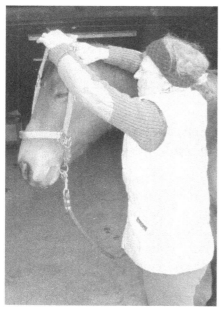

Step two, the halter has been pulled up over his nose, and I am carefully putting his left ear under the crownpiece.

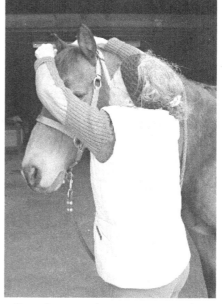

Step three, reaching across to put his right ear under the crownpiece. If he was taller, I would walk around. The finishing step is to fasten the throat latch, making sure the jaw strap is centered, everything fits comfortably, and nothing is twisted.

If the halter does not unfasten at the throat, you use a different technique both for putting it on and removing it.

1. Stand in the same place, behind the horse's head. Place your right arm over the horse's neck, as far back as you need to so you can reach comfortably. Pass the halter under his neck and take the end of the crown strap in your right hand. Then take the halter with your left hand at the buckle.

2. Bring the halter up quietly around the horse's nose until the nose band is snug around his face.

3. Now hold it up with your left hand while you bring the crown strap across.

4. Fasten the crown strap and check the halter as in the first method.

You can also put the crown strap around from underneath instead of putting your arm over the horse's neck, which might work better with a very tall horse. It takes some experimenting to hold the crown strap short enough so you can control it but long enough so it reaches over his neck. Try to flip it across and back far enough so you don't hit his ears by mistake. You'll need a little practice to flip it hard enough so that it comes over the horse's neck, but not

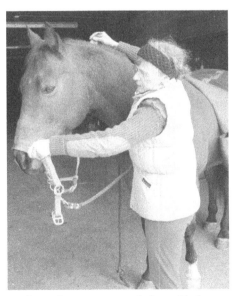

Preparing to put on a halter with the crownpiece open. This method is used with most rope halters, or with horses who are head- or ear-shy.

so hard that it frightens him. If you do it just right, you will be able to catch it with the fingers of your left hand. Check the fit as previously described.

The purpose of having a halter on the horse is so that you can either lead him or tie him. For leading or tying with one rope, fasten the rope to the ring under the center of the horse's jaw. For cross tying, fasten one rope on the lower cheek ring on each side. If the horse stands quietly and you want to give him some extra freedom, the ropes can be fastened to the upper cheek rings instead.

Taking the Halter Off

If you are removing the halter to turn the horse loose in a field, always stand him facing the gate or fence. If he is facing the field, in his eagerness to go out he may rush past you and kick out, not maliciously but from excitement. By having him face the gate, you can step out of the way when he wheels to go out.

1. Stand behind the horse's head as you did when you put the halter on, and slip your left thumb under the crown strap just below his ear.

2. Lift the strap over his left ear, then slide your hand along the strap a little way and lift it off his right ear. Your left forearm will now be across his face with the crown strap in your hand.

3. Slide your forearm down his nose until the nose band drops below his chin, then bring your arm down and away.

By removing the halter in this way, you will never accidentally pinch the horse's ears, as can happen if you try to pull it off over both ears at once. Sliding your hand down his nose prevents him from throwing his head up before the halter is completely off, in which case the halter can catch on his nose and jerk on him.

To remove a halter by the crown strap, simply unbuckle the strap and let the halter fall down and away. Sometimes a horse who has had the halter removed roughly over his ears will be more comfortable having it removed this way.

Bridles

Once you have become competent at haltering, bridling really isn't much more difficult unless the horse is very resistant. If you don't use a bit, the procedure is almost identical, except for some preliminary steps.

1. Bridles are always hung up with the front facing outward. As you take the bridle off its hook, hang it over your left forearm with the front facing you. Loop the reins over your forearm as well. Check to be sure the throat latch, caveson nose, and curb chain, if any, are all unfastened.

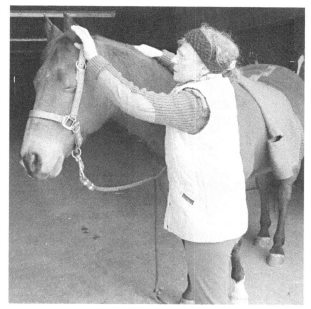

Removing the halter, the first step. Notice where I am standing, and that I am only lifting it over one ear at a time.

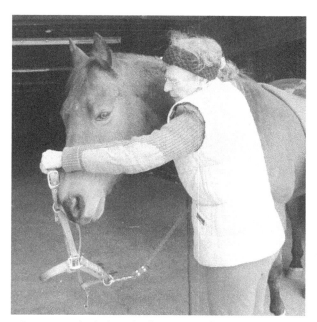

Removing the halter, the final step. After it is safely off both ears, I slide my forearm down the front of Sammy's nose. This keeps him from throwing his head, and he is less likely to try to bolt if I am turning him loose.

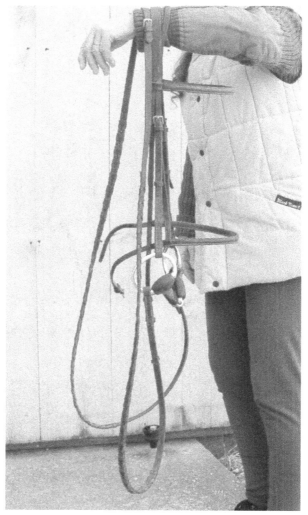

The proper way to carry a bridle. It won't get tangled, and it's all ready to put on. If necessary, you can carry several bridles at once this way.

2. Stand in the same position you took to put on the halter (page 58). With a continuous rein bridle, take the reins off your left arm with your right hand and place them over the horse's head, but only a few inches behind the ears. Be sure you don't twist them so they are crossed. With the reins in this position, if the horse decides to walk away, you can grab both reins under his throat and have some leverage to control him. With a split rein bridle, you can let the reins drop, wrap them around the horse's neck as above or leave them over your arm.

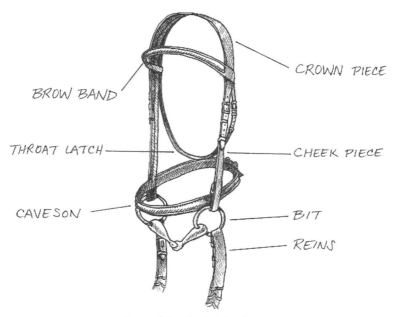

BROW BAND

CROWN PIECE

THROAT LATCH

CHEEK PIECE

CAVESON

BIT

REINS

Parts of the English bridle.

3. Undo the rope(s) and remove the halter, setting it aside or hanging it over your right shoulder. If you are very inexperienced with bridling or the horse is a little fussy, you can drop the halter down off the horse's nose, then slide it back around his neck. (This is not recommended for a horse you don't know—a few horses are not comfortable being restrained by the neck.) For safety reasons, never leave a halter hanging attached to a crosstie or on the ground under the horse's feet.

4. Hold the crown piece of the bridle in your right hand, just as you did with the halter. If there is no bit, you can put the bridle on almost exactly as you did the halter, just making sure the caveson nose is placed *in front* of the horse's face as you pull the bridle up.

5. If there is a bit, hold the middle of it on your lightly curved left palm and use your right hand to lift on the crown piece and bring the bit gently up against the horse's teeth. Slide the bit up and down a little against the teeth until you feel the place where the top and bottom teeth meet.

6. Pull gently up with your right hand, and many horses will open their mouths and take the bit. If not, slip your left thumb into the left upper corner of the horse's lips between his gums. Alternatively, you can reach across and slip your left fingers into the right upper corner of his mouth. Some horses

respond better to one technique than the other. If he still doesn't open his mouth, dig your thumbnail firmly into his gum. In any case, be sure to keep pressure with your right hand so the mouthpiece of the bit stays against the place where it can go into his mouth. This takes a bit of practice, so talk nice to your horse until you become less clumsy!

7. When he finally opens his mouth, *do not* yank the bit suddenly up into his mouth. Some horses have tense jaws and have trouble keeping their mouths open. Lift the bridle smoothly with your right hand as the horse allows it.

8. Once the bit is in his mouth the hard part is over. Now continue as you did with the halter, except that you have to guide the horse's ear between the crown piece and the brow band, or through the ear loop with a Western bridle. It should not feel too tight as you pull it over his ears, which would indicate the bridle was adjusted too short. In a correctly adjusted bridle, a snaffle bit just pulls the corners of the mouth enough to make a couple of little wrinkles, a curb rests in the corners but doesn't pull. You should also peek inside the horse's mouth to make sure the bit doesn't rest against the tushes, found in male horses.

9. Fasten the throat latch so it crosses the horse's jaw just above the middle. You want to avoid placing it where it would dig into his throat when he flexes at the poll. The caveson should hang about where the halter nose fits and should be adjusted to be snug but not tight. Curb chains should be unwound so that they lie flat, then adjusted to make a 45-degree angle with the shank of the bit. When putting on an English curb chain, hold the chain vertically, then on the right side put the *front* of the chain down over the hook, and on the left side put the *back* of the chain over the hook.

Tidbits & Supplements

If you need to leave the horse in his stall with the bridle on for just a minute or two, you can hook the reins behind the stirrups to keep him from accidentally stepping on them in your absence. However, if you want to leave him for a longer period, or if he isn't wearing a saddle, for his safety and comfort you should twist the reins up. First undo the throatlatch. Then bring the reins about a third of the way up his neck, and twist them around each other under his neck until they are snug at both the bit and the neck end. Now pass the throatlatch *between* the two reins in the center, and refasten it. Be sure there isn't a big loop near the horse's chin that he can step on if his head is down.

Removing the Bridle

The technique for removing the bridle, as with putting it on, is almost identical to removing the halter with the crown fastened.

1. Undo the throat latch, caveson, and curb chain, if any.

2. If you're turning the horse loose, bring the reins forward so they lie next to the crown piece. If you're planning to put the halter on, bring the reins about halfway up the horse's neck.

3. Standing just behind the horse's head and facing forward, use your left thumb to slip the crown piece gently over the horse's ears one at a time, starting with the left ear. If you are turning him loose, bring the reins over at the same time.

4. Slide your left arm with the crown piece down the horse's nose and hold it just below his eyes until he drops the bit. Occasionally a horse is slow to relax his jaw, so if you bring the bridle down too fast, the bit gets caught. Relaxing your own jaw helps with horses like this. Usually they just need a little extra time.

Now you can either let the horse loose or put the halter on. If there is a rope attached to the halter, bring the halter up *between* the two reins to avoid tangling when you take the reins off.

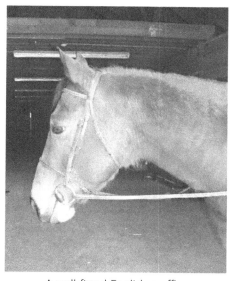

A well-fitted English snaffle.

THE BAREBACK PAD

For many years I have started nearly all my riders, no matter what their level of riding when they begin with me, on a bareback pad. Most bareback pads you buy at the tack shop are not really practical. They are not thick enough to protect either rider or horse; they sit on the horse in such a way that most of your leg hangs out in front, and the surcingle is so narrow and rough that it makes the horse tense.

An arrangement of pads that I find works for most situations consists of three or four layers. Next to the horse is an underpad of cotton, either quilted or thermal. This serves the dual purpose of keeping the other pads clean, since it is easy to wash, and, being cotton, prevents overheating of the horse's back. Next comes a thick Western pad—double fleece with foam between—then, if you want extra protection for horse or rider, a closed-cell foam pad, and finally, a double-faced fleece English pad. You might think with all this padding that you would get no feel of the horse whatsoever, but because everything is soft and flexible every motion is transmitted from one of you to the other. You can also ride the horse "bareback" for extended periods without hurting either him or yourself.

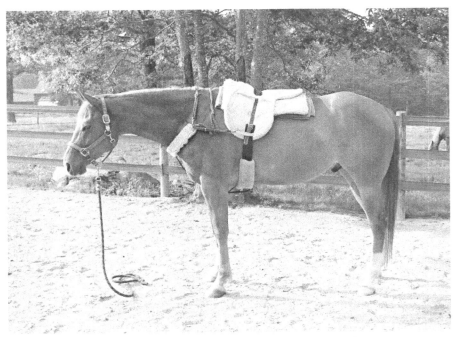

What the well-dressed horse wears for "bareback" riding.
The breastplate is perhaps a little high on his gullet.

The only way you can determine the combination that will be best for you and your horse is to experiment. Just remember it is essential for *both* of you to feel really comfortable when you are sitting correctly at whatever gaits you are riding. That means you have to pay attention to how your horse moves as well as how he behaves; changes in his gait, his carriage or his attitude can mean he is uncomfortable. Probably no one will have to tell you if *you* are uncomfortable, but if you find that you need to cheat a lot on your position to keep from getting sore, then you need to inspect your horse's equipment and perhaps make a change.

Surcingles and Stuff

You will need to fasten the pad or pads to your horse in a way that is both secure and comfortable for your horse. For this you will need a surcingle, which is a strap that goes completely around the horse and fastens to itself, usually with a buckle and strap. The surcingle should be at least three or four inches (7 to 10 cm) wide, and a fuzzy cover can be used as well.

Canvas or webbing surcingles can usually be purchased at tack shops, which sell them for use over blankets and turnout rugs. Avoid surcingles that have padding at the top to keep them centered and off the horse's spine. This is necessary with a stable blanket but is not comfortable to sit on! Don't get the kind that are made completely of elastic—they stretch too easily to hold the pad securely. You will need to measure your horse beforehand to get the correct length. Be sure to allow for stretch and for the thickness of the pads.

You can also make a surcingle quite easily using your horse's girth and two stirrup leathers or similar straps, or a cinch and a single wider strap. Lace the stirrup leathers or strap through the buckles on the off side of the girth or cinch, then pull the straps all the way through so that the buckles of both articles are together on the right side. Place the straps over the top of the horse's back, bring the girth or cinch up under the horse's barrel on the left side, and fasten the straps to the girth or cinch buckles on the near side.

Besides the surcingle, some sort of breastplate is a good idea, especially if you plan to do fast work or trail rides, where the pads could slide back. The breastplate is also a vehicle for a neck strap, which is essential for learning to ride bareback in a relaxed and confident manner.

Tacking Up with a Bareback Pad

The pad is placed differently on the horse than most people think. The tendency is to place the pad in the middle of the horse's *back*, rather than in the middle of the *horse*. As you look at the horse, you see that the lowest point of his back, where you will end up sitting (because it *is* the lowest point), is right behind his withers—that is, toward the front of his back.

As you look at the pad, you think you want to be sitting in the middle or even toward the front of it, to leave room for your seat. But it is really your knees that take up the space, and for your knees to be on the pad your seat needs to be just *behind* the middle of the pad.

With those points in mind, place the bottom pad with the middle of it about on top of the horse's withers, and then slide it back a few inches (which smoothes out the hair) so the middle is just in front of the "sitting place" on your horse's back. Now place any additional pad(s) centered over the first pad. If your horse shakes his body or drops and raises his head several times as you are dressing him, you may have to readjust the position of the pads. To avoid roughing up the hair, always pick the pads up, place them in the original position and slide them back into place. Never drag them forward.

When you place the surcingle over his back, hold on to the strap end, place the buckle end quietly over his back and allow it to drop on the other side. If you are using a breastplate or neck strap, put it on at this point, pass the surcingle through the side loops of the breastplate, then the loops on the saddle pad and then through the breast strap between the horse's front legs before fastening it on the horse's near side. Be sure to see the section on girths and girthing (page 74) to learn how to adjust the surcingle so the pads are secure and the horse is comfortable.

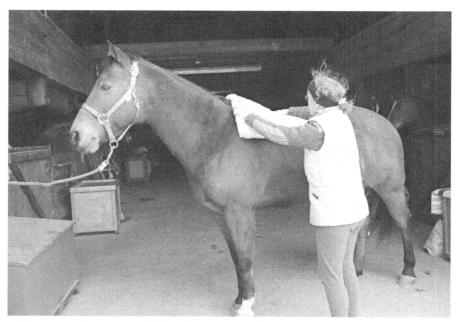

Placing the bareback pad. My right hand is on the low—sitting—point on Sammy's back. You can see that there is plenty of room for the rider's thigh on the pad.

Most of the early part of this book describes work that is best done on the bareback pad, so if you are either learning from scratch or planning some serious reconstruction of your riding skills, you will probably want to set yourself up with bareback pads. And of course, riding on bareback pads is also a lot of fun!

SADDLES

Let me say first of all that if you are serious about riding you should have your own saddle, even if you don't own a horse. Since the part of the saddle that touches the horse is padded, most saddles can be adjusted with additional padding to fit most horses adequately, unless you are riding for extended periods. The part of the saddle that you sit in, however, is rigid. If it doesn't fit you, forcing you to ride incorrectly, the horse will be far more uncomfortable than if the saddle isn't absolutely perfect for him.

Buying a saddle is something that should be approached with the help of the professional who is teaching you. If that's not possible, the professional at a reputable saddle shop should be able to fit you correctly. I hesitate to recommend buying a saddle by mail order, since every saddle is handmade and no two are alike. I once tried four supposedly identical saddles and only found one that was comfortable for me. And *comfortable* is the operative word. Nobody but you can tell how the saddle feels under your seat, and the right one just feels right.

Saddling Up

The same principles apply to the saddle that applied to the bareback pad. That is, the place where you sit, which is the lowest part of the saddle, should be over the lowest—and strongest—place on the horse's back. However, the saddle, unlike the bareback pad, has a rigid frame (called the tree), which has to be placed correctly relative to the horse's shoulder blades for him to be able to move his forehand easily.

1. Place the saddle and pad on the horse's withers and slide them back just as you did with the bareback pads. Look for the moment when you feel the saddle drop into place behind the horse's shoulder blades.

2. To check the position, slide your hand under the top front of the saddle and make sure it is sitting just *behind* the shoulder blade, *not* on top of it.

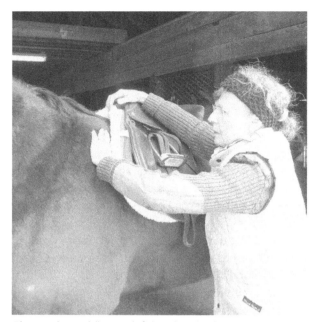

Placing the saddle. My left hand is checking to make sure
the saddle is sitting behind Sammy's shoulder blade,
while my right hand lifts the pad up off his withers.

3. For an English saddle, check the pad to make sure it isn't rumpled and is adjusted so that the billet loops are tight with the pad placed evenly under the saddle. The pad should project out about an inch all the way around, especially under the cantle. With your fingers, pull the pad up into the throat of the saddle.

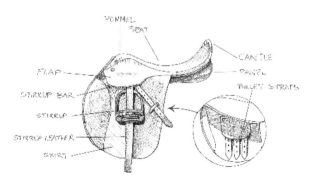

Parts of the English saddle.

Tidbits & Supplements

It is very important that the saddle sit level on the horse's back. This is not always easy to tell by eye, but you can tell when you ride. The most common way for the saddle to tilt is back, so the cantle is lower than the seat. You find yourself sliding toward the back, and leaning forward to compensate. On a short-backed horse the saddle will sometimes tilt forward. You find yourself up against the pommel, and arching your back or using your stirrups to get back again. Your horse may also be sticky because your center is too far forward relative to his.

I prefer to use soft, neatly folded towels to raise the saddle as necessary. The foam you buy for lifts nearly always compresses so easily that it quickly becomes worthless. You can buy saddle pads with pockets to put the towel in so it looks neat. Closed-cell foam inserts are another option. Of course, for the long term if you own your own horse you should have the saddle adjusted to fit the horse properly without additional padding.

If your saddle was tipped and you make it level, you will be astounded at the difference it makes in your balance!

Putting on and Removing the Neck Strap or Breastplate

Neck straps and breastplates are put on after the saddle or bareback pad is placed on the horse's back but before the girth is fastened. If they're put on beforehand and the horse puts his head down, they can slide down his neck and he can step on them or put his foot through a loop. The only real trick is making sure you put neck strap or breastplate on with the attaching straps facing the back. It is all too easy to put it on inside out!

The shoulder straps should not be attached to the saddle or pad until after the girth is fastened. If the horse spooks with the girth unfastened and the shoulder straps done up, he could end up with the saddle hanging around his neck. Not a good situation!

Hunting breastplate shoulder straps should be fastened to the D rings that are nailed into the tree of the saddle, not the ones that are stitched into the seam at the front of the skirt. The side straps on a polo breastplate or on the neck strap should be placed *above* the girth loops on the sides of the saddle pad, to keep them from sliding down and chafing or cramping the horse.

The chest strap that goes between the horse's legs *must* be placed in the exact center or it will cut into the tender inside of the horse's leg. This position must be checked after the girth is tightened, as well.

When removing the neck strap or breastplate, unfasten the shoulder straps before unfastening the girth. Once it is free, remove it from the horse's neck as quickly as possible to minimize the risk of him putting a foot through it. Slip it over the horse's head the same way you remove a halter or bridle.

GIRTHS, CINCHES, AND COMFORTABLE HORSES

This gets a separate heading because girthing is the cause of so many problems. I am going to use the word "girth" because I am accustomed to it, but the same rules apply for both girths and cinches. First let me say that a too-tight girth is *not* a substitute or a cure-all for improperly fitted tack, poor conformation or bad riding.

Our perception is that the girth is what keeps the saddle on—that is, without the girth the saddle would simply turn and fall off. This is not entirely true. What the girth does is hold the saddle in the correct position on the horse's back so that the horse's conformation can keep the saddle in place. When my mother was a child growing up in Virginia, she initially rode bareback. Then one day she found an old saddle up in the loft. It had stirrups but no girth. However, her old horse had very high withers so the saddle stayed on pretty well except going up hill, when she had to hang on firmly to the mane!

One day she was riding with her cousin when he challenged her to a race. Down the road they flew, neck and neck, and my mother thought she might even win. Then they came to a sharp bend in the road. Cousin and both horses flew around the turn; mother and saddle flew straight ahead. There are limits to what even high withers can do!

If the horse has well-developed withers to keep the saddle from turning, an evenly muscled back to keep it level, a good shoulder to keep it from sliding forward, and well-sprung ribs to keep it from sliding back, you need only to do up the girth snugly and ride in the center of the saddle with even weight on both irons to keep it in place.

As it happens, not all horses have this wonderful conformation, so adjustments and adaptations must be made. Unfortunately, the most common adjustment is to tighten the girth as much as humanly possible. I say "unfortunately" because an overly tight girth leads to all kinds of training and soundness problems.

A too-tight girth can be more dangerous than one that is too loose. In the latter case your saddle could turn and you could have a nasty fall. But we tend to forget that the girth goes around the horse's rib cage, which is fairly inflexible bone, and when it's too tight it can interfere with his ability to breathe comfortably. If the girth is too tight—and this is a matter of the *horse's* perception, not yours—the horse can respond with explosive bucking, rearing, bolting or throwing himself on the ground, any of which can get you badly hurt. On a sensitive horse, it will act just like a sharp spur if the horse takes a sudden, tense breath. (Tense breaths come from the chest muscles, relaxed ones from the diaphragm.) A less sensitive horse may accept the discomfort but still be tense, especially in the beginning of the ride. This tension often settles in the horse's back. The rigid back then weakens performance by interfering with the horse's function, and also may contribute significantly to hind leg breakdown. And of course, horses who are fearful about girthing can bite or kick quite nastily to avoid it.

Something you may not have considered is that when the horse has been standing around the stall or field, his muscles are tight, which is to say, compressed. As he moves around more vigorously and warms up, his muscles get longer and the horse actually gets physically thinner. Unless the horse runs around a lot in his field—and few horses do—he won't be as warmed up as you think. Lacking this knowledge, you may try to tighten the girth enough in the beginning to compensate for this. You might even believe the horse intentionally made himself fatter so the girth would loosen up later on. And of course, some horses do learn to do this in self-defense.

Overtightness of the girth is compounded if the girth has elastic ends. The purpose of the elastic is to allow the girth to be tightened firmly enough so the elastic is lightly stretched. Then when the horse exerts himself, as over a jump, the elastic stretches the rest of the way to give some freedom. However, if the girth is tightened until the elastic is fully stretched, not only is there nothing left for expansion, but the horse cannot find relief by relaxing because the girth contracts with him. (Think of putting a tight elastic band around your finger!)

Girthing Up

Besides the final adjustment of the girth, the *way* the girth is tightened has a lot to do with how the horse reacts to it. Biting and kicking while being girthed are nothing more than the horse trying to tell the handler he is being frightened or hurt. Many people have the attitude that this is nonsense and the horse shouldn't mind, but the horse obviously *does* mind and needs to be handled accordingly.

Because of the tendency many horses have to object to girthing—due to bad handling!—safety is an important consideration, especially if you are working with an unfamiliar horse. Unless the horse will stand well ground-tied, he should be tied or crosstied. Be sure the girth is long enough, and is adjusted on the far side so it will reach easily around at least to the first hole of the billets. For most horses, if the end of the girth hangs just above the hoof, it comes out about right. You can—and will—adjust it on both sides later.

The first point at which the horse may give trouble is when you reach under him for the girth. For safety, stand directly facing the horse's front leg. Rather than bending over, bend your knees so your head is in a position from which your eyes can see both ends of the horse—the end that bites and the end that kicks. If you are on the horse's left side, and expect the horse to nip, reach under with your right hand and pick up the hanging girth. If kicking is more likely, pick it up with your left hand. As you bring it under, don't bring it up against the horse's belly immediately. Instead, stand up while holding it away from him, then bring it smoothly and quickly up against him just until it makes firm but not uncomfortable contact. Hold it there for a minute so he finds out that you aren't going to yank on it.

The horse must be holding his head level, not down close to the ground, when you adjust the girth. When his head is down his back is lifted and he is bigger around. Thus if the girth is a little short you won't be able to get it around him, and when he raises his head it will immediately go slack.

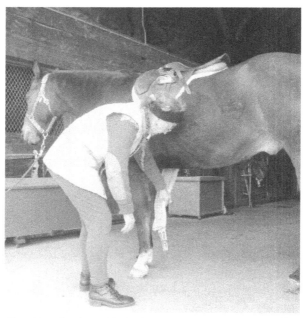

Reaching for the girth. In this case I am positioned as for a horse I expect might kick. If I were concerned that he might bite, I would reach under with my right hand instead, which would position me facing more forward so that I could watch his head.

Tidbits & Supplements

A not uncommon error when passing the strap through the girth buckle is to thread it through the inner half of the buckle, below the little central reinforcing bar. If you then tighten the girth up, it is almost impossible to get it off again. *Always* put the strap through the outer half.

Next, slip the point of the front billet strap through the front buckle of the girth. At this point most people lift up on the point of the billet and pull the girth up against the horse's belly. *Wrong!* This puts all the pressure on the horse's sensitive midline. Imagine if someone stood behind you and grabbed your belt and pulled! The pressure would all be on your stomach, like being punched. Now think about how you tighten your belt. As you pull the strap it pulls the belt a little away from your stomach, and the pull all comes against your spine, then you ease it and the pressure distributes itself evenly. To do the same thing on the horse, pull *down* on the billet strap first, which will create a little slack, then pull smoothly up to take up the slack and put the tongue in the nearest hole. If you can't get the tongue in a hole without pulling hard enough to upset the horse, it's too tight. After you do one strap, do the other one. Always try to have both straps adjusted to the same holes so the straps stretch evenly.

There are two ways to check the tightness of the girth. One is to simply take hold of the billet and lift up on it. If there is *enough slack* to tighten it, do so. If not, don't. This is the best way to check the girth when mounted, rather than trying to feel under the girth from the top of the saddle, which can be dangerous. Be sure to only adjust one strap at a time. If it comes up easily, pull until it feels tight, then do the other. Don't do both at once, in case something happens to disturb your horse while the girth is unfastened.

The second way, from the ground, is to slide your hand between horse and saddle. Most people (including me, for decades!) do this incorrectly. They slide their hand under the girth just *below* the saddle. Because of the thickness of the saddle and the shape of the horse, there is more space here anyway, which misleads one into thinking the girth should be tighter. Instead, slide your hand in—from front to back to avoid ruffling the hair—under the saddle at the horse's widest part. When removing your hand, press outward against the saddle so as not to drag against the hair.

How tight should the girth be? As tight as the horse can accept comfortably. If the slack is taken up in a smooth pull, without jerking, eventually you'll reach a point of firm resistance. When you slip your hand under the saddle the girth will feel firm but the horse will feel soft. Sometimes the girth will feel as if it would go up another hole, but when you go to tighten it the horse tightens up as well, which means he isn't ready to accept more tightness at that moment—something you ignore at your peril! (You can check by pulling up another notch, at which point the horse will harden under your hand and pinch your fingers, showing that he is tense and resisting.)

As the horse warms up the girth needs to be rechecked a number of times during the course of the ride: before mounting; immediately after mounting, especially if thick or foam pads that compress under the rider's weight are used; after about 15 minutes of warm-up, or when the horse blows out, showing that his abdominal muscles have relaxed; and before beginning the active part of the session, such as galloping or jumping; and of course, any time the saddle feels unstable. If the girth is tightened one step at a time as the horse's body is ready, it will always be as tight as necessary but the horse will still be comfortable.

With a Western saddle, tightening the cinch while riding is not easy, so it is important to spend time on the ground first, walking the horse around, then snugging up the cinch, then repeating until the necessary tightness is reached. Use the same technique as with the English saddle of pulling down on the strap, then taking up the slack. Some horses will accept more tightness sooner—you just have to watch how the horse responds. With a young horse you might want to plan to dismount after 15 minutes and tighten up the cinch a final time.

Removing the Saddle

Many people are thoughtless in the way they remove the saddle, either through ignorance or because they forget that the saddle is held on by the withers. They try to drag the saddle straight off the side, which is very uncomfortable for the horse and often not even possible for a small person with a tall horse. Instead, after undoing the girth and all breastplate or crupper straps, slide the saddle and pads back until the pommel is *behind* the withers, when it will slide off easily. If it doesn't, look for something that didn't quite come undone on the off side, or something that got caught.

All aspects of grooming and tacking need to be considered and performed carefully. Even if you are an inexperienced or tense rider, you can make a big difference in your horse's comfort and thus his attitude during riding by the way you work with him beforehand. Not to mention the quality time you are having together!

5

Leading
Be in Charge without Being Controlling

Recently I went to watch a demonstration of vaulting (think of circus riders) at a nearby stable. Most of the horses being used in the demonstration were brought from other stables. One horse in particular was very nervous in his new surroundings, and his handler was leading him around to help him settle down. While she was obviously a competent and caring horseperson, I could see that she had never been taught the basic concepts of leading. She allowed him to walk with his head well in front of her shoulder. This is a position that puts the horse psychologically in control, since in a herd situation the horses' pecking order is determined by their place in line, with the dominant horse in the lead.

The horse I was watching was apparently young and had no idea how to deal with all the unfamiliar horses and activities surrounding him. When his handler conveyed to him that he was in charge by allowing him to walk in front of her, the horse, being too inexperienced to deal with the situation, became very disturbed. His instinct was to try to hurry away to a safer place, while she tried, ineffectively, to block him with her body. The horse kept pushing against her, nearly stepping on her, which didn't help her confidence either. She also kept a very tight pull on his lead rope in her effort to control him. This restriction, which cramped the horse's body, made him uncomfortable and even more nervous.

Because of the basic errors she was making in leading, which increased both his physical and emotional tensions, the relaxation process took much longer than it should have.

∾

Leading the horse is simply the process of getting him from one place to another, following your direction. This can be much more difficult than it sounds, and is probably one of the most neglected areas of teaching. Learning to be led is one of the very first things a foal is taught, and much importance is attached to teaching him correctly, since a horse must be willing to be led

---

Tidbits & Supplements

A friend of mine once bet on a horse in a horse race because he was the only one who was being led correctly by his handler. My friend figured that horse's trainer really must know what he was about, and she was right. The horse won!

(which, oddly enough, we refer to as "leading") if you are going to be able to handle him at all. Unfortunately, comparatively little time is spent on teaching *people* how to lead, with the result that you often see handlers being dragged around by their charges, or interfering with them unnecessarily.

Before we start with leading, there are certain principles to be kept in mind. Webster's dictionary defines "lead" as "guide, persuade, be or go first." Being the leader also implies being the one in charge, the one who gives directions. When horses run together they often contend over who should be the leader, because **the one in front is the one in charge**. So when you lead the horse, you should be guiding him from in front of him and you should be persuading him, not attempting to force him.

This leads us to another principle: **Movement in the horse is always generated by the horse himself.** The average horse weighs about half a ton, and the strength of a human is not enough to move him anywhere. **Therefore physical strength, in the sense of power, has no place in your interactions with the horse.** When the horse does what you tell him to do, it is because he wants to. Your goal is to get him to want to. Try thinking about the horse as a person (the horse's brain) driving a car (his body). You are standing outside the car giving directions with your body postures and gestures. You would never think of grabbing the car by the bumper and trying to drag it where you want it to go.

With that in mind, before you start leading you should be very comfortable in the horse's presence and comfortable being in the same space with him—even as confined a space as a stall. If you are a beginner, you may feel uncomfortable at first with any horse, just because of your lack of familiarity with the animal, and because of his size. For that reason I do not recommend that brand new beginners be asked to lead their own horses, even though this is standard practice in most lesson problems. I have observed that most bad leading habits originate in this practice.

If you are more experienced, you should make a point of noticing if being around a particular horse makes you uncomfortable; if you don't trust him. You may want to do some Parelli or TTeam work with the horse before trying to lead him anyplace where he could get upset or try to take over.

Holding the lead rope correctly is an important safety consideration. If you get caught in the rope when the horse is pulling, you can get seriously hurt. For leading the horse from the left, which is most common, the rope is held in your right hand about a foot from where it is attached to the horse, with the excess coiled loosely in the *fingers* of your left hand. Never wrap the coil around your hand or put it anywhere near your neck. Never, *ever* tie the rope to your clothes or body even for a second. Many people advocate holding the excess rope in flat loops across your palm so there is no possibility of the rope pulling up tight around your hand. If you can hold it comfortably this way it is safer, but if your hand is too small and the rope slips out, the danger of having the excess dangling around your feet is probably a greater risk.

PREPARATION

The best way to learn to lead is with the help of another person. However, if this is not possible, try to work through the exercises described below, at least in your mind, so that you have a clear idea of how the horse will be affected before you start working with him. It is easier to lead the horse in a way that is comfortable for him—which means he will be more likely to respond well—if you understand leading from his point of view.

For the following exercises you will need another person and a soft lead rope. To begin, you play horse and the other person is the leader. Keep in mind that you are supposed to be an obedient, well-trained horse who is only waiting for the correct signals.

1. Tie the rope around your left wrist, just tight enough so it won't slip off.

2. Have the other person hold the other end of the rope as described above. First have her stand facing you and give a tug on the rope. Notice how it feels awkward to try to move with her in that position. She seems to be in the way, and what she wants isn't very clear. When someone is facing you, your instinct is to face her, either in a conversational or confrontational way, depending on how she is behaving. If she is being very aggressive and you don't want to deal with it, you might turn your back and walk away. Or, if you felt aggressive yourself, you might want to knock her down. It would not naturally occur to you to walk past her.

3. Next, have her stand beside you on the left side, just a little in front of you and with both of you facing in the same direction. For the moment you will only be working in a left-hand circle. Ask her to look at a place a little distance away and then start to walk toward it. As she starts to walk, have her give just

a little tug on the rope, then immediately let it go slack. She can also say something such as "Come on," or "Let's go," to let you know that she wants you to come with her. Notice how natural it is to follow someone when she simply asks you and walks away herself. She should hold the rope so it is comfortable for you to stay a foot or two to her right and a little behind her.

4. Do the same exercise again, only this time have her pull on the rope the whole time, as though she were pulling a wagon. (She shouldn't pull too hard. Since you probably weigh only about an eighth as much as a horse, the pull should be relative.) Notice how tiring and awkward this is, and how it causes you to want to pull away from her.

Now change so that you are the leader and your partner is the horse. Run quickly through the first five of the Seven Steps (see Chapter 2), so that you are well grounded. Be sure as you start up you have a mental goal of a particular place to go or of continuing around the circle, not just wandering vaguely. Have your partner tell you how the rope feels to her. Think of the pull on the rope that asks the "horse" to move as similar to a little tug on someone's sleeve that just gets his attention without annoying him. *If your "horse" is doing what you want, the rope should be slack.* The feeling should be one of two people walking pleasantly hand in hand, with one leading a little bit—except that you happen to be joined by a rope.

Stopping

Stopping a horse on the lead is a little more difficult than it seems. You have to give the horse time enough to understand what you want before you actually stop, or he will go past you and you will no longer be leading. One often sees someone attempting to stop a horse by stepping back near the horse's shoulder and dragging on the rope. Both because of the drag on the rope and because he is now in front, which he perceives as putting him in charge, the horse will tend to stop only reluctantly.

Again, let's try this using an exercise:

1. Reattach the rope to your own wrist, so that you are the horse again, and have your partner lead you around as before. Walk fairly briskly.

2. Ask her to stop at some point without giving you any warning. You will find that you shoot past her for a step before you can stop. Now try again, and this time have her pull back hard on the rope as you pass her. This feels very awkward, especially if she catches you at a time when you are not quite in balance.

3. Next, while you are walking have her drop behind you and pull on the rope as though she was going to drag you to a stop. This is similar to when she was pulling you around like a wagon, but now she is dragging backward. To maintain your balance, you will find it easiest to lean forward and drag against her until you can stop yourself.

4. Start walking again and have your partner hold the lead a little closer to your hand. Ask her to turn her head toward you slightly, reach back with her right arm and give a gentle backward tug on the rope, releasing as soon as she feels any resistance and immediately repeating the tug. She should be careful not to slow down more than a little and not to allow you to walk past her shoulder. The gentle backward tug will tend to make you slow down. As you do so, she should slow down with you, repeating the tug as necessary, so that you both stop *at the same time, still facing forward.* Again, you should find that this feels very logical and natural.

Now trade places and experiment with stopping. It takes a little practice to feel how long to hold the tug before letting go and at the same time not lose your position in front of the horse. This is that same tug on a sleeve kind of pull, which is a suggestion, not a demand. Be sure you only turn your head a little toward the "horse" while she is moving. After you have both stopped you can turn to face her, indicating that you want her to stay there for the moment.

Turning

Because you are walking on the left side of the horse, turning the horse is not the same in both directions. Turning to the left is quite easy. Take up the role of horse again, but this time, instead of walking in a circle have your partner pick a point on a straight line across the arena. When she gets near her goal have her pick another point to the left of the first and turn toward it, giving a soft little tug on the rope to indicate that you should follow. After she does this a few times, it will seem very natural to you to follow her movement.

Now change places and try some left turns yourself. You will find that when asking for a turn, if you give a little tug in the direction you want to go when the "horse's" foot on that side is just leaving the ground, she will find it easy to respond, and will give softly to your tug. If you pull at a time in her walk when she finds it difficult to respond, you will feel some resistance to your tug. Instead of pulling harder when you feel the resistance, ease up for a second and then try again.

Turning to the right is a little different than turning to the left because the "horse" is on your right, and therefore a bit in the way. To keep in front of the "horse" as you turn, you have to slow her down a little so you can get past her to where you want to go. You also have to speed up your walk a little so that you can cross in front of her, at the same time giving a little stopping tug on the lead to keep her from speeding up when you do. As soon as you have crossed her path, if necessary give a little forward tug to bring her around with you. Be sure to look where you want to go, not directly at the "horse's" face. You can look down at her body to see what it is doing, but don't look at her as though you were going to stop and talk.

Try each part of the exercises, playing the role of both the horse and the leader, so that you get thoroughly familiar with the moves. Also practice leading from the opposite side to teach your left hand the feel of the tug. Then you are ready to try with a real horse.

LEADING THE REAL HORSE

Learning and practicing leading the horse are best done in an area where there are no distractions for the horse, such as grass or other horses. Unless you are both experienced with clicker training, do not have any treats in your pocket that might make him nudge and push at you. The horse you work with should be quiet and lead willingly. He should be wearing a halter with a six- to eight-foot (two- to two-and-a-half-meter) lead rope attached to the ring under his jaw. If you are a beginner, someone experienced should bring the horse to the practice area for you.

Begin by spending a little time in "conversation" with your horse. Scratch him in his favorite place or whatever you would like to do to establish a little rapport. Now that you are going to be asking the horse, who is so much bigger than you are, to accept direction from you, you may tend to feel that you need somehow to be aggressive and controlling to get him to listen to you. However, if you consider that you would probably react to an aggressive, controlling person by becoming aggressive and controlling in return, or by becoming nervous, you can easily see that this is not a good attitude with which to approach the horse. What you are after is a nice balance of being friendly without being overindulgent.

By asking the horse to lead as described in the first exercise (on page 81, number 3), you are using his natural instinct to follow those he trusts, which all herd animals have. The rope only serves to give him an indication of your intentions and recall his attention if it starts to wander.

It is a good idea to *start* the horse moving in the general direction in which he is already facing, even if only for a step. Because of his length and because his center of gravity is close to his front legs, it is awkward for the horse to be asked to turn sharply sideways from a standstill. Consciously choose a goal to move toward, such as a place on the fence, but try not to aim directly for the gate since the horse may then assume the lesson is over and be annoyed when it isn't—like hearing the bell ring at the end of school, then having your teacher tell you that you have to stay another half an hour!

1. When you are ready to begin moving, take up your leading position just a little in front of the horse's head, facing the same way he is. Run quickly through your first five steps of growing, breathing, and so on, but without using your arms. Look at your chosen goal, give a cluck and shift your weight forward in preparation to starting walking. *Let your right arm, with the line in it, dangle back loosely.* Make your first step fairly short and feel with your arm whether the horse is coming along or not. If he is coming, leave the line loose and gradually increase your pace to a normal walk. Since this horse knows how to lead, it may not be necessary to give him any other signal than the movement of your body and a cluck.

2. If the horse does not move forward with you, stop where you are and repeat step 1, adding a light tug on the line. Do not turn around and face him. If he still remains anchored to the ground, glance around and make sure there is nothing distracting him. If his head has come up and his ears are pricked, it means he has seen something distracting. Allow him to look for a few seconds, then use a couple of light tugs on the rope to regain his attention. If he is just standing there, to get him started take a step to your left and bring his head to the left with you using a gentle pull on the line, followed by a release if you feel

Starting up leading. My arm is swung back so the line is loose. My eyes are on the point where I want the horse to look—about 10 feet ahead.

resistance. The pull should be in a direction that asks him to move forward a little as well as sideways. Bringing his head to the side a little bit will put him slightly off balance and he will move a front foot to rebalance himself. Repeat the pull as necessary, experimenting with the timing of the pull-release and the amount of pressure until he takes a step. Moving one foot is nearly always enough to get him started.

3. Once the horse is moving, praise him with your voice and start walking in a left-hand circle around the workspace. Be sure you walk with a long enough step and brisk enough pace that the horse can walk comfortably at his normal stride. At first, plan to stay near the gate end if it is a large area, to avoid the problem of having the horse hurry on his way home. Walk around several times just getting used to the feeling of having the horse walking close to you. Resist the temptation to stiff-arm the horse if he seems to be too close. Periodically check to make sure you still feel centered and grounded. Remember to keep the rope a little slack, but not hanging loose or long. Step 4 of the first section in this chapter (on page 82) explained the most common mistake people make in leading a horse, which is keeping the line taut all the time. The more you pull on the line, the more awkward it is for the horse and the more he wants to pull away or hold back. You should be holding the line 12 to 18 inches from the horse's halter. The looseness comes from having your arm and shoulder loose, not from having the line long. Think of holding the hand of a very small child.

4. If the horse starts to walk directly behind you, give a gentle push outward with your arm, so that the rope moves him back to a position just to your right. If he tries to walk with his head in front of your shoulder turn sharply to your left, which will put him behind you again, then circle back to your original track.

5. Some horses have the habit of wanting to walk a little in front all the time. With a horse like this, every time his nose starts to pass you, take a big step forward, and at the same time reach back with your right arm and give a backward tug on the rope to slow him down. Each time he returns to his proper place, give him a word of praise.

6. Next you are going to ask the horse to slow down a little, then walk on again. As you pass the gate, shorten up on the line by sliding your right hand toward him without increasing the pressure. Then turn your head slightly toward the horse and say "whoa" in a low-pitched voice, dragging out the word as though you were slowing it down. If you get no reaction from the horse, follow with a smooth backward tug on the line. If you feel him leaning on the rope, release the pull and try again. As you feel the horse respond, slow down with him, then praise him and walk on again at your original pace, using a

Sammy is trying to sneak past Peg—you can just see a little bit of his nose above her left hand. My left hand on her shoulder is telling her to step forward, while my right hand is guiding her right hand to pull back smoothly on the line.

cluck to indicate to him that you want to walk on again and being careful not to pull on the rope if he doesn't respond immediately. Practice this several times until you feel comfortable with it. If he stops accidentally, that's fine. Praise him and ask him to walk on again as in step 1.

7. Now you are ready to try a stop. You will be asking for it just beyond the gate, so the horse will stop easily. Start out as in step 5, but this time continue to ask him to slow down in small increments until he stops. Slow your own pace with his, but keep your feet moving as long as his are moving. Try not to feel that you *have to* make him stop at a particular place, just take your time and keep asking as you learn the feel of it. When he first comes to a stop, the line should be slack and you should still be in the same relative positions, your bodies facing the same direction, although your head should be turned toward him and his head slightly behind your shoulder. If he stops ahead of you, it means you stopped too quickly. Once he has stopped completely, you can turn to face him and make a fuss over him. Practice stopping a few more times, but space it out so the horse gets a chance to stretch out in between each stop.

8. Finish the lesson by trying some changes of direction using the same techniques for turning as you used with your human partner.

Stopping. My eyes are turned toward Sammy to ask for the stop, but my feet are still facing straight ahead so I can easily take another step if he hasn't quite finished moving.

Turning right. I am looking and turning slightly in front of Sammy, but not blocking his forward movement. My leading arm is very soft and relaxed, and he is taking a nice, flowing forward step.

Leading with a Bridle

There are several ways of leading the horse when he is wearing a bridle, rather than a halter and lead.

1. You can take the reins off the horse's neck, put them together and use them exactly as you did the lead rope. The advantage of this is that if the horse does something unexpected, you have a length of rein to let out to avoid hauling or being hauled upon. This is the best method if you expect to lead the horse for some time.

2. You can leave the reins on the horse's neck and use just the one on the side nearest you, again just as you used the lead rope, except that the end is over the horse's neck, rather than in your other hand. If the horse raises or turns his head suddenly, the rein should be allowed to slip through your hand so you don't jerk on each other. The advantage to this is that if the horse gets away, he is less likely to break the reins. It also avoids the problem of trying to get the reins back over the horse's head, which is often done clumsily by novice riders, especially if they are small. This is the best method to use with novices, or when you are leading for a short distance.

3. You can leave the reins on the horse's neck and hold both reins about six inches (15 cm) behind the horse's chin. This is the method most often seen, but is the most difficult for both horse and leader. It is very restrictive and thus annoying and unbalancing for the horse. And if he startles and throws his head up, it jerks the leader's arm very painfully since there is no way to release without letting go altogether. This method is really only useful with a horse who nips, or chews his reins.

TURNING LOOSE

Once you know how to lead, there comes a time when you want to let the horse go, either in his stall or in the field or arena. This is one of those things that even experienced horsemen can get careless about, sometimes with very serious results.

The first rule about letting a horse go is *never* let him go in such a way that he has to pass you to get where he's going. Many horses respond to being turned loose by rushing away. If they do that going into a stall, they can hit the doorway, which can lead to a horse who is nervous about doorways and tends to rush through them, trampling whoever is around in the process. Horses turned loose in a field often will start out with a big buck, with the handler in danger of being hit by a flying hoof. Broken arms and jaws can be the unfortunate result.

The procedure for turning the horse loose is the same whether you're in a stall or an open space. In this case the halter is to be left on, but the general rules would be the same if you were removing the halter, except that even more care should be taken.

1. Begin by leading the horse into the space, then turning him and your-self around so your back is to the door or gate and close to the opening, so that you can step back into it easily.

2. Spend a minute with the horse, scratching him or feeding him a little treat so that he is thinking about you rather than about being turned loose.

3. Lightly hold the nose of the halter while you quietly undo the snap on the rope. If the horse pulls away when he hears the snap being undone, don't attempt to hold on to him. The next time you turn him out, plan to give him a treat as you undo the snap, rather than holding the halter, so he is busy eating at that point.

4. If the horse waits, quietly take your hand off the halter and step back into the gateway at the same time. Thus, even if the horse wheels and bucks, you will be well out of range and protected by the gate, as well.

If you follow this procedure religiously *every* time you turn a horse loose, you will never get hurt and your horse will never develop bad habits about being turned loose. Horses who break away are a training problem that can take a long time to fix.

USING THE STICK

The instrument of communication I find the easiest for the rider to use and the horse to understand is the stick. When you are comfortable with leading the horse, you can use those skills to teach the horse to accept and respond calmly to the stick aid. This will prepare you both for later use when riding.

Now, as soon as I say "stick," your immediate reaction might be "cruelty," "abuse," "punishment." If I had said "voice," you would not have had that reaction, but the voice can equally be a weapon of abuse—as anyone who has had a sarcastic teacher knows all too well. Of course the stick can be used in an abusive way, but since abuse comes from a person's heart, the stick itself is innocent. So with the stick, you need first to realize that it is just another means of communication. You use a stick with the horse because your arm is not long enough to reach behind the horse to signal him when you are standing near his head or sitting on his back. It is quite natural for the horse to move away from a little pat on his behind, just as it is for a person. If you use the stick with more force than necessary for the horse to understand you, he will respond with fear or anger, telling you to ease up and change your method.

Sticks (also called whips, bats, crops, quirts, etc.) come in a great range of lengths, thicknesses, and flexibility. For groundwork you want one that is long enough for you to reach the horse's rump while standing near his head. Three and a half to four and half feet (one to one and a half meters) is about the right range. It should balance nicely in your hand and not be tiring to carry or use. It should be fairly flexible but not floppy. It should have a knob or button on top so it doesn't fall out of your hand too easily.

For normal riding work, you hold the stick in your softly closed fist using all four fingers, with your thumb and index finger on top, nearest the knob, and the body of the stick projecting from the bottom of your fist (see the photo on page 159). For greater maneuverability and reach, and for most groundwork, the stick can be turned around so that your thumb and index finger are point-ing up, the body of the stick projects upward and the knob rests against your little finger. Practice changing from one position to the other until it is easy.

Teaching the Horse to Accept the Stick

Although, as I said, there is no need to use the stick abusively, so many horses have been abused that it is not uncommon to find a horse who is what we call "whip shy." This can take many forms, from simply being overreactive, to buck-ing, and even to total panic. Therefore, with any horse, before you use a stick on him the first time, you must find out how he reacts to it. The first stick exer-cise is about testing and, if necessary, accustoming the horse to the stick. At any time during the exercise, if the horse shows fear, stop immediately, bring the stick to your side and return to the previous step until the horse is calm again.

However, do not stop the work altogether if the horse moves or shows fear, since this would be rewarding him for that behavior. Parelli recommends that you keep performing the action the horse is afraid of until he stops moving away from it, but this may take more skill than you have. For the novice, the best way to go is advance and retreat, that is, to back off a little, then gradually return to the point where the fear began. Unless the horse has been badly abused, he will usually gain confidence quickly when he finds you aren't going to hurt him.

1. Stand facing the horse, a little to one side, and hold the lead in your left hand or have your helper hold the horse. Hold the stick in your right hand in position 1, down by your side, partially concealed by your side. Begin by talk-ing with the horse, scratching him or whatever is needed until you are both relaxed and comfortable. Then bring the stick quietly up near his muzzle so that he can sniff it.

2. Letting the lead rope out as necessary, step back by the horse's shoulder and rub him with your hand with the stick in it. Gradually allow the stick to rub him too. Be careful *not* to touch him so lightly that it feels like a fly.

3. Turn the stick around quietly so that you are holding it in position 2. Continue stroking the horse gently but firmly with the stick, going all over his body except his flanks, which are sensitive. Also bring it forward and stroke his neck near the shoulder. It is not necessary to touch his legs for this exercise, although it is perfectly all right to do so if the horse is comfortable with it. Repeat on the horse's right side.

4. Step a little away from the horse and slowly wave the stick up and down about two feet from the horse's body, moving forward and back so that he gets used to seeing the stick move up and down in different places relative to his body. Repeat on the other side.

5. Finally, stand directly in front of the horse and move the stick slowly up and down about two feet from his head, then bring it under his chin and repeat on the other side, changing hands if necessary. Then bring the stick in a big cir-cle over the top of the horse's head. (Skip this part if the horse is very tall and you are not.)

Throughout these exercises continue to talk to your horse and observe him, making a point of praising him when he stands quietly so that he under-stands that just moving the stick around quietly does not call for any response whatsoever. Once he has this clearly in his mind, you can carry a stick that he will ignore until you start to use it for communication.

Teaching the Horse to Respond to the Stick

Now that you have carefully taught the horse to ignore the stick, the next step is to teach him how to respond to it. The first response you want is for the horse, on feeling a tap with the stick, to quietly increase his pace—so if he is standing still, for example, he should walk. If he is walking he should walk a lit-tle faster or jog, depending on the other signals you give him. In any case the transition should be smooth and relaxed, but still prompt.

1. Place the horse so that there is space in front of him to move toward. Stand by his left shoulder, facing forward. If you face the horse's shoulder or his tail, you are giving him a signal *not* to move. Hold the lead in your left hand or have your helper hold him, but leave the lead slack, and hold the stick in your right hand, thumb pointing toward the tip (position 2). Now bring the stick up and smoothly place it on the horse's rump. If the horse walks away immediately, bring him to a halt again as soon as possible without being rough, then try again. You want him

to wait for a clear signal, not try to second-guess you. This habit of moving before the signal is often an evasion rather than a response. The horse is saying, "I'm not going to wait to see what you want, I'm just going to leave *now*."

2. Now give a little light tap with the stick on the horse's rump and see what happens. If there is absolutely no response of any sort, not so much as a flick of an ear or a slight raising of the head, it means that he didn't "hear" you. That is, the signal was so light that he blocked it out. Count to three and tap again a little harder. Continue until you get some sort of response. You need to watch very carefully to be sure you don't miss it. The response might be just a slight tensing of his body or a movement of his eye or ear. If you got a response but no movement of the feet, it means he "heard" you but isn't quite sure what you said. Count to three and tap the same amount as before. The count ensures that you give him sufficient time to interpret the signal and react. If you get any sort of weight shift forward, as though he is thinking about moving, immediately praise and take a little time out.

3. If you are getting a response but no attempt at movement, after a couple of tries add a cluck. If he still doesn't get it, add a forward shift of your body as though you were about to walk. Be sure you are facing forward, not facing the horse. If there is still no reaction, reach forward and give a leading tug on the rope to get him started. Be very aware of his slightest effort toward movement and be effusive with praise.

4. Practice until the horse is responding promptly to the first tap of the whip—but be sure he continues to wait for the tap. If he moves before the tap, quietly stop him, then ask again. Practice only halt-to-walk transitions, allowing the horse to walk a few yards, then quietly halting him and allowing him to stand for 15 seconds or so before asking him to walk again. Be sure that when he moves, the line stays slack until you're ready to stop him. If you believe in hand-feeding, the halt break is a good time to give him a tidbit; otherwise, some scratching in his favorite place will keep the lesson from getting too boring.

Tidbits & Supplements

It is *extremely* important in the early stages of stick training that **at no time should you apply the whip hard enough to hurt**, even a little bit! This is a very difficult lesson to learn, especially with a horse who seems unresponsive. However, when you create pain the horse tenses up, and when he tenses up it makes it *very* hard for him to move. In some cases this can escalate into a really difficult problem.

It usually takes only a few minutes for a quiet horse to figure out what you want. An abused horse may have difficulty even after you get him over his fear of the stick. In some cases it simply has never occurred to the horse that you are trying to communicate with him! He thinks, "Sometimes people hit me and sometimes people feed me, but it doesn't really *mean* anything." When he finally figures it out, it is like revelation. "Oh, is *that* all? You just want me to move on when I feel that little tap on my butt? I can do that. That's *easy*."

CORNERSTONES OF COMMUNICATION

The principal concept you have learned in this lesson, that of pulling smoothly on the rope, then *easing* your tug instead of pulling harder when you feel resistance, is the basis for correct use of the reins later on. Resistance to a pull is nearly always caused by the horse needing to use his head for balance at that moment in a different way than what you are asking. By allowing him to regain his balance and then asking again, you avoid starting an unnecessary fight. With a little practice you will be able to feel when the horse can respond easily to the pull and when you need to release. Your own balance is essential in order for you to feel this, which is why grounding is important and why you wait to use the reins when mounted until your position and balance are relatively secure.

The second concept, of using the stick in a way the horse responds to by moving easily but without fear, helps you to develop a more immediate understanding of "forward" (which is discussed in Chapter 19). This, combined with your knowledge of how to get the horse to respond to the reins, is one of the cornerstones of all your riding communication with the horse.

6

Mounting and Dismounting
Riding Confidence Starts Here

Years ago my husband and I, along with a small group of riders from our stable, used to hunt fairly regularly with the local pack of foxhounds. We would take the horses in a trailer to the meet, unload them and mount up, ready to go for a morning's fox hunting. There were usually 20 or 30 other riders there from the surrounding area. At one such hunt, my husband had just finished mounting when a woman rode up to him. Almost gushing in her enthusiasm, she said, "I teach riding to one of the local Pony Club groups every week. I wish I could get you to come and demonstrate mounting to my students some time. You do it so effortlessly and gracefully!" My husband blushed a little and thanked her, and told her truthfully, "It wasn't hard. Anyone can learn to mount just as well."

Mounting is an action that often makes both horse and rider nervous. Many people don't ride their horses because they're afraid of mounting. This is because most mounting techniques cause rider and horse to lose their balance at some point, which leads to tension and fear. That does not need to happen.

This chapter contains more methods for getting on and off a horse than you ever thought possible. The technique you use will depend on your agility, the relative sizes of you and your horse, the equipment available and what you and the horse are wearing.

I think if I were going to trail ride frequently for long distances bareback, someplace where there weren't rocks, hills, and tree stumps, and if I couldn't remount alone, I would do what my great-grandfather did: train my horse to lie down on command.

My great-grandfather was a general in the Confederate Army during the Civil War. Confederate officers brought their own horses to the war, and Great-grandfather brought his favorite horse whom he had raised and trained himself. During one of the battles—I think it was Bull Run, but don't hold me to it—he was shot in the hip at the beginning of the battle and fell unconscious to the ground. The battle went on all day, and seven cavalry charges passed over his body without a horse stepping on him. That night, when he came to, he found his horse standing by his side. Great-grandfather gave the horse the command to lie down, then managed to drag himself over the saddle before he passed out again. When he awoke, he found himself back at his unit. The horse had managed to find his way through the Yankee lines to the unit, which was in an entirely new location. Or so the tale was told to me.

Anyway, if your horse was trained to lie down on command and you fell and got hurt, you might be able to use the horse to get home again. I saw a television show once about a paraplegic who taught his horse to lie down so he could mount, from a wheelchair no less.

You can also teach a horse to kneel, so that you can put your foot in the stirrup and balance yourself over the saddle or lie over his withers if bareback, then have him stand up and swing your leg over as he stands.

My oldest brother, who as a child was very small for his age, taught his 16-hand horse to bend his foreleg and hold it there. My brother would then put his foot just behind the horse's knee and mount bareback.

When we were quite little and wanted to get on bareback, we would wait until our pony put his head down to eat. We would swing a leg over his head so we were sitting on the neck just behind the poll facing backward. Then we reached out and tapped with a stick, the pony picked his head up and we slid down his neck to his back and turned around. The ponies didn't mind, because they got to eat and we probably weighed 50 pounds soaking wet!

I have also seen it recommended to tie a thick, soft rope around the horse's neck, loose enough so it fits behind his withers and hangs down fairly low in front. You then put your foot on the loop from back to front, being very careful not to let it slip through, and use it like a stirrup to mount. There is also a gadget that fastens to the horse's off-side foreleg. It comes across his back and ends in a loop into which you can put your foot and mount in about the same way.

So there are a lot of tricks. You just have to be creative. You also have to be very careful, because they all require some training on the part of the horse if you are not to invite an accident.

The method I like best is to find someone who brags that he can always mount from the ground and invite him along on all of my trail rides. Then if I drop something, he can get off and pick it up, or if I have to get off he can also get off and give me a leg back on!

If none of these techniques seems quite right for you, perhaps the serious techniques that follow may be more useful. And even if you are experienced, it would be a good idea to read the section on preparation for mounting (page 105).

BAREBACK

If you follow my recommendations, most of the time when you ride bareback you will be using a pad, but there may also be times when you ride the horse without any sort of attire—on the horse, that is! Following are descriptions of different ways to get yourself onto a bareback horse.

Mounting a Naked Horse

Vaulting onto a bareback horse from the ground, as seen in the movies where they face the rear of the horse, put the left hand on his withers and swing up and over with their right leg, is extremely difficult for many people to do at all, much less well. Most of the people who do it end up dragging themselves up with their heel tucked firmly in the horse's off-side flank. My brother used to be able to do it, but he was very athletic and he didn't do it on really big horses.

If you decide you want to try it, practice on a fence until you are skillful before you subject the horse to your efforts.

Virtually everyone except movie stunt riders uses some sort of mounting block for bareback mounting, unless the horse is quite small. A mounting block could be a tree stump, a log, a large rock, even standing uphill from the horse; all can make mounting easier for both. Small plastic step stools that can be purchased from the hardware store are easy to move and won't injure the horse even if he steps on one.

> ### *Tidbits & Supplements*
>
> Very good mounting blocks can be found at marine supply stores. They are used on the dock to help people to climb onto large boats, and are perfect for mounting horses. They come in all different heights, and are solid but still light and reasonably portable. They are not inexpensive, but are virtually impervious to damage and so, well worth the investment.

Mounting from a fence should be approached with a little caution, because of the possibility your foot could slip or catch on the rails. Best of all is a solidly constructed mounting block of the appropriate height.

There are times, however, when no mounting block of any sort is available, and in those situations you might want to try the following technique.

To learn this technique, the horse has to be naked—no bareback pad or anything—and the rider has to be dressed in light, nonrestrictive clothing, especially if the horse is very large. In my athletic youth, I (who am about five-foot-five) could mount a bareback 17.2-hand horse from the ground using this method.

1. Stand facing the horse's shoulder and withers. Even though the horse is taller here, he is also thinner and flatter on the side. Also, as you mount and turn to face forward, your hips will end up quite a bit behind where your shoulders are. If you are too far back, you may end up sitting on the horse's loins, which many horses object to!

2. If you are mounting a bridled horse, make sure the reins are without twists, lying with the buckle on the horse's withers. Pick up the buckle in your right hand. Put your left hand on both reins, palm down, and pick them up. Slide your left hand down the reins until you have the contact (amount of pressure) you want.

3. Place your left hand (when applicable, with the reins in it) on the front of the withers and *grab the mane firmly.* Place your right hand at the back of the withers. *Be sure to keep both hands in place until the end of the mount.*

4. Keeping your head up, bend your knees, push off with both legs and pull with your hands at the same time. It's a good idea to practice this move on a

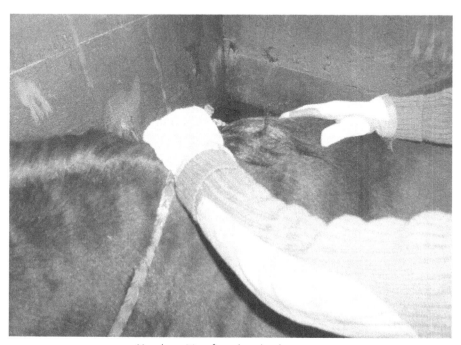

Hand position for a bareback mount.

rail fence or something similar, so you get the trick of coordinating hand and leg. You want to be able to jump up so you are "standing" on your straight arms on an ordinary four-foot rail fence. Be sure you really bend your knees and push off hard, and think to jump *higher than* the horse at first, not over or onto the horse's back. Do *not* try to swing your right leg over the horse.

5. You only have to be able to jump high enough to hook your elbows over and be "standing" on your elbows, then you can wriggle a little and hook the bottom of your rib cage over the horse's withers; another little wiggle and you'll have your navel over his withers (don't let go of the mane with your left hand or collapse your hips and back at this point!).

6. Finally, bring your right knee across the horse's back and hook it on the other side of his spine. Your right foot will still be on the near side. Use your knee to help you turn your body so you are more or less facing the horse's head. Using your knee this way keeps you from digging the horse in the flank with your right foot.

7. When your body is lined up with the horse's, swing your leg over the rest of the way, sit up straight and allow your legs to fall down the horse's sides.

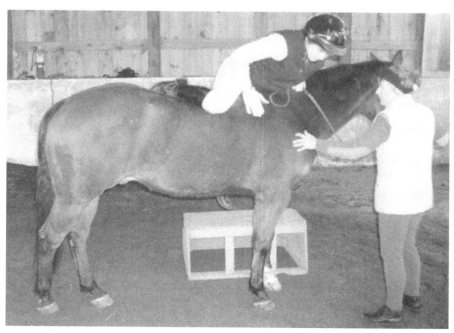

Peg is hooking her knee over Sammy's spine. This was her first try, and she's doing very well except that she moved her right hand off of his withers, looking for the nonexistent "handle" on his off-side shoulder. Not very safe!

Although it sounds rather clumsy, this is fairly easy for the horse to deal with because you stay close to him and right over his front leg, making it easy for him to balance you. Of course, even a little slope with you on the uphill side makes it easier for you both.

Having to wiggle up is why the horse has to be naked—you would get stuck on a pad. But the big trick, and the hardest to teach yourself to do, is *not* to try to swing your leg over *at all* until the very end. Once you push off from the ground, you keep your legs under you, either dangling or kicking (as in swimming) to help get your torso over his spine. Only when your body is securely on the horse can you then swing your leg over and sit up.

Mounting a Padded Horse

If you are going to be riding on a bareback pad fairly regularly and there is no one available to help you mount, you will probably need some sort of mounting block. I will describe two methods of mounting, depending on the height of the mounting block. Since a bareback pad uses a surcingle, the same girthing considerations apply as will be described later in this chapter (page 105) for saddled mounting.

Method 1

If the block is high enough so that your crotch is about level with the horse's back, this is the easiest method to use.

1. Place the horse next to the block so that his withers are opposite the middle of the block.

2. Stand on the block opposite the horse's withers, facing the horse. Keep your eyes up and soft throughout the mount. If you allow yourself to look at the ground on the far side of the horse, it may make you tense.

3. Take both reins in your left hand and place that hand on top of the withers. Place your right hand next to it.

4. Lift your right leg up high enough to *clear* the horse's croup and swing it over the horse, but do not put it down or try to sit.

5. Using your hands to help support your weight, give a small hop off your left leg, turn and land *gently* on the horse's back just behind the withers, at the lowest point of his back

If you cannot lift your leg high enough in step 4, use Method 2.

Method 2

This method is used if the horse is tall or the mounting block isn't. However, unless you are very athletic you will need to be at least high enough so that your lower ribs are level with the horse's withers. This is the same technique you use to mount a naked horse, except that since you are standing on a mounting block, you don't have to scramble up the horse's side. However, it is essential that you jump up high enough before trying to get on, or you'll get stuck on the pad. You need to get your navel about over the horse's spine on your jump. From there, you can hook your knee and finish the mount.

With all the bareback mounting methods described in this chapter, once you have figured them out, within reason the faster you do them the easier they are, since your momentum will carry you through.

Dismounting Bareback

Dismounting is also a time when horses can become irritable and accidents can happen. Again, this has to do with the horse's balance.

There are two secrets to dismounting safely and easily while bareback. One is keeping your center over the midline of the horse until your right leg is all the way over onto the horse's left side. If, as is common, you let yourself slide off to the left first, your right leg will instinctively start to grab, making it almost impossible to swing it up clear of the horse's back. The second secret is the importance of keeping a firm grip with your hands on the horse's mane until both legs are on the left side of the horse and underneath you.

Tidbits & Supplements

The combination of the horse's height, slipperiness, and strangeness creates a great deal of tension during mounting. As a result, the tendency, especially in the novice, is to rush, both mounting and dismounting, to find a secure place. Like climbing a tree, you tend to want to hurry to get your leg over the branch. The hurrying then creates more tension, which interferes with your balance, causing more tension, and so on. You'll see an example of this in the photo on page 111. So while you're learning, try to make your moves slow and focus on keeping your balance all the time. Once you have that down, you can speed things up and still be safe and relaxed.

Tidbits & Supplements

Some people like to dismount quickly by swinging their leg over the horse's neck instead of the croup. This works fine until the horse throws his head up or until you catch your leg in the reins. It then becomes a quick way to die.

If you are not really comfortable with bareback yet, you may still have a tendency to grip with your thighs and may find it difficult to let go—which obviously is necessary in order to dismount. Read the section on preparation for mounting on page 105. In addition, here is an exercise to help you free up. Practicing with both legs improves your balance and confidence, even though you usually only need to have the right leg free to dismount.

1. Keeping both hands on the neck strap, lift your right foot, with the leg straight, out in front of you as high as you can. The first time you try this, do it gradually to make sure it won't disturb the horse. You will find that leaning back a little makes it easier. Then let the leg fall into normal position; repeat a couple of times until your leg swings freely. Repeat with your left leg.

2. Place your hands, still holding the neck strap, toward the front of the withers so that you can lean forward comfortably. Turn your head so you are looking to your right. Now, keeping your right leg straight, swing it back, leaning forward as you do so. Be sure to try this slowly the first time to check your horse's reaction. Sit up again, then repeat, speeding up the action so that you kick your leg up high behind you. *Do not bend your right knee.* You should find yourself lying out almost flat on the top of the horse's back, but try not to let your left leg come up as well. Keep practicing until you can swing your right leg up to a point above the horse's croup. Do *not* allow your body to slide off to the left as your leg comes up. Repeat with your left leg, turning your head to the left as well.

3. Once you can easily let go of any thigh grip, you are ready to dismount unassisted. Place your hands on the horse's neck, far enough forward so that you can bend forward easily, but not so far that you feel unbalanced or disturb the horse's balance. The fingers of both hands should be on the right side of the horse's neck, curled up to hold a hank of his mane. Do *not* lock your thumbs on the left side of the horse's neck; they should be on top, pointing the same way as your fingers. This may seem like an awkward position, but it prevents you from spraining your wrist or thumb if you come off quickly.

4. Now lean forward and swing your right leg up and over the horse's croup, as you practiced. Keeping your head and eyes up will help you maintain your balance. It is all right if your leg touches the horse as it slides over, but try to get it up high enough before you bring it over so that you don't kick him. Once your heel is clear, you can bend your knee. As your leg starts to cross over, *without letting go with your hands* and keeping your body as straight as possible, let your upper body turn to the right so that you keep your center over his midline. You should not have any sensation of starting to slide off at this point. Let your right leg come around until it is hanging down beside your left leg. (The first part, swinging the right leg over, should be done very quickly. The second part can be done either quickly or slowly.)

> ### *Tidbits & Supplements*
>
> An additional—and rather entertaining—exercise is to get as far as step 2, then, instead of dismounting, bend your right knee, bring your right leg over so you can hook with your knee and get back on again. This tests your ability to stay in the middle of the horse, rather than starting to slide off too soon. Just be careful not to hook the horse with your heel as you bring your leg over.

5. Now you have a choice about coming down to the ground. If you want to come down slowly, perhaps because the horse is tall or your feet are cold, still without letting go with your hands, lie on your stomach over the horse, then allow yourself to slide down slowly until you touch the ground. A very small person on a very tall horse sometimes needs a "catcher" to help the first time or two. If you want to come off more quickly, turn your body to face the front of the horse and slide down on your right hip. In either case, breathe out as you come down, land on the balls of your feet and let your knees and ankles bend to absorb the shock.

USING THE SADDLE

Mounting a Saddled Horse

Mounting into a saddle presents problems of its own. On many horses the saddle has a tendency to turn, stirrup length is a factor and the additional height of the cantle requires an adjustment in the movement of your right leg.

In this section you will learn how to mount a horse while standing by the cantle facing forward—rather than facing the rear, as is often taught—mostly because mounting the horse facing forward is *much* easier on the horse. As I

Tidbits & Supplements

If you have a group of people, Scrambles is a wonderful game to play to practice mounting and dismounting. The rules are simple. There is one rider on each (bareback) horse, with her partner leading. All competitors walk in a circle delineated by cones or something equally safe. There is also one cone in the center of the circle. When the whistle blows, the riders dismount, run in and touch the cone and *walk* back (so as not to panic the horses) to their own horse. They then give the other rider a leg-on. An extra helper may be necessary to make sure the horse can't walk away during remounting. As soon as the rider is mounted, she raises her arms in the air.

The last mounted rider to raise both arms in the air is either eliminated or, if you want the practice, gets points against her. The last team remaining, or the one with the fewest penalties after *X* number of rounds, is the winner.

Direction is changed every *other* time, so that each rider has to dismount from both sides. (Mounting is always from the left.) The teams can be quite easily handicapped by putting more and less athletic riders together or giving the quicker ones bigger horses.

One caution: Some horses don't mind this or even enjoy the game, but if a horse starts to get irritable, it is a sign that he is not enjoying himself and he should be removed from the game.

A game like this, which involves some competition but can't be taken seriously, is a great help to those who have a fear of falling off. It is hard to be scared when you're laughing so hard you can barely stand!

---

have already pointed out, the horse cannot be overbalanced to the rear because of his hind legs, but overbalancing him to the front is all too easy to do. Having the rider stand in front of the saddle so that her weight pulls the horse forward is very hard for him to adjust to, and many will not do so.

One caveat: *Never* mount an unfamiliar horse without someone to hold him, unless the owner is an *experienced* horseman *and* can vouch for the horse's dependability. Some of the worst vices are associated with mounting, and since you are in a sort of limbo between ground and saddle, you risk serious injury.

Aids to Mounting
Although every physically healthy rider should be able to mount unassisted from the ground into the saddle in an emergency, to avoid stress on the horse use a mounting block of some sort whenever possible.

Adjusting the stirrup is another aid to mounting, especially if you have to mount a tall horse from the ground. If you can get your foot into the stirrup, unless the horse is exceptionally tall you should be able to get on.

The one "aid" to mounting that should *never* be used is over-tightening the girth to keep the saddle from slipping (see Chapter 4).

> ### Tidbits & Supplements
>
> There is a special stirrup leather that is made so it can be let down six inches and raised up again without changing the permanent adjustment of the stirrup. It's useful if you don't like adjusting your stirrups every time.

Holding the Stirrup

If either rider or horse is inexperienced, or the rider is heavy or the horse is round-backed so the saddle turns during mounting, it is a good idea to have someone hold the stirrup. This is done safely as follows.

1. The holder places herself on the horse's off-side beside his head, facing the saddle. She takes his right rein in her right hand, about eight inches (20 cm) from the bit, and holds it loosely.

2. Next she takes the stirrup in her left hand and leans back against it so she is using her weight to hold it. This stabilizes the saddle against the pull of the rider mounting.

3. After the rider mounts, the holder places the stirrup so the rider can put her foot into it. When the rider has picked up her reins, the holder releases the horse's head.

Preparing to Mount

Check the girth *before* you begin. Many horses are tense at the mounting block in anticipation of having the girth or cinch yanked up. Also check your stirrup length. Too short, and as you stand in the stirrup you will be too high above the horse, which makes it difficult to balance. If the stirrup is too long, you won't be able to swing your right leg over easily. A good rule you can use to check stirrup length from the ground is to place your fingertips on the stirrup bar, then bring the stirrup up under your arm. It should reach about to your armpit. This is only an approximation, of course, and the stirrups will probably need to be adjusted after mounting.

As in other exercises, we are assuming that your horse is trained to stand reasonably well for mounting. These directions are intended to include the use of a mounting block, and can then be easily adapted to mounting from the

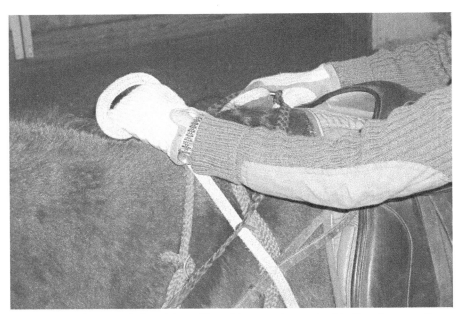

Mounting a horse with flat withers. The white rope is attached to the stirrup on the other (off) side of the horse.

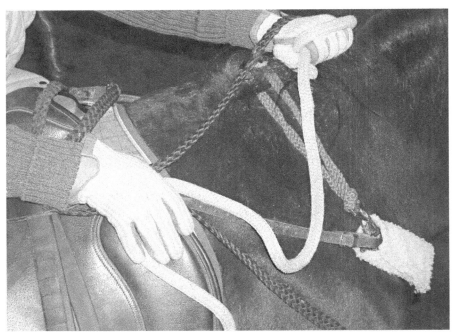

Mounting a horse with flat withers. In addition to holding the rope in my left hand, my right hand is pressing down on the right saddle flap, preventing it from turning—a useful thing to do during any mount.

Tidbits & Supplements

If you have a round-backed horse and no one to help you, there is still a way to mount without over-tightening the girth. Take a soft lead rope with a big snap and fasten it to the off-side stirrup. Bring it under the horse's barrel, laying it against the girth, then bring it up to the horse's withers. After you have used your left hand to place the stirrup, take the lead rope up snugly, wrap it firmly around your left fingers and take a firm hold of rope and mane together. Then mount as described. The rope will prevent the saddle from turning more than a very small amount. Once you are on, drop the rope from your hand, lift up the stirrup and unsnap the rope. If you are going on the trail, you can fasten the rope around your horse's neck or around your body in a safe manner, so it is available if you have to dismount on the trail.

   You will need to spend a little time getting the horse used to having the rope dropped and then drawn up on the other side. Also, if he is *very* cinchy, he might be bothered by the pressure against his girth during the mounting, so he should be accustomed to that before you actually try the mount.

---

ground. The directions are for a normal mount from the horse's left side. Learning to mount from the right is good training for both horse and rider, but also more difficult for both.

   1. Place the horse next to the mounting block. If you are using a portable block, place it on the horse's left side so that the cantle of the saddle is about opposite where you will be standing. Stand on the block facing the horse's head.

   2. Make sure the reins are without twists, lying with the buckle on the horse's withers. Pick up the buckle in your right hand. Put your left hand on both reins, palm down, and pick them up. Slide your left hand down the reins until you have the contact (amount of pressure) you want. Let go of the buckle with your right hand, then put it around both reins, close to your left hand with your thumbs together. Let go of the reins with the left hand and place your right hand, holding the reins, on the pommel and grasp it firmly.

   3. Adjust the length of the reins as necessary so they are a tiny bit slack. They should be short enough so that a small movement of your hand will create pressure, but there should not be any contact with the horse's mouth. This leaves your left hand free to handle the stirrup. You can wiggle the saddle back and forth a little to make sure the girth has not loosened up. If it has, and the horse is at all tense about the mounting block, move him away while you tighten the girth, then bring him back. Wiggling the saddle can also be used to teach the horse to brace his front legs, thus putting him in a more solid position to accept your weight. Now you are ready to mount.

4. With your left hand, take the stirrup and turn it counterclockwise so that the outside is toward you. Place your left foot in the stirrup so that the tread of the stirrup is solidly under the ball of your foot, not under the toe or the instep. Notice that your foot is pointed forward, not in toward the horse's barrel. Thus there is no danger of accidentally poking the horse with your toe as you mount.

5. Place your left hand on the horse's neck, wherever you can comfortably reach, and grasp the mane firmly. Do not pinch the top of the horse's neck. If the horse is comfortable with it, you can take a little feel on the left rein, turning his head slightly left and shifting his weight over to his right shoulder so he can balance better. Be sure you continue to face the front of the horse so that when you mount, you will be mounting along the horse's long axis, from back to front, rather than across him from side to side.

Preparing to mount in the saddle. Note that Peg is facing forward, which will cause the minimum of difficulty for Sammy as she steps up. Because she is a novice and I am holding the horse, her reins are slack.

You are now in a very secure preparatory position. With both hands firmly holding on, you can use them to support yourself if the horse moves suddenly. I have had a horse rear and gallop away with me as I started a mount from this position, and I was able to jump off safely and even stop the horse. Not that this is something you expect to happen in the ordinary course of mounting, but you should try to always have a safe avenue of escape in case the unexpected occurs.

With both hands holding on, if the horse moves forward, he will take you with him and you can either continue to mount or remove your foot from the stirrup, dismount, stop the horse and start again. For small movements on the part of the horse, it is easy to roll your right hand a little to give a correction with the rein and still keep a grip on the pommel.

Mounting

The two most common mistakes made in mounting are collapsing the left hip joint and trying to swing the right leg over too soon. If you collapse your hip, the thrust you gave to lift yourself up is lost. If you try to swing your right leg over too soon, before your left leg is fully straightened out, your left leg will give way and your right leg will be hanging over the horse, leaving you scrambling in an undignified way to get yourself into the middle of the saddle and perhaps landing on the horse's back with a thud. The following steps will help you avoid these problems.

1. With your body positioned as described above in Preparing to Mount, stand as straight as possible and push off with both legs. As you push off, try to think about going *up* rather than about getting on. Have a mental picture of thrusting your body straight up into the sky. Most of the thrust should come from your legs. Don't let your arms pull you *over* the saddle. You should end up standing in the left stirrup with both legs straight. You should be leaning slightly in toward the horse so you are over his midline, but don't bend over to do so. *Don't* swing your right leg over yet. It should remain hanging beside the left leg. Allow your weight to swing toward the horse so that you are balanced over the horse's midline, not just over the stirrup. Your left ankle should be relaxed so that your heel is down.

2. After you have the knack of this move, if your saddle tends to slide as you put weight on the stirrup, you can quickly move your right hand across the saddle so that you are grasping the stirrup buckle flap and pushing down on it, preventing the saddle from turning. If the mounting block is high enough, you can place your right hand on the flap instead of the pommel when you are preparing to mount. Be sure that in either case you don't accidentally pull

on the reins. If the horse shifts his weight or moves a step or two, allow it. Another reason horses become cranky about mounting is if they are forced to stand still before they have learned the knack of adjusting to the thrust. If you simply get the horse to stop as soon as convenient and give him a reward, he will quickly learn to stand still—not out of fear, but in expectation of the reward.

3. If your horse is quiet, you can practice steps 1 and 2 a couple of times, but not more, since it is stressful for the horse. Before returning yourself to the mounting block, rest your weight on your hands and *kick your left foot out of the stirrup*, then let yourself slide down.

4. When you are comfortable with bringing your body into a standing position in the left stirrup, quietly swing your right leg over the saddle and let yourself gently down onto the horse's back. If the horse has trouble with your weight when he is first mounted, or if you expect any difficulty, slide your right foot into the stirrup before you sit.

I am balancing over the center of the horse before swinging my right leg over. Note the straight leg and minimum hip bend, but my head should really be up as well! This is also the next-to-last step of the dismount.

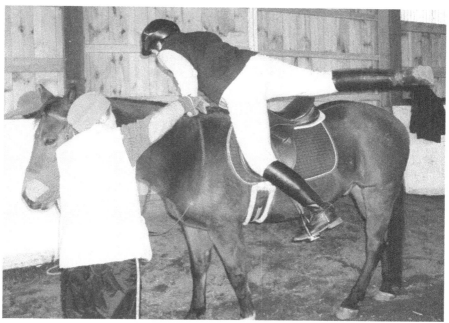

This could be either the next-to-last step in the mount, or the second step in the dismount. Peg has hurried, bent her left knee, and thrown her weight too far forward, so her heel has come up. Besides being awkward, this might upset some horses.

If you follow the instructions correctly, at no time during the mount will either you or the horse be made uncomfortable or feel out of control due to loss of balance. Horses accustomed to this method of mounting are thus far less prone to violent behavior during mounting.

Dismounting from the Saddle

The method of dismounting described below, like all mounting and dismounting methods in this chapter, is easy and safe for both horse and rider. It is a very controlled method of dismounting from the saddle, in which the balance of both horse and rider are taken into consideration.

1. Take both reins in your left hand, placed just in front of the horse's withers and grasping a piece of mane to give you a firm grip. Place your right hand on the right side of the pommel.

2. Slowly and smoothly shift your weight forward slightly and stand up in both stirrups. Moving slowly gives your horse a chance to adjust himself to the change in your position. Keep your back flat and be sure you are standing with your legs as straight as possible without lifting your heels up.

Tidbits & Supplements

I have found the "traditional" English method of mounting facing the horse's tail to be difficult for both horse and rider, and rarely performed correctly anyway.

The accepted reasoning behind this commonly used method is twofold: one, to avoid the possibility of being kicked, since the rider stands by the horse's shoulder to start; and two, if the horse moves forward during the course of the mount the rider will be swung upward into the saddle. In actual practice, almost everybody who uses this method to avoid being kicked, although they start at the horse's shoulder, hops around to the side or back in order to get in an easier position, which defeats the purpose. Also, some horses feel so threatened by this method of mounting that they will bite if the rider tries to mount standing near their head. With regard to the forward movement of the horse throwing the rider into the saddle, since many horses move as soon as the rider puts weight on the stirrup, she is far more likely to be dumped on her back on the ground.

This method also often causes the rider to hold the cantle either instead of or in addition to the pommel when mounting. Pulling on the cantle is bad practice because the horse's back is flat there and the saddle will come off very easily. In addition, it tends to put a torque on the saddle, which is bad for the tree. Putting both hands on the saddle rather than one on the horse's mane also means if the saddle slips at all, all stability is lost.

This is not to say that it is not possible to mount from the ground facing the rear in a way that many horses can handle, but it has been my experience that the method explained in this chapter is far easier and safer for both rider and horse. If you are accustomed to the traditional method and decide to change, you will find that the new method feels awkward at first (especially the position of your hands and the way you hold the reins), but if you practice it step-by-step, your body will soon learn the new technique.

Occasionally you find a horse who insists on facing you, especially if you are trying to mount from something like a tree stump. In this instance the traditional mount will work just fine, particularly if you are fairly high up.

3. Take your right foot out of the stirrup and carefully swing it over the horse's croup. If your left leg is straight, you should have no difficulty with this. *At the same time*, turn your upper body to the right so that you are looking across the horse, and bend forward a little so that *you stay over the midline of the horse's back*. If you have done this correctly, as a practice exercise you should be able to easily swing your right leg back over and sit down on the horse again (just as you

did when mounting). Because you have stayed over the midline of the horse, neither you nor he has become unbalanced. Thus you can practice the leg swing a couple of times without bothering the horse (see the photo on page 110).

4. With your back and arms straight, rest your full weight on your hands and remove your left foot from the stirrup. Then roll over on your right hip so you are facing the front of the horse and slide slowly to the ground. To help you to land softly, breathe out and land on your toes, letting your knees and ankles flex as you land.

Turning to face forward before you slide down helps avoid having your clothing—buttons and belt buckles and the like—catch on the saddle, possibly hanging you up and certainly damaging the saddle. As soon as you are well on the ground, turn toward the horse, slip your left arm through the left rein and put your stirrups up before leading the horse away.

When you are comfortable with the moves of both mounting and dismounting, without rushing, speed the process up so that it becomes a fluid whole.

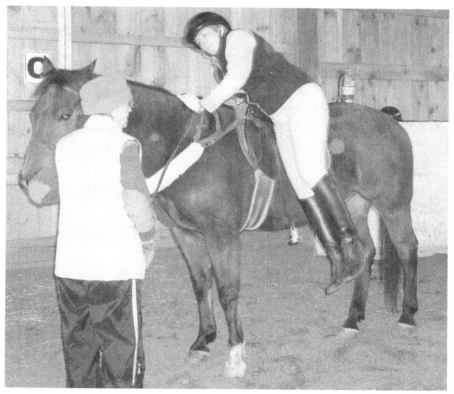

Sliding down. Peg's ankles are relaxed, so she will land fairly softly.
Just as well, because it was pretty cold!

THE LEG-ON

Having another person help you mount—give you a leg-on—is very common, and often performed very unsafely. Here's how to do it right, both for the "legger" and the "leggee." Read both descriptions, so you will know what you should expect from the other person.

Giving a Leg-on

Always either slip your left arm through the rein, or if the person is small and light, hold the rein in your left hand. If the horse is very fidgety, have another competent person hold him. One of the most dangerous things is if the horse moves off suddenly when the rider is halfway up, so that she lands *behind* the saddle. This nearly always sends the horse into a bucking fit, and sitting where she is, the rider has little choice but to take a bad fall. It is not enough for the rider to be holding the reins—she will not be able to stop the horse when she is halfway on.

1. If you are using both hands, face the rider and put your left hand under her bent left knee and your right hand around her lower calf so you are holding her shin bone. If you are using only one hand, put your right hand around her upper calf. Stand as close to the horse as possible.

2. Keep your back straight and bend your knees.

3. Count one, two, and on three straighten your knees and stand up quickly. Be sure to come straight up with your arms, not forward or back or out. Keep a firm hold with your right hand so that the rider cannot straighten her leg until she gets all the way up, then allow her leg to rotate as she turns to face forward and swing her right leg over.

Sometimes if the rider is inexperienced, she will collapse her hip or try to reach over too soon with her right leg on the first attempt. Rather than trying to push her on anyway, it is best to let her back down and (politely) point out her mistake, then try again. If you are strong and the rider is light, be careful not to throw her up so high that she goes over! Watch what she is doing and keep a hold on her leg until she is safely seated.

Getting a Leg-on

How you handle your body when you are being given a leg-on will make all the difference in whether or not it is successful. If you can do it right, even a fairly small person can help you on.

Giving and getting a leg-on. Peg is a good deal
bigger than I am, but using this method I was still able
to help her up. She did straighten her left knee a little,
making it harder for both of us.

1. Stand facing the horse, opposite his withers. Take the reins in your left hand and place it on top of the withers. Place your right hand close to your left hand if you are bareback, or on the pommel of the saddle. Keep your head up and look up above the horse.

2. Bend your left knee and lift your foot so your calf is at a 90-degree angle to the ground. Keep your left knee lightly pressing against your right knee. Bend your right knee a little, but keep your hip and back straight. Your helper will now take your left leg.

3. As the helper says "three," spring off with *just* your right leg and pull up with your arms at the same time. Once you have left the ground, let your right leg dangle straight down; don't try to swing it over the horse's back at first. Keep

your hip joint locked and your back straight, and imagine that you are going to go right up past the horse (see the photo on page 115).

4. When your crotch is about level with the horse's back, *not before*, bring your right leg up and over, turn and sit down gently.

REBREAKING: PREPARING TO MOUNT FOR A NERVOUS HORSE OR RIDER

Mounting can be difficult or even traumatic for many riders and horses. This problem arises in our initial approach to mounting, whether we are training the horse or the rider. **We approach mounting with the idea that once we're up, the idea is to stay there, no matter what!** This immediately adds an element of forceful invasion of personal space, from the horse's point of view, or a feeling of being trapped on top of an unpredictable animal, for the rider.

You may be an experienced rider working with a new horse or a horse who has a problem with being mounted. You may also be a novice rider, mounting for the first time. Or you may be an intermediate rider who has developed a fear of mounting, probably as the result of a fall. Whatever the circumstances, there is a better way to approach mounting. Think of being asked to dance, at least the way it was when I was young. The man approached the woman, perhaps smiled and bowed, and either said, "May I have this dance?" or "Would you like to dance?" If the young lady was properly brought up, unless she had a previous commitment she smiled and thanked him, and off they went to the dance floor together. What happened after that depended on his charm and skill as a dancer, but at least they started off in harmony.

Mounting is the introduction to your dance with the horse. The horse should look forward to being ridden with the same pleasure a girl has looking forward to a dance, and much of this depends on how the mounting is handled, especially the first time. Imagine if the young man just grabbed the girl by the wrist, hauled her to her feet, put his arm around her and held her in such a way that she felt she couldn't get away! Even if he was a good dancer and an attractive man, she would still feel very uncomfortable.

So first of all we must change our thinking about mounting. In the initial approach to the horse, rather than saying, "I'm going to stay on no matter what!" we're going to say, **"I'm going to slide off as soon as I feel the smallest amount of tension in either mine or my horse's body."** Later on we will modify this, of course, but in the beginning we want to make it very plain both to our own and the horse's body that we're not going to force things in any way. Once a good level of confidence is created, then we can be a little more demanding without appearing threatening, because trust has been established.

And how are you going to do that? Begin with advance and retreat, always the best way to reassure yourself or your horse about a new procedure. In this case, if you're starting at the very beginning, you introduce the horse to the idea of you standing on a small step stool, beside his shoulder. If introduced during grooming, this soon becomes a comfortable part of his routine. This is a very important step for the horse, because he instinctively fears any predator who appears above him. That is by far the easiest way for a lone predator to take down a horse, since it can jump down onto the horse's back to attack his spinal cord.

For this work, the horse should be wearing only a bridle or halter and lead rope, and perhaps a neck strap, especially if he has no mane or your arms are short. Just be careful that the neck strap doesn't slip down his neck where he could step in it.

First let him get comfortable having the step close to him. Then stand up on it and step down, then repeat, staying a little longer each time until he shows that he is not bothered by it. Once he is comfortable having you stand close to him on a fairly high box or mounting block, the next step is to start stroking him with your hands, along his back, down his other side and up across his croup. Touch the croup with a sweeping motion, as though it were your leg swinging over. He needs to get very comfortable about something rubbing along his side and up over his croup, because this is a movement many horses find threatening. You also should gradually add movements such as swinging your arms and legs about, and even flapping things up above him to get him comfortable with all kinds of odd movement in an area that he can't see very well.

The next step to put pressure on his back to get him used to the idea of weight. A useful thing to do here is to tie him so that he can reach the ground with his head, or just ground tie him. Then put a small pile of hay on the ground so that he keeps his head down. (You might want to put it in something like a feed or a clean manure tub so that he doesn't have to chase it around the floor, preventing him from standing still.) Having his head down places his back in the best position for carrying weight, so he learns early on how to support you in the most efficient way. Use a mounting block that places you at least waist high to his back. Then start leaning on him, first on your hands, then your elbows, and gradually draping your whole body over him so that you are lying on your belly across his back. Combine this with the patting, stroking and swinging of your arms wherever you can reach.

The next step is to add a little hopping of the sort you will use when you go to jump up on him. Standing on a mounting block, place your left hand at the front of his withers and your right hand on the backward slope (see the photo on page 98). Be sure he is standing fairly square. Gently rock his withers from side to side, so that he spreads his front legs a little, giving him a firmer base. Praise him effusively for this. Now hop so that your weight goes onto your hands and off again.

When he stands quietly for this, you are ready for the actual mounting. Using the techniques for mounting a bareback horse (with no pad) and for dismounting, proceed one phase at a time. The phases are:

1. Hop up so that you are resting with your torso on his back.

2. Hook your right knee over.

3. Rotate so that you are facing forward with a leg on each side.

4. Sit up straight.

After each phase, you dismount again. Repeat each one as often as necessary until you are confident that you and the horse are both completely comfortable and happy with what you're doing, before skipping the dismount after that phase and proceeding to the next phase. If you find that you are grippy with your seat and thighs when you reach phase 4, try doing a thigh squeeze at phase 1 to release some tension.

When you reach the point where you feel the horse is comfortable with you sitting up straight, really focus on the first five steps described on page 20. If he walks away—which may happen in his effort to adjust to your full weight—as long as he is walking quietly just keep doing the seven steps, keeping your following seat (see Chapters 7 and 8) very slow to encourage him to stop again. If you feel that either you or he is getting tense, immediately dismount, return to the block and start again. Be sure to quit while you're ahead—that is, end the session at a time when you both feel reasonably calm, not nervous.

Dealing with Fear of Mounting after a Fall

Sometimes when you have had a fall or other bad experience, you find that when you go to ride again, not usually the same day but a few days later, you get a sudden rush of tension when you go to mount. If you are taking a lesson, ask your instructor to hold the horse while you mount and continue to hold him until you are ready to go on your own. Usually, once you have gone through the Seven Steps described in Chapters 2 and 7 and walked around being led or longed for a few minutes, the fear recedes.

If you are alone, it may not be so easy, so a reintroduction becomes necessary. It is basically the same exercise as I just described, but it is done with the saddle and from a slightly different viewpoint, in that you are more concerned with your own reactions than the horse's. You also will try for a little more self-control to deal with your panic reflex.

Begin with the preparatory work associated with grooming (Chapter 4). Then, after tacking the horse up and checking the girth, go to the mounting area. If you are mounting into the saddle, take one step at a time, returning to standing on the block after each step. In other words, put your foot in the stirrup, then take it out, then put it back in, put some weight on the stirrup, take it out and return to the block. Proceed this way through the full mounting routine, finishing with sitting in the saddle for a few moments, keeping one hand on the pommel or horn for security, then quietly dismount again using a regular dismount, not an emergency dismount. Repeat each step as necessary until you find your comfort zone. If the horse becomes restless, take him away from the block and lead him around for a minute, then bring him back. Offering a small treat when he stands quietly may make it easier.

Once you have done this, then, depending on your confidence level, you can either proceed to whatever level of riding you feel comfortable with, or you can simply repeat the mount a few more times and call it a day. The next time, it is important to get to at least the same point and if possible push the envelope a little, so that you gradually regain your confidence. You are creating the awareness that *you* are in control of the situation, not your fear. You don't allow your fear to control you to the point where you start doing less and less, rather than more and more.

Learning to manage your fear in a very controlled situation, such as step-by-step mounting, will build your confidence. Then, if you have some fear to deal with in a more difficult situation, the knowledge that you have controlled it before will make controlling it again that much easier.

EMERGENCY DISMOUNTS

If you ride often enough and long enough, eventually it will happen to you—probably sooner than later. A horse panics in a situation where there is not room or time to maneuver, such as near a road. A piece of essential equipment breaks. A rogue horse decides he's going to take over *now!* Whatever the cause, you are in trouble and it could be serious trouble. But you have a little time; you are still on top of the horse and in control of your own body, if not his, and there is something you can do. You can get off! If you know how to do an emergency dismount, you can get out of trouble safely and probably regain control of your horse at the same time.

There are three situations most riders would rather not face. One is falling, either off or with the horse. The second is losing control of a horse who is running, bucking or otherwise misbehaving in a threatening manner. The third is being on the horse and not being able to get off in an emergency, such as running out into traffic.

Tidbits & Supplements

It is a very secure feeling to know that if your horse starts to "throw a wing ding," you don't have to try to hang on until you fall. From the point of view of the instructor, knowing that a pupil will dismount on command if you see that she is getting into trouble takes a lot of the stress out of teaching beginners.

Most of the time when any of these problems arises, there is a period of time during which you can see the trouble coming. You are probably trying to do something to stop it from happening, but sooner or later the inevitable occurs. If you are lucky, nothing suffers but your temper—and your confidence. However, if, during that period when you realize things are getting out of control but you are still on top of things, you can perform a safe emergency dismount, the situation can be saved.

Emergency dismounts are easy to learn, but they require practice until you can perform them almost without conscious thought. Mounting and dismounting are hard on the horse, so don't practice more than a half dozen dismounts in any one session.

The question always arises, "Should I hold on to the reins?" One school of thought says, "Yes, otherwise you might have to walk home." My own observation is that if you land safely, that is, standing up and at least partially in control of your body, go ahead and keep hold of the reins. If you fall on landing and your horse doesn't stop *immediately*, let go. Getting dragged, even by the reins, is no fun, and a panicky horse will kick at you. Also, if you fall in front of him, you force him to step on you if you're holding tightly to the reins.

Emergency Dismount from Bareback

The emergency dismount is easiest to learn bareback, particularly at the standstill and walk. Once you have perfected it bareback, you can try it in the saddle. The emergency dismount, whether from bareback or from the saddle, is very similar to an ordinary bareback dismount. In both instances you need to get enough momentum for your right leg to clear the horse's back. To begin with, you may want to practice the standard bareback dismount (see page 101), even if you never ride bareback and have therefore skipped the appropriate instructions. Then move on to the instructions below.

The first thing to consider is that any dismount must be a safe dismount, if possible leaving you on your feet and in control of your body. In order to come down feet first, your hands must be the last thing to leave the horse. Therefore, a good handhold on something that won't slip, such as the mane, is essential.

1. Start with step 1 of bareback dismounting (page 102). Practice grabbing the mane with both hands, as described, until you can do it quickly from any position. Don't bother to put your reins in one hand, but don't let go of them either. You can let your stick fall from your hand if it feels awkward, but be careful not to throw it—it might frighten a scared horse even more. Don't be surprised if your horse stops every time you throw your weight onto your hands; this is a natural reaction and will make the dismount easier.

2. Now practice the leg swing, as in steps 2 and 4. Practice until leaning forward, grabbing the mane and kicking up the right leg become one rapid move. Be sure to keep your head up and turned to the right, and stay on top of the horse.

3. Continue into the dismount as in steps 4 and 5. See how quickly you can get to the ground from start to finish.

4. Do another dismount, but this time as your right leg crosses over, give a strong push with your arms so that you land at least 18 inches away from the horse. Remember to keep hold of the reins unless you lose your balance and fall.

5. Now repeat, but as you push off with your arms, turn in the air so that you land facing the same way as the horse. Turning your head to the left first will help bring your body around. Take a step or two after you land to get used to the idea of keeping moving.

Although the emergency dismount is very similar to an ordinary bareback dismount, the ordinary dismount would not be safe on a moving horse. In an ordinary dismount, one often lands facing the horse and very close to him. In an emergency dismount, it is essential to land facing the direction in which the horse is moving. If you don't, inertia (the force that keeps you going in the same direction and at the same speed until something stops you) will tip you over your leading leg and sprain or break it. It is also essential to land far enough away that the horse doesn't knock you down by accident.

Try to land on your toes and let everything bend a little as you hit, and take a couple of steps in the direction you were going. It should not be uncomfortable, but if you do find yourself hitting the ground pretty hard, practice jumping off a low log or fence until you get the knack of landing softly. Older people get out of the habit of jumping around like the kids do, but they are just the ones who need the protection of safe dismounts.

When you are comfortable dismounting from a standing horse, try it from a walk—and a jog, if you like—from the bareback horse a few times. Ninety-nine horses out of a hundred will stop before you hit the ground, making the moving dismount surprisingly nonthreatening.

Tidbits & Supplements

Here are two exercises to help you get used to standing on something less stable than the floor. Find a flight of stairs with a railing to hold on to. Holding the rail, stand on a step with your feet close together and the bubbling spring point on the edge of the step so that your heel is hanging off in space. Let your knees bend a little and play with the first five of the Seven Steps until your leg muscles relax and allow your heel to drop. Try letting go of the rail. It is surprisingly hard at first to stay relaxed without holding on—which gives you some idea of how hard your body finds it to cope with stirrups.

The next piece of equipment you need is a round or octagonal wooden jump pole lying on the ground and either another person or, again, something to balance with. A second jump pole set in front of you on standards at about elbow height works well. Take the same position on the ground pole that you took on the step and again work on relaxing your legs until your heels will drop. The unsteadiness of the pole mimics the stirrup fairly well and helps you learn how to find the technique.

A variation on this is to have another person face you and hold your hands, or even have the other person balancing on a pole herself as you hold hands and both try to stay balanced.

Emergency Dismount from the Saddle

Emergency dismounts from the saddle require an additional move. Before doing anything else, you must kick your feet free of the stirrup irons. *Never* try an emergency dismount until you *know* your feet are free. If I find myself getting into a dangerous situation, the first thing I do is to slide my foot as far out of the stirrup as I can without losing it. Then, if I have to bail out, I know my feet will come loose immediately.

Adding the first step of kicking both feet free from the stirrups, practice the emergency dismount from the saddle going through the same steps as described for the bareback emergency dismount. Pay attention to the following additional thoughts:

• Even when you are doing an emergency dismount from the saddle, always grab the mane, not the pommel; sometimes the reason you need to get off is that the saddle has slipped!

• Because of the height of the pommel, which gets in the way of leaning forward, and the cantle, which gets in the way of your leg swinging over, you need to practice swinging your leg clear again.

As soon as you feel confident, try a dismount from a slow trot. You will be surprised and pleased to find that the bounce of the gait helps get you clear of the saddle, so the dismount is actually easier. The same is even more true at the canter. Just don't try the faster gaits until you can consistently land facing forward and clear of the horse. (The horse will nearly always stop, even at the faster gaits.)

Once you become proficient at emergency dismounting on the horse's left, you should also learn to do it from the right. In either case, you must become sufficiently comfortable with the emergency dismount so that, faced with a threatening situation, you can do it before it's too late.

Putting It All Together

To summarize, here is how the emergency dismount should (after you've practiced it) be ingrained in your muscle memory.

1. If dismounting from the saddle, kick both feet free from the stirrups **first**.

2. Place both hands on the horse's neck, fingers on the right side and thumbs pointing the same way, grabbing the mane with both hands and keeping the reins loosely in both hands. Drop the stick; don't throw it.

3. Turn your head so you are looking to your right, keeping your head and eyes up. Lean far forward and swing your right leg straight back, high behind you.

Tidbits & Supplements

Most horses who cause problems when riding can be more easily handled if you are on the ground. At least part of the difficulty with a horse who behaves aggressively when you ride him is that he knows he has your number. He can sense your insecurity, so he is less apt to listen to your commands. On the ground you feel more secure and have a better chance of getting him back under control. In any case, getting to the ground becomes your idea, not his.

When you start the emergency dismount, throwing your weight onto the horse's neck puts your center ahead of his and tends to cause him to at least try to stop. Your body will continue to go forward, so you land ahead of him. As soon as you catch your balance you can stop and face him, which is the best position from which to control a difficult horse. By keeping a feel on the rein, but not letting the horse get a hold and start pulling, you can do whatever is necessary to regain his attention.

4. Bring your right leg all the way across and let yourself swing down. As your leg crosses over, push off with your arms and turn in the air so you land facing the same way as the horse and at least 18 inches away from the horse.

5. Land on your toes first and let your body bend a little as you hit the ground. Remember to keep moving after you land and keep hold of the reins unless you are unable to stay on your feet.

If You Ride Western

A Western saddle does not lend itself to emergency dismounts as described above. The horn prevents you from throwing your weight forward as far as necessary to lift your right leg easily over the cantle and the horse's croup. However, Western saddles are a good deal harder to *fall out of*, as well. It is helpful to practice the emergency dismount bareback and then, if you do find yourself starting to fall, rather than trying to hang on with your legs, your instinct will be to get hold of something with your hands, so that you go down feet first. Once you know you're going to go, while still holding with your hands try to take your feet out of the stirrups and kick free with your legs so that they slide off and down. If you're strong enough, and the horse's gait is lifting you off the saddle, you can push off the horn to help get your legs free.

There is a fast dismount that can be done in a Western saddle if you have a little warning. This is the same dismount used by rodeo cowboys prior to tying a calf. They generally dismount on the right, but it could be done on either side. Watching rodeo on television will give you a very clear picture of the moves.

Tidbits & Supplements

Some instructors teach the emergency dismount technique as the standard dismount from the saddle. This is not a good idea, for two reasons. First, it is difficult to swing the right leg clear of the cantle when the horse is standing still, so the rider often gets hung up with her heel buried in the horse's off-side flank. Second, it is hard for a standing horse to balance against the sudden thrust of the rider's weight forward. As a result, horses dismounted in this way often become nasty about being dismounted, and will throw their heads or buck.

Tidbits & Supplements

I have heard of trainers who advocate throwing your arms around the horse's neck so you can hang on. I consider this *extremely* dangerous, and have seen at least one serious fall result from it. When you are dangling around the horse's neck you are unbalancing him badly and also interfering with his use of his front legs, which will very likely *prevent* him from stopping. If he can't stop, eventually one or both of you will fall, and you will be on the bottom of the heap!

Begin by getting a good grip on the front of the saddle with both hands and stand up in both stirrups. If you are dismounting on the left, stay upright, take your right foot out of the stirrup, swing your right leg over the horse's croup and bring it immediately down toward the ground. As it comes down, let your weight come back so your left foot swings forward. This will tip the stirrup so your left foot slides out. When you're sure your left foot is free, as it comes down let go of the saddle but keep hold of the left rein if you can, at least for a moment.

Unlike an English emergency dismount. which puts your center in front of the horse's, thus making him likely to stop, the Western quick dismount may even send him forward unless he has been trained to stop. Having a hold on the left rein will pull his head toward you and his hindquarters away from you so that he doesn't hit you with his hindquarters, or perhaps kick out if he runs past you.

As in the English and bareback dismounts, practice this first at the standstill, then at a walk and trot until your left foot comes out of the stirrup easily and consistently.

Which method of mounting or dismounting you choose will depend on the horse, the tack and the equipment or help available to you. In making your choice, safety should be the first consideration and comfort for the horse your second. You should familiarize yourself with all the techniques, so that you can use whichever one is the best for the situation at hand.

Part II

Riding without Fear
Bareback or without Stirrups

7

Sitting on the Horse
The Seven Steps, Part Two

When my mother was in her 80s, she spent her winters in Mexico, where she had a horse and rode almost every day. In the summer, in Rhode Island, she didn't ride at all.

One fall her visit happened to coincide with an invitation we had to hunt with one of the local packs. She asked if she could go along, and I was able to get her an invitation. But I was afraid a long day in the saddle for someone her age, who had not ridden in months, would be far too much. My fears were unjustified. Riding was so effortless for her that she came home after four hours of hunting as fresh as a daisy. Of course, she was one tough lady!

People will often say to me, "Oh, I used to ride and would love to ride again, but I'm *sooo* out of shape. I would just be in agony for weeks." To which my (hopefully unspoken) answer is, "Nonsense! Riding should be no more effort than walking. In fact less, since the horse is making the effort to hold you up and move you forward." Nearly all the factors that cause stiffness and pain for the beginning rider are the result of bad technique.

In Chapter 2 I covered the first five of the Seven Steps as they relate to working with the horse on the ground. Now that you are ready to begin riding, we need to see how those steps relate to being on the horse and add the last two steps, which have to do with following the movement of the horse. You should begin by reviewing Chapter 2 briefly just to refresh your memory of the steps on the ground. Then I will discuss any adaptations that have to be made to allow for sitting on the horse. The page number that accompanies each step refers to the page in Chapter 2 where the ground exercise may be found.

While you are learning the Seven Steps on the horse, avoid attempts at control as much as possible because you cannot expect to influence the horse in any beneficial way when your position causes you to get in his way. However, riding using the Seven Steps makes it much easier for the horse to function correctly even before your skills are fully developed, which means the horse will be more relaxed and control will be less of a problem. You will find it faster and easier to embed the Seven Steps correctly in your muscle memory if you can avoid using any aids at all except the voice and the stick. Since you will not be attempting to guide the horse, you must work in a situation where control is not necessary for safety; ride in a small, safe area such as a round pen or a 60- to 80-foot (20- to 25-meter) paddock or corral, with no obstacles that can injure either you or your horse and *no other horses in the same space*. If you are a beginner, a capable hand leader is essential, and a ground person is handy for the more advanced rider as well.

I have found it is easiest for most people to learn the Seven Steps on a horse equipped with a bareback pad rather than a saddle. The rigidity of the saddle tends to force the pelvis into a position that may not be correct. However, if you feel very insecure without a saddle, use one. Using the stirrups, which are unstable, creates tensions and makes it hard to find the feeling of grounding, so try to avoid them or even remove them from the saddle. Once you are comfortable at a walk and perhaps a sitting trot, learning to ground in the stirrups is much easier (see Chapter 12).

If you do ride bareback, the shape of the horse's back will be a factor in your leg position. Saddles are shaped to follow the contour of your pelvis and leg, and some horses are too. But some horses are quite wide and flat in the back, which is comfortable for your seat but means dropping your leg down the horse's side will force your legs to spread apart wider than they can easily do. Therefore, if your horse has a wide, flat back you will have to let your knees come up in front of you a bit. Over time your inner thigh tendons will lengthen to allow your knees to drop, but it is a mistake to try to force your leg down before this happens. **The "long" leg comes when the thigh and pelvic muscles stretch naturally and eventually relax, allowing the legs to get wide enough to fit around the horse.**

Very narrow, bony horses can be coped with by adding more pads. You should never feel as though you are going to be cut in half up the middle by the horse's backbone! If you do ride bareback for extended periods, you might get some rubbing on the end of your tailbone, but that is the only discomfort you should feel.

The first-time beginner should have a capable ground person steady her by putting a hand on her thigh just above the knee for the first few steps. These usually take place as the horse is moved away from the mounting block. Since the student has not had a chance to begin the Seven Steps, she is especially insecure. The ground person should warn the student before moving, "I'm just going to put my hand on your thigh for a minute to steady you while we walk over there." Later, after the rider has been through the first five steps, she can compare how much easier the movement is with her corrected position.

THE NECK STRAP

If the horse is bareback, you will need a neck strap, and it would be desirable with an English saddle as well. **In the initial stages of learning or relearning correct position, you should have at least one hand gently clasping the pommel, horn or neck strap at all times, except where noted.** If you use a neck strap, it must be adjusted so you can hold it easily without leaning forward.

The neck strap, sometimes called a neck yoke, is the name given to any device placed around the horse's neck that the rider can use for greater security. The horse's mane is frequently used for this purpose and is adequate for work standing in the stirrups, but is out of reach for bareback work. Also, some horses fuss if you pull on their manes a lot, and the mane can get thin in the area you use the most. A neck strap gives a better handle and I have found it more practical for serious position work. The mane can be used for competition if necessary, where a neck strap would be inappropriate. Directions for making a neck strap, or adapting other equipment for use as a neck strap, can be found in Appendix A.

A neck strap has several purposes. One is to keep the rider from falling backward, so in the case of the beginner learning to post or a rider learning a more advanced skill such as jumping, it saves her horse from having his mouth jabbed by the reins or his back thumped on while the rider is searching for her balance. You might think only an inexperienced rider needs a neck strap, but in reality there are times when riders of any level can find the neck strap very useful. For example, if a trainer is working with a green horse, holding a neck strap enables her to place her body behind the motion when the horse is reluctant to go, say, into water, and still not risk hitting him on the mouth or back if he suddenly leaps forward, as horses so often do. In another area, jockeys in Quarter Horse races sometimes use them because the horses break away from the starting gate so fast that it is almost impossible to stay with them without something to hang on to.

But the most useful purpose for the neck strap is to give the rider something to balance and ground with—as opposed to hang on by—while her body becomes familiar with the horse's motion. This is similar to a toddler learning to walk. In the beginning he holds on to something all the time, but rarely does he hold on hard. Just having hold of something lightly is enough to help a baby balance.

The neck strap also offers psychological support both to the rider's conscious mind and to her reflex brain. Think of your first impulses if something frightening happens. If there is someone nearby, you instinctively grab their hand or arm with your hand. The conscious knowledge that there is something there to grab onto, if necessary, is very comforting if you're a nervous rider. Since the neck strap is connected to a comparatively fixed place, it also gives the beginner a much more confident feeling than grabbing onto the reins and having the horse react with his head.

At the same time, holding on to something with your hands seems to send a message to your reflex brain, so your body relaxes much sooner. I had some bad experiences with a horse who was explosive about mounting and the first few minutes afterward. For a while I had someone lead him on the ground until he got past his initial panic. Then I discovered that if I put my hand on the neck strap or pommel, he would relax much sooner. I realized that my expectations were making me tense, which he was picking up on. When I held on for a few minutes, my body quickly relaxed and then his did too.

Unfortunately, with all their virtues, neck straps are frowned on by instructors who don't understand how they work. Their perception is that they don't want the rider to hang on the horse's mouth (naturally), and they think if the rider learns to ride by holding on to the neck strap or mane, she will then be unable to balance without it. The truth is that we learn most balancing skills by holding on with our hands at first, starting as toddlers. And don't you remember how you clung to the handlebars of your bike when you were first learning? Later on, as we become more adept, we gradually lose the need to use our hands for balance: "Look Ma, no hands!"

If the unbeliever is an instructor who doesn't think school horses can suffer, or thinks suffering goes with the territory, she will allow her students to hang on by the reins, perhaps offsetting the pull with a standing martingale. This sets up all sorts of bad patterns in both horse and rider with relation to the rein aids. If, on the other hand, the instructor cares about her horses' mouths, she may insist the students not hold on to anything with their hands. The result of this will be riders with tense legs and shoulders as their bodies struggle with the unfamiliar movement and height. This kind of tension is one of the most difficult habits to unlearn later on.

As you start learning the Seven Steps, you will use the neck strap to help you to ground more deeply and securely. At first, the neck strap is held with the first two fingers of both hands, to keep you square on the horse. Later, as you begin to use reins and stick, you will hold the neck strap with only one hand, and eventually stop using it altogether except in very challenging situations. One reason for using the neck strap consistently at the early stages is that it develops a reflex, so that you instinctively reach for it—or some other secure support—in case of trouble. Riders without this reflex tend to grab the reins in a tense grip, which often causes the horse to react in unpleasant ways.

In order to ground yourself more securely, you must establish an elastic connection with the neck strap. You do this by lifting up on it as though you were lifting a basket by the handle, but with your hands on the sides of the handle rather than the top. The neck strap needs to be adjusted so that your hands are a few inches above the withers, your elbows softly bent and falling just in front of your shoulders. The pressure on the neck strap should be enough to make you feel solid, but not so much that it creates tension in any part of your body. The pull on the neck strap should flow evenly up your arms and down your back and be felt in your seat (see Chapter 9, page 191). If you take a stronger feel on the neck strap you will feel an equal increase of pressure under your seatbones. Later, when you become somewhat experienced with the reins, you will establish a grounding connection with the reins through the horse. The use of the neck strap is important preparation for this work.

Now let's go on to working with the Seven Steps while mounted on the horse.

1. GROWING

Growing (see page 20) on the horse is almost exactly the same as it is on the ground. The main difference is that you are far more likely to be tense and unsure on the horse, so you will be more aware of the changes in your body that occur as the result of the exercise. Just as you began growing on the ground by grounding onto your feet, so on the bareback horse you should begin by grounding into your seat. Think about letting your hips become very wide, having your thighs resting on the horse very lightly at first and letting your seatbones sink into the bareback pad. After you finish the growing exercise, think about grounding into your seatbones again.

2. SHAKE-OUT

Begin the shake-out (see page 23) with your arms exactly as described, but as you finish with each arm be sure to return it to the neck strap.

When you do the leg shake-out, simply allow your legs to dangle and shake out first the left leg, then the right. A novice rider should stop at the knee; a more advanced rider can hold her thigh away from the horse and shake it as well. (The allover shake while mounted is too unbalancing for most purposes.) Don't forget to check your growing and grounding when you have finished.

3. BREATHING

I cannot emphasize enough the importance of good breathing (see page 24) in riding. The effect it has on controlling tension in the horse is astounding. Here are a couple of little stories that help make the point.

The first story is about a very common circumstance that occurred when I was teaching breathing to a group of riders. Horses and riders would be standing in a line or small circle and the riders would be focusing on relaxed breathing. Then we would hear first one horse, then another breathe out in a long, soft sigh, indicating they also had relaxed. Very often we would all chuckle as the new students realized what was happening.

The second story took place in quite different circumstances. I had a horse who once had a very bad experience with the mounting block and threw me badly at least once when he accidentally touched it. However, at the time of this story I'd had the horse for a year or more and he seemed to be better. I was mounting off a small, portable block and had just seated myself when he stepped forward a little awkwardly and brushed the block with a front leg. I could feel him tensing up to explode but still hesitating, almost as if he were saying, "I'm frightened. What shall I do?" I told him with my own breathing, "Just breeaaattthhhe." Again he hesitated for a second, then let his breath out—which he had been holding—and walked quietly away. We both breathed a sigh of relief and went on with our session.

4. SOFT EYES

Soft eyes (see page 26), as I explained earlier, help you to relate your body to its surroundings. When you are riding this can mean in relation to other horses or to difficult terrain. For example, if you are riding in a ring crowded with other horses, using soft eyes will make it much easier to work around them without collisions. On the trail your soft eyes will help your body to follow the movements of your horse as he picks his way down a twisty trail. They can also help you regain your position if the horse does something violent enough to unseat you. I was riding a young horse in the field one day not too long after I had started with Centered Riding. It was close to dinnertime and the sounds of the other horses being fed reached my horse's ears. He decided he wasn't going to miss dinner and that I was preventing him. He spun, bucked hard and bolted for the barn, leaving me hanging off to one side struggling to get back on. In the middle of this I looked up to see whether the gate to the field was open or closed. This required soft eyes, and suddenly I found myself back up in the saddle! The soft eyes had told my body where it was in relation to the horse, and it was then able to do the right thing to get me back on.

5. TEETER-TOTTER (LONGITUDINAL CENTERING)

Longitudinal centering (see page 26) is another very important exercise because it affects not only your balance but the horse's, and loss of balance causes about 90 percent of the serious "misbehaviors" in horses! Horses have an extreme fear of falling, going back to when they were small, tasty little animals whose only defense from predators was running. If a horse fell down, he was toast!

1. Comfortably seated on the horse, remove your hands from the neck strap and hold both arms straight out in front of you. If the horse is being held and/or you are very secure, close your eyes.

2. Keeping your back straight and *bending only at the hips*, lean forward until you start to feel uncomfortably out of balance. Try *not* to hold on with your legs or let them swing back. Notice where your lower body and inner thigh muscles are tense.

3. Slowly lean back, still keeping your back straight, until you feel unbalanced backward. Again notice the tension, this time in your lower back and buttocks.

4. Slowly teeter back and forth several more times, finishing in the leaning back position.

5. Focus on the tension in your buttocks and lower back, and teeter forward very slowly *just* until that tension disappears. Keep your body tall, bring your arms down and think about how that feels. Check and make sure your legs are hanging softly. Without changing your upper body, shake your legs out a little, if necessary. Allow yourself to ground completely.

At first this may feel strange. Often you feel as if you are leaning back. But notice, if you start to lean forward even a little, the muscles in your upper inner thigh will tighten slightly. When you are seated correctly, with your center over your seatbones, it will not require any obvious muscular effort to stay in that position when the horse is still.

On the ground there is a much greater range of motion before you feel tension, because the base of support when standing (your feet) is much longer from front to back than the base of support when sitting (your seatbones). You might think that with the greater margin for error, standing would be easier. However, because when you're sitting your center is much closer to your base, sitting usually feels more secure. Think of riding a rocking train standing up or sitting in a seat.

This is the last of the exercises that don't require movement. At this point you should go or be taken for a little walk in a straight line while you review what you have learned and apply it to the horse in motion. When you reach a corner, if you have a helper she should support your inside leg as before. However, now she will pull down slightly to keep you centered on the turn.

6. LATERAL CENTERING

Now we move on to the exercises that require motion. There is some preparatory groundwork involved, so you will probably find it easiest to deal with these two exercises in a separate session.

On the Ground

1. Stand (in front of the mirror, if possible) with your feet a little more than hip width apart and with your knee and hip joints unlocked but not bent. Your toes should be pointing straight ahead. Spend a little time experimenting until you find a secure, comfortable place and are well grounded.

2. Grow as in step 1, but finish with both arms over your head. (Stop the exercise and bring your arms down when they tire, rest and go on.) *Without rotating your body or bending forward from the hip,* swing your raised hands slowly to the right so that your right shoulder drops and your hips go to the left. Feel how your weight has to shift to your left foot for you to keep your balance. Now do the same exercise in the opposite direction. Be sure to stay tall and let your *whole hip* swing

Leaning to the right moves
the center to the left.

through to the right, not just your waist. Your body should feel evenly curved from head to foot. What this shows you is that when you lean in one direction with your shoulders, *your weight and your center* go in the opposite direction. Therefore, leaning *into* a turn with your shoulders is counterproductive.

3. Same exercise, different thought. With your arms over your head, stretch your left side by reaching up with your left arm, and at the same time move your hip to the left. Do not let your body twist. A good mental image here is to imagine that you have a fairly large, heavy ball in your center, just below and behind your navel, and that you are opening a door in your left side to let the ball roll out. Your upper body will bend to the right as you stretch your left side. Feel how the weight shifts to your left foot. You have "moved your center" left. Now try it to the right. This is not as easy for your body. To get it correct, keep your left arm long and reach your right arm up past it to open your right side and let your hip slide right. Continue going from left to right and back again, trying to see how smoothly you can move the ball, and your center, from side to side.

On the Horse

You should have a ground person if at all possible. If not, a small square or rectangular paddock is the best place for this exercise. Even a large stall would be good if the footing is safe and there is no danger of hitting your head.

1. Begin this exercise by quickly going over the first five steps. You should be sitting tall but not stiff, with long, loose limbs, centered and grounded over your seatbones, breathing easily and with soft eyes.

2. If possible, have someone lead you in a very small turn to the left while you hold the neck strap, pommel or horn with both hands. As the horse turns, try not to compensate, but *allow* your body to slide to the *outside* (right) in response to the inertial force of the turn. (Experienced riders often have trouble with this at first, since they are so accustomed to making some adaptation when the horse turns.) Then, without moving your body, have the helper stop and feel how the horse is *not* under your body. If no one is available to help, with your reins hanging loose (but not in such a way that you or the horse could get tangled in them), ask your horse to walk and then allow yourself to slide to the outside when he turns the corner. Compare this with having the ground person holding your inside leg down.

3. Next, have the horse stand still on the rail near a left-hand corner or have your helper ready to lead you as directed. Hold the neck strap with both hands and open up your left side (think of lifting your left armpit instead of

raising your arm). Then move your seat (and your center) to the left until you feel you are starting to slide off to the left. Do not twist. *Do not try to hang on with your thighs.* Now have the horse move around the corner. Feel how as the horse turns left, *he moves over underneath you* so that you no longer feel as if you are falling. When he stops turning, notice that you again feel insecure. Move back into the center of the horse again.

4. With the horse standing still, holding your neck strap with both hands, move your seat to the left until you feel slightly insecure, then grip with your right thigh. Do not twist. Notice how as you tighten the thigh, the right leg draws up, especially in the saddle, forcing you even more to the left. **Gripping with the thigh will never give you a secure seat.** Now, grow and at the same time push your right leg firmly a little away from the horse and down, and give a wiggle to push your hips to the right, back into the center of the horse. Practice several times sliding off to one side, then growing, wiggling, and lengthening the opposite leg until you can recover your lateral center effort-lessly. Be sure your legs stay very loose and slippery. They should be long

Centering left on a moving horse. The pattern on his shirt clearly shows that Douglas's spine is vertical, as it should be. The relaxed left leg tells us he is laterally balanced, not hanging on.

This is surprisingly good right centering in a rider of this age and experience, as shown by his vertical spine. It almost appears that his center is *too* far to the right, but the relaxed left foot tells us this is not so. Rather, the horse is turning more sharply than it appears.

without being stuck down. Think of them as heavy, wet towels lying over the horse's back, not sticks.

5. Now practice walking, moving your center laterally to stay over the horse's center as it moves from one side to the other—to the left when he goes left, to the right when he goes right. When he walks in a straight line, keep your center in the middle. *Do not* move your center too soon; wait until you feel the horse start to turn, then go with him. Move your center by lifting either the arm or the armpit on that side, then letting your imaginary ball roll over in the direction the horse turns. Do not push your inner leg down, just let it fall by itself. If you go too far and your outer leg starts to come up, do the little shove down of the outer leg and hip wiggle to get back over the horse again. When going right, lift your left side first, then bring the right side up past it before you try to move your hip to the side. If possible, try it with your eyes closed.

What you are finding out is that **as long as you keep the horse directly under you, you cannot fall**, since the only way to fall is down, and *there is a horse in the way.* You are also finding that you keep the horse under you by moving your center over his center of movement, which is moving from side to side as he turns first one way and then the other. By using your body this way to stay on the horse, rather than by gripping with your thighs, you have a much softer, more flexible seat, which allows you to sit deeper and does not interfere with the horse's back.

7. FOLLOWING SEAT

On the assumption that you are reading this chapter through before you try these exercises on a horse, this is a little game you play on the ground, with another person if possible, but you can play it alone if necessary. The name of the game is Horsie.

Hold your forearm horizontal with the palm down, to represent the horse. Ask the other person to place her fingers, which represent the rider, lightly but firmly on your forearm (or place the fingers of your other hand there). Then start to move your hand and forearm forward in a circular motion—forward and up and down and back—to imitate a horse cantering. After a few moments, have the other person begin to move her fingers around on your arm but keep the pressure constant, like a rider shifting her weight around on the horse. Then return to the steady pressure. Now have the other person grab your arm hard and hold it (or hold it yourself with the other hand), like a rider gripping with her thighs. Again, return to the original pressure. Finally, the "rider" should hold her hand entirely still while the "horse" continues to move.

What you both will observe is that it is easiest for the "horse" when the rider stays soft and still on his "back." When the rider moves around, even lightly, it is very distracting to the horse. When the rider grips the horse with her "legs," the horse feels *very* restricted. When the rider locks her "body" and keeps still, she bangs on the horse, who is moving. So we observe that the easiest thing for the horse, and therefore the way he can perform the best, is when the rider's body is still *relative to the horse's movement*, that is, the rider's body must move as much as the horse's body moves—no more, no less.

I was once working with a horse who had an extremely rough canter. I felt as though I were being tossed all around on his back! When I finished, one of my pupils who was standing by the fence said, "I just love to watch you ride. You always sit so *still!*" I was startled by her comment, to say the least. But when I thought it over, I realized that if the horse's gait was very bouncy, then I must be equally bouncy. What was important, and what made it look right to my pupil, was the fact that the horse and I were moving *together*.

On the ground, sit on a straight chair, preferably unpadded. Without sliding around on the seat, wiggle your hips from side to side and feel where your seatbones press against the chair. Then slide one hand underneath your seat from the side and feel the seatbone. It is quite far under, almost in the center. Now you're ready to get on the horse.

On the Horse

1. Begin this exercise by checking your position using steps 1 through 5. Then have the horse walk around while you think about how his back feels under your seat. Notice that it does not feel like a moving car or a bicycle, which both have wheels and, except for bumps in the road, move very steadily. The horse's back drops, first on one side and then the other, as he steps along. Some people feel this as back-and-forth, some as up-and-down or side-to-side. It doesn't make any difference how you interpret the movement; just notice it.

2. With the horse standing still, use your left hand to feel your seatbone. Bring your hand back to the neck strap. Now imagine that you have a strip of Velcro stuck to your left seatbone, and the other strip of the Velcro is stuck to the saddle or bareback pad. Start the horse walking in a straight line and think about your seatbone being stuck to the Velcro. If it is stuck, when the horse's back goes down, your seat will go down with it. When the horse's back comes up, it will push your seatbone up. Your seatbone is *following* the motion of the horse's back, which results in a hip movement like backpedaling a bicycle. Keep your body long and flexible and try to keep your shoulders level so that

the movement all occurs below your rib cage. Imagine your hip joints are made of ice or something equally slippery. The pressure on your seatbone should be the same all the time, just as the pressure on your forearm stayed the same in the horsie game you played earlier.

3. When you have the left seatbone following nicely, think about the right one until it is following as well. Now you should feel equal, steady pressure on both seatbones as they move up and down, first one side, then the other. Experiment by stiffening your back and hips and squeezing with your thighs to see how it feels and how your horse reacts, then grow, check your center both forward and back and side to side, and go back to following.

It is easy at this time to confuse lateral centering and following seat, because they both involve your hips and lateral pressure. It helps to remember that in lateral centering you *purposely* slide your hips (and your center) to one side to follow the horse as he turns, whereas in following seat you allow the *horse* to move your seat up and down, but your center remains in place.

The goal is to keep *even* pressure on both seatbones; *even* in the sense of constant, and *even* in the sense of being the same amount of pressure on both sides. **Therefore, as the horse turns, lateral centering is necessary for you to keep even pressure on your following seatbones, and in fact, if the pressure on your seatbones is *not* even during a turn, you will know that you are *not* laterally centered.**

GROUNDING ON THE HORSE

In Chapter 2 I referred to grounding, which is the goal of the Seven Steps. At that time you were only concerned with grounding into your feet. Now that you are sitting on a moving horse, you need a slightly different viewpoint. To understand grounding when seated on the horse, imagine your seatbones are the prongs of an electric plug and your horse's back is a portable outlet. For your seat to stay firmly "plugged in" no matter how the outlet is wiggled around, *all* the Seven Steps must be correctly applied.

This flexible connection to the horse is what enables you to be on the horse in a way that is comfortable and secure for both of you. It is also the indicator that you have achieved *true* balance, because without balance your body will retain tensions that prevent you from grounding completely.

The first time you use the Seven Steps you may well be astonished at how comfortable and secure you feel, especially if you previously rode with tight thighs.

To complete the picture of the Seven Steps, let's see what happens to you and your body if you are faced with a threatening situation, then look at how the Seven Steps can bring you back into harmony with the horse.

A typical threatening situation is one in which the horse is walking down a trail when something surprising occurs ahead and to one side. The horse jumps off to the other side and stops. When he does, inertia carries you straight ahead, so you find yourself unbalanced both longitudinally and laterally as you feel yourself falling forward over the horse's shoulder. In addition, there is the fear that the horse may do something even more threatening.

Your first reaction will be a gasp, an inhaling chest breath. Your eyes will focus down onto the horse's neck, becoming hard, and your body will try to curl up into a tight ball—the fetal position. Your legs will be gripping the horse. Your arms will be drawn back to your body, making the reins tense, and this puts you at risk of being pulled still more forward if the horse snatches the bit. I call this the uh-oh position. If you allow yourself to remain in this position

Peg *before* doing her Seven Steps. You might be misled into thinking this was a good position. She is sitting up straight, her heels are down and her hands are neatly up in front of her.

your horse will pick up on your tension, and unless he is a very solid citizen, he may proceed to violent action such as wheeling and bolting. And of course your brain will be saying things like, "Oh no, here we go. I'm falling and I'm miles from home and if I get hurt how will I get back on?!"

Using the Seven Steps, your first responses, begun almost immediately and together, should be to lift your head and eyes—allowing your eyes to become soft—and then to grow, which means relaxing your hold on the reins, and begin breathing with a long exhale. Softening your eyes will help your body to locate itself, growing will release the worst of the tension, and the breathing, besides helping you relax, sends a strong message to your horse that things are okay. You should then use your hands on the neck strap, mane or saddle to help you get back on the saddle and regain your centered position, both laterally and longitudinally. Keeping one hand on the saddle, you can now quickly shake out your shoulders and arms to release tension on the reins, and shake out your legs to allow them to fall into a natural position again. At this point you will be

The *after* photo. Looking at this, you can see how tense and posed Peg was in the previous photo. Now she almost seems to melt into the horse.

Uh-oh! I need my Seven Steps!

pretty well grounded, which helps the horse to ground, and as he moves off, your following seat will encourage relaxation of his back and regularization of his gait, helping him overcome his tension as well. And you're soon on your way as though nothing happened!

SOME PROBLEM SOLVERS

In working with the Seven Steps, many people discover tensions in themselves of which they were previously unaware. Here are some exercises and games to help you work through these tensions and have a little fun at the same time.

Swan Neck

Because the head weighs a lot, the neck very easily becomes compressed and stiff. This exercise is a safe way to loosen the neck muscles.

1. Imagine there's a balloon on a string attached to the top of your head, then nod your head smoothly back as far as it will go comfortably. Next, still thinking about the string, nod slowly forward, again as far as you can go without forcing.

2. Continue nodding back and forward several more times, each time thinking about letting your neck grow longer.

3. Notice how your range of motion increases appreciably, so that you can tip your head both forward and back much farther without feeling any cramping.

4. Finish with your face vertical, which feels like a very slight arch in your neck (similar to what you would like to see in your horse's neck). If you look in the mirror, you should *not* see a bunch of double chins, which would indicate tension.

This exercise can also be done from side to side and around in circles, but the change in range of motion will probably not be as noticeable. Do not ever attempt to force any more range of motion than is comfortable.

Playing with Blocks

This exercise helps relieve tension along the whole spinal column.

1. Bending from the waist upward, not at the hips, allow your whole spine to round and your head to fall forward as far as it will go easily.

2. Then picture your spine as a set of children's blocks. There are 5 in your lower back, 12 in your upper back, and 7 in your neck.

3. Starting from the bottom, slowly straighten up by imagining you are stacking the blocks on top of one another, one at a time. (Tip: The sixth block in your upper back should come about in the middle of your shoulder blades.)

4. Finish by placing your head on top, with your ears in line with your spine.

Finding the Middle of the Horse

One of the mental barriers to maintaining correct longitudinal (front to back) centering is our incorrect perception of our center in relation to the horse's base. We perceive ourselves to be sitting in the middle of the horse's body, the way we sit in the middle of a bicycle, because of the visual illusion of his head and neck. Actually, we are sitting just behind the front of the horse's base.

Another barrier is our instinctive fear of falling backward, especially from a height. We feel (incorrectly) that the safe way to lean is forward, because the

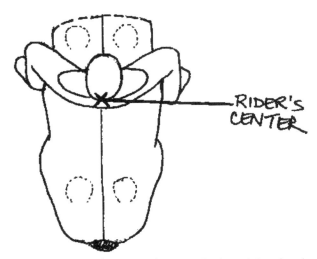

RIDER'S CENTER

Reality check. When you take away the horse's head and neck, there really isn't much in front of you, is there?

horse has a long neck reaching out in front (with a convenient hairy "handle," as well), while behind us is a big drop to the ground—since we don't have eyes in the back of our head to see the horse's back stretching out behind us.

The following exercises will increase your awareness of yourself in space and of your longitudinal relationship to your horse. They are best done on a bareback pad, if possible. The horse should be a mature, quiet animal.

The first exercise helps you overcome the body's belief that the horse's head and neck offer secure protection from falling forward. It is this belief that makes you tend to crouch forward when the horse starts to act up. Allowing your weight to come forward unbalances the horse and often will cause actions such as crow-hopping or dropping the shoulder. You can use a ground person to help with this exercise, if you like.

1. Take the horse out to a grassy patch and make sure he stands with his head and neck in normal position.

2. Hold your hands out in front of you, keep your back flat and bend forward from the hip as far as you can without letting your legs swing back and without feeling in serious danger of falling over.

3. Now, *without straightening up*, allow your horse to drop his head to the ground or let your helper do this with a treat. You will immediately feel extremely insecure! You can then straighten up until you feel secure again.

By deliberately dropping the horse's head when your body is already in an insecure position, you become aware both mentally and physically that the horse's head and neck do not offer secure support; that they are, in effect, an illusion that can disappear without warning.

The next exercise increases your awareness of longitudinal position. Practice until you can lean forward and backward easily with a minimum of tension. A variation is to add a two-armed growing stretch and centering each time you sit up straight. If you are in the saddle, take your feet out of the stirrups.

1. Turn your head so you can see as far behind you as possible and reach back with one hand, both for support and to feel the horse's back. Allow yourself to lean back from the hips as far as you can.

2. Reach back with your other hand as well and turn your head to face forward again. If you're using a bareback pad, you will now be able to lie all the way back with your head on the horse's rump. A beginner may need the ground person to help her lie all the way back the first time. If you're in a saddle, the cantle may get in the way so you can only rest on your elbows. Allowing your knees to come up a little will take the strain off your back.

3. Remain in this position for a minute or two and become aware of how secure a spot this is. That is, it is not possible to fall off the horse backward without great difficulty, first, because your body does not bend backward easily and second, because the horse's back is long enough that it will always offer adequate support if you fall back. The only exception would be if you were riding without reins or neck strap and the horse leaped or bolted forward very explosively.

Katy is finding out that there's plenty of room for a nap.

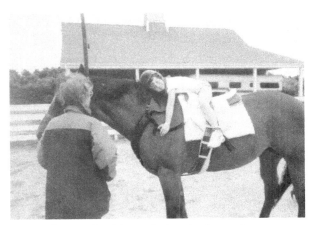

When you're this small, there's plenty of room everywhere on a 16-hand horse. But notice that Katy's center is slightly behind Miss Kitty's center, which makes this position comfortable for both.

4. Slowly sit up again. With the horse's head in normal position, bend forward from the hip, turning your head to one side, until your upper body is lying on the horse's neck. At the same time as you bend forward, if you are on a bareback pad you should slide your seat backward, using your arms to push yourself, if necessary, so that your center stays *behind* the horse's withers. You can either use your arms for support as you bend forward, or allow them to dangle, or hug the horse around the neck. Your legs should not be allowed to swing back or grip the horse's sides.

You should become aware at this point that just as it is easier for you to fall forward than backward, it is—unfortunately—also easier for the horse. That is, because of the way his body bends and the position of his center just behind the front legs, the horse can stumble and fall in front comparatively easily— another reason it is important for you not to ever let your center get in front of the horse's center. On the other hand, it is nearly impossible for the horse to fall backward (unless he is standing on his hind legs, which is why rearing is such an undesirable vice). The part of the horse that is behind his center is supported by his hind legs, so you can lean back as far as you wish without ever endangering the horse's balance.

Wringing Out the Old

Two major areas of tension are the shoulders and hips. The following exercises specifically address those tensions.

To release tension in a muscle, you need first to identify it. You do this by delib- erately tensing the muscle group until it becomes uncomfortable, then consciously releasing the tension you have located. To release, breathe the tension out by taking deep breaths with long exhalations. Try to let the tension out of the muscles one small area at a time. It should take four or five breaths to reach full relaxation.

1. For the shoulder area, tense by drawing your shoulders up to your ears. Hold the tension until it hurts a little, then begin the release as described above. Think about allowing your shoulders to get wide, then drop down, until your shoulder points feel really low. (Think of the ladies in 17th-century portraits with elegant, sloping shoulders.)

2. For the hip area, tense by squeezing your buttocks and thighs together as hard as you can, then hold as above. For the release, start in the middle of your back, just below your waist, and let it get very wide. Then release your buttocks outward and downward, and continue releasing in this spiral down the outside and tops of the thighs. Finally, let the inner thighs fall open. If you feel this last move leaves your knees poking out, you probably didn't release your middle back and buttocks far enough.

Building a Shelf

I always loved the description of a large-bosomed Victorian lady as having a shelf instead of a chest. Of course, the Victorians were sticklers for good posture—which did not mean rigidity of body, although they were noted for rigidity of mind! The secret here is not to try to pull your shoulders back, but to release your front so it can come forward and up.

1. Begin with your collarbones. Imagine they are getting longer and longer, finally extending out over your shoulders like the yoke farmers used to use to carry buckets of water.

2. Now tie an imaginary balloon to your breastbone a couple of inches below the collarbones, and just let your chest float upward until you feel your breastbone is well out in front.

Don't make the mistake of trying to open your chest by lifting your chin. If you have done the swan neck exercise first, your neck muscles will be nice and soft. Now you want to bring your chest up toward your softly flexed jaw. Again, think of how you want your horse's head, neck, and forehand to be.

Letting Go of the Branch

We seem to have an instinct, when sitting on something high, to want to hold on with our thighs. I call this the tree branch reflex, based on my memories of climbing trees as a child. The following series of exercises provide different ways to teach your body to be independent of the leg grip for staying on—that is, to encourage true balance through adjustment of the center. If you are in a saddle, your feet should be out of the stirrups.

Knees Up

This is a very simple exercise that, besides removing the possibility of leg grip, also helps you find your seatbones. This exercise is easiest to do in an English saddle, but can be modified for Western or bareback.

1. Lift your legs one at a time and hang your calves and feet in front of the knee roll of the saddle flap, so your thighs are about level with the top of the horse's withers and your feet are in front of your knees, resting on the horse's shoulders. It is similar to your leg position if you were sitting in a chair. If there is no saddle, your knees can still be lifted into this position but will require a little effort of the top thigh muscles to keep them there, since there is not much for them to rest on.

2. Teeter-totter slightly to find your center over your seatbones. Do a buttock-thigh squeeze and release to let yourself all the way down onto your bones. With your legs in this position (and holding the pommel or neck strap for security), you are forced to depend on the adjustment of your center for balance. Walking (and later jogging) in this position is very easy and beneficial. Watch for tensions in your buttocks and thighs at first, and don't try the faster gaits until you are completely balanced at the walk.

Knees up. Douglas is sitting firmly and comfortably on his seatbones.

3. Finish by bringing first one leg, then the other, back into normal position. Only bring the legs down as far as you can while still staying on your seatbones. Many riders, in trying to make their legs long, push them too far down and back, so their weight ends up primarily on their inner thigh rather than the seatbones, and they find themselves gripping again.

Knees up can be done at the canter on a smooth-gaited horse. It is also a good exercise standing still if you are a beginner whose inner thighs are uncomfortable with the unaccustomed stretching of sitting on a horse. Bringing your thighs together puts them in a less stressed position, so you are not as likely to be stiff after the lesson.

Sidesaddle

This exercise is sometimes frightening to the novice in the very beginning, so a ground person may be necessary for the first walking steps. To avoid getting tangled in the reins, which can be dangerous, the reins should either be left lying on the horse's neck or, if you are holding the reins, have them all in your left hand and don't lift the left hand off the pommel, but swing your leg *over* the reins. I know this sounds wrong, but because of the relative length of your arms and legs, if you try to put your leg *under* the reins, it is difficult not to catch a toe.

1. From a normal sitting position, place your left hand on the pommel and your right hand on the back of the seat of the saddle near the cantle, and hold the saddle with both hands. If you are riding bareback, the left hand goes on the neck strap and the right hand on the surcingle just behind the right leg.

2. Now lift your right leg forward, keeping the knee fairly straight, and swing it over the horse's neck. Bend your knee when it reaches the left side, so your right calf and foot rest on the left side of the horse's neck, while your right knee lies right on top of the horse's mane and your inner thigh rests against your left hand. Your hips and shoulders should continue to face straight ahead, not twist to the left, and your seatbones remain squarely on the saddle or pad. The left hand inside the right knee prevents the leg from sliding down, and the right hand tucked under the cantle or surcingle gives additional security.

3. Walk (and later trot) around the arena in this position for a while and notice how this is very easy and secure once you get past your initial fear. I have seen very athletic riders canter and even jump in this position, but that isn't for everyone.

4. Practice sidesaddle on the opposite side as well. Most riders will find this a more awkward position, but growing helps make it feel more natural.

Sidesaddle. Notice how Douglas's left hand supports his right leg, and how his pelvis is straight across the horse, not twisted to the left.

Round the World

This is one of the most common exercises used to teach confidence and balance. It is most beneficial if you consciously think of the first five of the Seven Steps as you do it. You should always have someone holding the horse, because if he moves off when you are facing backward you could have a nasty fall. If you have no help, practice going from facing forward to facing sideways, and then forward again. Avoid facing the rear.

This exercise helps your body become willing to let go with the legs when you are in a precarious position. It should be practiced until your legs will release easily to swing over the horse. For an additional challenge, it can also be done with your eyes closed and/or your arms folded. I have heard of it being done on a trotting or cantering horse, but I suspect that takes an exceptionally smooth-gaited and well-mannered horse. I have never tried it myself.

1. Begin by putting your right hand on the pommel or neck strap and your left hand on the cantle or surcingle. You will move each hand as needed to let the leg go by, and to change your hold as you turn.

2. Swing your right leg over the horse's neck and turn your torso until you are sitting sideways.

3. Now swing your left leg up and over the horse's croup, being careful to lift it far enough so that you do not kick the horse accidentally. If your horse is quiet, you can lie down with your head on his croup at this point, or simply lean over and pat him. Be careful not to grab hard with your knees in this position, because the area near the horse's flanks is quite sensitive.

4. Continue on around, one leg at a time, until you are facing forward again.

If you ride with a group and the horses are quiet, round-the-world races are fun and a good exercise. Children especially love them.

Roll Over Rover

This is a different way to return to the astride position from sidesaddle. It is also useful if you start to slide off accidentally and don't want to be bothered with remounting. Try it bareback first, if possible.

1. With your legs on the left side of the horse, in the sidesaddle position, allow your seat to slide down the left side of the pad a little. At the same time, move your left hand forward and grab the mane, turn your head to the right and roll over onto your front so that your center is over the horse's midline. Keep your head up and your back flat. Don't let go with your right hand, just turn it as necessary.

2. Now swing your right leg over as in a normal mount and sit up.

3. Try it from the other side as well.

Jumping Off

Jumping off a standing, walking or trotting horse from the side can be practiced in conjunction with the sidesaddle position. Jumping off the horse is an important exercise to build confidence. The knowledge that you have a way of escaping safely if the horse becomes uncontrollable gives you a great feeling of security. Every reasonably athletic person should learn this skill. (Emergency dismounts from the astride position are covered in Chapter 6.)

With the legs already on one side, so no leg grip is possible, jumping off is easy. If you are uncomfortable with the height, a ground person can take your hands and help break the force of the jump.

1. When jumping off a standing horse, keep your head up and exhale as you jump, landing on the balls of your feet and allowing your leg joints to flex to take up the shock. If you are not very athletic, practice jumping off a low object on the ground until you get the knack of landing softly.

2. To prepare for jumping off a moving horse, where you must turn in the air and land facing the direction in which the horse is going, practice at a standstill first. Keep one hand on the saddle or touching the horse for balance, but if you hold the reins, do so in such a way that you can let go of them easily if you fall on landing. Under no circumstances should you loop your arm through the reins.

3. Now practice jumping off a moving horse. As practiced at the standstill, you must turn in the air and land facing the way the horse is going, so you can easily continue to move in that direction after you land.

The game of Scrambles, described on page 104, can be played sidesaddle to perfect jumping-off skills.

Some Other Games

Other games that can be played in class or used as part of a gymkhana include:

Simon Says is the classic game you played as a child. Moves include touching your toes, touching the horse's ears or tail, and similar moves.

In **Follow the Leader**, the leader just has to remember to wait for everyone to complete one task before going on to the next, or you end up with everyone lost and horses all over the ring. For riders who are not yet steering, this game can be played with hand leaders.

In the **Potato and Spoon Race**, riders line up at one end of the ring holding a potato on a spoon. The rider may not touch the potato with her hand. At the far end of the ring is a bucket for each rider. The rider must carry her potato down the ring and put it in the bucket, then return for another potato, and so on. If she drops the potato she must go back and get another. A time limit is set, and the rider with the most potatoes in the bucket wins. This game can also be played with teams, and hand leaders can be used for less experienced riders. This is a great game for practicing soft eyes.

Red Light, Green Light can be the first control game, or it can be played using hand leaders. If the riders are beginners, the leaders do all the controlling while the riders concentrate on maintaining lateral and longitudinal balance. If the riders have learned to use the stick, the leaders are only allowed to bring the horse to a halt and to steer him. It is up to the rider to make him go. The instructor can make the game more interesting by penalizing players for mistakes, such as leaning forward to get a transition.

The person who is "it" stands facing the other players, who are lined up facing her. The distance can be varied depending on the skill of the riders. The more advanced they are, the greater the distance. The "it" begins the game by turning her head away or closing her eyes, then saying "green light" and count-ing to 10 at an even speed. Again, the speed is determined by the skill of the players. However, the tempo of the count must stay the same so the rider or handler can plan ahead and not be forced to jerk the horse suddenly to the stop. The "it" can try to draw the players into a mistake by turning her head, then turning it quickly back before she says "green light," in hopes of catching someone moving before "the light changes." However, once she says "green light," she must continue the count. When she reaches 10, she says "red light" and opens her eyes or turns her head. Anyone whose horse is still moving has to go back to the beginning. (The game can be adapted by specifying that the horse cannot move more than one foot after "red light" is called.)

The object of the game is to be the first one to reach the "it" and tag her. Once she is tagged, in an advanced game the "it" then chases the others back to the start, trying to tag someone who will then be "it" for the next game. In a beginner game, the rider farthest from the "it" when she is tagged is "it" for the next game.

These are only a few of the many games that can be played to occupy your mind while your horse teaches your body how to ride. Perhaps the best exercise of all at this stage is not to take yourself, and especially your mistakes, too seriously. Check your position regularly, but don't dwell too much on your weaknesses. Instead, try to notice when it feels right and give yourself some praise. Have a little fun!

8

Communicating Considerately

*The Stick, the Seat, the Center, the Weight,
and the Eyes*

I have a web page, and frequently visitors to the page will e-mail me with questions about their problems. Not long ago I received a query from Mary, who wrote, "Why won't my horse go when I ask him? I kick and kick and he doesn't move. I think he's really stubborn!" I wrote back and suggested that perhaps when she used her legs vigorously, her upper body swung back and forth. I explained that this interfered with her horse's response, since it threw him off balance. She wrote back to me very excitedly that this was exactly what was happening. I sent her a simplified version of the Seven Steps, plus some guidance in using her stick, seat, weight, and legs. After a week or two of following my suggestions, she told me her problem was solved!

This is one of the more common problems that riders run into; the other is the horse who won't stop. The cause of both is very similar. These problems result from the student being taught to use her reins and legs too soon. With her body unstable, the rider develops ways of using her reins and legs that are incorrect and ineffective. At the same time, in her efforts to control the horse she is no longer able to focus on her position, so it becomes less secure instead of more. This interferes with the horse's balance and he becomes even more "disobedient" and "stubborn."

There are many other aids, besides the reins and legs, that have an important influence on the horse. The aids the rider learns first should be aids she can easily learn to use correctly without having to worry about losing her position and creating tension. The aids covered in this chapter release rather than create tension, and don't affect the rider's balance. Thus they can all be learned without interfering with her work on correct position.

The first of those aids is the stick. In Chapter 5 you read about basic stick handling, how the horse should be accustomed to the stick before riding and most important, the philosophy of using the stick.

USING THE STICK WHILE MOUNTED

The easiest kind of stick for the novice to use is what English riders call a crop. Crops are sort of medium everything. Choose one that comes about to your armpit when you are holding it in your hand. If it's too short, you won't be able to reach the horse's rump easily; too long, and it becomes difficult to control. Try to find one that has a sort of flat button on top, so you can hold it with a relaxed hand without dropping it. At all costs avoid the kind that has no knob on the top at all, causing it to immediately slip out of your hand. It should also have a nice balance to it and feel comfortable in your hand.

Handling the Stick

Before you do anything with the stick, get accustomed to handling it, first alone (see page 91), and later with the neck strap and the reins.

Besides the knob or button on top, most sticks have a hand grip, a body and a tip, which may or may not have a loop or lash on it. Crops very often have a leather loop attached to the handle, but I don't recommend that you put the loop around your wrist because if the tip gets caught on something, you could get hurt. Slipping just your thumb through the loop helps you avoid dropping it accidentally.

When riding, the stick should be carried so that it is resting on your thigh, not pointing down the horse's shoulder. This keeps your hand and wrist in the correct position for using the reins.

Changing the stick from one hand to the other while mounted frightens some horses if it is done carelessly. If you are using a short stick such as a crop, the safest way to change it to the other hand is as follows.

1. Hold the crop as in the photo on page 159 in your right hand. With your left hand, grab the knob or top of the crop and pull it *halfway* up out of your right hand, so you are holding it in the center.

2. Now place your left hand palm up under the crop, close to your right hand.

3. Grasp the crop with your left hand and pull it the rest of the way out of your right hand. As you pull it out, slip the tip over the horse's withers so it is on the left side of his neck.

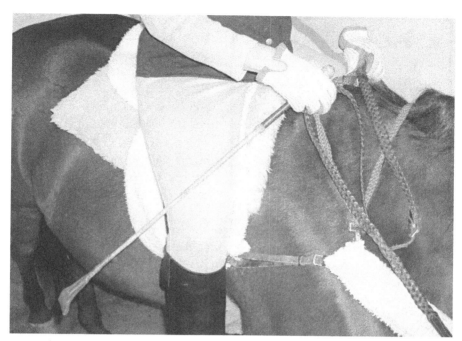

Peg is holding the stick correctly, resting on her thigh. You can also see how she uses her fingers to keep the neck strap, reins, and stick separate.

4. Push on the knob of the stick with the palm of your right hand, to push it down into your left hand.

This sounds much more complicated than it is. It is actually a very simple way of changing your stick hand while keeping it completely under control

If you are using a longer stick, such as a dressage whip, you need to use a different technique that the horse may find more threatening. Therefore, you will need to be more careful the first time you try it and be prepared to spend whatever time is necessary to get him accustomed to it.

1. With the whip held in your right hand as before, rotate your left hand 180 degrees clockwise so the back of your hand is toward you and your thumb is to the left. Then reach over with your left hand and grasp the stick below your right hand.

2. Let go of the stick with your right hand and rotate your left hand and the stick over the horse's withers until it is pointing down on the left side. The stick should describe a nearly vertical arc over the withers, not point forward over the horse's neck.

Tidbits & Supplements

A horse who has been badly abused with the stick may appear to be cured after training, only to have a new position or use of the stick trigger the fear reflex again. Or the horse may trust riders he knows well, but not strangers.

Practice changing the stick from one hand to the other on the ground until you are comfortable with the moves of both techniques. Later, when you are on the horse and he is accustomed to the stick, practice while holding the reins, which should be held in a half bridge in the same hand that is holding the stick at the beginning of the change. Use a fairly confined space for the first couple of tries, until you know how the horse will respond. However, if you have done the groundwork correctly, there should be no problem.

When mounting with the stick in your hand, if you are mounting bareback it is best to put the stick in your left hand, holding it with your thumb toward the top of the handle and the stick pointing down the horse's left shoulder. If you are mounting in the saddle, have the stick in your right hand, thumb on top, and the stick on the far side of the horse. This leaves your left hand free to handle the stirrup. In either case, before starting to mount, wiggle the stick up and down a little so the horse knows it's there and so you know whether the horse might react when he sees it moving.

While it is possible with a long stick to use it on the horse's rump while holding the rein in the same hand, this is a very advanced concept. It is difficult not to tug on the rein *at all* when using the stick behind the saddle, which causes many horses to become either unresponsive or overreactive (bucking) to the stick. Therefore, these exercises will describe how to use the stick *without* the rein in the same hand. While you should be able to use the stick with either hand, since the right hind leg is the primary driving leg most horses do better if you carry the stick in your right hand most of the time.

When you are not using the stick, you will be holding a rein and perhaps the neck strap in the same hand. The rein and neck strap are held as described in Chapter 10, with the stick also in your hand. You will have two fingers around the neck strap, three fingers around the rein, and all four fingers around the stick, so that each is under separate control.

Get yourself seated comfortably and correctly on the horse, holding the neck strap and reins with both hands and your stick in your right hand. First, you need to get rid of the rein that you're holding with your stick (right) hand. Take your right hand off the neck strap and carry it across to your left hand. Take the right rein into your left hand in a half bridge (see page 206) and put your right hand with the stick back where it was on the neck strap.

Keeping your upper body centered over your seatbones, look back over your right shoulder toward the horse's rump. Now reach back with your right hand and gently lay the stick against the horse's rump on the right side. Let it rest against him firmly enough so it doesn't tickle. Be sure it is far enough back. It should not be touching his flank. If he walks away, quietly stop him, if possible while the stick is still resting against his side. This exercise is to teach him not to overreact or second-guess you if you bring the stick back in preparation.

Turn your head so you are looking forward again and think about how your arm feels when the stick is in the correct place. Then, with your head still facing forward, bring your hand and the stick forward until your hand is back on the neck strap, and then back to its place against his hindquarters. Turn your head and look back to make sure it is in the correct place.

Practice this exercise a few times, until you can easily place the stick on the side of the horse's hindquarters without looking back. **Be sure that your upper body position doesn't change at all and that you don't tighten your buttocks or inner thighs when you bring your hand back, either of which would interfere with forward movement and confuse the horse.**

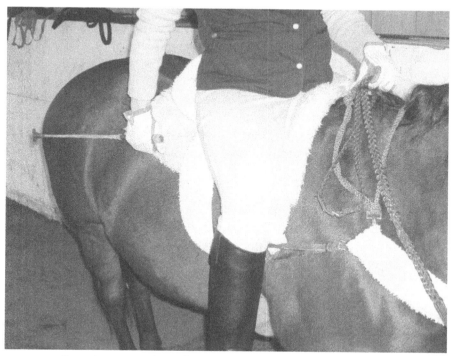

Preparing to use the stick. Note that Peg is sitting well centered, not leaning in any direction.

Now you are finally ready to actually ask the horse to respond. Be sure you have a firm hold of the neck strap or pommel, and that if you are holding the reins, they are looser than the neck strap, so there is no chance of you grabbing the horse's mouth if he steps forward more quickly than you expect. Your eyes should be ahead of you; choose a spot you would like the horse to move toward.

Bring the stick back and lay it on his hindquarters. Then tap him with the stick exactly as you did in the ground exercise described on page 91 in Chapter 5. Some people who have had bad experiences instinctively grab with their thighs or lean forward as they use the stick. To avoid this, lean very slightly back and think about lifting your feet forward and away from the horse. You don't have to actually do it, but just direct your body that way, which will keep it from tensing.

If the horse doesn't walk right away, continue as you did on the ground, waiting for three seconds, looking for a response and asking again using the same or a stronger tap as necessary. You can also add a cluck or any other voice command the horse responds to, until he begins to respond to the stick alone. Don't make the mistake of tensing or wiggling your body if he doesn't respond immediately.

Once the horse understands you want him to move quietly forward in response to the stick, you can use it to get a more active form of the gait he is in or to move up to a faster gait. Later on, when your position is more established, you will be using a leg aid for this, but for now the stick will give you very adequate results without causing position problems.

Summarizing the Stick

1. Choose a stick that is a comfortable length for you and is easy to hold. Practice holding it in the two different ways, changing from one position to the other and from one hand to the other.

2. Accustom the horse to the stick on the ground so he is relaxed about it, then teach him to respond to it by moving quietly forward.

3. When using the stick while mounted, keep your body passive so that you do not confuse the horse or interfere with his response.

4. Look for a prompt but quiet response, with no signs of anger or tension.

THE SEAT AIDS

The seat as an aid has been a source of controversy for many years. I attended a professional meeting once where several highly respected gentlemen almost came to blows over the subject! Certainly it has some effect on the horse, but how—or if—it should be used is often a cause of disagreement among experts. I find the problem less confusing if one divides the seat aid into three parts: the seat, which includes the upper thigh; the center; and the weight, primarily of the upper body. The eyes have a related effect, so they are also included.

The seat aid, as defined in this book, is most effective if the rider is in full seat. The centering and weight aids, however, are equally effective in half seat. The horse can both feel and see where the rider's center is, whether she is sitting or standing. With regard to the weight, when a rider is standing in the stirrups, the pressure on the stirrups is carried up the stirrup leather to the tree and from there to the panels of the saddle. For example, if the rider puts her weight in her left stirrup, the horse feels the pressure on the left side of his back.

The Passive Seat

The seat is the principal point of contact between rider and horse. You can drop your reins and take your lower leg off your horse, but unless you fall off, your *seat* is going to be there, maintaining a connection. What kind of connection this is can have a major effect on the comfort and even the soundness of your horse.

Try a little experiment. Hold one forearm horizontal with your palm down, then place the heel of the other hand flat on the forearm muscle. Jiggle the forearm up and down like a horse trotting, keeping constant pressure on it with your hand. Now press down as hard as you can while continuing to "trot." Continue for 30 seconds or so. Next, instead of keeping a constant pressure, hit your forearm with the heel of your hand, first not too hard, then harder.

What you will notice is that no matter how hard you press, even though your other arm gets tired it won't hurt, but as soon as you start hitting your forearm, it quickly gets sore and stays sore for several minutes afterward. So a heavy rider will tire a horse faster than a light one, which should be no surprise, but even a light rider banging on the horse's back will quickly cause pain. If this is a regular part of the way he is ridden, the horse will soon develop a sore back. The tension produced by a sore back usually results in hind leg problems and big veterinary bills.

For the next little experiment you need a foam pillow, not too thick. Put it over your arm and press on it with the heel of your hand, then hit it as before. Cushioning makes a big difference in the amount of discomfort! But banging is still not great.

Some of the cushion between rider and horse comes from the saddle and pads, but the majority is the result of keeping the soft buttocks and thighs we have been talking about in this section. The combination of softness, lack of tension and following the horse's motion creates the *passive seat*, which you have been practicing and which we use nearly all the time.

The Active Seat

The term "use your seat" is one of the most misleading phrases in riding. ("Drive with your seat" is even worse—we'll cover that later in this chapter!) The image that "use your seat" immediately brings to mind is tensing of buttock and thigh muscles, which is, in fact, the way many riders use their seats. But as we know, tensing those muscles lifts you off the horse, makes you bounce at the faster gaits and makes the horse tense his back in response. None of which is exactly going to aid him to do anything!

However, you do actually use your seat as an aid, you just don't use your seat *muscles* in the process. Let's see what muscles you do use instead, and how.

Ground Work

Place one hand flat below your waist with your thumb on your belt buckle and the back of the other hand just below the waist in back, and walk around briskly. If you watch your hand carefully, you should be able to see, and also feel, that your hands are being pushed forward and back with each step by the movement of your body as you walk. That is, your lower spine is flexing with each step, and since your pelvis is fastened to your spine at the sacrum—where the back of your hand is—it too is rolling back and forth. As you probably know, the movement of the horse under your seat has the same effect on your body as the movement of your own legs. Therefore, as you will see when you are mounted, your pelvis, and thus your seatbones, are constantly moving forward and back on the horse's back in addition to the lateral following seat motion. All this without any effort in your pelvic area whatsoever. *This movement is the passive aspect of the seat.*

The active aspect is the same movement but exaggerated a bit. Walk around as before, but now move your hand up higher on your front so that your little finger is over your belt buckle. Put the hand in back in the same place, just below your waist. As you walk, using *just* the muscles directly under your front hand, push your hand forward a little extra with each step, then let it come back—still in the same rhythm as before. With the hand in back you can feel that your pelvis is moving a little more vigorously than before. Try walking with and without pushing your hand forward to feel the difference in the activity of your pelvis. Notice also that your buttock and thigh muscles aren't doing anything special except holding you up.

You can do this active seat movement while seated in a chair, to give you a little idea of how it will feel in the saddle. Sit straight in the chair as though you were sitting on the horse and place your hand on your front as above. Have your knees about a foot apart. Push your hand forward with your stomach, then let it come back. Notice how you roll from the back of your seat bones to the front, but without changing the pressure on the chair. Now try pushing your seat forward by squeezing your buttock and thigh muscles. Notice how this lifts you *up off the chair* and drops you down again. Not exactly what you want!

On the Horse

If possible, try this next exercise on a horse with a good forward walk. The trail might be a good place for it, or walking down a very slight incline, to give you more of a feel of the movement. After warming yourself up with the Seven Steps, with special emphasis on relaxed thighs and buttocks, try the same exercise you just did on the ground, beginning with the passive aspect: one hand in front, one in back, and feel the movement. Loop your rein over the fingers of your front hand. Let yourself be passive and soft in the seat and thigh, and just feel how the horse moves you.

Now become conscious of your seat on the saddle or pad. You should feel a little roll in your seatbones, as though they were a paint roller moving just a short distance back and forth. If you are sitting level, you should feel yourself roll from your seatbones up to (but *not* on to!) your crotch bone and back again. You should *not* be rolling from your seatbones *back* to your tailbone and then forward, which would indicate that you were rounding your back too much, thus making your buttocks tense. This can happen, especially with men, if the saddle is a little short or sits you too close to the pommel, or if you are riding bareback on a high-withered horse, any of which would create pressure *under* your crotch bone. Even light pressure on the crotch from underneath is uncomfortable, and your body will try to avoid it.

Once you understand the feel of the passive seat, move your front hand up and push against it just as you did in the groundwork. Be very sure you *only* use the muscles up high in your abdomen to create the extra movement. Your buttock and thigh muscles must stay soft and passive. You will feel your pelvis moving more, and you will also feel the "paint roller" making a bigger movement.

You can also use the active seat unilaterally, by moving your hand over to your hipbone, on the side just below your waist. You then use just the abdominal muscles on that side to move just that side of the "paint roller," which is to say, that seatbone.

This movement is the active seat. But what does it do? Is it a driving aid? That is, will it make the horse go faster? Or is it a stopping aid? The answer is, neither. The active seat helps the horse *relax his back muscles*. It works just like a nice, gentle back rub. And what does that do for the horse? If the horse's back is tense, he can't step under freely with his hind legs, which means all movement will be more difficult for him. Therefore, your active seat loosens his back and helps him move forward more freely. It also helps him stop more softly and effectively. When you use it unilaterally, it loosens up one side of his back more, so that hind leg will step farther underneath him.

Try it yourself and see how it feels. Hold your back very stiff and straight, then try to lift one knee as high as you can. Now relax your back and feel how much easier it is to lift your knee. For the horse to step forward easily, he also has to be able to "lift his knees," that is, swing his stifles forward.

Returning to the paint roller metaphor for a moment, if your seatbones are the paint roller, your pelvis and spine are the handle, and the hand that is push-ing the roller is way up above your belt. The roller itself isn't doing any of the work at all. Which is another way of saying that even when you "use your seat," the muscles in your seat themselves are still soft and passive.

THE CENTER

The center as an aid is most easily understood if you think about using it on the ground. If you are trying to catch someone, whether a person in a game of tag or a loose horse, you unconsciously use your center to control their direction. That is, if you move (your center) to your left, the chasee will move (his cen-ter) to your right. If you get behind him, he will run away from you. If you get in front of him, he will turn and go the other way. This is called using an active center.

The other way to use your center is passively. If you are giving someone directions by showing them the way, or if you are leading the horse, you move your center away and the person or horse follows your lead.

In either case, on the ground your center is not forcing any action. That is, the horse or person you are trying to catch can choose to confront or run over you, and the horse or person you are leading can choose not to follow. This does not apply while riding, as you will see.

Using your center as an aid while riding involves the same principles as using it on the ground, but far more subtly. Relative to the horse, you actively move your center as an aid to get him to move away, and passively to get him to follow. The big difference is that unless he bucks you off, the horse cannot evade your center completely. If he tries to push past you and you don't allow your center to be shifted, he can't get past. It is surprising how most horses will give up trying to evade your center as long as you are not abusing them in some other way.

However, moving your center in the saddle shifts your weight as well, which affects both yours and the horse's balance, and this must be taken into account when moving your center either forward or side to side. Because the horse's hind legs keep him from falling backward, moving your center and weight even exaggeratedly to the rear does not adversely affect his balance.

Let's begin by talking about the *horse's* center. To understand how the horse moves and responds, I find it easiest to think of him as having three different centers. The first is his physical center, which is the point at which a line drawn horizontally through the horse on the girth line just below his widest point intersects a line dropped vertically through his midline. (Obviously, this is a generality and will vary somewhat from horse to horse. For example, the physical center of a short-necked long-backed horse will be farther back than that of a long-necked short-backed horse.)

When you sit on a horse of ordinary conformation, with or without a saddle, you should be sitting on the lowest point of his back, just at the base of his withers. This places your center—which should be directly over your seatbones—several inches behind the horse's physical center, which makes it easier for both of you to balance longitudinally, as explained on page 26. However, on a pony or small horse the distance from where you sit to his physical center is often very short, making it difficult not to get ahead of him if he slows down abruptly. Laterally, however, your center is directly over the horse's physical center, since both are on his midline.

The second center is the center of motion. As described on page 136, when the horse changes direction or speed your body tends *not* to follow. That is, the

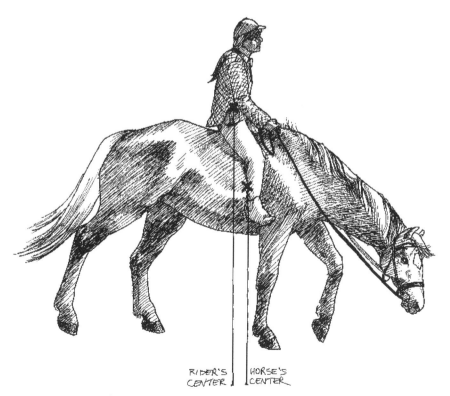

RIDER'S CENTER   HORSE'S CENTER

Relative positions of the horse's center and the rider's.

Tidbits & Supplements

The concept of using your center as an aid may be new to some people, but once you start to use it and find out how simple and effective it is, you will wonder how you ever worked without it.

---

horse exerts force to change what he is doing, and in order to stay with him you must exert effort with your body. We say that you have to stay over his center of motion. If the horse is turning left, his center of motion is to the left; if he is stopping, his center of motion is back. Thus, if you do *nothing*, when he turns left you will fall to the right, and if he is stopping you will fall forward. But you have probably already discovered this in a more direct way!

The third center is more subtle. I call it the center of force. This term describes what is happening when the horse is making an effort to move in one direction but, due to some influence such as your other aids, is not really succeeding in doing so. The most common example is a horse who doesn't want to stay out on the rail. Because of your other aids he is not actually cutting in or moving to the inside, but you can feel his resistance pushing against you. Thus, if he were trying to cut in going left hand around, we would say his center of force is to the left.

Now let's talk about how you can use your center to direct your horse while riding. In this case the use of the word "direct" is most appropriate, because we are concerned only with *direction*, not flexion, bending, response to the bit or any of the things that can make communication so complex.

Turning

Using your center to ask for a turn is the easiest centering aid to understand. Notice I say "ask for a turn," not "make your horse turn." As I explained earlier, the center is a nonforcing aid. It simply tells the horse what you want, without interfering with him physically in any way. Some horses, for example young horses who are more sensitive, will respond to the centering aid correctly right from the beginning. Others, especially school horses who have learned to ignore the movements of the rider's body, at first may not respond at all.

Ground Work

Many horses have been taught to respond to a weight aid to turn. That is, the rider shifts her center—and weight—in the direction of the turn before or at the time of applying the other aids, and before the horse actually turns. The problem with this is that it is really a weight aid, and essentially causes the horse to "fall" in the direction of movement, making for a heavy, clunky movement instead of a balanced one. It would have an especially adverse effect if you were turning toward a jump. (This will be examined in more detail in the section on the weight aid, page 175.)

Moving your center in advance of the horse also has the effect of blocking him, just as you block him when doing ground work by placing yourself on the side you want the horse to turn away from. In addition, your weight interferes with the freedom of the horse's leading legs. However, you should realize that a horse who has been taught to respond to a weight aid may initially respond to your centering aid by going the opposite way from what you intended.

Here is a short ground exercise to help you understand how the horse under tack feels the difference between moving toward your center and moving away from it. You will need another person to help you. You should be in a fairly large space.

1. Stand behind your helper with your hands resting lightly on her shoulders. Ask her to walk with you walking directly behind her, staying in step so you move together.

2. Continuing to walk forward, take half a step to your left. This will put a little weight aid on your helper's left shoulder and she will probably move to the left as well.

3. Ask her to walk again and this time, when she feels you step to the left, she should turn smoothly *away* from you, to the right, instead of left.

Your helper should find that when she turns *away* from your center it feels much easier, freer and better balanced than when she turns *toward* your center. You, as "rider," should also notice the difference in the way she moves. Try it both ways several times, and in both directions. Then trade positions and see how it feels yourself.

On the Horse: Using Your Lateral Center

Choose a riding area that has straight sides and no obstacles or temptations to distract the horse. The horse should be well warmed up and you should be sitting straight and level. If you are a beginner, this exercise can be done with a ground leader, provided she remains completely passive, neither guiding nor interfering with the horse. Depending on the horse's training, you may have to try the exercises in different parts of the ring.

Unless otherwise indicated, "outside" refers to the outside line of the turn, and "inside" to the inside of the turn.

1. Start with the horse walking around on the rail. Let your reins out to the buckle and put your hands on the pommel to keep yourself from using the reins unconsciously.

2. Keeping your body long and *being careful not to twist*, shift your center to the outside (toward the rail) so that your weight is on your outside seatbone. The movement is *very* slight. Do not move so far that you feel insecure, only just enough to feel your weight shift, that is, more pressure on your outside seatbone than the inside one. At the same time turn your head a bit so you are looking away from the rail. Wait and see if the horse moves away from the rail, but *don't* try to force him by making the aid stronger—it will only unbalance you both. It may take a while before he decides to move away from your center.

3. As soon as the horse responds to the aid by turning in even a little, *shift your center to the inside just enough so that you follow his movement, that is, until the pressure on your seatbones becomes even again*. You are then moving your center over his **center of movement.** When he has stopped turning and is walking straight, move your center back over his **center of gravity.**

4. Allow him to walk a few steps in the new direction, then move your center to the opposite side from step 2 and wait for him to start back. When he does, follow the movement as before.

5. On some horses you may find it easier to ride down the center line, then ask the horse to move off to one side and back in a flat serpentine pattern. Another good place to try this exercise is on a wide, flat trail or road.

6. It usually takes awhile for the horse to respond at first, especially if he isn't thoroughly warmed up, so be patient. If you think the horse just doesn't understand or believe that he should respond to the centering aid, and you are accustomed to using the reins, use a light inside rein aid to encourage him. Be careful *not* to shift your weight away from the outside as you use the rein. Praise the horse when he responds correctly.

After you and the horse have developed some feeling for using your lateral center to tell him which way you want to turn, if you are accustomed to using them go ahead and add your usual turning aids. You should find that if you use the centering aid before the other aids, and assuming the horse has no prejudice about direction, you need far less rein aid to get the turn.

Something to beware of is a tendency, when the horse isn't moving in the desired direction, to try to "go there yourself." By doing so, you start to lean strongly in the direction you want him to go. This, of course, blocks him very thoroughly, and if he really *wants* to go in the opposite direction, it puts you in a position where you can easily fall. The other mistake would be to try to force him by moving your center too *far* to the outside, away from the desired direction. This causes your weight to unbalance him, and he would have to step to the outside to regain his balance.

Your lateral center has other uses than just preparing your horse for a turn. It is extremely helpful for keeping a horse on a line, especially when you want to keep rein use to a minimum. Suppose you are trying to ride a straight line down the center for a dressage test, or perhaps to a jump. The gate to the arena is off to your left and the horse wants to drift toward the gate. (This is that center of force thing we were talking about earlier.) You can feel the horse pushing against you to get over to the left. If you keep your center a little to the left of his, so that he can't push past you, he will tend to straighten up and go on.

If you are approaching a jump that has one side that would tempt your horse to run out, place your center a little to that side, which will block the horse and make him more likely to jump straight.

If you are trying to ride past something your horse wants to shy at, keeping your center a little away from the fearsome object again acts as a block to keep the horse going straight. In addition, if he jumps sideways or spins, since your center is already a bit on that side, you are far less likely to get dropped in the mud.

When riding circles, you can use your lateral center to increase or decrease the size of the circle. Riders frequently have a problem with the horse spiraling inward, especially to the right. This is nearly always caused, at least in part, by your center sliding to the outside, because of the inertial force of turning. As we saw earlier, your center on the outside tends to move the horse inward. If you can shift your center a little to the *inside of the center of motion*, the horse will move out again. And, as one of my students once said, "It's more than you think." Meaning the center of motion is often a stronger force than you realize.

Directing the horse with your lateral center is such a useful tool that it is well worth spending some time and practice to perfect. Since it reduces the

---

Tidbits & Supplements

Very often if a horse seems very crooked or unresponsive to your lateral aids, when you check your lateral center you will find that it is telling the horse to move in the opposite direction from the one you want. For example, the horse is cutting in and in doing so has pushed your center to the outside, which tells him to cut in even more.

Tidbits & Supplements

I once watched a World Cup competition in which the competitors had to ride one another's horse. One rider's center was consistently way off to the left, and at one point the horse he was riding—who was not accustomed to his peculiarities—almost jumped the right-hand standard!

need for a rein aid, it is much easier for the horse to keep moving forward through the turn. Remember, moving your center to the *right* correctly takes lots of practice, and perhaps some help from a keen-eyed observer.

Increasing Pace

When you think of increasing pace with the horse on the ground, you think of getting behind him. When you are riding, your seated center is already behind the horse's center, so using your center to increase pace is really a matter of maintaining what you have. The reason you may have difficulty is that your natural impulse when asking the horse to go forward is to lean in that direction. You tend to feel that if you go, the horse will follow. This is especially true if you are moving into a gait that involves standing in the stirrups, which brings your center forward.

For this exercise it is best if you can get the horse to move with either your voice or a stick, since using your legs may change your balance.

1. With the horse standing still, use the first five of the Seven Steps to make sure your position is correct. Leave the reins slack.

2. Think about how your weight feels over your seatbones, and perhaps open your hips just a little (lean your upper body back from the hip) to put your center a bit more over the back of your seatbones. Be sure not to go back so far that your buttocks start to tense up.

3. Use a cluck or a tap with the stick to get your horse to move forward, concentrating on *not* allowing your upper body to swing forward *at all* by firming up your back (but not your buttocks). Think of a pocketknife that is halfway open. If you open it just a little more, it wants to open the rest of the way. That's how you want your hip joints to feel. Be careful that you don't tense your thighs when you are asking the horse for movement.

This method is particularly important with so-called lazy horses, who are nearly always horses who have grown accustomed to having the rider get in their way every time they try to start. Sometimes the horse will take a step or two then stop, expecting that the rider's center will move forward and block him. Generally, as soon as the horse is convinced his rider will not move, he becomes much more responsive. (Actually, "more responsive" is not really what is happening, since the horse was responsive before, but was responding to an incorrect command!)

This is a time when many riders try to drive with their seat—that is, they lean back so their lower back and seat become hard. In some cases this will increase the horse's speed, but that will happen either because the hard seat is hurting the horse's back or because the tension causes him to lose his balance. In neither case will he end up going *forward*, he'll only go *faster*.

When asking the horse to move into the trot or canter, you have a choice. You can either stay seated until the transition is completed, which is usually the best way, or you can take an open half seat (see page 252) to be off the horse's back *before* asking for the transition. Because the stirrup is farther forward (relative to the horse) than the seat of the saddle, your center moves slightly forward when you go from full (sitting) to half (standing on the stirrups) seat. What you want to avoid is moving your center forward—moving from full to half seat—*during* the transition, which makes it far more difficult and confusing for the horse.

Decreasing Pace

Most of the time you will use your center passively to ask for a decrease in pace. This is because if you move your center to get in front of the horse, which is using it actively, you will also unbalance him and possibly yourself, and may well find yourself farther in front of him than you had planned!

Tidbits & Supplements

I once had a class of riders who had been jumping for about six months. They were at the stage where they were having a lot of trouble finding the "right spot," that optimum place from which the horse should leave the ground. As an experiment, I had them put their horses into the canter, then ride toward the fence in half seat without using any leg at all, but just concentrating on keeping their centers back until the horse came off the ground. Without exception the horses jumped more willingly and smoothly and found better spots by themselves.

Tidbits & Supplements

The active center can also be used to stop the horse, but generally speaking should only be used as part of an emergency dismount. If you are an experienced rider, you no doubt have noticed that if you try to dismount when the horse is walking, he will nearly always stop before you hit the ground. This is because when you throw your weight forward onto your hands to dismount, you are throwing your center in front of his, as well as unbalancing him, so the stop is almost automatic. The only times this will not work are if the horse has been trained to keep going, like a trick-riding or vaulting horse, or if he has lost his balance so badly that he *can't* stop. Sometimes pretending that you are going to dismount by throwing your weight onto your hands will cause the horse to stop, without your actually having to complete the dismount. This is useful for some of the exercises in this book. I have also used it successfully when a rein or bridle broke while I was riding at speed.

Using your center passively when riding is almost a mental exercise. Think of allowing a bicycle to coast to a stop. You begin by stopping pedaling, that is, you become passive with any driving aids you might be using to keep the horse going. Then you allow your following seat to gradually slow down while keeping yourself centered over your seatbones, being careful *not* to lean back, which would tend to send the horse forward again. And you think about allowing the horse to slow down by letting yourself be very passive and quiet.

The easiest downward transition is usually trot to walk. If possible, try to wait it out and not use any rein aids. The beauty of *allowing* the horse to stop is that he can learn to stay balanced throughout the transition, which many horses find very difficult, and he is less likely to become frightened or tense about it. Once he understands what you want, as he becomes better balanced and stronger you can begin to add aids to make him slow more promptly.

Maintaining Pace

This is simply a matter of learning to pay attention to where your center is at all times. Since the horse's movement tends to affect your center, you have to make constant adjustments. However, with practice these will become automatic.

If your center is either too far forward all the time or rocks back and forth too much, the horse will have difficulty maintaining an even pace. Depending

---

Tidbits & Supplements

One day I was teaching a fairly advanced rider who was new to my methods. We were working on the sitting trot and the horse kept breaking to the walk. Since he was usually more than willing to maintain his trot, I was at a loss to figure out what was bothering him. Then I noticed that the student's inside leg kept getting tense, then relaxing, and I realized she was slipping to the outside, then grabbing with her thigh to regain her balance. When I got her to focus on keeping even pressure on her seatbones, rather than allowing her weight to slide from side to side, the horse maintained his trot perfectly.

---

on a number of factors, he may go too fast in an awkward, out-of-balance way or keep stopping. Lateral imbalance of the rider will also cause the horse to be irregular as he struggles to maintain balance.

A useful exercise to improve your lateral centering is to walk or sit trot over ground poles and see if you can keep yourself centered throughout your horse's step over the pole. As the horse lifts each foot over the pole, it increases his lateral movement.

Summarizing the Center

Your center is the least invasive, and thus the first aid to be used in most situations. It can be used either actively to send the horse, or passively to allow decrease in activity or following.

For a turn, use the active center on the opposite side. For an increase in forward motion, hold your center firmly behind the horse's center. For a decrease in forward motion, allow your center to become passive.

Using the center too strongly or moving it too far to one side turns it into a weight aid, which changes the intent.

THE WEIGHT

As you will see, the center and weight aids are very similar, but they aren't quite the same. The weight aid is a definite physical influence, while the center is somewhat more abstract. To clarify a little, you can use a centering aid effectively from the ground, but not a weight aid. As you work with them both, you will find it easier to sort out the difference.

Weight and Turning

When I first wrote the section about using the center for control, I ran it by a couple of friends who ride Icelandic horses. Both of them reacted very negatively to the idea of the horse moving away from your center, since it was their experience that their horses moved *toward* their center. That is, if they moved their center left the horse turned left. I thought about that for a while and came up with the reason for the apparent contradiction.

In the years since I discovered using the center as an aid, I have worked almost entirely with large, mature horses. But on searching my memory, I found that when I had worked with smaller or younger animals they did indeed move in the direction of my center shift. This gives me a good opportunity to further discuss the difference between the rider's weight and her center. Your weight is just that—the influence of the mass of your body as it shifts around. It can be used both positively and negatively. If you've ever carried anyone piggyback, you have an idea of how weight shifts affect the horse. Your center is far more subtle. It is a place, but it is also a force, as in when you chase someone on the ground. It has very little to do with size and a lot to do with personal confidence and power.

If you are riding a small or not very well balanced horse, your weight will have a great effect on his feet—far more than with larger or more experienced horses. So if you shift your weight far enough to the left, the horse will step to the left with his left front foot to regain his balance. Since a turn begins with the front foot on that side stepping in that direction, you have the start of a turn. So you can teach the horse to respond to weight shifts to the left or right to get the amount of turn you want. However, the horse will be turning in response to your *weight*, rather than to your *center*.

Here is a ground exercise that shows how the horse's balance responds to moving *toward* your weight, as opposed to moving *away* from your center.

1. Stand with your feet together, your arms by your sides and even pressure on both feet.

2. Move your center to the left until you feel your weight is mostly on your left foot.

3. Continue to move your center to the left until you lose your balance and have to take a step to keep from falling. Notice how heavily you step over. This is the way the horse responds to *following* your *weight*.

4. Center to the left again, as in step 2.

5. Now pick up your right foot and place it to the right. Notice how you are in complete control of the foot and can place it anywhere without losing your balance. This is how the horse responds when he moves *away* from your *center*. Try it in both directions.

I believe the problem with teaching the horse to follow your weight (although if it works well for you, you will probably stay with it anyway) is that it puts weight on the horse's forehand at the beginning of the turn and tends to make the horse's hind leg step to the outside, rather than staying to the inside to support his hindquarters on the turn. Some horses can deal with this, others cannot; that is, some horses don't mind being a little on their forehand on a turn, others find it very threatening and can get quite resistant about turning as a result. I worked with one horse who had developed the most unpleasant habit of waiting until you put your weight in one stirrup and then deliberately spinning the other way, right out from under you!

So it is my opinion that the weight should *not* be used as an active aid in lateral work. That is, except for the very slight weight shift associated with the centering aid, your lateral weight should stay directly over the horse's lateral center of motion or force. However, weight does play a positive role in longitudinal work—specifically, in keeping the horse going forward.

Weight and Forward Movement

When you ride in a car, the only time you notice movement is when it changes. There is no thrust unless there is a change in speed or direction. That is, once the car on a straight, smooth road reaches a certain speed and *remains there*, whether it is going 10 miles an hour or 100, it will feel the same to your body.

This is less true on a horse, because the horse has legs instead of wheels so the thrust is not constant, as it is in a wheeled vehicle. Every time the horse pushes off with a leg he throws the rider back, and every time his foot hits the ground he throws the rider forward. The smoother the horse's gait, the less the rider feels the thrusts, but they are always there.

When we talk about the rider being thrown forward or back, most of the time we are talking about her upper body. Unless the thrust is extreme her legs stay more or less in place. So if you do nothing about it, your upper body will be rocked back and forth as the horse moves. This is most apparent when a novice rider canters, but it exists to some extent at all gaits.

Ground Work

This exercise demonstrates how you can use your upper body weight to either help or hinder your horse's forward movement. You will need a chair with wheels, such as an office chair, if possible (another excuse to think about riding while at work). Otherwise, you can use a straight chair and some imagination. Place the chair on a hard floor, not carpet. You will also need a rope tied to a heavy chair or table leg, or another person sitting on the floor to hold it.

1. Sit in the chair holding the rope. Bring your feet back so your toes are resting lightly on the floor under your seat.

2. The rope represents the force that would pull you forward if the horse was stopping. First, pull on the rope and allow your upper body to come forward. Notice how you start to fall off the front of the chair, which moves forward little or not at all, though it may start to *tip* forward. This is what happens if you allow your hip joint to close when the horse slows down. Your center gets ahead of his, blocking his movement and causing you to fall.

3. Now pull the rope while holding your hip joints open. Be sure to keep your buttocks relaxed so you feel your seatbones firmly on the chair. The chair will roll forward if it has wheels, or will feel as though it could if the floor were slippery enough. There is no feeling of the chair tipping over. Instead of your body falling forward, the force travels through your body, into the seat and into the chair, sending it forward.

This is part of the law of inertia. A body in motion will tend to continue to move in the same direction and speed unless something occurs to stop it. How far it will move is directly related to its mass (size and weight) and the speed at which it is going. Your legs are fairly well stopped by the saddle; but if you allow your hip joints to close, your body in essence "breaks" in half, with the top half free to fly ahead of the horse. If you keep your hip joints open so your body stays joined together, the momentum has no place to go except into the saddle.

To get a clearer picture of how your weight affects the horse's forward movement, you need another person, preferably someone smaller than you are.

Stand behind her and place the palms of your hands on either side of her back, below her shoulder blades. Press upward as though you were going to pick her up from behind. This is how your weight presses into the horse's back through the saddle. The stronger you are, the more you can lift her up. Then imagine that instead of standing up, she is on all fours. Now the pressure would send her forward. You also have her body under very good control, and she would find it difficult to get away from that lifting pressure. This is a technique that most parents have used at least once on a small child having a tantrum! Change places and have her try to lift you, so you can feel it.

Tidbits & Supplements

It takes some practice to keep your hip angle open without locking your hip joints so that you lose the following seat. If you do, the downward transition becomes stiff or the horse may have trouble stopping.

To further clarify, your friend represents the horse, except that her body is vertical rather than horizontal. Your hands represent the pressure of the saddle with the rider's weight on it. If you use your weight correctly, it travels through your seat and the saddle into the back of the horse's withers and shoulder blades to send the horse forward (or your friend's body upward).

Now, to see how your weight can affect the horse adversely, let's do another chair exercise.

1. Sit in the chair and hold the rope as before, but this time put your feet flat on the floor in front of the chair (and your center).

2. Bend forward quite a bit and pull on the rope, bracing with your feet to keep from falling forward. The chair will roll backward!

This is the "feet on the dashboard" position that we read so much about. It results from having the stirrups mounted too far forward relative to the seat of the saddle, or from trying to push your heels down. Or it can be the result of the saddle sitting tilted back on the horse—something often found in poorly made saddles, both English and Western. We'll talk more about this in Chapter 12. Suffice it to say for now that bracing with your feet doesn't help your horse. What it does is push your weight into the horse in opposition to his movement.

Now let's get your friend back and see how this position affects the horse. Instead of your hands pressing upward against her shoulder blades, they are going to slide down and press downward into the small of her back. Instead of picking her up, they will tend to hold her down and also hollow her back in an uncomfortable way. You also will find that you have far less control of her body, because she can now wiggle away from you much more easily. Have her try it on you so you can see how it feels. All of this is also true for the horse.

Worse, at the same time the weight through your seat is hollowing the horse's back and *not* sending him forward, your upper body weight is ahead of his center, unbalancing and thus further hindering him. And again, the bigger you are, the worse it will be.

I think this matter of size/weight/momentum explains, in part, why some men are such very effective, capable riders and some are absolutely appalling. Men in general weigh more than women, especially in their upper body. Therefore, when the weight is used correctly it helps the horse more, and when used badly interferes more. This is particularly true during jumping.

Another way your weight can affect the horse adversely is if it gets *ahead* of the horse's center. This often happens with a poky horse at a trot, when the rider tries to keep him going by posting "harder." She throws her center and weight ahead of his at each step. This has the double effect of unbalancing him and also of allowing him to get behind her.

Get your friend to help again, and place your hands on her back just *above* her shoulder blades. Now you find that when you try to lift her up, your hands just slide up her arms. It's quite easy for her to slip out from under your hands. Similarly, the horse finds it quite easy to avoid going forward if you get ahead of him.

On the Horse
Start, as you always do, by running through the Seven Steps.

1. If you are in a saddle or riding with a thick pad so you can do it easily, take up the "knees up" position (see page 150.). If the pad is too thin to hold your knees up without strain, and you are comfortable with it, you could sit sidesaddle instead. The object is to get your thighs off the horse for a minute so you can really feel your weight pressing into the horse through your seat. If you can do neither of these comfortably, you will need to think a little more about keeping your thighs from tensing.

2. With your horse at the standstill, take your neck strap or the pommel of the saddle and pull on it, just as you did on the rope when you were on the ground. Try to pull evenly, and let all the pull go *through* your body into your seat. Be sure to keep your upper body a little back so your hip joints stay open, and think about keeping the pressure on the same place on your seatbones.

3. If possible, with someone either leading or longeing the horse at the walk, get your following seat working smoothly, then add the pull on the neck strap and see if you can keep your hip joints open and still moving to follow the horse, without letting your upper body fall forward.

4. Now have the horse walk freely, then have the ground person slow him down fairly abruptly. As he slows, keep your center back so your shoulders are not tipped forward by his change of speed. Instead, that force will go into your seatbones, pressing them forward against the backs of his shoulder blades, just as your hands pressed on the other person in the ground exercise. This is rather subtle at the walk, but if you focus on where the pressure is on your seatbones, you can feel it. Don't allow your center and weight to rock forward so that you feel more pressure on the fronts of your seatbones, but don't lean so far back that your buttocks get tense.

5. Allow the horse to walk forward, then slow down again. This time, as you hold your center and weight back, use a little cluck to encourage him to walk on. Try to feel how your position helps keep him going.

6. Again, allow him to walk forward and slow down, but this time allow your body to swing forward so that your thighs tighten and your weight comes up on his forehand. Feel how you have lost control of his body. He feels as though he was slipping out through your legs to the back. Most horses will immediately stop, but some will get very unbalanced so that they can't stop and will speed up instead. This is particularly likely in the faster gaits.

What is happening is that as the horse slows down, your body wants to keep going. When you keep your upper body from falling forward, its momentum is sent back into the horse, sending him forward again. The more strongly the horse tries to slow down, the stronger the aid becomes, and the easier it is to feel.

In summary, unless it is over his center, your weight tends to unbalance the horse. The exception to this is if your weight goes back. Used as an aid, holding your weight strongly back—resisting the thrust that is throwing you forward as the horse slows down—sends the horse forward again.

THE EYES

When we speak of using your eyes, we mean that you virtually always *look* in the direction or toward the place you want the horse to go. If you want to turn left at the end of the center line, you look slightly to the left as you approach the end of the arena. If you are jumping, you look down the line to the *far* side of the obstacle.

Like the center, the effect of the eyes is subtle and rather abstract. Two main things happen when you look in a particular direction: first, a slight centering shift is created; second, an intent is created in your mind. It would seem that this could have no particular effect on the horse, but as every instructor knows, the rider's eyes have a very strong influence. Over and over we see it: The rider is trying to get the horse to go past a scary place or over a jump without success. The instructor calls out, "*Look* where you're trying to go. Think about getting to that place!" And the horse goes past the scary place or jumps the jump.

Using your eyes does not mean that they have to become hard, as described in Chapter 2. The focus can still stay soft; only the direction or the distance changes.

The eyes can also very easily hinder you. For example, if you lose your balance forward and start to fall, if you look down at the ground (which is your instinct), you will very likely end up there Your horse will also follow your eyes if they are heading the wrong way. Whether this is a matter of telepathy or simply the result of the centering shift is debatable.

Tidbits & Supplements

When I was first learning to drive a car, my teacher told me that if I was driving on a narrow road, especially at night, and another car came toward me, *not* to look at it. He explained that if I looked at the other car I would instinctively steer toward it! If I looked off to the side of the road ahead of me, that would keep me in my own lane. The same effect is at work when you ride.

PRACTICING THE AIDS

Since the aids discussed in this chapter are often used in combination, you should practice them until you can use them together. Choose a situation in which getting results is not important and where you won't need reins. Walking in an empty arena or field, or down a wide trail or road are good places.

Begin by combining your eyes and centering aids to get moderate turns. Then you can add the active seat on the side toward which you want the horse to turn, to help that hind leg move more freely. Be *very* careful that your center doesn't move to the inside at the same time, before the horse has begun the turn. This takes quite a bit of practice.

Another exercise is to combine your eyes, center, weight, and active seat to keep the horse walking at a steady pace in a difficult place, perhaps past the gate or down the road away from home. Your eyes and center create a strong intent, your center keeps him straight, your weight keeps him going forward, and your active seat helps him relax.

It is, to a great extent, from the correct use of the aids described in this chapter that "invisible aids" arise. The horse's body is directed in a nonthreatening way, so that hand and leg aids can be reduced to a minimum.

The Seven Steps have taught you to have a passive position on the horse, instead of interfering with him. Thus, the horse becomes aware that you are listening to his needs and helping him to deal with being ridden, which creates trust. Now, by using *aids* that don't interfere with him, you make it easy and desirable for the horse to listen to you.

9

Free at Last!

Riding without Reins, Sitting the Trot without Stirrups

As a beginning rider Julia was told repeatedly that she must control her horse at all times to avoid getting hurt. Since this was virtually impossible due to her lack of experience, she did the only thing she could do: She kept the reins very tight, like a beginning driver clutching the wheel of the car. As with any repeated action, this became a habit. Some years later, she came to me as quite an experienced rider. To my amazement, the first time I asked her to ride without holding the reins she was panic stricken. She was so in the habit of holding them tightly, and so convinced that the horse must be "controlled" with the reins at all times, that she felt seriously threatened without them, even when walking in a small space.

My experience with Julia resulted in a major step forward in my understanding. I realized that one of the primary blocks to relaxation, and thus one of the most difficult problems for many riders, especially adults, is the need for control. If you are riding in or on a vehicle and you are holding the controls, then at all times you feel you must be the one to decide what the vehicle is doing. The reason for this feeling is obvious: If you are driving a car and you do not continuously steer, accelerate, shift, and brake as needed, you will have an accident, perhaps a life-threatening one. The same is true of bicycles, boats, and any other vehicle we are accustomed to driving. However, *it is not true of the horse.* **Control of the horse's body comes from the horse's brain and only from there.** We can use aids to stimulate the horse's reflexes, but the horse can choose to ignore them. I recently heard someone describe a horse who got tangled up in the trailer and went berserk. (He got out of it safely.) The point she made was her impression of the raw power a horse can produce. Four people all stood there helplessly until the horse worked his way out of the trailer. Stories such as these remind us that the horse is an animal of such tremendous size and power that we cannot hope to control his body by any physical means.

However, most people are taught that they *should* be in control of the horse, and not just be carried along. They are especially taught that if they do not have a bit to control the horse, he may at any moment do something disobedient or even dangerous. Therefore, they learn to be afraid to let the horse control his own body. Allowing the horse to control his own body is not the same as allowing him to do whatever he likes! It is simply understanding that at any given moment, only the horse knows for sure how his feet are meeting the ground and what his balance is. Horses who blow up and are violently disobedient are almost without exception horses who feel they are out of control of either the situation or their own bodies, and are reacting the way any frightened (and therefore angry) person would.

To clarify your thinking about control, try looking at it this way: The horse's *body* is the car. The horse's *mind* is the driver. The rider is the *passenger*. As a beginner, the passenger doesn't know enough to give any instructions at all to the driver. If she tries, she often does things like waiting until the car is at the intersection in the far right lane and then suddenly deciding she wants to turn left. Since this is not possible, the driver doesn't respond and then the passenger gets upset. Because she doesn't know what she did wrong, the passenger is probably also frustrated. She may even try to interfere with the driver's ability to control the vehicle.

As the rider-passenger begins to understand better how the vehicle works, she gives better directions and interferes less, and the vehicle goes pretty much where she says, unless the driver-horse really has a priority to be elsewhere (such as back at the barn at suppertime). Later still, the passenger has enough skill that she can begin to help the driver learn to handle his vehicle better. At that point, the driver-horse begins to be very responsive because of his respect for the passenger's knowledge. In addition, if a good relationship has been established, the driver cares about the passenger and wants to please her, so he tries to do what she wants. Alternatively, you have the situation where the driver fears the passenger, so he tries to do what she wants but there is a certain reduction in the quality of performance, due to his fear.

In these and all situations, the horse's mind is still the actual driver in control of the vehicle. This needs to be especially noted when you are riding an unfamiliar horse or one who is obviously upset. What gets riders in serious trouble is when the horse's mind is slightly unbalanced mentally, for whatever reason, and the rider gets onto the horse anyway. This is no different than getting into a car with a drunk driver, and the results can be equally disastrous.

However, seriously disturbed horses are not common, and our concern is with riding a pleasant, ordinary horse and learning to communicate with him in a way that is best for all concerned.

Tidbits & Supplements

The way you "control" your horse is not with a bit or a halter or any other piece of equipment. These are just some of the ways you *communicate* with the horse. Control comes from making intelligent choices about what can be expected of the horse. A good horseman does not take a half-crazy four-year-old fresh from the track into the hunt field! A good instructor does not put a beginner on an aggressive, tense horse and start her cantering toward the barn.

One reason that what are often referred to as natural horsemanship approaches are so successful is that they teach you how to reach the horse's mind, so that he *wants* to please you, and thus control *himself* for your benefit.

RIDING WITHOUT REINS

This may be the first time you have purposely and totally given up control to the horse. The first time you try this exercise, make it at the end of a lesson of more familiar work, so you and the horse are both warmed up and relaxed.

For this exercise, you will need your horse, preferably with a bareback pad, your stick and a small workspace from which the horse cannot escape. A round pen is preferable to a square one, since there are no corners for the horse to stand in. You can use a larger space if the horse is quiet. If you need to divide a larger space, be sure to use solid dividers such as poles, set about four feet high for a horse, lower for a pony. Do not use rope or anything similar, which the horse could try to duck under and perhaps entangle you. There should not be any other horses or any obstacles within the workspace, except a mounting block, since you may be dismounting and will need to be able to remount. There also should not be anything such as grass or hay for the horse to eat.

Twist your reins up into the throat latch, as described on page 66, so they are safely out of the way but still available if the horse needs to be led. It is important for this exercise that the reins *not* be available to you, because if they are there, it is very difficult to resist the temptation to grab them.

The object of this exercise is not to discover that you can control the horse without the reins, but to discover that if you *don't* control the horse, nothing bad will happen. The only thing you are going to ask him to do is to move, just so you get the feeling of being in a moving vehicle without holding the "steering wheel."

Tidbits & Supplements

If you're a beginning rider, this should be the first time you are riding without a ground person leading the horse. Still, if you don't have an instructor on hand, you should really ask an experienced friend to keep an eye on you, so you feel safe and relaxed at all times. Anyway, since you will not have any reins, you will need someone to lead your horse into the workspace and close you in. Alternatively, you can mount in the workspace, but unless your horse is very well trained, you will still need someone hold him while you mount.

Even though you are not in control of the horse's body, you are still in control of your own body. And you have learned one method of controlling a potentially threatening situation—the emergency dismount. Your plan is that if, at any moment, the horse even *begins* to do something that you find even slightly disturbing, you are going to dismount immediately. This is not supposed to be a game of chicken, where you see how long you can hold out in a potentially threatening situation. Instead, you want to tell your body that safety is just a dismount away. This is probably one of the most significant aids to overcoming fear.

Begin the exercise by being mounted on your horse, standing still if possible, without reins but with both hands on the neck strap or pommel. You should also be carrying a stick, unless the horse responds very well to voice commands. At first do nothing at all except grow, breathe, center, and soften your eyes, and any other exercises you have found to be helpful for relaxation. If both you and the horse are very relaxed, he will probably remain standing still.

If the horse remains still, the next thing to do is get him to walk, using the stick or your voice as a signal. (If he starts walking by himself, that's okay too.) Once you have him walking, just go with him, continuing to think about your Seven Steps and allowing your body to get used to this new idea of riding with no one guiding the horse. He may walk around the enclosure or he may go and stand near the fence. If he stops, allow him to stand for a minute, praise him and scratch him if he likes that, then ask him to walk on again. Don't ask at all aggressively, especially if he is facing the fence, where it may take him a minute to figure out that he has to turn.

Sometimes a horse will be so persistent about standing by the fence that you find yourself getting frustrated. Just remind yourself that even though standing still may be boring, it is not dangerous! Also remember that feeling annoyed because the horse is not moving is another symptom of wanting to be in control. Take advantage of the fact that the horse is still to practice some of the exercises in Chapter 8. You are still in control of what *you* do, and that is the important thing.

If you want to continue to try to ask the horse to move away from the fence, that's okay, as long as you don't take it too seriously. Ask the horse again to move by using the stick and try to convey the idea that, while you are not going to get angry or abusive, you are going to continue to ask. See if you can notice even the slightest shift in weight or turn of the head that indicates the beginning of movement, and immediately praise the horse. Using your centering and weight aids as well as your eyes will help the horse understand what you want.

Some horses keep going no matter what. A horse, by nature, is like any other vehicle: If there is nothing telling him to keep going, he will gradually coast to a stop. However, the horse may be a bit nervous, or he may have been trained that once he has been put into a gait, he should keep going until he is *told* to do something else. In either case, practice seeing how quiet and passive you can be. Let your breathing be very slow and let your following seat movement be just a little slower than the horse's. Don't make the mistake of leaning back too far; it will make your buttocks tense and might even be interpreted by the horse as a driving aid. Try to notice if the horse slows down even a little, and praise him.

If you *really need* to stop for some reason, you can often fool the horse into stopping by starting an emergency dismount, throwing your weight forward onto your hands and starting to swing your right leg over. Suddenly putting your center in front of the horse's in this way will usually cause him to stop; it's as though you suddenly stepped in front of him. If he stops, smoothly resume your normal position. If he doesn't stop, complete the dismount and stop him from the ground.

Tidbits & Supplements

Even though you have the stick, if you were so rash as to try to use it in an abusive way, you would risk having the horse react in a very aggressive manner, since you have no reins to restrain him with. Many riders' "conversations" with their horses are conducted along those lines—punish the horse with the stick, then, when he reacts violently to the unfair treatment, punish him with the bit. This exercise helps you overcome your need for such "discussions."

Tidbits & Supplements

If you are accustomed to asking a horse to go forward with seat and leg aids, you may be tempted to use those in addition to the stick and voice aids. Remember, however, that the purpose of this exercise is to give up control, not just give up the reins. It's okay to *ask* your horse to move; it is not okay to try to get physical with your body in an effort to *make* him move. If you are unable to keep from tightening your legs and seat, try riding sidesaddle if you are bareback, or with your knees up if you are in the saddle and the horse is trustworthy.

If you have any sense that the horse is beginning to get tense, such as see-ing him raise his head or quicken his pace, immediately dismount. Stand with the horse and again go through your steps until you feel comfortable again, then remount. However, you are most likely to find that the horse walks for a few steps or a few minutes, then decides nothing much is happening and stops.

Now spend some time wandering around the arena in this manner. This exercise should be repeated until you feel very comfortable riding in a small enclosure without reins. Once you are comfortable with the idea, you can also trot and canter in a somewhat larger space if you have the skills and the horse is sufficiently well balanced to handle the turns comfortably.

Notice that what we have done here is almost completely take away your perceived ability to *control* the horse, while still allowing you to *communicate* with him. Most likely your horse just went on plodding around and responded quite well to the very few voice and stick aids you used to direct him. Without reins, the horse does not all of a sudden start a self-induced training program for the Derby or the Grand National! Most runaways are caused by the rider, not the horse.

In dealing with people, getting the results you want comes from learning when to *give up* control, developing awareness of the other person's priorities and respecting them. The discovery that you can do this same thing with a horse, and by so doing gain his attention rather than losing it, will increase your confidence when the horse seems to be "taking over." Combining this knowledge with improving your basic riding skills through the Seven Steps will mean that you can just go along for the ride without any trouble.

Once you are comfortable with the concept of giving up control at the walk, you will find that going on to slightly faster work is not at all threaten-ing. So it's time to start working on a slow trot.

SITTING THE TROT WITHOUT STIRRUPS

When my husband was a little boy, he summered not far from the local riding stable. He loved horses but was unable to take any lessons. However, the stable kept some ponies turned out in the back field, so he would occasionally sneak over and ride them. Naturally, he had no saddle or bridle, so he just had to climb onto the pony and manage as best he could. In describing his rides to me, he said, "If I could get the pony to go right from the walk to the canter, I was okay. I could hold his mane and canter for quite a ways. But if the pony trotted, I always went bump, bump, bump, THUD onto the ground!" Since he was young and the ponies were small, he thought it was very funny. Right away he would scramble back on and try again.

It is surprising how many people have trouble sitting the trot easily. Yet unless the horse is very stiff in his back, which sometimes occurs as the result of bad riding at the sit trot, it is not a very difficult thing to do, and far easier than sitting the canter correctly. We are talking now about what really might be called a jog, not a full-fledged trot, which requires a highly trained horse to provide the soft, flexible back that makes the trot sittable. Sitting a jog, however, can be learned by any rider who has practiced the Seven Steps at the walk long enough to be secure.

Once you are fairly comfortable working without stirrups—and preferably without reins—at the walk, you're ready for the trot. If you have access to a horse who will easily pick up a nice, comfortable, slow jog, then the sitting trot should be your next step. However, it is important that the horse have an easy

---

Tidbits & Supplements

Although the gait is different, using a horse who does one of the faster four-beat gaits—single-foot, running walk, etc.—is also a very good next step, especially as a confidence builder. If I had my way, I think I would start all my novices on horses who had a four-beat speed gait. This enables the rider to get accustomed to the physics of the speed—which is mostly adjusting the body to the faster turning rate—without the threatening aspect of being bounced around. This, in turn, builds confidence so the rider accepts speed without fear. Thus, when she begins to work at the trot she is better prepared both physically and psychologically. Also, the motion of the canter is closer to the four-beat gaits than to the trot, so the rider should find the canter easier as well.

gait and be content to go at a slow speed until you are ready for a faster gait. Having a ground person to lead the horse is the ideal, but if that's not possible or if you don't have such a horse, you will be better off going on to the fixed leg and posting trot (Chapters 11 and 14), or to half seat work in the saddle (Chapter 13), and coming back to the sitting work later. Some people have problems with their build, or perhaps have a minor disability that would make the sitting trot too difficult at this stage, so they should also go the other route.

If you are working on a bareback pad, you really need a neck strap. If you are working in the saddle, there should be enough clearance under the pommel so you can fit at least two fingers of each hand into the pommel without being pinched. If not, use a neck strap.

Absorbing the Bounce

The trot tends to be the bounciest gait, so both you and the horse have more shock to absorb than at the walk. Shock absorption is mostly a function of conformation, but can be improved greatly through training both horse and rider. There is also a lot of interaction; a tense rider will tend to create a hard-trotting horse, and vice versa, while a rider who sits softly and correctly can improve the horse's gait.

The movement of the trot is absorbed in your body in two areas. The primary area is the inner thigh and seat where the weight of your upper body actually makes contact with the horse's back. If you keep those muscles relaxed and soft, they act like a cushion to absorb the shock. If you tense them, they become like a rubber ball and bounce you up and down. This is one of the main reasons you must learn to center your body over the horse both longitudinally and laterally. If you get the least bit off center, those muscles will tense automatically to try to keep you centered. (It doesn't work, of course, but try telling your body that!)

The second area is in your waist, that is, the space between your pelvis and your ribs. This is where growing becomes important. If you keep that space long and stretched, it stays flexible. If you allow yourself to scrunch down and curl up, it becomes rigid. A flexible waist enables your following seat to work effectively, which in turn enables you to sit the trot.

Let's start by seeing how trotting affects your own body.

1. Review the first five of the Seven Steps. Then, on foot, walk and then jog slowly with your hands on your hips, feeling the change of motion from one gait to the other. There is a very distinct bounce to the jog that isn't there in the walk.

2. Keep reviewing the five steps as you jog, trying to see how softly you can hit the ground, which means you are absorbing the shock well.

3. Try jogging with your hips and thighs pinched, and also with your shoulders hunched. Notice how much harder you hit the ground.

On the horse, no matter how smooth the trot, you are still going to be bounced a little, just as you were on foot—it is the nature of the gait. The first thing to realize is that the feeling of extra movement is normal. However, you should not feel your seatbones lifting up off the saddle completely. Until your body becomes accustomed to the new movement, you are going to need a little extra help from the neck strap or pommel.

1. At a walk, work your way through the Seven Steps with special emphasis on lateral centering and following seat.

2. Take hold of either the neck strap or pommel with two fingers as usual, with just enough contact to feel the pressure.

3. With your horse walking, increase the pull on the neck strap or pommel, consciously opening your buttocks and thighs as you do so. Lean back very slightly if necessary to keep from tipping forward, but not so far that your buttocks and lower back begin to tense. You should feel additional pressure on your seatbones, but nowhere else. Increase and decrease the pull with your arms and see if you can feel the changes in seat pressure.

Douglas is learning how to use the neck strap
to deepen his seat, in preparation for his first sitting trot.

4. Run your "mental eye" through your whole body, looking for areas of tension and consciously releasing them. Think about your following seat again and make sure it is very fluid even with the firm pull. If you find yourself unable to stay loose, ease up on the pull until you find a place that is comfortable. The pull should be enough to make you sit deeper into the horse, but without tension.

Starting the trot is often the hardest part. As the horse picks up speed at the walk, your tendency is to lean forward to stay with him. This causes your thighs to tense, so when the horse begins to trot you immediately start to bounce a little, which may cause the horse to tense up, making things even worse.

1. With the horse walking, take your snug hold on the neck strap as above.

2. Ask the horse to walk faster. As he increases speed your shoulders should swing back, but instead you may find yourself leaning forward to prevent this. (Your body doesn't like the feeling of falling backward from seven feet in the air!)

3. Ask the horse to slow down, then speed up again. This time think about allowing your shoulders to swing back a little for a second, then come smoothly forward until you are centered again. The neck strap can help to hold you in place if you allow your arms to straighten and bend a little as necessary.

Practicing the Trot

Now you are ready to ask for the trot. If at all possible, get someone to lead the horse. Longeing is not a good idea because the tight circle makes it difficult to stay laterally centered and relaxed. Plan on only a few steps at first, in a straight line. Also plan that if you find yourself starting to bounce at all uncomfortably, you will walk and start again. If that is not possible, and you already know how to do so, fix your leg and post. If you are accustomed to using the reins, use them to bring the horse back to the walk. Otherwise, do an emergency dismount. Continuing to trot when you are bouncing will make you more tense about it. Also, it is very uncomfortable for the horse and can lead to both short- and long-term problems.

1. Position the horse so that when he starts the trot there is enough room to do 8 or 10 strides in a straight line. The ground should either be level or slightly uphill, *not* downhill.

2. After checking your position, think about jogging yourself, and at the same time ask your horse to jog. Continue only as long as your seatbones stay fairly well connected to the horse's back. Stop before you have to turn a corner.

3. Continue in this pattern until you feel comfortable.

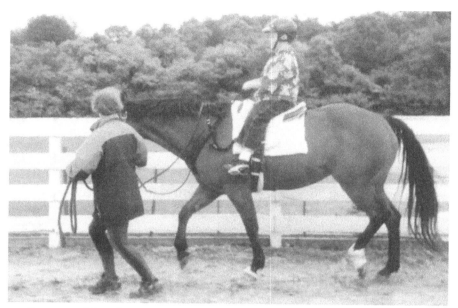

Pretty good for a first trot! Douglas's lower body is very soft, and the neck strap is doing its job of keeping him down on Miss Kitty's back.

The main difference between walking and trotting on turns is the speed, which creates greater force to throw you to the outside. Also, because you are being bounced up a little, you tend to be pushed more easily toward the outside as your outside seat drops.

1. At the walk, ride your horse on a smallish circle to the left.

2. Each time your inside seatbone drops, move your center a little extra to the inside by lifting your inside shoulder and shifting your hip. Don't twist, and be sure neither thigh tightens up.

3. Without squeezing the horse or swinging your foot back, pick up your outside knee a little to help keep your weight to the inside. Imagine a string tied to the top of your knee that is pulling it up.

4. Practice this a few times. When you feel comfortable, try riding in the other direction. Centering to the right is much more difficult, as was pointed out in Chapter 7. If necessary, review the section on lateral centering (see page 136) so that you can get your center over your right seatbone with your spine vertical.

5. Now, riding counterclockwise (to the left), try the trot, starting on a straight line with a good, loose, following seat. As you come to the corner, be very conscious of the pressure on both seatbones and shift your weight as you just practiced in the walk, but only as strongly as necessary to keep your center from slipping to the outside.

6. When you are really balanced to the left, try going to the right. (This may not happen on the first day.) The thing to remember about moving your center to the right is that it's more than you think!

If possible, have someone watch you from behind and see if your spine stays vertical and your center pants seam stays over the middle of the horse's spine (not the saddle; many horses throw the cantle of the saddle to the outside on turns — it's the *horse* you need to be in the middle of).

SPECIAL FOR MEN (SOME STUFF FOR WOMEN, TOO)

Starting the sitting trot is when some men decide that men weren't meant to ride. I remember a male pupil who could only be convinced the sitting trot was possible when my brother got on a horse and rode at the sitting trot bareback. I think they also had some private discussion afterward! My knowledge of these problems is obviously not firsthand, but my husband has been a very accomplished rider for many years and was able to offer some pertinent advice.

His first advice is that men should wear boxer shorts, not jockey shorts. (However, I have heard other male riders adamantly contradict this advice.) With boxer shorts the significant parts hang inside the thigh, below the pubic bone and in front of the thigh bone and the big tendon that runs down the inner thigh. Thus they are fairly well protected from being crushed between the pubic bone and the saddle, provided the rider sits correctly. Jockey shorts really are only comfortable in an English saddle if the saddle is very flat—that is, there is no pommel projecting upward to bump into. And of course, before World War II boxer shorts or the equivalent were all there was, and the majority of riders were males. One has to assume that if riding with the more natural boxer shorts was really uncomfortable, the men would have either figured out something else or not ridden at all!

The tendency among most novice male riders is to try to protect themselves by squeezing with their thighs in an effort to stay away from the seat of the saddle, and drawing their hips back by rounding in the back to stay away from the pommel, which tightens the thighs even more. As with so many things we do instinctively on the horse, this is exactly the wrong thing to do. Squeezing the thighs diminishes the available space between them and makes the thigh muscles hard, so they are more likely to crush anything in the way. It also causes the rider to bounce severely, which can only lead to trouble. And if you ride at the jog for long periods, your thighs just get too tired to squeeze!

Instead, you must focus on sitting correctly on your seatbones, as described in Chapter 7, and allowing your pelvis to get very wide and your thighs very soft. The exercises under the heading "Letting Go of the Branch" in Chapter 7 may also be useful. As you sit correctly at the walk, you will notice that as the horse moves and the small of your back flexes with the movement, you roll slightly on each step from your seatbones to your crotch bone and back. It will be as you roll onto your crotch that you tend to tense up.

The other common mistake is to roll from your seatbones onto your tail-bone, especially if the horse is bony or the saddle is too short (women will make the same mistake for similar reasons). If you have learned to follow the move-ment correctly—that is, from seat to crotch—it's no big deal if you find your-self on a bony horse and are forced to try to follow the wrong way, from seat to tail; you will find this easy to correct. However if you *only* learn the wrong way, you will have trouble with all the faster sitting gaits, because your buttocks and spine are less flexible in this position.

If you practice enough at the walk to develop confidence that you can be safe and comfortable sitting correctly—that is, wide and loose in the pelvic area and upright in the spine—and if you choose a horse and saddle to learn on that will make the process as smooth as possible, you should find that you can sit the trot very successfully.

Once you are fairly comfortable, you should combine the sitting trot and riding without reins exercises. This will give you lots of practice and will also teach your body to follow the horse, since his movements may be somewhat unpredictable. Sitting the trot without reins and with your eyes closed, if the horse is steady and you are in a safe area, will help you develop a very secure seat.

To summarize, you should be very secure with your Seven Steps at the walk, especially the following seat and lateral centering, before trying the trot. Use your hand on the neck strap or pommel to help you sit more deeply. If you start to bounce even a little bit, stop and start again. Use a horse with a smooth gait, and stick with short distances in a straight line until you get the knack of it.

PROBLEM SOLVING

If you feel very uncomfortable and bouncy, go back to checking yourself through the Seven Steps. A weakness in any one of them can cause problems at the sitting trot—which is why so many people have trouble with it! You can also try trotting:

● Slightly uphill: Adjust your upper body angle if necessary to avoid tension in your thighs and buttocks.

● Knees up (see page 150): This is often the easiest way to sit the trot on the straight line. It's best done in the saddle, but also works bareback, since it forces both lateral and longitudinal centering.

● Sidesaddle (see page 151): Some people find this even easier than knees up, especially if you're riding on a bareback pad.

Any of these exercises can also be done without reins and with your eyes closed.

It is very important to learn to sit the trot correctly, especially if you ride in a discipline where it is used a lot. Poor technique will interfere with all your aids; but what is more important, it will hurt the horse. This can result in anything from bad gaits to serious and debilitating lameness. Once you understand the principles, however, you should be able to sit the trot on any horse who will allow it. Enjoy your new skill!

10

Handling the Reins
Goofproof Your Moves

The need to teach rein handling as a separate subject came to me, as so many things have, while giving a lesson. My student that day was Sheila, a well-coordinated woman in her early 30s who had been riding for some 15 years. She was on a pony who was being especially poky at the canter and kept breaking to the trot for no apparent reason. I asked her to use the stick lightly to remind him, but she didn't. I asked her again, and still no stick. Finally, thinking she might be frightened, I called her into the center and asked her why she wasn't using the stick. She explained that she had her stick and reins tangled up and didn't know how to use them separately, and felt very confused. She also confessed to being somewhat frightened, not by the idea of cantering faster but by her feelings of disorganization and incompetence.

I have known many otherwise skilled riders who handled the reins awkwardly, causing them to be tense in situations they should have managed without a problem. In fact, you see it all the time: riders getting pulled forward by the reins, riders with their reins too short or too long, too tight or too loose, all of which causes discomfort to both rider and horse. Much of the problem is the rider's lack of balance, but a surprising amount has to do with the rider's inability to handle the reins easily and skillfully. Anyone *can* learn to deal with the reins, but it requires both knowledge and practice.

As everyone knows, the reins are a major route of communication between rider and horse. However, communication of any sort, to be successful, must transmit a clear message from sender to receiver. If you are talking on your cell phone and there is a lot of interference, no matter how intelligent your message, the listener will not be able to act on it because he won't receive it clearly. Similarly, if your rein contact is bouncy, unbalanced or tense, the message you want to send to the horse will be unclear.

Tidbits & Supplements

For those of you who are fairly experienced, I still suggest reading this chapter. Since these skills are rarely taught in any depth, it is not uncommon to have missed out, and you may find some ideas here that will help make your responses quicker and more effective.

So, in order to *communicate* successfully with the reins, you must spend some time learning to *manipulate* them so that you are comfortable with them. This is comparable to learning touch typing so that you don't have to hunt for the keys to type a letter. And the faster the letter has to go out, the more essential it is for you to be able to type effortlessly. However, just as good typing starts with a good position at the typewriter or computer, so good rein handling starts with a good position on the horse. It may seem as though we should have been talking about using the reins long ago, but without all that groundwork we've been laying so far, trying to use the reins would just get both you and the horse in trouble.

Before you even think about transmitting information to the horse through the reins, your balance must be secure. Otherwise, whether you mean to or not, your hands will instinctively be moving as necessary to help you balance. Luckily, with the use of the Seven Steps (Chapters 2 and 7) you can attain balance at the walk fairly quickly, so you can begin working with the reins. At the more advanced gaits, using the neck strap with one hand to maintain balance enables you to communicate at least rudimentary messages with the reins. However, advanced work with the reins at the trot and canter, especially in half seat, should wait until your balance at those gaits is secure.

To handle the reins comfortably, you must learn the following skills:

- Picking up the reins

- Holding the reins

- Releasing and lengthening the reins

- Bridging and shortening the reins

- Manipulating the reins, stick, and neck strap

You will need your horse with reins attached to a bridle, halter or whatever, and a neck strap and stick. In some of the exercises a helper is called for. These directions are intended for ordinary reins that are joined with a buckle at the center. They describe holding the reins in the English fashion. If you are a novice rider, try not to put any actual pressure on the bit while you're learning to handle the reins, and release if the horse does so.

PICKING UP THE REINS

I once went out on a trail ride with a group who were not the most thoughtful people. We were walking and I had put my reins down, looped over the pommel so that they wouldn't slide down the horse's neck, while I made an adjustment to my helmet strap. Without warning, as she came into an open field the leader of the ride picked up a canter! Naturally the rest of the horses, including mine, immediately either cantered or pulled themselves together to do so. I was very grateful that I knew how to pick up and adjust my reins almost instantly.

Generally speaking, when you are mounted you will have hold of the reins at least by the buckle, but there may be times when you have put them down on the horse's neck for the moment. The method of picking up the reins described here works equally well in either situation.

1. To practice this skill, begin with the reins lying on the horse's neck with the buckle on his withers. With your palm down, put your left hand on the buckle and pick it up so that your hand is about chest high. Check to make sure there are no twists in the reins.

2. With your thumb toward you and your palm down, put your right hand around both reins a few inches below the buckle, inserting your ring finger between the reins.

Tidbits & Supplements

When first learning rein skills, see if you can find a group of other riders who are also learning and have races or play Simon Says to give you all more practice. More advanced riders can practice these skills while cooling down or walking on the trail. It is also very good practice for the horse who anticipates, because it helps him learn not to overreact every time the reins are picked up or shortened.

Picking up the reins. This is also the way to shorten the reins if you're riding "on the buckle" and need to shorten in a hurry.

3. Now slide your right hand down the reins until you have the contact (amount of pressure) you want. At this point you would have some communication in case you had a frightened horse. Right now the reins should have a little slack.

4. Let go of the buckle with your left hand. Then hold your right hand over the horse's withers at waist level and take only the left rein into your left hand, holding it the same way you picked the reins up with your right hand—that is, with your thumb toward you and your little finger toward the horse's mouth. Give a half twist to the reins if necessary so that the rough, unfinished inside lies against your fingers. This gives a better grip.

5. Separate your hands, flipping the bight (leftover length) gently forward so that the buckle hangs between the two reins on the right side of the horse's neck.

6. The reins will now be lying over the tops of your forefingers, with the smooth, finished side of the reins up. Place your thumbs on the tops of the reins, which will then be held between your thumbs and forefingers. This enables you to relax your fingers as much as you wish without having the reins slip through your hands accidentally.

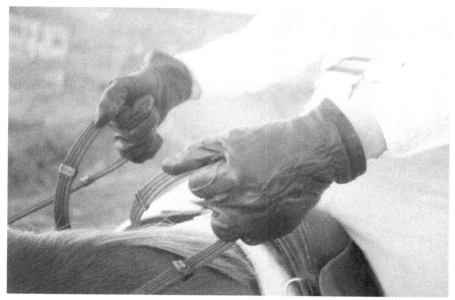

Holding the reins (English). Notice that the knuckle of the thumb is lower than the wrist and the hands are curved very slightly inward, which creates the best communication between your body and the horse's.

This method of picking up the reins is much quicker and more efficient than trying to pick up the reins one at a time. You can pick up the buckle with either hand first. Practice with each hand until the moves flow together smoothly.

HOLDING THE REINS

As you will see in Chapter 18, how you use your hands to hold the reins is crucial in establishing soft, relaxed communication with your horse. The goal is to have no tension in your hands, wrists or arms. This can only happen if you are in balance, since your hands will always tense up when balance is lost. You can look at a photograph and instantly tell how well a rider is balanced just by looking at her hands. If her hands are pulled down and back you know she is too far forward and has drawn her hands back to compensate; if they are high she is too far back. Either of these situations can occasionally occur with even the best riders.

Holding the reins correctly starts with holding your arms and hands correctly.

1. With the reins dropped, run through the first five of the Seven Steps. When you have finished, allow your arms to fall completely relaxed at your sides. The backs of your hands will be away from you.

2. *Leaving your right hand and wrist completely limp,* use your left hand to pick up your right forearm just above the wrist, allowing your elbow to bend, until your hand is in front of you just over and to the right of the horse's withers. Your elbow will hang just in front of your rib cage. (How far forward your hand will be relative to the horse depends on the length of your arms.)

3. Curl your fingers slightly and let your thumb rest on top of your index finger. Notice how your whole hand is lower than your wrist, and the back of the hand curves lightly to the left from the wrist. The slope of the back of your hand should be approximately the same as the slope of the horse's shoulder. Study your hand for a minute so you have its appearance clearly in your mind. Bring your left hand up to match it. Try raising and lowering your hands by bending and straightening only your elbows. No bend should appear at the base of your thumb.

4. Now pick up your reins as described in the previous section. Do not grip them in your fists, but let your fingers curl softly around them. Many people make the mistake of opening their fingers out straight in the belief this will make their hands lighter. Besides being dangerous (it is easy to jam your fingers against the horse's neck), you actually lose the sensitivity and flexibility you get from having the reins held in the curled fingers.

5. Grow and shake out your shoulders gently, letting your hands fall from the wrist as in step 3. Leave your little finger on the outside of the rein unless the horse has a high head carriage. If the horse's mouth is well below the level of your hands, the pull around your little finger will tend to bend your hand upward, making your wrist stiff.

This hand position is essential to maintain if you want a soft connection to the horse's mouth (see the photo on page 201). Anything other than a slight variation will result in locking the wrist or elbow, which the horse will notice instantly.

RELEASING AND LENGTHENING THE REINS

One of my favorite stories concerns a woman to whom I sold a horse for trail riding. She complained that he constantly pulled, even though she rode him "on the buckle." I knew the horse went perfectly quietly on loose contact, so I asked her to show me how she held the reins. She carefully picked up the reins by the buckle and then pulled the buckle firmly up to her chest! Naturally, the reins were quite tight, and since she wasn't a very well-balanced rider, the horse was quite annoyed (though polite). I tactfully explained that the reins, while *long*, were not *loose*, and suggested that she hold them a bit shorter and then rest her hand on the pommel when she felt insecure.

So, before we begin this exercise, we need some definitions. Releasing has several connotations. In this case it refers to letting go of the reins when the horse pulls them tight, so that the reins become loose. Lengthening (and shortening) the reins has to do with the *amount of rein* between the rider's hands and the bit, *not* the amount of tightness.

Releasing the Reins

Many instructors fail to realize that the horse needs to be allowed freedom of his head and neck, especially with inexperienced riders whose bodies and hands put severe demands on the horse's balance mechanisms. These instructors insist the rider hang on tightly to the reins when the horse endeavors to get his head free, which he does by thrusting his head suddenly out and downward. "Don't let him get away with that!" is their favorite phrase. It is often followed by, "Are you okay?" as the unfortunate student, pulled forward by her tight reins and arms and the movement of the horse's head, hits the ground! Releasing the reins easily and effectively is useful for all riders, but is a particularly important skill for small riders, children or adults, because they so easily get pulled out of position by the horse, which results in their riding in a tense, defensive position.

This exercise can be done on the horse if the reins are long enough; otherwise it is best performed on the ground. You can either stand or sit in a straight chair with your legs back under you so that only your toes are touching the ground. You will need another person to help you. You will also need a pair of reins or the equivalent.

1. Take your position either standing or sitting, holding the reins as described in the previous section. Your helper should be squatting or sitting below you, fairly close, holding the bit ends of the reins.

2. Have your helper give a sharp tug on the reins without warning. Your instinct will be to close your fists and resist the tug. When you do this, your whole body is pulled forward—imagine how much more so when it's not a person tugging but a horse! Once you are pulled forward, you are totally out of balance and defenseless against a sudden move.

3. Have your helper repeat the tug, but this time let your arms relax and stretch out, soften your fingers and allow the reins to slide through them without letting them go completely. *Your body should not move at all.* You are in a secure position and still have control of the reins.

Lengthening the Reins

In the preceding exercise, the "horse" pulled the reins out of the rider's hands with a sudden tug and the rider released the reins, making them loose, to keep her position secure, while giving the horse the freedom he obviously needed. Sometimes, however (most often when warming up), the horse's neck will start to lengthen only gradually, as a result of which the reins will begin to get tighter, which you may not notice immediately. When you do notice it, you have to make an adjustment. For a small amount of lengthening, you can allow your elbows to straighten a little, but never so much that your arms approach being straight. As the horse lengthens more, simply allow the reins to feed through your fingers as he takes them. Here you are *lengthening* the reins without making them *looser*.

Sometimes you want to lengthen the reins yourself, even though the horse is not pulling on them. To do this, again relax your fingers and this time slide your hands up the reins toward the buckle, then move your hands, with the lengthened reins in them, back into position over the withers after you have achieved the length or degree of looseness you want. In this instance you *loosen* the reins by *lengthening* them.

BRIDGING AND SHORTENING THE REINS

Releasing is a comparatively easy skill to learn, but shortening the reins quickly and efficiently takes some practice. As a result, it is a skill many people never learn. One of my most experienced students, Ellen, has often complained that she doesn't like to release the reins when the horse drops his head because she will have to shorten them again in a minute. Similarly, she tended not to shorten the reins when preparing to give a hand aid or when the horse raised his head a little. We finally focused on it one day, because she became aware that it was affecting her balance. She worked on it for a while, and began to see how keeping the reins the right length improved her balance and thus her sensitivity to the horse's mouth.

When it was my turn to ride, she watched my hands closely and said with surprise, "Your hands never move [forward and back] at all. They just stay in the same place and you constantly adjust the length of the reins." I hasten to add that she did not mean I was not following the movements of the horse's head that related to gait, but that as the horse extended and shortened his neck in his efforts to work out his balance problems, I simply adjusted the rein length while keeping my hands where they were, which enabled me to keep my body still.

Bridging the reins and shortening the reins go together, because the hands are used in the same way to achieve both. Bridging is mostly used to ride with the reins in one hand while still keeping the reins somewhat independent of one another.

Bridging the Reins

1. Pick up the reins and hold them the way you learned earlier in this chapter.

2. Turn your hands so your palms are down and your thumbs are together. Be sure the bight of the reins is in front of your hands.

3. With the first two fingers and the thumb of your right hand, grasp the left rein from above *near your left thumb* and hold it firmly. Do *not* grasp the left rein *below* your left hand (near the little finger).

4. Let go of the left rein with your left hand and put your right ring finger around the left rein as well. You will now be holding both reins in one hand, so the left rein enters your hand on the left (thumb) side of your right hand, and the right rein enters on the right (little finger) side. The reins cross over inside your hand.

5. Finally, turn your right hand, now holding both reins, to the correct position with the thumb on top. The bight will fall forward on the right side of the horse's neck.

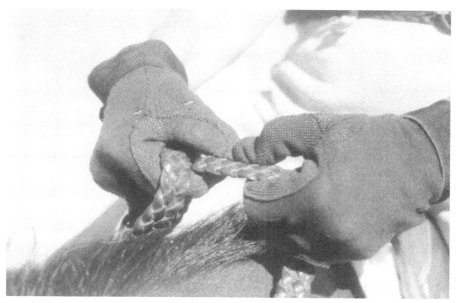

The first step in forming a half bridge, or preparing to shorten your reins when riding with your reins in two hands.

A half bridge—the correct position of hand and reins when you ride with the reins in one hand. While freeing up one hand, this position still enables you to use the reins separately, though not as accurately as having them in two hands.

This is called a half bridge, and is the best way of riding with your reins in one hand. By rotating your hand, you can put pressure on each rein individually; and with the reins kept separate, it is very easy to take the reins into two hands again. Practice making a half bridge with each hand, then taking the reins back into two hands again.

Shortening the Reins

Many riders shorten the reins by climbing down them with their fingers, as though they were playing the flute. This is awkward both for you and your horse, and unsafe if you need to shorten the reins quickly. The habit is usually developed by riding horses who have been punished for slow responses, and who now anticipate upward gait changes and either become very tense or simply pick up whatever gait they think is going to be called for. Since a request for a gait change or transition is usually preceded by shortening the reins, as soon as such horses feel the reins being adjusted, they are off. Very disconcerting, even when you expect it! The answer to this problem is, of course, to spend a little time with the horse teaching him that it is okay *not* to react like a firecracker to a request for a transition.

There are a couple of correct ways to shorten the reins. If you are holding the reins in one hand by the buckle or loosely in both hands, the quickest way to shorten them is to proceed almost as though you were picking them up: Grab both reins in both hands, one above the other, and slide the lower hand down the rein until it is the length you need. You use this technique if the horse startles suddenly and goes from a long neck to a short neck in a hurry.

For normal shortening of the reins, use your hands as though you were going to make a half bridge. Again, you begin by turning your hands palm down and hooking the index finger of your right hand on the left rein. Then:

1. Instead of letting go with your left hand, slide it down the rein toward the bit, straightening your arm as you do so. Thus you *shorten* the rein without tightening it. Check your center to avoid leaning forward as you shorten the rein.

2. Let go of the left rein with your right hand. Your left rein is now shorter than your right one. If you keep your left hand extended, both reins will be equal in pressure. If you bring your left hand back beside your right hand, the left rein will then be *tighter* as well as *shorter*.

3. Repeat steps 1 and 2 using the opposite hand.

4. Repeat steps 1 and 2 first with one hand, then the other, until both reins are evenly shorter.

Now review this chapter so far and practice the releasing, lengthening, and shortening skills together. Slide your hands up the reins until the reins are long, then shorten first one and then the other. Be sure to practice starting with different hands until you are equally adept either way. Have your helper pull the reins out of your hands, then shorten them again using both the pick-up and the bridging methods. This is an activity you need to be very good at because horses, especially in training when they are trying to find their balance, frequently need to lengthen their necks, which pulls the reins out of your hands. Then they raise their heads again almost immediately, requiring constant adjustment of the reins.

Tidbits & Supplements

Not only will you need to adjust your reins when the horse does something to change them, but you will also use shortening as an essential part of using the reins to direct the horse. Many riders send confusing signals to the horse because the reins are too long, which puts the rider's hands in an awkward place and thus affects her whole balance and position.

MANIPULATING THE REINS, STICK AND NECK STRAP

The purpose of learning the rein skills in this chapter is so that you won't have to consciously think about them every time you want to use the reins. You also need to learn to handle the reins, stick, and neck strap (if you are using one) with equal dexterity. These skills are useful even for advanced riders. One day at a horse trial I was riding a not-very-experienced horse over his first cross-country course. Like many horses at that level, when faced with an unfamiliar obstacle he would first slow way down, then overjump. To keep both of us reasonably safe and comfortable, I needed to be able to use the stick to remind him to keep going, still have hold of the neck strap if he overjumped so I did not accidentally yank his mouth, and of course have the reins available for both grounding and control. I was grateful for all the practice I had in handling all these tools at the same time.

Luckily, Nature gave us four fingers on each hand, which we can use to separate the reins, neck strap, and stick.

Reins and Neck Strap

The neck strap is held with the first two fingers; the reins are held in the first three fingers. Thus, the pull on the neck strap is felt on the middle finger, the pull on the reins is felt on the ring finger. Have someone tug on first the neck strap, then the reins, so you can feel the different pressures. When you are holding neck strap and reins together, the reins are passive, so **the pressure on the reins should always be less than the pressure on the neck strap.** Only then can you be sure you are not using the reins instead of the neck strap to hold on.

Practice all the variations of one or two hands on the neck strap, until you can take your hands off and put them on easily without dropping the reins in the process. When you take your hand off the neck strap, extend your arm forward a little to be sure you don't unconsciously pull on the reins. Check your center each time to make sure you don't lean forward accidentally as well.

Reins and Stick

Any skillful rider should be able to touch the horse with the stick on any reachable place on his body, as well as keeping it passive, so she needs to be able to go easily from holding reins and stick together, to holding the stick separate from reins. There was a time in my life when I could change the stick from one hand to the other and shorten my reins at the same time while in mid-flight over a fence, without even thinking about it. A very useful skill to have in jumper classes! I can probably still do it, because it is so ingrained in my reflexes.

When the stick and the reins are held in the same hand, three fingers are around the reins and four fingers are around the stick. Thus the feel of the reins is in the ring finger, as before, and the feel of the stick is in the little finger. The knob on the end of the stick rests on top of the reins, in the hollow at the base of the thumb. Resting the end of your stick on your thigh will help keep your wrist in the correct position (see the photo on page 159). If you are carrying the stick reversed, the knob will be just outside the little finger and the end of the stick will protrude from between your thumb and forefinger, following the path of the reins. To use the stick separate from the reins, make the beginning of a half-bridge using the hand that is not holding the stick. That is, if the stick is in your right hand, use the forefinger of your left hand to grasp the right rein by your right thumb. Then let go of the rein with your right hand, keeping your little finger firmly around the stick so you don't drop it as well (see the photo on page 161)! Practice putting the reins in one hand, reaching back with the stick as though to tap the horse on the croup, then bringing it forward and taking the reins in two hands again. Also practice changing the stick from one hand to the other, and from normal to reversed position (Chapter 5), both while holding the reins.

Once you are comfortable with reins and neck strap, and reins and stick, you can put all three together. It may seem like a lot of trouble at first, but these skills can also keep you *out* of a lot of trouble, and are well worth learning.

To develop effortless communication with your horse, you must practice all the combinations of rein-handling skills until they are firmly ensconced in your muscle memory. Only then will they be available immediately when needed.

It is also important to have these skills *before* you try to learn to transmit the actual commands. You can really only focus on one thing at a time, and if you still have to remind yourself to *hold* the reins correctly, you will not be able think about *using* them correctly, and one skill or the other will suffer. As you will see if you look at the table of contents, the next chapter on using the reins doesn't come for quite a while, so you have lots of time to practice!

Part III

Riding without Fear
Back in the Saddle and Using the Stirrups

11

Settling into the Saddle

Adjust to the Difference

In addition to the beginners in my riding program, I also had many adults who had some previous riding experience. I explained to one student, Jeannie, as I had explained to the others, that she would get the most benefit from the program if she spent some time starting over, that is, relearning her basic position with the Seven Steps. This included riding on a bareback pad, something she had never done. After a certain amount of trepidation, her reaction to the bareback pad was, "Oh, this is so much easier than the saddle and stirrups!"

Eventually the time came when she went back to the saddle. Initially, she found it difficult and even frustrating, since the bad habits she thought she had eliminated now tried to reestablish themselves. Typically, she reverted to gripping with her thigh and drawing her leg up, and when that was corrected, pushing the stirrups forward and leaning forward to compensate. However, she soon found that the relaxation and balance she had learned on the bareback pad could be adapted to the saddle and stirrups, ultimately making her more secure than ever before.

Up to now we've talked mostly about riding bareback. And while bareback, with or without a pad, has a very important role in riding, the reality is that almost everyone rides in a saddle most of the time. **A saddle is nothing more than a rigid, padded frame from which stirrups can be hung. The frame fits over the horse in such a way that the stirrups can be stood on by the rider without causing the saddle to slide around the horse.** When we talk about riding in the saddle, what we're really talking about is **riding with stirrups.**

Those pesky stirrups! They're supposed to make riding easier, but sometimes they seem to make it impossible: trying to stand up in them for jumping, trying not to lose them at the sitting trot, trying to keep your heels down and worst of all trying to keep the stirrups and your legs from swinging when you post or canter!

Back in Chapter 2, I described grounding and explained that the ability to ground is essential to any athletic endeavor. **Perhaps the single biggest barrier to developing a good, secure seat on a horse is the difficulty of grounding into the stirrups.** Unfortunately, by their very nature stirrups are an extremely wiggly, unstable platform on which to try to stand! Our bodies instinctively resist putting weight on anything that is wobbly or insecure. That is, we do not want to commit to grounding on something that might give way. (Think of how you walk on icy pavement.)

However, without grounding it is impossible to find your balance, and without balance it is impossible to use your stirrups effectively and have a secure position. Getting comfortable on the stirrups, which means being grounded and balanced, is essential to all your riding skills. This principle is not easily grasped by most people, so they tend to have less-than-perfect security on their stirrups unless they are very experienced, and the common perception is that you must ride a long time before you can expect to be balanced. However, I have found that if you are willing to work at the basic principles described in this chapter and the next two, you can learn to ride well in stirrups no matter what your level. Luckily, because of the time you have spent building a solid foundation *without* stirrups, you should be able to find a good, safe and even elegant position without too much difficulty.

Chapters 11, 12, and 13 represent quite a long span of riding time. The best way to work on them is to intersperse the exercises with other riding that you are comfortable with, as suggested in the Introduction.

So, to work!

Tidbits & Supplements

There is a theory that you should not put all your weight in your stirrups in case the stirrup leather breaks, which does occasionally happen. For this reason some people are taught to always grip with their knees or thighs, "just in case." We have already discussed at some length why gripping is not desirable. I have also observed that any rider who has learned to balance herself properly has no trouble dealing with an unexpected broken stirrup leather. And, as a practical matter, there is no way you can ride comfortably for extended periods while gripping with your thighs rather than allowing your weight to fall onto your irons. And that, after all, is what the stirrups are for!

A LITTLE BIT ABOUT THE SADDLE

If you are to ride well in the saddle, it must fit you well and put you in the right place on the horse, that is, over the deep place in the horse's back just behind the withers and his center. It must seat you level so that you are not being pitched forward or back. It should feel comfortable when you are sitting with your feet out of the stirrups. The stirrup bars should be placed on the tree so that when your foot is in the iron correctly, the stirrup leather is hanging vertical, with your toe lined up with your knee and the back of your heel under your pants seam at the hip (see the photo below).

If you are serious about learning to ride and don't yet have your own horse, you should still buy your own saddle as soon as possible. Visit a good saddle shop, preferably one with a knowledgeable professional who can help you. Saddles are all made by hand and vary even within the same brand and style, so trying them out is essential.

The saddle must also be comfortable for the horse. It should follow the contours of his back without pinching. It should sit level on his back when viewed from either the side or the back. It should sit clear of his spine, especially at the

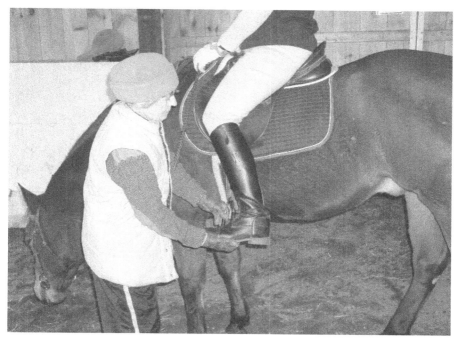

I'm checking to see if the stirrup on this saddle is in the right place for Peg.
It looks pretty good, although the saddle seat is a bit tight.

withers, where you should be able to fit three fingers vertically under the pommel. A well-made saddle will fit most normal horses, possibly with the addition of a special pad. It should stay in place without you having to make the girth unnecessarily tight—that is, a breastplate, crupper or foregirth should be used if needed. If the girth makes the horse tense while riding, it is too tight.

Safety stirrups are an excellent option, especially if you ride alone at all. The best ones are are hinged to open under the sort of pressure that would occur if you fell. Whatever type of stirrups you choose, they should be adjusted to be even before you mount. To find the approximate length (you will be riding with them quite long at first) before mounting, put the fingertips of one hand on the stirrup bar and use the other to hold the stirrup up under your arm. It should reach into your armpit. After adjusting one stirrup, adjust the other one to be even with the first. To check, measure from the bottom of the saddle to the top of the stirrup on each side. You can also flip the stirrup upside down on the bottom of the leather and compare the distance from the bottom of each stirrup to the bottom of the flap. (Because of the way the horse moves and stands, looking at both stirrups from the front is rarely accurate.)

Once you are riding in the saddle, rather than bareback, your own riding attire must be considered. The easiest, most comfortable garments to learn in are well-fitting stretch jodhpurs (or tights) and "riding sneakers" or similar footgear that just covers your ankle bones.

Clothing to avoid includes tight pants that do not stretch, because they make it almost impossible to relax your buttocks and thighs. Pants with loose legs tend to bunch up under your knee and can rub you raw in a very short time. Chaps and high boots are both stiff when new and need to be correctly broken in. Since your leg position won't be perfectly correct at first, you run the risk of breaking them in in the wrong position and having great difficulty with them forever after. High-laced paddock boots, because they need to be laced tightly to look nice, tend to be even more restrictive than high boots. Rubber boots should be avoided at all costs until your leg position is thoroughly confirmed, because it takes some effort to make them accept any sort of ankle flexion. Whatever footgear you use, be sure it is wide enough so that your foot can spread out and feel the stirrup.

One other point: If you ride in cold weather, it is essential to dress so that *you do not get cold!* Your feet are especially important because cold, tense feet make stiff ankles, which make your whole shock-absorbing system ineffective. You can buy lined footgear, or just buy a shoe size larger or wider so that you can wear thicker socks without pinching. (Tight shoes make your feet *really* cold.) For the rest of your body, lots of *loose* layers do the job. This means long underwear of a fabric that wicks away moisture, then adding layers as needed. Don't forget your legs! Cold feet come from cold legs. Many people wear turtlenecks, sweaters, vests and coats on top, then cover their legs with just a thin pair of jeans or breeches over long johns. Their legs don't *feel* cold, but they are losing heat because the tightly layered covering provides almost no insulation at all. Chaps are good once your leg position is confirmed, or you can buy insulated trousers intended for riding. If you're showing and have to wear the tight clothes, keep yourself covered until just before the class. Necks and ears should also be covered, but stay away from long scarves, which can be dangerous. I make the assumption, of course, that you will be wearing a safety helmet.

For all the initial work in the saddle, your horse should be wearing an adjustable neck strap. At times a ground person would be very helpful. You won't want to use leg aids at all, since that would confuse the issue, so if your horse doesn't respond easily to a cluck, carry a stick. It would also be best if you can do without the reins, so if possible use a ground person or a horse who responds to the voice for downward transitions. If you have not used the saddle before, check Chapter 6 on mounting first. It is a good idea to practice some emergency dismounts from the saddle as soon as you are comfortable (you'll also find those in Chapter 6).

GROUND WORK

Your leg begins up in your pelvis, where muscles that connect to the pelvis and spine on one end connect to your leg bone at the other end to move your leg in various directions. If there is any tension in those muscles, it will affect your leg position. The muscles in the back of your pelvis and buttocks tend to pull the tops of your thigh bones back, rotating your knees outward and causing you to ride on and perhaps grip with the backs of your legs. This is one of the reasons you don't want to squeeze your buttocks.

The real troublemakers, however, are the muscles on the inside of your thigh, which so desperately want to help you stay on by squeezing whenever you lose your seat even a little. The trouble is, when they squeeze they make it *harder* for you to stay on the horse, for several reasons:

• When you contract these muscles they become hard, making you tend to bounce up off the horse rather than sink into him.

• The horse feels the tension and becomes more tense himself, and thus more difficult to sit.

• Because the horse is round, and narrower on top, squeezing tends to move you to the narrower part—that is, up off the horse. This is similar to trying to hold a large ball by squeezing it with your fingers.

• Squeezing the thigh tends to draw your whole leg up, raising your center of gravity.

Just to make sure, in case you have some tensions you haven't completely dealt with, let's look at what a loose leg should be.

1. Stand where you can hold on to something with one hand, such as the back of a chair. Stand sideways to it. Get nice and tall and comfortable.

2. Place a hand on the chair to balance yourself, then take your other hand, bend over and place it behind and just above your knee on the side away from the chair. Leaving your leg muscles as relaxed as possible, pick up your leg with your hand until your foot is six inches or so off the ground. Keep your hip joint bent, and straighten your upper body.

3. Shake out your lower leg. Your hip joint will be bent more or less as though you were sitting, but the rest of your leg should just hang there.

When your leg just hangs there with all the muscles relaxed so there is equal tension on all sides, your knee is only slightly bent and you can see pretty much your whole lower leg right down to the ankle and foot. This is the way your leg should look on the horse.

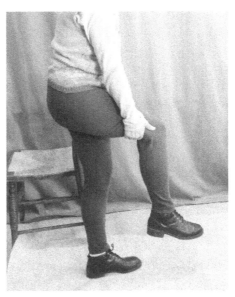

Finding your relaxed leg on the ground. It's very common to have small tensions that you aren't aware of, but that will show up in your leg position.

ON THE HORSE: GETTING USED TO THE SADDLE

As soon as you have mounted, take both feet out of the stirrups. With the horse standing still, go through the first five of the Seven Steps. If you have not been riding in the saddle it will feel quite strange at first, so your body will take a bit of time to adjust to the new feeling. However, it should still feel comfortable, especially under your seatbones!

What is really different about sitting in the saddle as opposed to the bareback pad is that the top of the saddle is comparatively flat and slippery, while the top of most horses is more of an upside-down V shape and the pad is anything but slippery. The flatness of the saddle is an advantage in enabling you to sit deep without feeling undue pressure on sensitive parts of your body, but you lose the lateral stability that resulted from the horse's shape and the friction of the pad. This tends to create a feeling of insecurity, and tension can be the result, so you may want to go through some of the exercises in Chapter 7.

Next, you need to spend a few extra minutes thinking about lateral centering. With your hands on the pommel for stability, slide your seat off to the right side the way you have learned to do to move your center laterally. Slide fairly far, so you are well off center but not in danger of actually falling. Then, *without twisting*, recenter by lifting your left shoulder, hiking your center and hips to the left and pushing down on your left leg. The first thing you should notice is that it is *much* easier to slide in the saddle than it was on the bareback pad. Later on you will see how the stirrups relate to this, but for now just be aware of it. What this means to you is that if you aren't paying attention, you can quite easily lose your lateral centering, but if you do start to lose it, you will find it easier to get it back—provided you catch it early enough! Practice sliding off and recentering a few times until you are comfortable with it in both directions.

Now allow your horse to walk pretty much at liberty while you focus on going with him. Use your voice or stick to keep him going, not your leg. You won't have quite as much feel of his movement in the saddle, but you'll have much more than you might expect. Notice that you have to really *think* about staying in the middle of him on the turns. You have to use that little lateral correction move from the previous paragraph on every stride on the corners. You should do this each time your inside seat drops. It's important to start working on this at the walk, because the tendency to slide to the outside is far greater at the faster gaits.

Think about your following seat and become conscious of the fact that when your left seat drops, your left leg does too. You don't have to do anything about this, but just think about letting your legs be very heavy—imagine you have sandbags hanging from your ankles. Don't try to push or force your leg down, which would make it tense. I have found that once a student gets past the stage of trying to squeeze with her thighs to stay on, the next phase is trying to push her legs down. This has the effect of making her narrower between the upper legs, which lifts her seatbones off the saddle—exactly the opposite of what you want.

Once you are comfortable sitting in the saddle, take a look down at your legs. Just as when you were on the ground, the lower leg below the knee should be hanging a little forward so that you see your whole foot. If your lower leg wants to hang straight down instead, or behind rather than in front of the knee, it means there's some tension in there somewhere. Of course, if you are so soft in the inner thigh or your horse is so slender that your knee can go effortlessly out and around his barrel, rather than forward, then your thigh will be more vertical and your lower leg as well, but your shin should never be *behind* the vertical when your leg is loose.

A test for a relaxed lower leg on the horse is to sit with your feet hanging loosely and have someone take your foot and see if it will swing back and forth easily. This tells you about the muscles controlling the knee. Then she should put her hand either under your foot or around your ankle and see if she can push your knee up easily and if it falls back down when she lets go. This tells you about the muscles controlling the hip joint, as well as about your inner thigh muscles.

FIXING THE LEG

Before you start using the stirrups, you need to first get a feeling for how your legs are going to be placed, since it is different from what you've been doing. When you do this without stirrups, it is called *fixed leg*, as opposed to the loose leg you have been working on. Until the leg muscle groups I've just described will let go and allow your leg to just hang naturally, you should not try any fixed leg work. Fixed leg allows your thighs to tense just the tiniest bit, which is like giving a little bit of whisky to an alcoholic; if they have any tendency to grip at all, they will go right back to it!

Once you feel that your loose leg is truly loose, you're ready to learn the fixed leg. You can be either bareback or in the saddle. The horse should *not* be one who is overreactive to the slightest movement of your leg. Check your basic position with the Seven Steps before starting.

1. With one leg only, straighten your knee without locking it, so your foot goes out in front of you. Keeping your knee straight, lift your toe up and out, flexing your ankle. Now turn your toe in and out, toward the horse and away. You will find that your ankle flexes somewhat more easily with the toe turned out. Let your toe and lower leg drop back into the relaxed position.

2. *Without lifting or allowing your knee to lift*, swing one foot forward and back until it is swinging freely. Then swing it back and stop it with your heel under the side seam of your trousers.

3. Lift your toe up and out as before, being careful *not* to let your shinbone rotate so that the back of your calf turns toward the horse—which it can do only when the knee is bent. Notice that turning your toe out brings your calf away from the horse a little and makes your knee and thigh lie more firmly against the horse. This is *not* the same as gripping with your knees, which involves the inner thigh muscles, although it *is* what instructors want when they tell their pupils to grip. Conversely, when you turn the toe in, your knee and thigh fall away from the horse a little, allowing your calf to come into closer contact with the horse. Just notice this, and later on you will see how each position applies in your riding. For this exercise, find the place between in and out where you can lift your toe the highest without lifting or turning out your knee or shin. You have now found the fixed leg.

Finding the fixed leg position. Notice that my knee and thigh are not drawn up at all. Except for the bend at the knee, my whole leg is completely relaxed.

The fixed leg. Compare this position and the one in the previous picture. The toe is lifted and turned out a little, so the ankle is flexed, but the rest of the leg is unchanged.

4. Return to loose leg by dropping your toe and swinging your foot forward to straighten the knee. Do a leg shakeout to be sure you have released all the tension.

5. Repeat steps 1 through 3 with your other leg, then with both legs, until you can switch back and forth between fixed and loose leg quickly and easily. Then try it with the horse at the walk.

Despite what you might have learned before, the fixed leg is not a particularly tiring or tense position. When you fix your leg correctly, most of the muscles you use are either on the top or on the outside of your leg, so there is little tension in your inner thigh. You should practice the fixed leg at the walk until you are very comfortable and relaxed before starting work with the stirrups, which you will find in the next chapter.

12

Solving the Stirrup Problem
The Seven Seats, Part One: Full Seat

Many years ago I had a friend, a good deal older than me, who also ran a riding program and for whom I had the greatest admiration. She was very kind and patient with me in my struggles to become a better teacher, especially in dealing with the parents of my pupils, also a good deal older. Since we usually saw each other at shows where only our pupils were riding, I had never actually seen her on a horse.

When I finally did, after some seven or eight years, I was appalled. Though an excellent instructor, my friend had rigid ankles and feet, something she would never have permitted in one of her students. She appeared in constant danger of losing both her stirrups and her balance. In all her years of riding, she had never learned the basic skill of resting her weight on the stirrups! Even at that time I knew the importance of a relaxed leg in riding with stirrups. Since then, my acquaintance with Centered Riding, which leads effortlessly to a naturally correct posture, has given me the necessary tools to teach any rider to use her stirrups effectively.

Finally, we're ready to start working with stirrups. Most instructors divide saddle and stirrup work into two basic seats: full seat (sitting), also called three-point; and half seat (standing in the stirrups), also called two-point, forward or jumping position. I have found that, in terms both of teaching and usage, position can be better divided into seven seats, of which three are sitting and four are standing. Some of these are only used for special situations, but they all serve a useful purpose.

The standing positions will be described in the next chapter. The three full seat positions, described in this chapter, are:

1. Full seat, legs in ∩ ("n") position

2. Full seat, legs in Λ ("A") position

3. Full seat forward

TWO LEG PLACEMENTS

Just now I referred to two different leg positions, ∩ position and Λ position. Your leg and foot have to be in a different position when you want to sit than they are when you want to stand in the stirrups. Let's discuss this in detail.

Your goal when you ride in two-point position, which is when your weight is up in your stirrups, is *maximum ankle and knee flexion to absorb the horse's movement*. On the other hand, what you want when you are doing sitting work is *maximum softness and openness in the buttocks and thighs* to enable you to sit and allow your lower leg to lie close to the horse's side for communication.

Your ankle is designed so that as you walk, when you first put your foot down your weight is on the outside of the foot, which tends to lock your ankle so that it doesn't collapse as your weight comes over your vertical leg. This also gives your muscles a little rest. Then, as your leg goes behind you, your weight shifts to the inside to allow your ankle to flex. As your weight swings forward, your foot comes off the ground and you start again. The knee and the ankle work together so that locking your ankle also locks your knee. Thus you can see that if you want your ankle and knee to be locked, your weight must be on the outside of your foot, while if you want them to flex, your weight should be on the inside.

This is one of those things your body finds confusing about riding. When you are in half seat, you are standing up but not walking. Your body thinks that to make it easy to stand still for long periods without tiring, the ankle and knee should be locked, so it wants to put weight on the outside of the foot. Next time you're in a group of people who are standing around talking, take a look at how they are standing. Some people actually stand so far to the outside of their feet that the inner edges are off the ground! The shape of the horse tends to encourage this as well. And then, of course, if you have been told to turn your toes in to keep your knees from sticking out, or told to keep your lower leg against the horse, you are faced with an impossible situation. You have locked your joints, which makes you more rigid rather than increasing your shock absorption, which is what you intended when you stood up on your irons.

Here is some groundwork to give you a clearer understanding of how your foot and ankle position relate to your whole leg position.

1. With your upper body vertical, stand with your feet pointing almost straight ahead and shoulder width apart, with your knees straight but not locked. Your weight will probably be slightly on the outside edges of your feet. Roll back and forth between the outside and inside edges of your feet to feel the difference.

2. Keeping your body upright and your weight on the outside edges of your feet, gradually bend your knees as far as they will comfortably go. Notice that to keep your center over your feet, your ankles have to bend as well. Notice also that you can't bend very far without feeling your ankles start to lock up.

3. Now, without changing anything else, roll your weight over to the inside edges of your feet. What a difference! Everything suddenly is much more flexible. Keeping your feet on the ground, try bouncing with your weight in each place and see how much springier you are with your weight on the inside edges. You can see that this is how you want your feet to be when you're working at the faster, bouncier gaits.

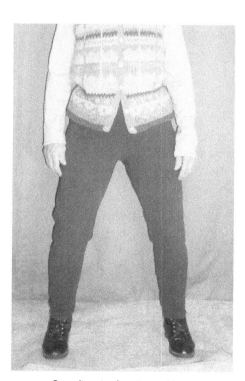

Standing in the ∩ position.

Standing in the Λ position. Notice the
difference in the knee and ankle flexion
between this photo and the preceding one.

But, you might say, why wouldn't I just want my feet to be like that all the time? Let's look at what happens to your leg bones when you shift your weight in and out.

1. Stand again in the position you took in step 1 above, with your weight on the outsides of your feet. Now look down at your legs. Notice that your shinbone is almost vertical while your thighs angle in gradually from the knee to the hip. This is what I call the "n" position, which will hereafter be designated in the text as the ∩ position. This is the leg position that allows you to sit softly and flexibly and use your lower leg aid freely without tension.

2. Roll your weight to the insides of your feet. What happened? Now your thighs are vertical and your shins angle outward from your knee to your feet. This is what I call the "A" or inverted V position, which will hereafter be designated in the text as the Λ position. Besides giving you greater flexibility, it also brings your knees in close to the saddle without gripping, so they stay tucked in behind the knee rolls. *Very* useful in case of sudden stops!

However, something else happens when you roll your weight to the insides of your feet while you're on the horse. When you roll your weight in on the ground, your thighs come closer together by several inches. But now there is going to be a horse's body in the way! This will keep your thighs apart, and therefore (gasp!) will move your lower leg away from your horse. Sacrilege! But that's the only way to retain all that nice flexibility. We'll go into this in more depth when we start talking about the leg aids (Chapter 16), but for now let me say that it is easier for the horse to go forward if your body is flexible and not interfering than if it is rigid. Also, most people's inner leg muscles are somewhat shortened. As these muscles soften and lengthen, they allow the lower leg to fall into a position from which you can use the leg aids quite adequately.

But if you are doing work that requires very active use of the leg, you really need to have it in the ∩ position. Also the ∩ position, as you have already discovered, is the only one in which you can really sit the trot, and later the canter. Therefore, there will be times when you need each leg position to ride effectively.

Many people have trouble keeping their knees from turning out at an angle, causing the backs of their thighs and calves to grip and losing the braking effect of the knee against the knee roll. Hopefully, you have worked out a

Saved by the knee rolls! Letting the reins run would have helped, too.

lot of this tension in your buttocks and thighs already, but trying to balance in the stirrups often brings it back. If it does, try this exercise.

1. Stand on the ground with your legs in Λ position. Shift your weight so you are standing mostly on your left foot (which will return to more of a ∩ position), but with the inside edge of your right foot still on the ground.

2. Keeping the front of your right foot where it is, slide your right heel out a few inches. Stay on the inside edge of the foot and don't roll it flat as you slide. If you ski, think of doing a stem turn or a snowplow.

3. Slide your heel to the inside of the original position, then slide it in and out while watching your kneecap. You will see that you can control the position of your kneecap by moving your heel. What you are actually doing is rotating your thigh bone at the hip joint which, in turn, moves your knee around.

4. Practice with both feet until you can place your knees where you want them. Notice that the more you turn your kneecap in, the further out your feet will go relative to the knee. For some people this means riding with their feet quite far out for a while until their bodies adjust.

I'm using my foot position to rotate my knee inward without gripping. My left hand is on the top of my thigh bone, my right fingers point toward my hip joint.

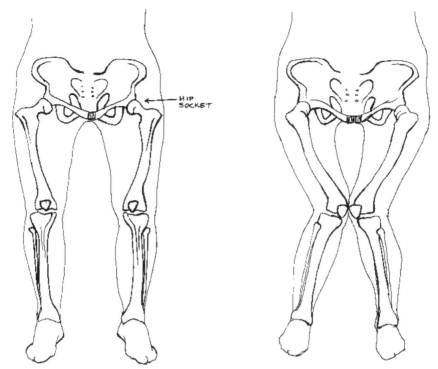

Notice how the rotation of the thigh bone turns the knee in. The muscles across your buttocks, which attach to the top of the thigh bone, need to be relaxed to allow it to turn.

PREPARING FOR THE STIRRUPS

Many riders find it difficult to relax their foot in the stirrup, which means grounding is impossible. Part of the trick is in having the stirrup in the right place. There is one particular spot on your foot that is intended to be the center of weight bearing. In martial arts this point is known as the bubbling spring. Riding with your stirrup under the bubbling spring will result in a foot and ankle that are truly relaxed and flexible, and will give you the feeling of strength and security in the stirrups.

1. Begin by sitting down in a chair with your shoes off. Bend over and slide your fingers under the inside of one foot just behind the ball. On a line between your big and second toes just back (toward the heel) of the ball of the foot is the bubbling spring point. There's a little hollow there and it feels a bit more sensitive than the surrounding area. Massage it with your fingers so you know exactly where it is.

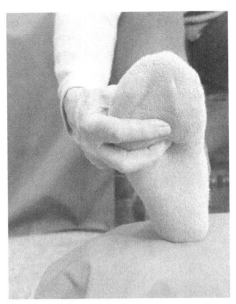

My middle finger shows the location of the
bubbling spring point.

2. Now stand up, preferably on a carpet or on grass, think about the location of that point and try to feel how it connects with the ground. If you do a teeter-totter (see page 26), you will find that when the bubbling spring point comes off the ground, that's when you lose your balance.

3. Stand with your feet shoulder width apart. Bend your knees a bit. Have your weight evenly balanced on the bubbling springs of both feet.

4. Straighten one knee. Your center will move to the opposite side, but you can keep the pressure on your feet about the same. Bend the knee again and let your center come back into the middle.

5. Try this on both sides until you get the feeling of how you can use the ground and your leg to move your center laterally without moving your weight very much or losing your connection to the ground on either foot.

6. Now stand on tiptoe. Your weight has to roll to the outside of your foot and your heels are now up, but notice how much effort and tension it takes to keep them there! All you have to do is release the tension in your buttocks and thighs, roll to the inside of your foot and *your heels will come down by themselves*.

Tidbits & Supplements

Many riders have been taught to place the stirrups close to the toes. The theory behind this is that your foot will come out easily if it needs to, plus it really keeps your toes up. However, with the stirrup in this position your foot will also come out easily when you *don't* want it to, plus having the stirrup in front of the joint between your toes and your foot creates a lot of tension. This makes your ankle stiff, so while your toes may be up, your heels won't be down.

---

7. Finally, sit down again in a straight chair with your feet flat on the ground and your lower leg vertical. Use your hand under one thigh to pick the leg up a couple of inches, then drop it. Feel how the whole leg drops solidly to the ground and rests there heavily and firmly. Try it with each leg. Now pick up your leg without using your hand and drop it again. It won't fall quite as heavily, especially in the heel area, because it isn't easy to release the muscle

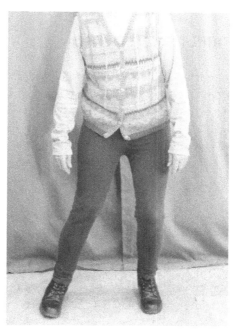

Using your leg to shift your center.
Straightening the right leg moves
your center to the left.

Tidbits & Supplements

I have often had a new student—especially one who has ridden quite a lot—say to me, "I have to ride with my stirrups uneven, because one leg is longer than the other." I say to her, "Gee, I didn't notice you limping!" Yes, most people do have one leg longer than the other, but the difference is tiny. Only if the difference is great enough to warrant an orthopedic shoe, or if there is, for example, an ankle injury that prevents the leg from functioning normally, do the stirrups need to be adjusted to compensate. The rest of the time, the uneven stirrups are the result of the rider feeling more comfortable with more weight on one leg than the other, and adjusting her stirrups accordingly. It is important to correct this, because sitting unevenly on the horse makes *him* uneven, which adversely affects all his movement and makes him more difficult to ride.

---

tension quickly. See if you can get it to drop as heavily as before. Practice a few times, sometimes using your hand and sometimes not, to see if you can get the same feeling either way.

TRYING THE STIRRUPS: ∩ POSITION

Now that you feel comfortable and deep in the saddle with either a loose leg or a fixed leg, and you have an idea of how you want your legs and feet to feel, you're finally ready to try the stirrups. Be sure you have adjusted your stirrups to be even. Begin by placing your legs in fixed leg position, but don't tip your toe out. Be careful not to lift your knee up at all. Your foot should be hanging not more than an inch below the stirrup, so adjust your stirrups if necessary. Count the holes so you don't lose the even adjustment you made on the ground.

If you have a ground person helping you, ask her to grasp your leg by the calf and lift your knee up a few inches and then drop it again. Try to make your leg absolutely dead weight so that you don't help her at all to lift the leg. If you don't have a ground person, try to lift your knee yourself and then let it fall again as you did in the groundwork. Do this a couple of times until you're sure there is no tension holding your leg up.

Why did we do this? There is a very common misconception that you have to push on the stirrups to keep your feet in them. But as you discovered earlier, if you are sitting in a chair with your feet on the floor, you don't have to push on them to make them stay down! Gravity, that is, the weight of your leg, will keep your feet on the floor unless you make a distinct effort to pick them up. The same thing will happen when you sit on the horse, *if you allow it!* That is, if you don't tense your leg muscles your feet won't come up out of the stirrups. Which is one of the reasons you spent all that time working on your centering, since it is mostly lack of centering that causes tension in the legs.

Now have your ground person turn the stirrup so the outside of it is toward the back, then pick up your leg for you and drop it into the stirrup. If she doesn't mind holding the bottom of your foot to lift your leg, you'll feel the effect better. If you're doing it alone, get your toe into the stirrup but not down on the tread, then drop your whole foot onto the tread. Either way, work your foot around until the bubbling spring point is resting on the back edge of the stirrup tread. Next, lift your leg and foot up, keeping your toe in the stirrup as before, and drop it a few more times until it feels very heavy on the stirrup. Your foot should rest fairly evenly across the whole stirrup, but many people have shorter inside leg muscles, so this may not happen right away. Remember that all the weight of your leg except the very top part will be resting on the stirrup, and since your leg is about a fifth of your body weight, it should feel nice and solid. Try to avoid doing anything tricky with your foot or ankle that you might have learned before.

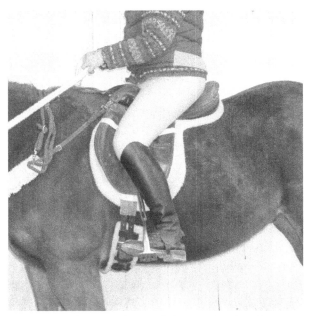

Gravity doing its thing. All the weight of my leg,
from mid-thigh down, is resting on the stirrup.
Thus, my foot is solidly in the stirrup, but my leg—
in ∩ position—is completely relaxed.

Tidbits & Supplements

Some people have a problem with stirrups that can be difficult to solve. For the weight of your leg to rest on the stirrup, the stirrup must be placed in such a way on the saddle that when your leg is in the correct fixed leg position, the stirrup will be in the right place under your foot *when the stirrup leather is hanging vertically.* If, as sometimes happens, the stirrup hangs too far forward, when you rest the weight of your leg on it, the stirrup will swing even farther forward. In many cases I have found this to be the root cause of the rider being unable to find a secure leg position or a comfortable centered half seat.

Don't worry if your heel isn't deep. As long as there is no tension in your leg, your heel (which, unlike your toes, has nothing under it to hold it up) will fall as deeply as your particular conformation allows. Some people's feet stay quite flat, others' heels go down.

Next, get your horse walking around. Think about letting your seat follow the horse and your legs follow your seat. The result should be that you have constant, even pressure on both seatbones and *on both stirrups.* The feeling of "following the stirrups" is very subtle, in the sense that you won't feel the movement the way you do with the following seat, but you should feel there's no way your feet would slide around in the irons. What you are after is the same sort of grounding you found in your seat during the bareback/without stirrups work. However, now you want the grounding to be at least partially into the stirrups. (When you begin half seat, the grounding will be *entirely* into the stirrups.) Using the same electrical plug image I described on page 141, imagine that each bubbling spring point has a plug that will be plugged into the stirrup so that it stays connected and follows the stirrup wherever it goes. Look down frequently and make sure your toe hasn't crept out in front of your knee, which would mean that you were pushing on the stirrup, instead of just letting your weight rest on it.

Everything will feel pretty much the same as when you were riding without stirrups until you come to a corner, but now you have a different and easier way to keep your lateral center during turns. As you start into the corner, add the straightening of your outside leg to move your center to the inside as much as necessary, just as you did on the ground (see the photo on page 221). What you should feel as a result is *even* pressure on both stirrups and both seatbones. You will still have to *open the inside of your upper body to make your center move,* but using your leg against the stirrup gives you a great deal of additional lateral security.

You have to be careful not to let this additional support lead you into sit-ting off to one side and compensating with pressure on that stirrup. Since peo-ple tend to stand or sit with more weight on one leg or seatbone, you have to constantly check yourself to stay even. Any crookedness on your part will affect the horse's overall balance and performance significantly. I never cease to be amazed at how many "control" problems magically disappear when the rider learns to stay centered!

This combination—full seat with legs in ∩ position—is one of the two you will use most of the time. It is used for virtually all sitting work, since it is the position that enables you to sit deep and easily follow the horse's motion. **Because your center is directly above your seatbones, and there-fore slightly behind the horse's center, it is the best position for most train-ing work.** And it is the easiest position from which to use your leg aids, since your weight is mostly on your seatbones and your lower leg is close to the horse's side.

FULL SEAT: Λ POSITION

You have no doubt figured out that up to now, except for the fixed leg work, you have been riding with your legs in ∩ position, both bareback and in the saddle. That's because we have been focusing on sitting work and on getting the leg to release and become long and heavy by itself. This is important not only for sitting but also, as we have seen, to persuade your body to accept the stirrups without tension.

Tidbits & Supplements

Dropping and picking up your stirrups using just your toes, not your hands, is a technique that should be mastered as soon as possible. Always insert your toe from the *outside* toward the horse so that the stirrup leather follows the contour of your calf instead of cutting into it. This means you have to turn your toe well in to hook the stirrup. Then use little wiggly kicks of your toes to turn the stirrup until it is perpen-dicular to the horse's side, *not* to your foot. When it is in the right place, let your weight drop onto the tread with the inside of your foot up against the inside post of the stirrup. Practice dropping and picking up your stirrups frequently until you can do it without thinking about it. You will be glad you did if you ever lose a stirrup when you are in the mid-dle of a bees' nest!

The next step is to put your legs in Λ position. As you found on the ground, you are going to have to do two things: the first is to put weight on the inside of your foot and the second is to move your lower leg away from your horse. They are interdependent, so you are going to do them both at the same time. Having previously said that you do not push on your stirrups when sitting, I am now going to ask you to cheat.

1. Begin by sitting with your feet in the stirrups and your legs in ∩ position. If your feet don't want to rest firmly on the stirrups, take them out and do a shakeout (page 23) and then put them back in. Hip and thigh squeezes (page 149) may also be necessary to release tension in your upper legs.

2. Move your feet around in the stirrups until the inside edges of your feet are resting against the inside post of the stirrups with the bubbling spring on the back edge of the tread.

3. *Without leaning forward,* push down on the *inside* edges of your feet and push your feet directly out to the side until your ankles are flexing easily and your knees are snug against the saddle. Notice that your toes will go out a little more than your heels, but use the heel rotation you learned earlier to keep your knees from rotating outward. With your ankles softer, your heels will also come down. Because your seat is behind the stirrups, when you push on your feet they will tend to move forward. To prevent this, think to bend your knees and *lift* your toes a little (without lifting the bubbling spring off the stirrups,) just as you did to get the fixed leg.

4. Once you have the feeling of the Λ position, you can experiment a little with letting your legs fall in a bit closer to your horse, but don't let them come in so far that your ankles stiffen up or your knees pop out. The closeness of your lower legs will be a function of yours and the horse's conformation and relative size. Some people find it helpful to slide a hand under the back of their thigh and pull the inner thigh muscle back out of the way to allow the leg to lie closer to the horse.

5. Try walking around the ring changing back and forth from ∩ to Λ position. If you have a helper, ask her to lead you in some tight turns. Notice how, especially on the turns, the Λ position really adds to your lateral stability. What you have done is widen and lower your base of support by pressing down and outward with your feet. *So easy and so helpful!*

The position you have found, full seat with legs in Λ position, has several uses, none of them very frequent. The first is as a training exercise to help your body get accustomed to the stirrups. That's what we're using it for right now. The second is to add security to the sitting position. Suppose you are walking along the trail and

Full seat, leg in Λ position.

you see something ahead that might cause your horse to spook and spin. Besides all that other Seven Steps stuff, you would immediately put your legs in Λ position to give you extra lateral stability, while maintaining your full seat to give you longitudinal stability. Another use is if you are sitting on a young horse or a horse who has a mild back problem and want to keep your weight distributed as much as possible over his back without leaning forward. Putting a small part of your weight on your stirrups, which happens when you are pressing them outward, spreads that weight over the tree instead of only under your seatbones.

The last use is when showing in equitation. So many judges are hung up on the concept of heels down that you really have to go the extra mile. Of course, some of them miss the point. Your heel is nothing more than the back of your ankle. As we have seen, when you release the tension in your leg and ankle, your heel will go down as far as your conformation allows. What the judge is *really* looking for, whether he knows it or not, is lack of tension in the leg, which demonstrates itself by the heel falling as far as it can.

FULL SEAT FORWARD

This position is just what it sounds like—sitting down, but leaning forward. It has some important uses, both for training and for everyday riding. It can be done with the legs in either ∩ or Λ position, but it is easier to learn with your legs in ∩ position.

Ground Work

One of the things that confuses many riders is what to do with their back. They are told they have to be flexible to follow the horse's movement, but they are also told to keep their back upright and firm and not allow it to collapse. Even though it sounds contradictory, it is possible to do both.

The growing exercise, which was the very first one you learned, makes your back tall and upright yet still flexible. However, a great many factors tend to make you lose this position, which is why you have to keep repeating it. One of these factors is the tendency in all of us to have stronger frontal muscles, which tend to make the back round. Fear will always add to the tension of those frontal muscles. But another factor, which we tend to overlook, is not knowing how and where to bend when leaning forward for half seat.

All bending and straightening of the upper body should take place in the hip joint. Many instructors use the term "closing the hip angle" to emphasize that idea. However, keeping the rest of your body still while you bend in only one place takes some practice. Since your hip joint is located fairly deep in the pelvic area, thinking about it is an exercise in abstract thought. Here is a method to help you find your hip joint.

1. Stand on one foot with your hand holding on to something for balance.

2. Put your fingertips on the outside of your other hip a few inches below your waist and find the top of your thigh bone, which is about the length of your hand down from your waist. The thigh bone is L-shaped at the top, so your fingers will be on the outer corner of the L. Rotate the leg around from the hip and lift and drop the knee, feeling how the bone moves.

3. Slide your fingers inward to the crease between your leg and torso. Continue to move your leg around to get a feeling for where the joint is.

4. Sit in a straight chair with your fingers over the hip joint. Feel your seatbones on the chair. Your hip joints are almost directly above your seatbones. Move your leg around and try to visualize the joint in your mind (see the pictures on pages 228 and 229).

Now that you know more or less where your hip joint is, the next thing to do is figure out how to use it to bend forward, instead of bending your back.

1. Stand with your back to the wall and your heels about six inches (15 cm) away. You should be standing straight and tall but not stiff. Growing must be kept in mind throughout this exercise.

2. Without bending your legs, reach back with your butt and touch the wall. To do that, you have to bend your hip joints, and when you do, your upper body comes forward. You bend over, but you don't *bend* anything in the sense of curving it, you just close your hip angles. Touch the wall and straighten up a few times until you get the feeling.

3. Now let's see what it feels like when you bend your back instead of your hips. To feel it, place one hand palm in with your thumb at the bottom of your breastbone and the other hand palm out on the back of your waist. Deliberately round and arch your back so you can feel the movement in your hands. Then keep your back still, and open and close your hip joints to feel the difference.

4. Finally, sit in a straight chair with your hands positioned as in step 3 and bend and straighten from your hips. Look for the slightest tendency in your back to round or arch. If need be, start with a very small movement and gradually increase it so that you bend in the hip as far as you can without bending anywhere in your back, but also without stiffening the back.

Standing close to the wall with everything straight.

I bend only at the hip to touch the wall.

Notice that you tend to *round* your back when you lean forward, and *arch* it when you lean back. Neither of these things should happen. Your back should stay the same no matter what you do with your hip joints

This may seem terminally boring to those of you who are never going to show in equitation, but *everything* you do regarding position has an important purpose. With your back, allowing it to round and arch as your upper body angle changes will affect your balance and also break the connection that runs from your feet or seat up through your body, down through the reins, through the horse's body and into his feet. This is one of the principal connections through which you communicate with the horse.

On the Horse

1. Begin by sitting in full seat with your legs in ∩ position and your feet in the stirrups. Grow, then place your hands on your front and back as in step 3 in the previous exercise.

2. Keeping your eyes level, close and open your hip angle so that your upper body swings forward and back into position. Don't go so far forward that you create a lot of tension in your thigh, or your legs go behind you. You should feel the weight mostly on the front of your seatbones, and your buttock muscles should stay soft.

3. When you feel your hip joints are working smoothly (imagine them coated with silicone spray), place your hands on the pommel or on the horse's withers and find a comfortable closed angle. Your hands should be pressing very lightly on the horse. If they are pressing heavily, you are leaning too far forward.

4. Now, *without pushing your stirrups forward*, use your hands to slide your seat back a little bit on the saddle. When you lean forward, your center moves forward. Pushing your seat back will move your center back as well. Now you can find a place where you are leaning a little forward but still feel balanced with no pressure on your hands at all.

This position, full seat forward, is the way you learn how to use your back and hip joints to control your upper body angle, but it has an essential everyday use as well. Step 4 of the exercise you just did is the bottom of the posting trot, so we will return to it when we start work on posting. Step 3 is occasionally used when your horse is stepping over something, so that you don't get thrown back if he hops it instead. It is also the position you use when asking the horse to back.

Full seat forward. My face should be closer to the vertical,
but my balance is good, so my arms and legs are relaxed.

You will want to work on these first three seats—full seat with legs in ∩ position, full seat with legs in Λ position, and full seat forward—for a while. Your
goal is to have the two leg positions and the closing and opening of your hip
angle fairly clear in your mind and in your body. Once you are comfortable with
them, you'll be ready to go on to the other four seats.

13

Solving the Balance Problem

The Seven Seats, Part Two: Half Seat

Johanna, who has ridden most of her life, took some lessons with me for a short time, while she was in her 20s. As her job responsibilities increased, the drive to my farm proved too long and time-consuming, so she moved to a stable closer to home. Some years later she called me and said she would like to come back and ride with me again. She said she was taking jumping lessons, and every week she fell off! Although she is an exceptionally brave person, she found, not surprisingly, that she was beginning to lose her nerve. She knew I would be willing to give her the time it takes to recover her confidence.

We spent a few weeks reviewing on a bareback pad, then she went into a saddle. As I had suspected, her ability to balance in half seat—standing in her stirrups—was severely limited. As a result, when she tried to jump, the least hesitation from her horse would send her flying. Her lack of balance also contributed to the horse's insecurity, causing him to approach the fence with very little confidence. We worked on this for some time, and her jumping improved dramatically. A year or so later she was hunter pacing and had to ride a rather inexperienced horse over some very large fences, which she did with great success—and also delight in her recovered skills.

Once your body has "accepted" the stirrups in full seat, it's time to get to the hard stuff. Standing in the stirrups, or half seat, is an essential skill for any rider who plans to do fast work in any gait but a four-beat, such as the rack or tolt. It is used for galloping, jumping and hills, and is an integral part of posting. When you lift your weight off the horse's back, the horse is allowed and encouraged to use his back more freely, and your body can absorb far more bounce than it can when you are sitting.

Merely standing up in the stirrups is not enough. You have to be able to *ground* and *balance* your body so that your position is secure at all gaits, and so that you do not interfere with the horse. It is mastering this combined ability to stay *still* relative to the horse while standing up in the stirrups that defeats many riders. Each of the steps described in this chapter must be practiced at length until you feel very secure and comfortable. You will be glad you did when your horse takes a rough jump or stops unexpectedly!

Even though I use the term "half seat" in the title of this chapter, there is also an in-between position that is included in the standing work. It is called the three-quarter seat.

Then there are three half seats (to finally bring us up to seven):

1. Half seat open position

2. Half seat closed position

3. Half seat balanced

When you have mastered all these seats, which won't take as long as it might seem, you will feel truly secure standing in the stirrups.

THREE-QUARTER SEAT

Three-quarter seat, as the name implies, is halfway between full seat and half seat. We use it as preparation for learning the half seat, but it is also used any time you want to get your weight off the horse's back a little bit.

Ground Work

Back in the days when gentlemen stood up when a lady entered the room, most men developed a little trick that they used when they were seated at a table and the ladies were coming in one or two at a time. Rather than going through the whole routine of pushing his chair back and standing all the way up, probably dropping his napkin in the process, the man would simply raise himself from his chair an inch or so, giving the lady a chance to say, "Oh please, don't get up!" Thus the formalities were recognized with a minimum of effort and everybody was happy.

Three-quarter seat is very much like that polite gesture, so let's talk about what your body does when you stand up. Unless you're sitting on a very special kind of stool, when you sit your center is over your seat but not over your feet, which are out in front of you. As you probably understand by now, if you don't want to fall down, your center has to be over your base. When you're sitting, that's your seat, but when you're standing, your base is your feet. Therefore, in order to stand, you have to move your center from over your seat to over your feet, which means you have to lean forward.

Our perception of standing up and sitting down is that we *lean forward* when we stand up and *lean back* when we sit down. When you see beginners posting awkwardly, that's what they are trying to do—and it looks very awkward indeed. Let's explore this concept a little further.

For the ground exercise, all you need is a chair or stool, but it should be quite high so that you can sit on the front edge with your feet flat on the ground without having your knees too sharply bent. An adjustable office chair is a good option, but don't let the boss catch you! You can also do this exercise on a regular chair, but it's not as easy.

1. Sit on the front edge of the chair, with your seatbones resting on it and your feet as far back underneath you as you can get and still keep your heels on the ground.

2. Close your hip angle to lean forward as you did for full seat forward (page 238), but this time place both hands behind you on your back, palm out, one at your waist and one higher up on your ribs. Your hands will be able to feel if you are bending your spine. Open and close your hip angle several times, checking to be sure your back doesn't flex anywhere.

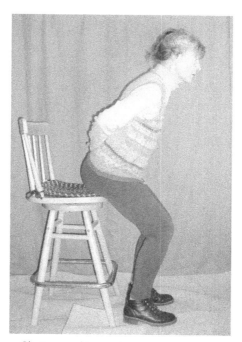

Closing my hip angle moves my center
forward until it's over my feet.

3. Keeping your hands on your back, very slowly get ready to stand up but don't actually take your seat off the chair. You will find you have to lean quite far forward—enough that your center, which is more or less behind your navel, is over your feet. Try to find the place where your center is exactly over your feet so you won't have to bend over any more than that to lift your seatbones up.

4. Now lift your seatbones off the chair just the tiniest bit, only enough so they're not pressing on the chair seat. Did you have to lean even farther forward before you could get up? Let yourself back down and try again. You're trying to learn the feeling of getting your center over your base, in this case your feet.

Once you have the feeling of leaning forward—that is, closing your hip joint—to get your center over your base in order to stand up, then you need to observe what happens to your hip joint as you go from sitting to standing.

1. Sit down again and go through steps 1 through 3 of the previous exercise.

2. Now stand up very slowly. Think about keeping the pressure on your heels and toes steady—don't rock forward or back. As your legs straighten, notice what happens to your hips and shoulders. As your hips come up they also come forward, so your shoulders, to compensate, come back. Your hip joints *open* as you stand.

3. Sit down and stand up again, but this time *don't* allow your shoulders to come back as your legs straighten. Guess what? If you don't bring your shoulders back when your hips come forward, you fall on your face! Well, probably not. You probably took a step forward to bring your base under your center, which was too far forward.

So, when you go up, your shoulders come back; that is to say, **when you stand up, you lean back** from the hip, not forward. Now let's look at sitting down.

1. Stand up in front of your chair with your feet in the same relative position they were in when you were sitting. The backs of your legs will probably be just touching the chair seat. Put your hands on your back.

2. Start to sit down very slowly. Imagine that you have severe sunburn on your bottom, so you want to sit down very gently! To do that, you have to keep your center over your feet, and to do that, you're going to have to lean *forward*. Your hip joints *close* as you sit.

3. Using a soft, heavy chair, try sitting down without leaning forward. Ka-thump! Aren't you glad that wasn't your horse's back?

Conclusion: **When you sit down, you lean forward** from the hip, not back. The misconception about when you lean forward and when you lean back arises because, as you found out, as you *prepare* to stand you do have to lean forward to get your center over your feet, and once you are sitting down and prepared to *stay* there you lean back to put your center over your seatbones.

Now we need to start thinking a bit more about balance. Sit in your chair, as near the front as you can, with your feet flat on the ground.

1. Keeping your back flat, bend forward from the hips until your center is over your feet. Let your arms dangle straight down from your shoulders.

2. Push on your feet to lift your seatbones up off the chair just enough so there is no weight on them. The seat of your pants will still be touching the chair, but your bones will be up. You should not have had to lean forward any farther to lift your seatbones. Let yourself back down on the chair again *without leaning back*.

3. Repeat step 2, but now think about keeping the pressure even on your feet, both relative to one another and over the whole length of the foot; that is, don't allow your weight to shift from side to side or more to the front or back of your foot as you lift and let down. You will find that if you lean too far forward, your heel pressure gets light; not far enough forward, and your toes get light.

4. Now become conscious of your arms and shoulders. They should be free of tension throughout the exercise and should hang loose and free. If you are leaning too far forward, your arms will come back and down; too far back, and they will come forward and up.

5. Repeat the whole exercise until you have it fairly correct. You will find this exercise is hard on your legs, but it is much less so in the saddle.

The purpose of this exercise is to help you find and maintain your longitudinal balance on your feet, which is the most difficult aspect of standing in the stirrups. The stirrups are hung so that they swing forward and back easily—a quality that is necessary for hills and jumping but very disconcerting to the novice trying to learn to stand up in them. You adjust your longitudinal balance by leaning more or less forward, which in turn moves your center. The pressure on your feet and the position and degree of relaxation of your arms tell you where your center is. When you are in the correct position, you will have even pressure on your feet and completely relaxed arms, and the stirrups will stay still.

***

Tidbits & Supplements

Here are two exercises to help you get used to standing on something less stable than the floor. Find a flight of stairs with a railing to hold on to. Holding the rail, stand on a step with your feet close together and the bubbling spring point on the edge of the step so that your heel is hanging off in space. Let your knees bend a little and play with the first five of the Seven Steps until your leg muscles relax and allow your heel to drop. Try letting go of the rail. It is surprisingly hard at first to stay relaxed without holding on—which gives you some idea of how hard your body finds it to cope with stirrups.

The next piece of equipment you need is a round or octagonal wooden jump pole lying on the ground and either another person or, again, something to balance with. A second jump pole set in front of you on standards at about elbow height works well. Take the same position on the ground pole that you took on the step and again work on relaxing your legs until your heels will drop. The unsteadiness of the pole mimics the stirrup fairly well and helps you learn how to find the technique.

A variation on this is to have another person face you and hold your hands, or even have the other person balancing on a pole herself as you hold hands and both try to stay balanced.

***

On the Horse

You want your stirrups shorter than before; by one or two holes, or possibly more. The neck strap should be adjusted so it lies just in front of the withers. You may want to change these adjustments later to find what works best for you.

1. After mounting, spend a little time without stirrups getting yourself fully comfortable and relaxed. Then pick up your stirrups and walk around with your legs first in ∩ position, then in Λ position until your feet are resting firmly on the stirrups.

2. Now, with your horse standing still and your legs in ∩ position, close your hip angle until you are in full seat forward. Place your hands on the neck strap with your elbows hanging just below or a little in front of your shoulder.

3. *Without lifting yourself off the saddle*, put your legs in Λ position, then adjust your hip angle if necessary until you feel you *could* get up. Straighten up again and allow your legs to fall back into ∩ position. Repeat this several times until it comes together for you.

4. Now you are ready for the big move upward! Except that it is going to be a very *small* move at first. *Pulling* lightly on the neck strap, for balance only, from the position you practiced in step 3, very slowly lift your weight off your seatbones. The seat of your pants should remain in contact with the saddle, but there will be no pressure on your seatbones. If you had to change your hip angle very much to get up, you need to practice step 3 a few more times with the angle that works for you. When you are up, your hip angle should be such that you are *pulling* very lightly on the neck strap.

5. Without changing anything else, let your seatbones down on the saddle, rest and lift up again. It is very important *not* to get into the habit of straightening up as soon as you sit. *Always* let your weight completely down onto your seat *while still leaning forward.* Then, if you wish to return to full seat, bring your shoulders back as a separate step.

Three-quarter seat.

6. It is also important to learn to release the tension in your buttock muscles when you sit. Just as your seatbones begin to press against the horse, relax your lower back and buttocks. Think about letting your lower back get a little round and your buttocks and thighs get a little wide. You should feel yourself sink into the horse instead of being perched on top of him.

7. Now start to be conscious of what is going on in your feet and back. The stirrup leathers should stay vertical at all times; that is, the stirrups should not move forward or back *at all*, though they will move out, away from the horse's sides. You should feel most of the pressure on the inside edge of your foot, and your heels should have dropped down a little in response to the extra weight over your foot.

If you can't keep the stirrups from moving forward or back, try lifting up even more slowly, and not lifting up completely until you figure out how to adjust your center forward or back to keep your stirrups still. Generally, to move your center back, push your hips back first, then adjust your shoulders. To move your center forward, lean your shoulders forward, then adjust your hips.

To understand this whole concept a little better, let's talk about how your stirrups move in relation to pressure. Put simply, if the pressure comes from behind, the stirrups will move forward; if the pressure comes from in front, the stirrups will move back. (The stirrups will also move out in response to pressure on the inner side, but will not move in very much because the horse and saddle are in the way.) What this means to you is that if your center is behind the stirrups, they will go out in front of you, putting your center even farther behind them; if your center is too far forward, the stirrups will go behind you, putting your center even farther forward. If your center is moving forward and back as the horse moves, your stirrups—and your feet—will swing back and forth as well. If your stirrups are swinging back and forth, you have an unstable base, making it almost impossible for you or the horse to maintain balance and grounding.

Unlike your seat, which is placed behind the horse's center (thus allowing a margin for error), the stirrups on most saddles hang almost directly in line with the horse's center, so when your center is over your stirrups, falling forward even a little puts the horse off balance. For this reason you practice three-quarter seat with your center just a tiny bit back of your bubbling spring point, which you compensate for with the tiny pull on the neck strap.

When you feel fairly comfortable finding and maintaining three-quarter seat at the standstill, practice at the walk both on the straight and on turns. This is a good time for quiet trail ride practice, since you need to spend quite a lot of time with three-quarter seat at the walk before going on. (Don't try it except on fairly level ground.) You have to work on the three-quarter seat until your body has learned the knack of balancing itself over the stirrups in the same way that you learned to walk, to ride a bicycle or to skate or ski.

> ## Tidbits & Supplements
>
> Three-quarter seat has an everyday use for everyone. Many people have the habit, when they first get on a horse, of shoving down against the stirrups with their legs while sitting down, with the idea of getting their heels down and their legs in a good position. Unfortunately, this doesn't work at all. Because you have to use muscles to do this, you create tension, and because of the position of the stirrups, most people just push their feet out in front of them. Instead, when you mount, develop the habit of immediately going through the first five of the Seven Steps to get your whole body correct, long and soft, then taking up the three-quarter seat for a few seconds. Since this puts your center over your base (the stirrups) and you are using gravity to drop down into your stirrups, you will get the leg position you want without effort. You can add this as an extra step any time you lose your position.

Things to look for to tell you when you have it right:

• It feels easy; your legs may tire, but keeping the position is not an effort.

• Light, *even* pull on the neck strap, not pulling harder and letting go, or falling onto your hands on the horse's neck. The pull on the neck strap should ground you, not make you tense. You feel the pressure on the neck strap in your feet.

• No pressure on the front of your knees (which would mean you were staying up by leaning against the saddle with your legs, not balancing).

• Toes approximately on a vertical line with your knees, not out in front of them.

• Soft relaxed ankles and feet, heels comfortably down, feet rest against the inside corner of the stirrup.

• Kneecaps pointing almost straight ahead (pointing out would mean you were tight in your buttocks and the backs of your thighs).

• Following the motion of the horse easily, indicating "slippery" hip joints.

If you continue to have difficulty, experiment with different stirrup and neck strap lengths.

HALF SEAT: OPEN POSITION

When you have learned to ride successfully in three-quarter seat at the walk, you are ready for the real world. Half seat is what you use any time the gait is too springy to sit comfortably, or when you want to give the horse extra freedom through his back. By placing your weight in your stirrups, it is transferred directly into the tree of the saddle and distributed over the whole area of contact instead of just on top of the horse's back. This is roughly the equivalent of you carrying something in a backpack instead of around your waist.

There are three variations of half seat, two of which—the open and closed positions—put your weight just a little behind the horse's center, while the third or balanced half seat puts your center over the horse's. As I mentioned earlier, when your center is directly over the horse's, there is no margin for error, so we use the open and closed positions when either horse or rider is learning. You would also use them any time you are in a situation where you might get thrown forward, since it gives you a little time to save yourself before you get the horse into trouble as well.

Half seat is not only used for jumping. It is also the up part of the posting trot, which, except for the walk, is the most often used gait. Being able to stay up effortlessly will make an enormous difference to your and your horse's comfort and endurance when posting, which you will learn in the next chapter.

I prefer to start with the open position, but some people do better working on the closed position first. You will probably want to stretch these exercises out over several sessions because they will be quite tiring at first, not to mention confusing if you try to do them all at once.

Ground Work

Refer to the ground work for the three-quarter seat (page 244), with particular attention to the way your upper body and hip joints move when you stand up from a three-quarter or full seat forward position. If you have a full-length mirror available, you may find it helpful to work in front of the mirror. You will also need a straight chair, or if your legs are very long, something like a tack trunk.

1. Place the chair so that you are facing the side of it. Stand with your feet a few inches apart and your toes directly below the edge of the chair seat. Be conscious of your centering and grounding.

2. Now stand on tiptoe, putting your hand on the chair back for balance, if necessary. Notice how you are still centered over your bubbling spring point. All of your leg joints are fully opened. Your arms should hang totally loose from the shoulder sockets.

3. Next you are going to close your leg joints one at a time. Practice each exercise several times. First, close your ankles.

4. Next, staying centered on your feet, allow your knees to bend by dropping them down and forward until they touch the edge of the chair seat. Keep your upper body vertical so your hips drop straight down, not forward or back.

5. Finally, keeping your knees against the chair, close your hip angle. Your buttocks will go back and your upper body will go forward. Your pelvis will rotate so your crotch will be the lowest point instead of your seatbones. The more you close your hip angle, the lower your pelvis will be. Practice with different angles, staying centered on your feet at all times and allowing your arms to hang straight down.

Except that your feet are closer together, this is your basic half seat position. The angle of your upper body will depend on the position of your stirrups relative to the center of the saddle and on the amount of thrust being generated by your horse's motion.

Your base of support when in half seat is a fixed triangle formed by your lower leg, your foot and the stirrup leather. Having your knees resting against a fixed point such as a chair keeps them from bobbing up and down, so the triangle doesn't change as your hip angle changes. It takes some practice to learn to do this without support, since our tendency is to bend and straighten both sides of the knee at once.

On the Horse

Because of the nature of the gaits, half seat is very difficult to do at the walk. Therefore, you will practice it first at a standstill and then go directly into trot work. Since the half seat is for the bouncier gaits, you will be higher up above the horse than you were in three-quarter seat to allow space for more up and down movement in your body. You therefore need to make your neck strap longer and raise your stirrups at least one more hole.

1. Work at three-quarter seat at the walk for a few minutes, which will get both you and the horse warmed up. Then halt someplace where the horse will stay parked and adjust your stirrups and neck strap, if necessary. The neck strap should be quite long for the first exercises.

2. Take up your three-quarter seat again. Now, holding your neck strap, just stand up, all the way, just as you would stand up from a chair onto the floor, so that your legs are straight but not stiff. Your seat will be quite far from the saddle. If you lose your balance, try to use your neck strap to keep from sitting

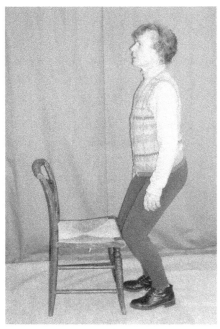

Centering over my feet with my knees bent as they would be when riding.

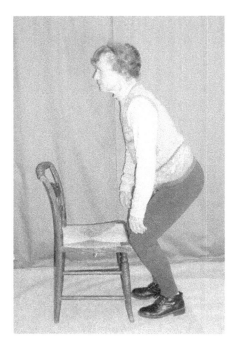

Closing my hip angle while maintaining both my centering and my lower-leg position.

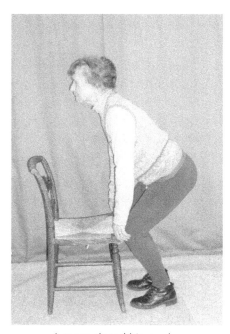

A more closed hip angle.

down hard on the horse's back. This is a very good time to use soft eyes to help your body figure out what's happening. When you are standing, you should be pulling a little on the neck strap. You should feel the only way you could possibly fall would be back, never forward (see the photos on page 257).

3. Most people have a bit of trouble standing all the way up at first, so don't worry about it. Sit down and stand up several times. Usually your feet tense up, so try wiggling your toes a little and imagine you have roots growing in all directions out of your bubbling spring points.

One of the problems riders have with half seat is that the idea of being less connected with the seat of the saddle is quite scary, so their bodies want to curl up and stay close to the horse. This, of course, makes them tense and stiff, which in turn makes their bodies even more concerned. Here is an image that should help. Imagine a carpenter's steel measuring tape. When your body is tense it wants to be a measuring tape and coil itself up into a little circle like a snail in its shell. Even when it is stretched out, it is still trying to coil into a circle again. Now imagine a carpenter's folding ruler. When it folds up, each part of it stays just as long; the parts simply fold up over each other. This is how you want to think of your body—as opening and closing like a folding ruler with each part staying separate and long, not all rolled up.

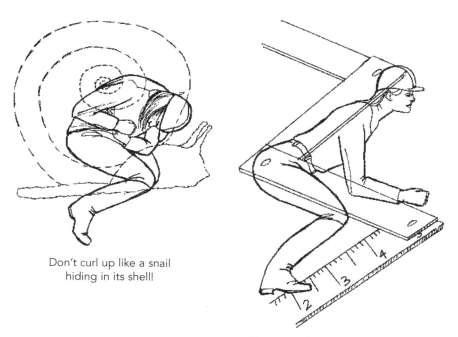

Don't curl up like a snail
hiding in its shell!

Keep your body long, then folded,
not crouched.

1. Start from your three-quarter seat, and this time have a picture of grad-ually unfolding yourself until you are standing up straight, then folding yourself up into three-quarter seat again.

2. When you are standing up straight, you should be resting only on your stirrups with a little pull on the neck strap. You should not be leaning against the front of the saddle with your knees. Continue practicing, going from three-quarter seat to standing up straight, and thinking about unfolding your joints while keeping your feet relaxed.

If you have a lot of trouble falling against your knees whenever you stand, you may be one of those people who in their daily lives are always on the run. As soon as they stand up from their chair they are off, and they get in the habit of letting their center fall forward as soon as they stand, then letting their feet catch up as they walk away. If you are one of these people, try to make a prac-tice during your regular day of standing up and counting at least to one to get centered before you walk away! Isn't your riding worth a few seconds out of your day?

Standing all the way up is what you might call a zero seat. Now you are ready to find the true half seat.

1. First you are going to try to stand on tiptoe. Start from your three-quar-ter seat and straighten all the way up to a tiptoe position. When you do this, your weight will go to the outsides of your feet. Find your balance so you are centered over the stirrups with just a light pull on the neck strap and standing straight up, not bent over. It should be exactly like standing on tiptoe on the ground. (If necessary, dismount and stand on tiptoe on the ground to remind yourself of how it should feel.) Being able to rest the insides of your legs against the saddle helps compensate for the wiggliness of the stirrups, but don't rest against the knee rolls or pommel. You should feel that if the horse disappeared, you could still stand there.

2. Now you are going to fold your joints one at a time, as you did in the ground work, starting with your ankles and moving up. Use your neck strap to help you stay centered over your stirrups as you slowly fold. Since you want to be higher up above the saddle, adjust your stirrups if necessary so that when your knees and ankles are bent, your seatbones are several inches above the seat. Practice folding each joint several times before you go on to the next. When you get to your hip joints, fold just enough so you are maintaining a light pull on the neck strap. You should feel that if you let go of the neck strap, you will sit down, but not hard.

Tiptoes. All the joints are fully opened.

Ankle joints are flexed and the heel drops down.

Now the knee flexes, and drops down and forward.

The hip angle closes to bring me closer to the saddle, but still leaves some room for shock-absorbing movement during the faster gaits. This "open position" keeps me safely behind the horse's center, and the neck strap lightly supports me.

Closed position. My closed hip angle enables me to follow an active forward movement, while my hands on the neck prevent me from accidentally getting ahead of the horse's center.

3. Now practice going from three-quarter seat to tiptoes and back into the open half seat as one slow, smooth motion without curling up. Remember that all you are trying to do is to get far enough above the saddle so that it doesn't hit you at the trot, and with your weight far enough back so that you don't feel you could tip forward easily. This is your half seat open position.

When you think you have found the right spot, try going directly from three-quarter seat to half seat; that is, just lift yourself up a little higher and straighter. Check yourself by going from half seat to tiptoes and back to be sure you stayed long, not curled up. As with the three-quarter seat, the half seat should feel easy although slightly tiring.

Trotting in Open Half Seat

The next step will be the trot. If, by any chance, you have access to a trampoline, especially one of the little ones, this exercise that I learned in Centered Riding is a great introduction.

1. Stand on the trampoline with your feet a few inches apart and your knees and hips unlocked. Grow and shake out to make yourself tall and loose.

2. *Without lifting your feet,* begin to walk in place. Your ankles, knees and hips will move, and your arms should swing a little as well. Walk until you are moving freely. Be careful not to sway from side to side.

3. Now increase pace until you are jogging in place. Again, practice until you are moving easily, but *keep your feet down so you stay grounded on the trampoline.*

4. When you are ready to stop, slow down gradually, *with* the movement of the trampoline, so that you stop together. If you just stop, you will feel an irregular jarring movement because the trampoline kept going. The same thing will happen to you on the horse, which is hard on both of you.

You can do the first three steps without a trampoline to get the feeling of only moving from the ankles upward, but it isn't quite as effective.

Trotting on even a smooth-gaited horse is different from "trotting" on the ground because the horse is moving forward and, because he has legs rather than wheels, the forward progression isn't absolutely smooth. When you first begin to trot, you may find it pretty unbalancing and your tendency may be to hang on pretty hard with the neck strap to stay up. Unfortunately, this tends to stiffen you up and make you even less balanced. This next exercise will teach you how to pull without tensing, something you will also be applying to rein use later on. You can try this on the trampoline or you can skip the ground exercise and try it directly on the horse if you like.

1. On the ground, put a rope around a heavy chair leg that won't move if you pull on it a bit. You can also stand facing the edge of an open door with one hand on each doorknob.

2. With your feet a few inches apart, take up a half-seat position with your knees and ankles bent and your upper body inclined slightly forward. Be centered over your feet. Hold the rope or the doorknobs so that your elbows hang just a little in front of your ribs and close to them without squeezing.

3. Begin gradually pulling on the rope or doorknobs. As you do, think about the balance over your feet and don't let yourself be pulled more forward, but don't try to compensate by leaning back and straightening your arms. Your body angles and centering should stay exactly the same, no matter how much you pull.

4. Slowly increase the pressure on the rope, and now start looking for tension within your body. As you pull, you have to oppose that pull with your body, but the trick is to distribute the pressure throughout your body evenly,

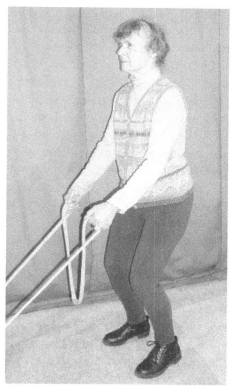

Learning to ground against the pull on
the neck strap in open position,
without getting tense.

not stuck in your shoulders or back. Don't let your toes curl up, which would stiffen your ankle. Instead, let your toes spread out. What you should feel is that as you pull harder, your feet press more heavily into the ground with no tension to speak of in between. You should feel *more* grounded, not less.

5. You will find that if you pull too hard, you will become tense no matter how you try to release the tension. On the ground you can just let go with your arms a bit, but if you are off balance on the horse, your arms won't want to let go. Instead, if you're pulling too hard, just close your hip angle and lean forward a little, which will move your center forward. If you start to tip forward, push your butt back first, then straighten up. Experiment with different hip angles and pulls to see how they affect your center and your grounding.

6. Try walking and trotting in place, as you did in the previous exercise. Do them with and without the rope to check your flexibility. You can also combine the rope exercise with the trampoline exercise.

The exercise is the same on the horse, except that you will be using the neck strap and you have the additional complication of keeping the stirrups from swinging. Remember, your goal is to be centered, grounded, and flexible.

You might ask, why bother with the neck strap? Why not just fold your arms or leave the reins loose so you can't pull on them? The answer is that if you are unbalanced, your body is going to try to hang on somehow, whether you want it to or not. It will either try to hang on with the legs, or if you can persuade it not to do that, it will tense your arms and shoulders. This last is particularly subtle and particularly difficult to eliminate once the habit is formed. Using the neck strap gives you constant feedback about what is happening to your balance. When it is poor, your pull on the neck strap will be heavy or jerky, and when it is right, the pull will be soft and even—which also happens to be exactly what you want for rein contact!

I find that using the exercise of balancing without holding on is not of much benefit to most people. If they are ready to do so, they don't have to practice it, and if they aren't, it simply creates tension. Of course, once you can do it, it's a lot of fun!

As soon as you feel confident, you can try the trot in half seat. If you have been trail riding, a good place to start is on a straightaway with a gradual uphill slope. If you are following another horse, start your horse trotting first so he doesn't see the other horse start and move off suddenly to catch up. The pace should be quite slow at first, but as soon as you feel a little confidence, let the horse trot on. If he is going more forward without getting fast, the half seat is easier to find. If you are in an arena or field that isn't quite level, avoid going downhill until you start to get the knack.

Adjust your stirrups and neck strap for half seat. Be sure the neck strap is adjusted so that your elbows are hanging a little in front of your shoulders when you are standing holding the strap.

1. Begin as usual, walking without stirrups and going through the Seven Steps. Then pick up your stirrups and walk in full seat A position, reviewing how you use your stirrups to keep yourself centered on turns. Next, ride three-quarter seat for a few minutes, thinking about the Seven Steps again, especially lateral centering and following.

2. Now halt your horse and practice a few times going from three-quarter to half seat and back. Think about staying balanced over your feet so the stirrups don't move at all as you change positions. You should maintain a light, even pull on the neck strap throughout.

3. If you are in the ring, put your horse back on the rail, going around to the left at the walk, and take up three-quarter seat. As you come around the corner into the straightaway, use your voice or stick to ask for a trot. As the

horse picks up the trot, come up into half seat. You may have to lean a little more forward at first to keep from falling back as he starts, but not so much that you get in his way. If the horse's trot is very smooth, you won't have to come up much. If it is bouncy, you will have to come up a bit more, but only enough so the saddle doesn't bump your behind.

4. Remember that the trot is a bouncy gait, and don't try to keep yourself *too* still. You should feel that the (light) pressure on your neck strap and the (firm) pressure on your stirrups is constant, and *everything else is moving and flexing*. The springier the horse's trot, the bouncier you will feel, but that just means you're moving with the horse.

5. As you approach the corner, remember to lift your inside shoulder a little to make room for your center to shift. Also, straighten your outside leg a little to keep you over the horse's center of motion.

6. When you are ready to stop, use the same technique you used on the trampoline. Slowing your own motion and using a voice command is usually enough to get the horse to walk.

7. If you start to feel very awkward, immediately bring the horse back to the walk, or if that is not possible, do an emergency dismount. Remember to kick your feet out of the stirrups first! Then check your basic position and start again.

When you are comfortable with going left hand around, try the other direction.

Some people start right off without problems, others find standing up at the trot very difficult. If you are having a problem, try to figure out what part of your body is tense. Check the following areas especially:

• Curling up or turning in your toes, which makes stiff ankles.

• Locking your hips against the pull on the neck strap, which interferes with your following seat.

• Tensing in the shoulder area against the neck strap, which will lock your hips as well.

• Stirrups or neck strap too short or too long.

• Stirrup feels slippery or uncomfortable; try a stirrup with a wider base, such as an endurance stirrup—your foot will find it easier to relax with the extra support.

• If you are losing it on the corners, practice lateral positioning again at the standstill; remember—it's more than you think!

Half seat open position is used in any situation where you want to be off the horse's back but are in a situation where he might stop. Riding a horse into water for the first time is a good example. And of course, it is *the* exercise for working on your balance in the stirrups. It can also be the up of the posting trot.

HALF SEAT: CLOSED POSITION

Closed position is the other half-seat position that places your center slightly behind the horse's center. It is used for riding up hills, for jumping and for learning to post, and is easier for some people to learn balance in the stirrups. It is not as suitable as open position for a situation where you really expect the horse to stop abruptly, or for a horse who tends to lose his balance easily, or for a horse who carries his head low. It is also not possible to do in many dressage saddles because of the high cantle and straight flap.

Most people think of the closed or jumping position as being a forward position. It is true that your center is an inch or two farther forward than it is in either full seat or open position. But at no time does or should your center get ahead of the *horse's* center.

Ground Work

The main difference between open and closed position is that in open position, you stay back by opening your hip joint so that you are leaning back a little more than you would if you were balanced; while in closed position, you stay back by bracing against the horse's neck with your hands, closing your hip joint, and pushing your hips—and center—back. The only equipment you need for the ground work is your dining room table.

1. Stand about 18 inches (45 cm) away from the table with your feet a few inches apart. Bend your knees until they are directly above your toes.

2. Close your hips until your upper body is at about a 45-degree angle. Watch your knees to make sure they don't move back as you close. Lift your chin as necessary so that your face remains vertical, but try to keep your neck soft (see "Swan Neck" in Chapter 7, page 144).

3. Place the heels of your hands firmly against the edge of the table, then push against the table as though you were pushing a lawn mower. Do not lean down on the table. Instead of letting your arms straighten so that your shoulders

Using your arms to keep your center back
in closed position.

go back, keep your elbows bent and as you push, allow your hips to bend more so that they drop down and back while your shoulders come down and forward.

4. Because you are pushing with your hands on something that is lower than your center, the tendency may be to let the weight come off your feet, especially off the balls since you are also pressing yourself back. Think about staying heavy on your feet and letting your knees drop forward to compensate.

5. Practice opening and closing your hips while pressing against the table. Make sure your knees don't slide back and you stay centered over your feet throughout. Notice that your hip joints have to be very slippery.

6. If you have someone around to help, have them grab your belt and try to pull you forward when you are closed. If you feel uncomfortable with the idea, you can have them push against your buttock instead. Resist the pull with your hands and feet so you stay in place. This tests your ability to hold your position during a sudden stop.

You can also feel the concept of pushing your center back by sitting in a wheeled office chair, bending forward from the hips and using your hands, not your feet, to roll yourself away from the desk.

On the Horse

When you close your hip angle, because you are made out of bones and not springs, when your hip goes back it must also go down. On the ground this is no problem because there is nothing under your seat, but on the horse the saddle is in the way. Therefore, you must have shorter stirrups to leave space for this. Also, because the cantle limits how far your hips can go back, the stirrups can be farther forward. Thus, those who find their stirrups are mounted too far forward for open half seat may be more comfortable with the closed position.

1. After warming yourself up, at the standstill use your neck strap to take up a zero seat tiptoe position to be sure you are fully stretched, then close your joints as described on page 256. As you close your hip joints, place your hands on the horse's neck wherever it feels comfortable. Close until your upper body is at about a 45-degree angle and you have light pressure on your hands (see the photo on the top of page 267).

2. So as not to develop a stiff hand position, press your *knuckles* against the sides of the horse's neck *with your wrists straight and the backs of your hands parallel to the slope of the horse's shoulder.* Your elbows should hang below or in front of your shoulders.

3. Practice pressing with your hands and closing so your hips slide back. This is how you are going to use your body if the horse slows down or stops suddenly.

4. At the same time as you press with your hands, press on the stirrups just enough to keep you from falling *down* on your hands. Don't push your feet forward, however. As with the open position, you should never have any feeling that you could fall *forward*, even if the horse were to stop and drop his head. At no time should you be leaning on the horse's neck; just using it to press back against. Think of pushing a lawnmower.

This closed position enables you to resist a stopping thrust that is throwing you forward, without the danger of having you fall back with your shoulders and sit down heavily on the horse's back when he goes forward again. Instead, your body slides back *along* the horse.

Showing closed position with my hands, arms, and feet keeping me from getting thrown forward if the horse checks.

This is how the body responds in closed position to a sudden thrust forward by the horse, such as over a jump or up a steep hill. The hip angle closes more and the body shifts back, but without coming down. From a correct closed position it is almost impossible to get "left behind."

Tidbits & Supplements

Especially for the novice, a small knee roll on the saddle is very important. It acts as a brake in front of your knee on the inside if the horse stops suddenly. Without it, it is all too easy for your leg to slide entirely past the saddle, and you can find yourself lying on the horse's neck!

Trotting Revisited

When trotting in the closed position, the same conditions should apply as when you are working at the trot in open position (page 259), and you should follow the same sequence of actions.

1. At the walk, take up the three-quarter seat but close your angle a bit more so you have a light pressure on the horse's neck. Slide your hips back a little in the saddle so your crotch is over the seat, rather than your seatbones, but don't let your toes sneak out in front of your knees. If you have a problem with this, your stirrups may need to be shortened.

2. As the horse starts to trot, straighten your legs a little to lift your upper body enough so you aren't hitting the saddle. Adjust your hip angle as necessary so you keep the same light pressure on the horse's neck.

3. Except that you are *pushing* against the horse's neck instead of *pulling* back on the neck strap, and of course your hips are much more closed, everything should be the same as described for the open position.

You should experiment with half seat in closed and in open position to find out which is easier for you for learning purposes, and because you will need both of them throughout your riding career. They need to be practiced *ad nauseam*, preferably in situations where you can be thinking at least partially about something else. Riding to music is a good exercise, as is any kind of trail work. When you've got it, you will have the feeling of standing there effortlessly while the horse trots or canters along beneath you.

HALF SEAT BALANCED

Half seat balanced is not something you learn as much as it is something that happens to you. For you to be balanced in your stirrups without needing the support of your hands, not only must you have the skills but the horse must also be moving in a way that supports you. That's part of what "going forward" is about.

Some years ago my farm used to sponsor an annual Hunter Pace, and everyone who could ride in it did. We had wonderful school horses and I would send out some of the less experienced riders on the good old schoolies. Many of these riders were not really solid yet at either the half seat or the posting trot, but over and over again riders would come back and tell me that after they had been out on the pace for a half hour or so, suddenly the horse would begin to feel different and the half seat and posting became easy. What they were experiencing was the horse relaxing and going forward, something that wouldn't happen to them in the ring.

After you have put in the necessary miles working on the different half seats, one day you will find that you're just cruising along comfortably without any support from your hands at all. Just like an experienced rider! And I, for one, will never tell a soul.

14

Posting the Trot
Perfection Is Perfectly Possible

When my mother was a little girl spending her summers on a farm in Virginia, there was an old horse who was used for light carriage work around the place—going down to the station to collect luggage or freight, for example. Since he was only driven, the sole riding tack was a bridle, so if my mother rode him, she did so bareback. One day she was taken to visit some cousins who had horses and was invited to ride with them. They had saddles, and while my mother of course had seen people riding in saddles, she had never ridden in one herself. She certainly wasn't going to admit that she didn't know how to ride in a saddle, so she watched what they did, managed to get her stirrups adjusted, and away they went.

Nothing seemed very different until they began to trot. What was this? They weren't just leaning back and sitting there on the horse's back as she had always done, they were leaning forward and going up and down! Well! She didn't want to appear ignorant, so she leaned forward and went up and down too. In a very short time she was posting as though she'd been doing it every day of her life. And you can bet she never told her cousins that she hadn't! Posting came very easily for her because she was relaxed and balanced already.

Correct posting is quite a natural movement. We use it every time we sit down or get up out of a chair. Since this is an action we perform many times a day, why do so many riders find correct posting so difficult? The problem is in the nature of the stirrups, combined with the movement of the horse. Normally when you get up from a chair it is onto a solid floor, but consider getting up from your seat on a moving bus or train. It is usually necessary to hold on to some sort of support while making the transition from sitting to standing. Once the action is complete, remaining standing isn't as difficult. But when you return to your seat, it's usually with a thump. Now suppose your feet were resting not on the floor, but on a couple of wiggly ledges that were moving separately from the bus and from one another. Standing up and sitting down would become difficult balancing feats, requiring much practice to achieve ease and grace.

If you apply that standing-sitting sequence to posting on the horse, balance becomes even more important. When the rider does not maintain her balance throughout the whole sequence—or, to put it another way, when she is unable to keep her center over her bubbling spring point—the post becomes incorrect. She may either let her center fall behind on the downstroke of the post, so that she lands hard, or throw her center too far forward on the upstroke, landing on her knees and thighs against the front of the saddle. Not infrequently, she does both. The change of center relative to the foot causes her feet to swing back and forth, so her base of support is lost and she is forced to grab with her thigh and/or calf—or the reins—to pull herself up. The tense leg muscles create stiff joints, making it more difficult for her to move with the horse's motion. They also pull her heels up and harden her seat, causing double bouncing. At the same time, the horse is being thrown off balance by her constantly changing center. This irregularity leads to pokiness, excessive speed or uneven gait. The banging on the horse's back also causes him discomfort—which he may show by souring his ears—and eventually will lead to back and hock damage.

PREPARATION FOR POSTING

You have already learned about sitting the trot with a loose leg. You have also learned about the fixed leg. Now you can use the fixed leg to learn the posting trot. Posting is an action of the hip joint, and most people can feel this more clearly without stirrups. First a little history, just in case you have some negative feelings about posting without stirrups.

The common misconception about posting without stirrups is that in order to post, you must grip very tightly with your thighs and lift yourself up. This fallacy was compounded by a misunderstanding of the way the cavalry and similar organizations taught their riders to have relaxed legs. When they were ready to trot, the recruits were more or less shown how to post, that is, told that they should go up and down, without stirrups, and then simply made to do it for about 15 or 20 minutes. Of course they tried posting by squeezing with their thighs, not only to post but also in an effort to protect the more tender parts of their anatomy. But after 20 minutes or so, they were forced to let go with their thighs. And they found, to their surprise, that they could post a lot better that way, for reasons I will explain in due course. And it helped their riding in many other ways as well.

This method worked for them because they were soldiers and had to obey orders whether they wanted to or not. Unfortunately, when this technique was carried over into civilian life, the teachers who used it missed the point. They had their pupils post without stirrups, but when the students got tired they were allowed to stop and rest, since they weren't in the army. When they tried it the next day, they were a little stronger and could grip a little longer, so instead of learning to post without gripping, they just learned to grip harder and harder. And nobody—horses or riders—liked it at all, except maybe a few sadistic instructors!

But as you found when you first tried to sit the trot, the bounce of the horse's gait tends to throw you up in the air and you have to make a conscious effort to stay down on his back. When you post correctly, with or without stirrups, you use the horse's motion to give you the lift. If you have ridden a lot of different horses, you know that some horses throw you quite high, while others hardly lift you off the saddle at all.

However, if you merely allow yourself to be thrown in the air every step, you will also come down with a thump every step. When the horse trots, one diagonal pair of legs pushes back against the ground, thrusting his body forward. Meanwhile the other diagonal pair is swinging forward through the air. It hits the ground and starts to push back as the first pair is swinging forward again. The thump comes when his feet hit the ground.

Since the rider is not part of the horse, the thrust that pushes the horse forward throws the rider's body not only up but also back. To offset that, when you post, you begin by leaning forward from the hip—closing the hip joint. This does two useful things. The slight tightening of the thigh makes the horse's lift more effective, and leaning forward combats the force that is throwing your shoulders back.

What you are going to do (which is what differentiates posting from just bouncing up and down) is resist the thrust of one pair of the horse's legs by swinging forward with it, then give to the next thrust and allow yourself to be thrown back. However, as you do this, you must keep your balance or you will go up with a lurch and come down with a thump—neither of which the horse will like.

Ground Work

First you're going to practice posting from a chair, focusing on what's going on in your hip joints, which is the secret of easy, graceful, well-balanced posting. The chair or stool should be quite high so your knees are only bent as much as they would be in the saddle. You can do the exercise in a lower chair, but it will be harder.

1. Sit on the forward edge of your chair with your feet as far back underneath as possible while still keeping your heels on the ground. (If you are in a low chair or have very long legs, you may have to let your heels come up to get

your feet far enough back.) Assume the closed hip position that prepares you for standing (as described on page 245). Be sure your center is really over your feet. Place your hands on your back.

2. Now, instead of thinking about getting *up*, imagine a string tied to your stomach, a couple of inches below your navel, that is being pulled forward. As it comes forward, remember to keep your center over your feet, that is, make sure you don't put more weight on your toes. Your hip joints slide open and your hips come forward, your shoulders and knees come back, and you will come up.

3. Once you are standing up, imagine a string tied to your tailbone, which is being pulled back. When your hips go back, keep your balance by letting your hip joints slide closed and your shoulders and knees come forward, and you will come down. Again, try to keep your center steady over your feet and not rock back on your heels.

4. When your seatbones feel the chair, *do not* lean back, which is your instinct. That's because you aren't going to stay sitting down. Instead, keep your hip angle closed and stand right up again. When you are upright, immediately sit down. Imagine for the moment that the chair seat is very cold, so you don't want to stay there long.

5. Stand and sit a number of times, thinking about your balance and your hip joints. This is where a higher chair makes it easier, because you don't have to go so far between sitting and standing.

Now that you understand how posting relates to sitting and standing, the next step is to try it standing up. This will be even more helpful when you start working with stirrups, but right now it will help you with the concept.

1. On the ground, stand facing the side of a straight chair so your toes are against or slightly under the bottom of it and your bent knees are resting directly above your toes against the seat (just like your leg position on the horse). A tack trunk also works well for this exercise. See the sequence of photos on page 254. Look at the photos from top to bottom and also from bottom to top.

2. *Keeping your knees and toes in place*, start posting using the string image you used in the previous exercise. Only go up and down four or five inches (15 to 20 cm). The purpose of this exercise is to learn to keep your lower leg in place. Thus it forms a triangle of support with your stirrup leather, giving you the solid base you need.

3. Let your arms hang loose, and if you are truly balanced, they will appear to swing forward as you bend forward and back as you straighten up. Actually, they will be hanging straight down the whole time while your body angles change.

Preparing to stand. My hip angle is closed so that my center is over my feet. My shoulders are forward.

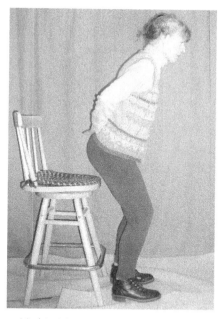

My hip joints open, my pelvis comes forward and my shoulders come back.

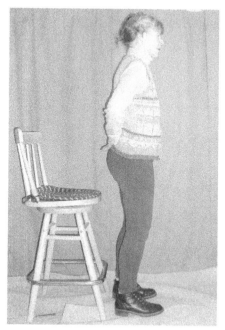

Standing all the way up. Notice the only things that change from sitting to standing are the angles of the joints, especially the hip joint. My shoulders are directly over my hips.

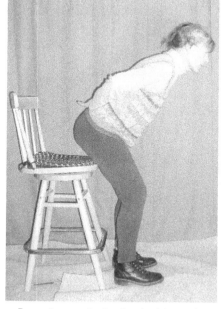

Preparing to sit. Again, the hip angle closes so that my center stays over my feet as I come down. My shoulders are forward again.

4. You want to feel how you go up and down *by swinging your hips forward and back.* Because your hips are fastened to your knees via your thigh bones, when your hips come forward they have to come up, and when they come back they have to come down. You can also imagine that someone is pulling up on a string on the top of your head and then letting it go. *Be sure not to allow your weight to shift back and forward on your foot.*

Try posting while squeezing hard with your buttocks and thighs. It doesn't work at all! That's why those soldiers had such a hard time. Practice doing it right a few more times.

POSTING WITHOUT STIRRUPS

The ideal horse for this is one whose slow trot is soft and easy to sit, and whose faster trot has good energy and impulsion. However, if your horse doesn't meet these criteria, you will have to adapt the exercise as necessary.

I find this exercise is easiest with a bareback pad because it isn't slippery. If you do use a saddle, wear chaps or breeches with suede insets if possible, so your knees don't slip as much. If you don't have them, a good coating of glycerin saddle soap well rubbed into the flaps of the saddle will help.

This first exercise is important to help you learn to keep your thighs relaxed and your hip joints flexible when you're on the horse. Before starting, with the horse at the walk, practice going from loose leg to fixed leg a few times.

1. Still at the walk, fix your leg (as described on page 220), then close your hip (bend forward) slightly. Place your hands palms down on the horse's withers. Since the horse doesn't bounce you up at the walk, you will have to use your hands to give yourself the necessary lifting motion.

2. Become conscious of your following seat. When you post, you sit as the horse's outside back drops and rise as his inside back drops.

3. Let your outside seatbone drop, then as it comes up, press on your hands to lift yourself up a little and at the same time think about bringing your belt buckle up and forward. Try to make a little extra effort with your inside hip. You should also feel your chest lifting up so your upper body is *more upright.* Keeping your head up will help.

4. On the next step allow your tail bone to come down and back, letting your outside seatbone drop to follow the horse's back. Your hip will close so you are *leaning more forward.* You won't be coming up and down or moving forward and back very much at all, just enough to give you an idea of the timing with the gait.

5. Repeat this at every stride as though you were posting at the walk.

The "down" of the bareback
posting trot with fixed leg.
My hip angle is somewhat closed.

The "up" of the bareback posting trot.
My hip angle is more open than in
the previous photo. Since Sammy
has a very smooth trot, I am hardly
being lifted off his back at all.

This exercise helps with the feeling of *straightening* as you rise and *bending* as you sit, as well as helping with the timing.

Now you are ready for the trot. It is best if you can avoid trying to use any leg to get the trot, since this will interfere with your posting at first. Either a cluck or another voice command or a stick is a better way to go. If you have someone to help and your horse will trot quietly behind another horse, that would be better yet. Having someone longe you is another option, but she should try to get the horse to make as big a circle as possible. Part of the difficulty with trotting is that the faster gait throws you more to the outside on turns, increasing your tendency to grip with your thighs. If you have never posted before, find someone to lead you so they can stop the horse if you have difficulty with the faster trot. Try to trot only on the straightaway at first.

1. With the horse walking around the ring, fix your leg and place your hands knuckles down on the horse's withers or neck with your fingers around the neck strap. Your arms should not be cramped, nor should you have to stretch far forward or round your back. Your elbows should hang a bit in front of your shoulders, with a comfortable bend.

2. Begin posting at the walk to find the timing, then ask the horse to trot.

3. As he begins the trot, continue the posting motion as described in the previous exercise, letting your outside seatbone slide back and down as the outside of the horse's back drops, then letting your belt buckle and inside hip come up and forward on the next step. If you are having trouble getting up off the horse's back at all, ask him to trot a little faster.

4. If you find you are bouncing rather than posting, you are probably squeezing with your thighs and tightening your hips. Stop the horse or do an emergency dismount and start again.

5. Keep trying short trots until you get a few steps that feel fairly smooth and effortless. Try to keep your toes up and out and your knees bent, as this puts your legs in the best position for posting.

6. When you start posting around corners, emphasize pulling your inside hip bone forward. This will tend to pull your center to the inside, compensating for the centrifugal force that is pushing you to the outside. If your inside leg tends to get "grippy," you are probably still sliding to the outside.

Practice posting until you can feel the rhythm, and keep posting for a little while without too much effort.

You may notice that when you sit, you are getting a little double bounce. This is because your seat muscles are tight. When you bend forward, your lower back and buttock muscles tighten to keep you from falling over, but to land softly on the horse's back you need to release that tension for a moment.

1. Begin posting at the walk.

2. As you sit, just as your seatbones begin to press against the horse, release your lower back and buttock muscles as described on page 250.

3. Continue to post at the walk, putting in a release of your back each time you sit.

4. As soon as you get the feel of releasing, try it at the trot. The post should now feel much deeper and softer.

If your ring isn't quite level, a good trotting exercise is to practice sitting the trot with loose leg on the uphill side, then fixing your leg and posting on the downhill side. Uphill makes the trot smoother and easier to sit, downhill makes the trot a little bouncier so the posting happens more easily.

Once you have mastered the hip movement, you are ready for posting with stirrups. As soon as you have mastered the stirrups!

POSTING WITH STIRRUPS

Since posting in the saddle involves standing on the stirrups, you must be able to remain in half seat for several steps, keeping your balance without gripping or falling down. Since posting also involves sitting, you must be able to sit softly at least a few steps of a smooth trot. If you have been learning from this book in sequence, by now you should be reasonably competent in these two skills. On the other hand, if you have been having trouble, posting may help you improve the other skills. Everybody learns differently, so do whatever works for you.

Your stirrups and neck strap should be adjusted for riding in half seat, and you should be riding in an area where your horse can move forward fairly easily in a straight line. The ideal conditions are either in a large arena following another horse or on a straight, wide trail such as a dirt road if your horse is quiet. The idea is for you not to have to think about anything except posting.

1. After you and the horse are thoroughly warmed up at the walk both with and without stirrups, take up your three-quarter seat with stirrups at the standstill, but in a slightly closed position so that instead of pulling lightly on the neck strap you are pressing lightly on the horse's withers with your knuckles. You should be using your hands to push your hips slightly back, not pressing straight down (see Closed Position on page 264). Hold the neck strap as well, in case you start to fall back.

2. Now go from the three-quarter seat partially into half seat, bringing your hips forward but trying not to let your knees straighten and pop back (see page 274). As soon as you are up, let your hips close and come back so that you come

right back down again, finishing in full seat forward position. Continue in a forward-back (up-down) pattern, thinking about staying steady on your feet and hands, having slippery hip joints and soft knees and ankles. Don't forget to release your back and buttocks to allow your seat to sink into the saddle as you come down.

3. If there is an experienced rider around, ask her to trot while your horse is standing still; you watch and try to post in the same rhythm. Most beginners tend to post too high, and thus too slowly, instead of allowing the spring of the horse's gait to give them the height and the rhythm.

4. You may find a tendency in yourself to pick up not only your seatbones but also your feet, by pushing too hard with your hands and feet. Since the motion of the horse will lift you up, you don't want to make any extra lifting effort (one of the causes of posting too high!).

TROTTING

If you are in an arena, you will be thinking in terms of outside and inside, which will change as you change direction. If you are on the trail, try to alternate between left and right where the terms "outside" and "inside" are used in this next exercise. That is, let your right side be the outside some of the time and your left side be the outside the remainder of the time.

1. Take up the three-quarter seat at the walk and start to feel the rhythm of the gait with your following seat. Even though the rhythm is different from the trot, since your seat follows the movement of the hind legs, it will help your timing.

2. Now begin to think about posting a little bit at the walk. Take up the rail to the left if you are in the arena. When your *outside* seat drops, that is the down position of the post, so as your outside seat drops, let your hip angle close a little and allow your seat to slide back on the saddle if it will. Then, as your *inside* seat drops, push a little on your feet (only because the horse isn't lifting you up) and let your hip angle open a little so your shoulders come up and back. Be sure only your hip angle is changing—don't let your back get floppy. Practice this until your hips are working easily.

3. Now think about your arms for a minute. For your hands to stay quiet, your elbows must straighten and bend as you rise and sit. If your balance is secure, your arm joints will be soft and this will occur fairly naturally. If you are still having a problem, shake out your arms one at a time. You want your pressure on his withers to remain absolutely even, which tells you your center is not rocking back and forth.

4. On the corners add a push with your *outside* foot as your *inside* seat drops. This will move your center slightly to the inside so that it moves over to your inside foot. This is to correct the tendency to slide to the outside on the corners. You can also push yourself up with your outside foot just a little (when you trot, the horse will be lifting you, remember) to start giving your body the up-down idea. You want to think *sit on the outside seat, stand on the inside foot.* However, don't let that lead you into shifting from side to side!

5. Continuing with your following seat in three-quarter position, ask your horse to trot. The best advice I can give you at this point is, don't try too hard. Feel the rhythm of the gait, allow the horse's bounce to lift you up and your flexible hips to let you down again. Generally speaking, the rhythm is quicker than you think. If you encourage your horse to trot a little more boldly than usual, as long as neither of you feels out of control or unbalanced, the posting will be easier because the bounce and the rhythm will be more distinct.

The "down" of the posting trot with stirrups. I am leaning forward so that my center stays over my feet as my hips come down and back.

The "up" of the posting trot with stirrups.
Again, notice the difference in the hip
angle. I am only leaning enough forward to
stay with the horse's forward movement.

TROUBLESHOOTING

When you get too disorganized and can't seem to find the post, either go into half seat or come back to the walk and start again. It is essential not to allow yourself to get really tense, because you will lose all feel of the horse if you do.

• If your feet won't stay down, think about letting your weight go down the *inside* of your legs to increase flexibility.

• Check to be sure your center isn't too far forward (that is, too much weight on your hands).

• If your heels come up in half seat as well as when posting, tense muscles on the backs of the thighs are also a likely cause.

• If your feet are swinging, it means your center is moving forward and back instead of up and down. Practice at the standstill again, and try to keep an even, light pressure on your hands and along the entire sole of your foot.

• If you are double bouncing or not really sitting each step, your inner thighs and buttocks are too tight. Imagine you have a long, heavy tail, like a crocodile, then allow the tail to fall through the horse to rest on the ground.

- If you are hitting the saddle with a thump, you need to close your hips and lean forward more as you sit. This is especially likely if you are having trouble getting back up again.

- If you are falling against your knees as you rise, you must open your hips and lean back more as you go up.

Once you are posting in rhythm, start reviewing your Seven Steps in detail. Anybody can post with a little practice, but posting in a way that is truly comfortable for the horse and effortless for you requires a little extra thought. If you have learned fairly good balance at the trot in half seat, and done the posting trot with fixed leg, posting with stirrups should come fairly easily. Again, once you have the idea a little, practicing to music or riding on the trail will give your right brain a chance to figure out what to do. Don't forget those soft eyes!

DIAGONALS

When you post, you move up and down as one diagonal pair of the horse's legs (that is, right front–left rear) is moving up and down. Generally speaking, when working in any space where you are turning in one direction, you want to be posting with the outside diagonal—that is, the diagonal associated with the horse's outside front leg. So if you are riding left hand around, the horse's outside leg will be his right leg and you will post on the right diagonal (see the photos on pages 281–282).

The reason for posting on the outside diagonal really has to do with the *inside hind* leg that is associated with it. As the horse turns, he needs to bring his inside hind leg well forward to support himself. When you post on the outside diagonal, you are coming up off the horse's back as his outside front and *inside hind* legs are in the air coming forward, which makes it just a little easier for the horse to swing that important inside hind leg. When you are riding on the trail for extended periods, it is important to use each diagonal equally so the horse doesn't get overmuscled on one side.

When we were talking about starting posting, both in this chapter and in Chapter 13, we said that you go down as your *outside* seat drops and up as your *inside* seat drops. This is somewhat confusing, but the horse's *back* drops as the *leg* on that side comes up. So when you sit as your outside seat drops, the horse's outside hind leg is in the air and his inside hind leg is on the ground. Then you rise at the time your inside seat (and foot) drop, and the horse's inside leg is in the air. Thus your following seat guides you into the correct diagonal.

You can check your diagonals by looking at the horse's outside shoulder point. You should be coming up as it is coming forward. Some people find it helpful to put a little tape on the horse's shoulder points so they can see them better. It also helps to count or use some phrase such as "up-down," so that you are going—and saying—"up" and seeing the outside shoulder come forward at the same time. However, you should try to learn to pick up the diagonal using your following seat, and just use your eyes to check. Be careful not to get into the habit of dropping your head when you look.

Changing diagonals is done by skipping a beat while posting. You can either sit an extra step or stand an extra step, but the first is usually preferred. Say to yourself while posting, "Up down up down up *down down* up," to change by sitting, or, "Up down up down *up up* down," to change by standing.

A very useful exercise to improve your balance and rhythm is to post three steps and stand three steps. You would say, "Down up down up down *up up up* down up down up down *up up up*," etc. Since you are staying up for three steps instead of two, your diagonal doesn't change.

When you get your posting right, the pressure of your hands on the horse's neck will be light and absolutely even. Your feet will stay still and your legs flexible. You will hit the saddle very softly, but your weight will come completely down for an instant. Your hip joints will feel very smooth and slippery. You will feel as though you could keep posting forever.

15

Cantering Basics
Just in Case

There was a little cartoon poster that was popular a few years ago. It showed a man taking his first riding lessons. First he walks and says, "Oh, there's nothing to it. I can ride pretty well." Then you see him trotting, and he obviously is thinking that this isn't quite so easy. Next comes cantering, and there he is with his hat over one eye, his stirrups flying around and both arms around the horse's neck!

This seems to describe the way a lot of people feel about the canter. No matter how they try, it seems to be a lot of work and, while it's exciting, it isn't very secure. It doesn't have to be that way!

Cantering (and galloping, which is closely related) is the *most* fun of all the gaits, provided you are prepared so you can canter fairly correctly. Students who have spent the necessary time on the Seven Steps in the walk and trot sometimes experience a little canter by accident, before they have had any instruction, and cope with it easily. This is what I hope you will do, too. I'm not going to go into any depth about the canter in this book; I'll just give you a little idea of what cantering is about and how to prepare for it, just in case.

When you ride a horse, the horse's motion acts the same way on your body as your own legs would. The movement of his back pushes your pelvis up and down in the same pattern when he walks as your legs do when you walk, and at the trot it's the same as when you run. That's why hippotherapy (riding therapy) is so effective for repatterning people who have lost the ability to walk correctly, such as stroke victims. We find walk and trot easy gaits to follow because they are the same gaits (walk and run) we use ourselves.

Most people think human running is just a fast form of walking, but if you watch the way racing walkers move, you can see that walk and run are quite different gaits. This is even more apparent in the horse, because if the relaxed rider allows her arms to swing naturally, they will follow the movements of the horse's front legs in both gaits—as her seatbones follow the movements of his

285

Tidbits & Supplements

I was watching a nature show about jungle primates not too long ago. To my astonishment, they showed a long clip of a primate "cantering" on two legs—that is, in an upright position. It was obvious from the narration that the photographer didn't know what he was looking at, because they described it as the animal being playful. But to my more educated eye, the rhythm and sequence of the canter were immediately apparent. The primate *did* look as though he was having fun, too!

---

hind legs—even though the footfall pattern of the horse's walk is quite different from that of the trot.

Canter, however, is not a gait a two-legged person would normally use, because it has a phase where all the weight is on one foreleg, and our "forelegs" (that is, our arms) don't reach the ground. So learning to follow the movement of the cantering horse doesn't come as easily. Incidentally, it isn't all about speed, because a fast trot is a good deal faster than a slow canter, but riders are far more likely to have problems with the latter.

Somebody asked me recently why the canter just felt so great. I talked about the footfalls and about the fact that the horse she was riding probably had good gaits. But then it occurred to me that perhaps one reason we find cantering so special is that it is something we had to give up when we took up walking on two legs instead of four. Could it be that at some deep level, our bodies miss it?

THE CANTER STRIDE

A little explanation of the canter stride may help you understand how it affects your body. Cantering is a three-beat, four-phase gait. It can be done acceptably in one of two ways, depending on which lateral set of legs comes farther forward or "leads" during the stride. That is, the canter begins off either the left hind leg or the right hind leg; the former results in the right lead and the latter in the left lead.

A canter stride starts with all of the horse's weight over his outside hind leg, which is forward under his body. He then pushes off onto the diagonal pair of inside hind and outside front legs. Next, the inside front leg comes down and

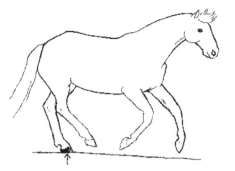

Phase one of the canter: Right lead, left hind leg support.

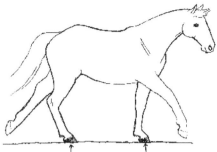

Phase two: Diagonal support, right hind and left front together.

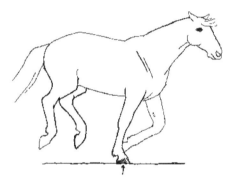

Phase three: All the weight is on the right front (leading) leg.

Phase four: The moment of suspension; you can see the left hind leg ready to hit the ground and begin the sequence again.

all of his weight shifts over that leg as the diagonal pair leave the ground. Finally, he pushes off and there is moment of suspension when all four legs are in the air. Then the outside hind leg comes forward and down once more and the next stride begins.

This sounds complicated, but it actually feels very much like the walk. In fact, the walk and the canter are much more similar than are the walk and the trot. Therefore, the transition from walk to canter is more natural for the horse, and if he is balanced, much easier for him than the transition from walk to trot. It is also easier for the rider to learn to sit the canter on a horse who will go directly from the walk to a slow canter, since her body is already moving in more or less the right pattern.

PREPARATORY WORK

Even though you don't necessarily plan to canter right away, there is some work you can do to prepare your body for cantering.

The first exercise is the same one you did for passive and active seat (pages 164–166). You should review it on the ground first, then later on the horse at the walk. If you can practice when the horse is walking fairly energetically, or walking downhill, it will be even more helpful, since the movements of walk and canter are very similar. This rolling of the pelvis over the seatbones is where most of the bounce of the canter is absorbed. Notice particularly the importance of *not* rounding your back, which would cause your buttocks to come under you and harden up instead of staying soft and absorbing the shock. The little bounce you often see at the canter results from this.

The next exercise is one that I love, and which I think really helps get the feel of the canter. But some people think it is nuts! You can be the judge.

You are going to learn to canter, almost exactly the way the horse does, on the ground on your own (four!) feet. As I said earlier, the canter is not a gait that we use, because of our upright posture, but the program for it is still in our brains—just like that primate I saw on television. All we have to do is wake it up a little. I started riding so young that I learned to canter on a horse very early in life, so it is quite natural to me to canter on my own as well. I have found that with a little practice, cantering comes quite easily to anyone who doesn't mind looking a little silly. (Behind the barn is okay!)

If possible, first look at some slow-motion video of horses cantering, or watch horses cantering so that you have a clear picture of how the canter goes. Then you need a fairly long, open space, 50 feet or so. We will start with the left lead, which is usually easier not only for horses but for humans as well.

1.   Start by standing with your feet together. Lift your left foot and at the same time lift both hands, mostly from your elbows, so your right hand is about at shoulder height and your left hand is lower, at chest height. All your weight will be on your right foot (beat one).

2.   Now reach forward with your left foot and right hand together and take a step (beat two). Your hand and foot should reach their farthest forward point at the same time. Your right foot comes off the ground, but not forward.

3. Then, *before* you step forward with your right foot, reach well forward with your left hand (beat three). Oops! Almost fell on your face, didn't you? That's because as you reach forward for beat three, you have to open your hip and let your shoulder come back to keep your balance. (Horses who canter heavily on their forehands lose it here.)

4. As your shoulders swing back, your right leg comes forward and steps down to start beat one again.

This is much harder to describe than it is to do.

After you have the sequence down slowly, speed up, add a little skipping/hopping to get your moment of suspension between beat three and beat one, and pretty soon you're cantering easily. Next you need to learn your right lead, and after that you can learn lead changes. Now you're ready for the dressage arena or the reining ring!

Once you are cantering easily, go back and think about your body movement from the hip joints up. At first your shoulders will be rocking back and forth, but now try to keep your spine vertical and let your hips and lower back work the same way they did at the walk. That means that, beginning from beat one, your hip joint will open as you progress to beat three, then close as you return to beat one. Feel how your chest lifts at each step. You can also try leaning forward and closing your hip angle from beat one to beat three, to see how heavy and awkward you feel.

Practice ground-cantering until your body can follow the movements of your feet smoothly and fluidly, and you feel balanced and grounded. After that, the transition to cantering on a horse should feel quite natural and be much easier.

The third exercise is useful if you have access to a swimming pool. When I was taught to swim at camp, we had to learn several different strokes to pass our swimming test. I always found the side stroke very easy, although I never understood quite why. Then my daughter pointed out to me that the one place where we can canter is in the water, and the side stroke is the equivalent swimming stroke. It tends to be a bit irregular, but the sequence is the same, and it helps you feel the moves. Swim on both sides to practice both leads, and try to keep the three-beat rhythm.

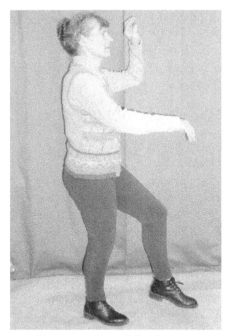

Phase one: The left lead canter,
human style, with the weight
on the right "hind" leg.

Phase two: Diagonal, the left "hind"
and right "fore" together.

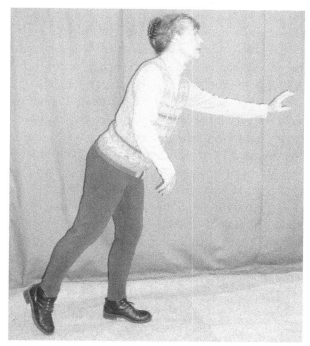

Phase three: My left "fore" would be taking the weight
if it could only reach the ground!

Another very helpful thing to do is get a videotape of somebody really good at the canter, such as the late Dr. Reiner Klimke, and just watch it and imagine yourself doing it with him. We now know it is more effective to watch a physical activity being done correctly and practice imitating it in our minds until we are comfortable with it—often several weeks—than it is to try to learn the skill by trial and error alone.

ON THE HORSE

One of the things we learned about sitting the trot is that if it gets too bouncy, so that you can't keep your seat right on the saddle—that is, if you are bumping at all—you should stand up in your stirrups. The same is true of the canter. If your horse breaks to the canter, if it's fairly slow, try to sit it first. This is easiest if he breaks into it from the walk, since your body is already moving the right way. Tuck your fingers under the pommel right away and lean back a little, then just think about centering and following, keeping your seat and thighs soft. Usually, unless he's following another horse, he will canter a few strides and then come back to the trot. The trot he comes back to is often a little rough, so be prepared to stand up or post right away.

Sometimes the horse will be spooked and will break suddenly into a rather fast canter. This can be scary if you're not expecting it, but it isn't all that hard to deal with as long as he canters on a fairly straight line. If he spins or suddenly jumps sideways, even the most experienced rider can lose her seat. That's why it's so important to spend a lot of time with the despooking games you can learn with one of the ground training disciplines (Appendix D). But let's assume for the moment that he takes off straight forward. The first thing to do is grab the neck strap, the horn or his mane, look up and try to ground in your stirrups. That means going through your Seven Steps as quickly as you can. It also means making sure your reins are not too tight and pulling you forward. That's what usually causes horses to crowhop—a little head-down hoppy action that is fun if you're leaning back with loose reins but scary if you're leaning forward with tight reins. Then focus mostly on keeping your eyes soft and following your stirrups with relaxed feet. Try "playing the piano" with your toes to release your ankle tensions.

Now, I can hear you saying, "You really expect me to do all this as my horse is taking off down the trail?" Yes, I do. It really isn't hard if you have been practicing the Seven Steps both on the horse and in as many other situations as are appropriate. Not only will you be able to at least start the procedure, but if you are concentrating on the Seven Steps, you won't have time to panic. And you'll probably find that as you go through the Seven Steps and start to ground, your horse will too. Unless you keep him going with your own panic and tension, a horse will only run mindlessly for about 50 yards. After that, if there is nothing to keep him going, such as other horses running, he will usually slow down quite quickly. If not, once you are organized and grounded, you can use some of the aids described in the following chapters to bring him back to you.

Tidbits & Supplements

If you are an instructor, teaching "ground cantering" in the stable aisle is a good lesson for a rainy day, especially for kids, who really get into it. It can then be incorporated into horseless horse shows, which can also include jumping.

Tidbits & Supplements

Whether you stand or sit, try to be very free in the waist and hips. The canter has a sort of spiral wiggle to it that will make you bounce if you don't stay very loose and soft from your waist down. Except in the case of fairly advanced riders, most riders' seats bounce on the horse's back at least a little bit at the canter. A lot of riders — and their instructors — consider that bounce normal and acceptable. It's not. At least not to the horse. Nor is it necessary.

As we said, this is only an introduction to cantering, just in case. But the time will come when all the walk-trot work you have been learning will be firmly embedded in your muscle memory, and you will look forward to having the horse break into the canter. You will know that you can deal with it, and that it will be fun for both of you.

Part IV

Helping Your Horse Do What You Want

The Leg and Rein Aids

16

Using Your Legs
No Strength Required!

When my daughter Karen was about 12 years old she went to visit her grandparents in Mexico for a few months. My mother, who lived there in the winter, was associated with a local riding program, so she signed Karen up to ride. The teachers prided themselves on being "old-school cavalry" and wanted all the riders to learn to ride with "plenty of leg," so no crops were allowed. Poor Karen was expected to get her horse to move with just her legs, on horses that were accustomed to large adult males with very strong legs. The horses had, of course, become completely dead to the leg aids, and Karen was soon practically dead from exhaustion! Her Mexican riding career lasted two lessons!

"Use more leg!" "Your legs aren't strong enough!" "*Drive* that horse forward!"—all comments that pretty well describe the way many teachers perceive the leg aids. This concept, that strength has an important place in our control of the horse, is false. Some of the most capable riders I have seen were well along in years or were disabled.

As you will discover in this chapter, when it comes to the leg aids, the more strength we use, the poorer the results. Looking at it from another angle, most riders think "invisible aids," that is, aids so quiet that they are not apparent to the viewer, are only possible with a highly schooled horse. However even the greenest horse quickly learns to respond to the nearly invisible soft leg aid described in this chapter.

Another misconception is that you cannot be an effective rider unless you have very long legs. This misconception results partly from the idea that strength is important, but also from a lack of understanding of the importance of centering. A rider who has short legs in relation to her body, especially if she is heavy, will have a higher center of gravity. This means it is more difficult for her to keep her center from disturbing the horse's balance. A horse whose balance is disturbed very often responds by being unwilling to go forward, and who can blame him? The rider, or her instructor, thinks the problem must be that her legs are not strong enough or are hitting the horse in the wrong place. Thus she is told to either use her legs harder or to try to force them down, both of which tend to tip her forward and interfere even more with the horse's balance. Finally, she is told that she doesn't have good conformation for riding, so she gives up and goes home. If, instead, she focuses on learning to stay centered before she tries to use leg aids, she can become as effective a rider as anyone.

The rider's legs are, in many ways, the most important aids. That's because they affect the horse's legs more directly than other aids, and after all, it is the horse's legs that take him where we want to go. Leg aids can ask the horse to move faster, to take longer steps, to gather himself together or to step sideways with one or both pairs of legs.

Like all the aids, the legs can be used either passively or actively. The passive leg, like the passive seat, is the leg you have been using all through this book. It lies quietly on the horse's side, without tension, following the movement of his barrel as it swings from side to side with each step. As your seat drops, following the horse's back, your leg drops as well. At that point in the horse's gait, his hind leg on the same side is coming forward and his barrel is swinging toward the opposite side to give the leg freedom to move. Your leg will naturally follow this inward movement if it is free from tension as it should be, so that the soft, passive contact of your leg never changes, just as the pressure of your passive seatbones on the saddle never changes. Even though your leg is touching the horse's side, no messages, annoying or otherwise, are being sent, because the leg is passive.

The active leg aid is often misunderstood and frequently applied with far too much force. It actually works most effectively when used lightly, almost as if you were tickling the horse. This causes the muscles on his sides to contract, very much the way tickling causes a person to curl up. However, if you keep tickling a person, she stays curled up—she is unable to let go and stretch out. Similarly with the horse, while the leg pressure brings him together, the *release* is what allows him to go forward. This is especially true when spurs are used. Spurs can contract a tense horse so much that the only way he can go is up! Even a quiet, "lazy" horse is far more sensitive than he appears. If a fly lands on his side, his skin will twitch and his tail will swish around. A horse who can feel a fly will feel your leg aid even though he may not respond.

Lack of response to the leg aid is usually the result of interference by the rider with the horse's ability to move. Too-tight reins, body weight uneven or too far forward, and tense thighs or buttocks are the most common causes. It is for these reasons that I recommend the rider wait until her position is fairly well confirmed before she starts using the leg aids.

THE SOFT LEG

The way most of us learned to use our leg is to bend the knee a little, turn the toe out a little and bring the calf and/or heel back and in. Maybe only a *little* back, but that's what we do. When you do that, you are using your inner thigh and back-of-the-thigh muscles. When you use those muscles, several things happen. It tends to lift you up and tip you forward—only a little, it's true, but even that little has a negative influence on getting the horse to go forward. In addition, tensing the thigh creates tension in the horse's back. For the horse to reach under from behind, his back needs to release. So when you use your leg in the way most of us were taught, you are actually *interfering* with the horse's ability to respond by going forward. Banging and thumping with the leg may create a response, but it forces the horse to break through the tensions that are created, so it will not be a relaxed, forward response. (A light tap with the stick is far more effective, because the rider can maintain correct position while using it.)

Some years ago I was serendipitously introduced to a far more effective way of using the leg. Nuno Oliveira was a Portuguese world-class dressage trainer who was in the United States in the 1980s doing a lot of clinics in my part of Connecticut. I went and watched him a few times, and managed to ride with him once. My regular horse was lame and I had to ride another one, and it was quite expensive but worth every nickel for this one thing I learned, which Oliveira called a "soft leg." Early on in the lesson he asked me use my leg. (He worked through an interpreter, but for simplicity's sake we'll leave her out.) Then he made some remark to the effect that of course I rode hunt seat because I had a grippy leg. I was deeply insulted, since I had always ridden balance seat and was quite proud of the fact that I did *not* use a grippy thigh. However, now that I understand the soft leg, I realize he was quite right. Although I did not grip to maintain my seat, I did indeed grip when I applied my leg.

Oliveira's technique is as follows. It takes a *lot* of practice in the beginning to get the feel of it. I will describe your left foot, and then you reverse it for the right one.

1. With your feet out of the irons and your leg loose, straighten your left knee enough so you can see your toe easily.

2. Now rotate your toe in a circle counterclockwise, so the toe comes up and out and down and in. *All the movement will come from your ankle joint.* Think of a clock face hanging vertically in front of and facing your toe. Your toe starts at three o'clock, goes to twelve, then nine, then six, then it returns

---

Tidbits & Supplements

Your leg is constructed so that when your knee is bent, the shin will rotate with the ankle if you aren't careful, which will create some tension in the back of the thigh. If possible, have someone check and perhaps hold your shin in place until you find the trick of rotating only in the ankle.

---

to three again. As your toe comes in, you may feel your knee and thigh coming away from the horse a little. That's okay.

3. Practice the movement for a while until you are doing it nice and softly, without tensing your leg. Then bend your knee, *without letting it come up*, so your foot swings back under you, and lift the toe so you are in fixed leg position, but in ∩ rather than Λ position, that is, your toe is not rotated very far outward—say about at 11 o'clock. Some part of your calf, depending on your and your horse's size and shape, should be in contact with the horse's side. It should be only a couple of inches of the wide part of your calf. (Trying to force your lower calf in is unnecessary.) Your thigh and knee will be a little off the horse, but your knee should not be *pointing* out.

4. Now do the toe rotations again, going from eleven to nine to six to three to twelve and back to eleven. You will feel that as your toe comes in to three o'clock position, your calf presses a little more firmly against the horse's side, contracting his muscles; and as your toe goes out, your calf presses a little less, releasing the contraction. *That's all the pressure you need!* Your toe won't come very close to the horse because of his shape, but imagine you are going to tap the girth with the inside of your stirrup.

You can vary the leg aid by making the release greater, letting your calf fall away from the horse so that when you put it back on, you get a little more of a *tap*. This tends to *increase the horse's speed*. If you keep the release minimal by keeping your calf in contact and just softening the pressure, you will make a little more of a *rubbing* effect on his side, which tends to *lengthen his stride*. You can also add a slight forward-and-back movement, bringing the leg a little back as the toe comes out and a little forward as it comes in, which acts on the horse's muscles to help draw the hind leg forward. Generally speaking, the horse will bring his hind leg forward to a point underneath where you are applying your leg.

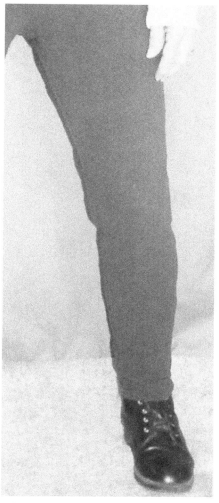

The leg in ∩ position. Note the vertical calf, which would lie against the horse, ready to be applied as an aid.

The leg in Λ position. If you were using your leg in half seat or posting, it would be returned to this position when it became passive.

Because you get the leg activity from the bottom by wiggling your toe, which uses only muscles on the front and the outside of your leg, no inner thigh tension is created, so the horse's back stays relaxed and allows him to respond effortlessly to the leg. You will be surprised at how much more effective your legs are once you learn to use the soft leg.

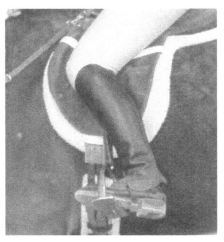

On this horse, my leg is pressing on him when my toe is only slightly inward (toe at one o'clock).

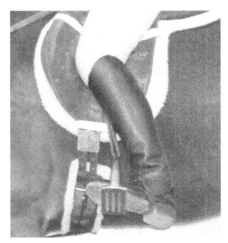

Rotating the toe outward during the release of the leg aid (toe at nine o'clock).

The soft leg contact from the front. This is a long-legged rider on a small horse. Her knee comes below the widest point of his barrel, so she has to bring her lower leg in quite a bit to reach his side.

On the other hand, she only has to bring her toe a little more than straight ahead to take her calf off and create a release.

Tidbits & Supplements

Not long after I learned Oliveira's soft leg and began teaching it, one of my advanced pupils, who was going to college to get a degree as a riding instructor, had to go there to take a preliminary test. She is a very large woman and they gave her a very large horse. She was terribly nervous, and found herself out in the ring for her test with no whip, no spurs and a horse who was apparently dead to her legs. She was too embarrassed to ask for a whip, so after clunking him a couple of times with her heels and getting no response, she thought "what the heck" and tried the soft leg routine. To her amazement, and to the amazement of the observers, the horse responded beautifully and she ended up getting a performance that no one even knew he had in him!

TIMING AND PLACEMENT

The horse can only respond to your leg aid when his leg—the one you are trying to influence—is off the ground. To get this timing you must combine your leg activity with a following seat, so if you want to influence the left leg you give the command when your left seat is dropping (and his left hind leg is in the air). At the same time, his barrel will be swinging to the right. So your left leg will naturally be dropping down and inward toward the horse, and it requires very little extra effort to apply the soft leg pressure at the same time. For example, if you want more lateral bend to the left, you use left leg at the girth as your left seat drops. This brings his hind leg farther forward, making the lateral bend easier.

When you want the horse to increase his pace or lengthen his stride, you can do one of two things. The American method is to apply *both* legs as the horse's *inside* leg is in the air. This indicates that you want him to stay straight. If most of your riding is on the trail, your inside leg would depend on which diagonal or lead you were on. At the walk you would change inside legs regularly. The second method is the European method, in which you apply each leg as the seat on that side drops, thus influencing each of the horse's legs separately. If done correctly, it will be a bit easier for the horse to use each leg. However, it can be difficult to do this without shifting your center or weight from side to side.

Here is simple way to think about where to place your leg on the horse's side.

● If the horse is crooked and you are trying to straighten him, try to feel where he seems to be bulging outward and use your leg at that point to press him back in again. This might well involve using both legs at different times to move his middle in one direction and his quarters in another.

● If you are trying to bend him, think about where you want his body to bend, which is right about at the girth, and apply your leg there. This asks him to give with his body and at the same time helps him bring the hind leg on the same side directly forward to support him on the turn.

● To get his hindquarters to step sideways, carry your leg somewhat back toward the quarters. This tends to block him from stepping forward, thus encouraging him to offer the sideways step. If you are using a leg back, *you first place your leg where you want to use it* (being careful not to draw it up), then use your toe action as before.

Forward and backward leg positioning should not be very great. The classic definitions are at the girth, forward of the girth and behind the girth. However, these refer not to the placement of the leg, but to the placement of the *stirrup* when the leg is applied. The difference between one position and the next should only be about an inch. Of course, in training one sometimes has to exaggerate a leg position to give the horse the idea, but try to return to the correct placement as soon as possible.

As with all the aids, you must observe the horse's *first* response to the aid, and praise and become passive for a moment. If your horse has learned to be very unresponsive, combine the leg aid with a click or another voice aid, or a whip aid, until he realizes you are actually trying to communicate with him with that soft little pressure. For lateral work, you may want to work with him on the ground until he understands the concept of stepping sideways to a light pressure.

When you use the soft leg aid your leg never gets tired, the horse never gets dead to it and it doesn't interfere with your position at all. Once the horse begins to understand it, you will find that you have achieved an invisible aid and a far more responsive horse.

17

Understanding the Rein Connection

Use Your Hands Effectively

There is an old adage, "Bad hands hurt the horse, good hands don't disturb the horse, educated hands help the horse."

It has occasionally happened that, when I am either riding in a clinic or schooling someone's horse, an observer has come up to me and said, "You have really nice [or sympathetic or gentle] hands." This always makes me feel very good. I have been riding for a great many years, so my educated hands could well be attributed to my experience.

However, I have also had judges say to me at shows, "Your students have such good hands!" Some of these students had only been riding five or six years. Traditionally, when I was a young rider, 25 years was considered the length of time it took to develop "good hands." And it was a given then that some people could never learn to have good hands. Nevertheless, it is my belief that anyone who is willing to spend the time to first develop good balance can have good hands.

In Chapter 10 earlier in this book you learned how to deal with the reins without trying to actually use them. Sort of like learning how to hold a golf club before you start to swing it. This chapter could be compared to learning how to swing the golf club before you try to hit the ball. The importance of learning how to use the reins without creating tension in your own body can *not* be overemphasized.

By far the most difficult aspect of riding is using the reins. While both rider and horse are able to *maintain* balance by adjusting their center over their feet, **during any loss of balance, the horse uses his head and the rider uses her hands to regain balance**. Since horse's head and rider's hands are connected through the reins, to maintain a connection between the two that is not threatening to either takes a great deal of experience. The most common scenario is for one or the other to pull a little too hard. This puts the other one off balance, who then gets panicky and pulls back. It makes no difference who starts it, but because the horse is larger and has four legs to use, he usually wins. The horse is then called headstrong, more severe bits are applied and a cycle of fear and failure begins.

Needless to say, this doesn't have to happen. With an understanding of how the reins function and of the techniques used to apply them, combined with an understanding of the horse's needs and, of course, a great deal of patience and practice, any rider can communicate effectively using the reins.

Ideally, before you try to do anything with the reins beyond merely holding them loosely, you should have perfected your seat—at least at the walk—to the point where you are as independent of your hands for balance as you are for walking on your own feet. Your total position is of great importance in working with the reins, since any lack of balance will cause tension in your arms and hands, interfering with your ability to feel the amount of rein contact.

Throughout this chapter, when the word "bit" is used, it should be taken to also mean any device, such as a hackamore or a bosal, that is used to direct the horse's head—unless specifically defined otherwise.

HOW THE REINS WORK

The novice rider or someone who doesn't ride is inclined to think the reins work like the brakes and steering gear on a bicycle; when you pull them both, the horse stops, when you pull one, he turns. The difference is this: On a bicycle, when you apply the brakes, little rubber pads grab the wheel and press on it, slowing it down; that is, the brakes are directly connected with the thing that is moving (the wheel). Similarly, the handlebars of the bicycle are attached directly to the front wheel, so when you turn the handlebars, the wheel turns (unless your older brother undid the bolt that keeps them together!). On a horse, however, *the reins are not attached to the "wheels" (feet)*, they are attached to the head and they *directly affect only the head*. **The attachment to the feet is through the horse's body and mind.** Therefore, pulling on the reins to either stop or turn, *by itself*, will not necessarily give you the result you expect.

The reason your reins can be used to guide the horse when you're mounted is that the horse's head is directly related to his balance. **Since the reins are attached to his head, when they are pulled or released they affect the horse's balance in some way.** The horse then does something with his feet to regain his balance. The goal, of course, is to use the reins in such a way that what the horse does with his feet is the result you are looking for.

To give a familiar example, if you are on the ground and pull the horse's head a little *forward* and to the left, the easiest way for him to regain his balance is to step to the *left* with a *front* leg. However, if you pull *back* and to the left more strongly, his easiest solution is to step to the *right* with a *hind* leg.

Many riders get themselves and their horses into trouble by pulling the reins incorrectly. For example, if, while riding, you pull on the reins hard enough to interfere with the horse's ability to reach out with his front legs, it will cause him to lose his balance. That's because the horse uses his front legs for balance, especially if he loses his balance a bit at speed. You do the same sort of thing with your hands if you stumble while you're running. When the horse loses his balance he speeds up, just like you do, and since, with the reins too tight, he can't use his front legs easily, he hangs on the reins instead. The rider, feeling him speed up and pull, thinks he's trying to run away, so she pulls harder, with the results you might expect. Many, if not most, situations where the horse "runs away" are a direct result of this sort of pulling.

There is a common misconception that the purpose of the bit is to control the horse by hurting him through pressure on his mouth. Of course it is quite possible, especially with severe bits, to do so, but there is no more reason to hurt the horse with the bit than to hurt him with any other aid. And there is every reason not to, since pain creates tension and a tense horse cannot respond as well as a relaxed horse.

If the bit is properly fitted to the horse, making allowance for the size and shape of his mouth, lips, and tongue, and the rider uses her hands correctly, the horse will find it quite comfortable and even comforting to accept a steady rein pressure on a snaffle bit for 20 minutes or half an hour at a time. Later we will see how this pressure helps the horse ground himself

You can try a little experiment to help you understand how the snaffle bit feels to the horse. Insert your index fingers from the side into the corners of your mouth about half an inch (2 cm) and then pull them back toward the hinge of your jaw until your mouth is firmly stretched. Adjust as necessary so you don't press your lips or cheeks against the biting surface of your teeth. Now let your head fall forward so the weight of it is resting on your fingers through the corners of your mouth. Unless your lips are very chapped, it really is not at all uncomfortable, and the horse's lips are much stretchier and stronger than yours. Incidentally, this is quite a lot more pressure than you would normally expect the horse to accept.

In the belief that the bit causes pain, many people prefer to use some sort of bitless bridle that works on the horse's nose instead of his mouth. For contrast, place your index fingers across the middle of your nose and again let the weight of your head rest on them. It's not any more comfortable, and in fact if your fingers are a little too low and are pressing on the part of the nose cartilage that is unsupported, it is quite *un*comfortable. In addition, if you experiment first with one position, then the other, you will find that your *neck* can be more relaxed with your fingers in your mouth than when they are on your nose. The tension or relaxation of the neck will, of course, be transmitted throughout the entire body of the horse.

This is not to say that bitless bridles do not have an important place in training and riding many horses, especially previously abused horses or those ridden by novices. Since communication to the ground is less direct, mistakes are less bothersome to the horse. I merely want to make it clear that the bit does not and should not work by causing pain.

GROUNDING

In Chapter 2 we introduced the concept of grounding, the essential basis of any athletic endeavor. **Just as grounding is necessary for the rider to be secure on the horse, so grounding is necessary for the horse to feel secure within himself.** A horse needs to feel that he can move quickly and safely in any direction if the need arises. The right contact on the reins, offered by the skilled rider, helps the horse to ground in the same way that a light, supporting touch on someone's hand helps a novice ice skater. Even though a well-coordinated horse doesn't need any assistance when he's on his own, when you add the weight of the rider there are times when grounding can be difficult for the horse. Naturally, you don't want him to become so dependent on this support that he is unable to function without it, but you do want him to know it is there and available to him whenever he needs it.

Thus, when you use the reins, besides affecting the horse's balance, you also affect his grounding. Your own grounding is affected as well. A rein connection with soft, elastic contact through your arms and body into your seat and stirrups gives you more depth and stability than riding without contact. I hardly need say that this must be practiced at length if it is not to disturb the horse, and the practicing is done using the neck strap (as described in Chapters 9, 13, and 14).

We could say the reins help both rider and horse to ground. Using the ice skating analogy again, pairs skaters help one another ground through the contact of their hands. Neither one interferes with the other's balance, as long as both are balanced themselves, and the help they give one another enables them to perform actions that would be difficult or impossible alone.

In riding, if the horse loses his balance, the rider can sometimes use the reins to help him regain his balance, while still keeping her own balance and grounding, but the horse should not be expected to do the same for the rider. If the rider loses her balance, using the reins to regain it would be abusive to the horse's mouth, to say the least. Yet another reason for the rider to develop the habit of reaching for the pommel, horn or neck strap in an emergency.

Tidbits & Supplements

Helping the horse to ground using the bit and reins can be done with a Western bit as well as an English one. I once saw a movie with some excellent Western riders. At one point they were galloping down a very steep incline, and had their horses in a beautiful light contact, enabling the horses to ground securely in a difficult situation.

USING THE REINS

Bringing it down to its simplest form, there are three basic things you can do with the reins.

1. Pull them, increasing the pressure.

2. Hold them steady, maintaining the pressure or lack of it.

3. Release them, decreasing the pressure.

Similarly, the horse can respond to the reins in three basic ways.

1. Pull against them, increasing the pressure.

2. Accept the pressure without increasing it.

3. Give in to the pressure, decreasing it.

However, the horse cannot change the pressure on the reins *by himself*. For him to put pressure on the reins, they must be fixed at the other end. That is, either the reins are attached to the saddle or surcingle as side reins, or *the rider must be pulling on the reins as well*. Similarly, for the horse to release the pressure, *the rider must release as well*. **That is, if the rider drops the reins, the horse cannot pull against them; and if the rider keeps pulling on the reins, the horse cannot make them loose, no matter where he puts his head.** People talk about the horse "spitting out" the bit or "taking the bit in his teeth," but this never really happens. The bit is attached and adjusted to the horse's head so that unless it or the bridle breaks, the horse cannot get rid of it, nor can he move it to where he can get his teeth on it very solidly (which would be very uncomfortable for him anyway). The rider, however, is another matter. She holds the reins in her *hands*, and can therefore easily adjust them to make a stronger or lesser feel on the reins. **Therefore, the rider is always the one who determines how much pressure there is on the reins.**

Most riding instructors do not like to use the word "pull" because it implies hauling on the horse's head. **I prefer to say it's okay for you to pull the rein. It is *not* okay for you to pull the rein in a way that causes the horse to resist.**

Combining pulls, releases, and staying steady (also called "passive" or "following") in different ways to get different results is called "hand effects." This is different from "rein effects," which have to do with the direction in which the hand effect is applied. Both hand and rein effects will be dealt with in the next chapter.

LEARNING REIN SKILLS: PULLING

Before you start to learn the hand effects themselves, you must first learn the techniques for performing those actions correctly. We will therefore begin by looking at the general actions involved in pulling and releasing the reins. By working on the ground, you can get a feel for the skills without confusing or aggravating the horse.

For the time being, we will assume the *direction* of the pull of the reins will always be along a line drawn from the bit to the rider's elbow, as viewed both from the side and from the top. In other words, we will not look at any other rein effects yet. This line of pull makes it easiest for the horse to maintain the connection through his body between the contact on the reins and the ground. It is also the position from which the rider can ground through the reins most easily.

Even when the horse's head is out of the correct position, it is still nearly always easiest for him to find his way back to the right place if the rider maintains this line. This means the rider always *bends* her elbow as she pulls, following the line upward and back, and *straightens* it when she releases, following the line downward toward the bit. Here is a little exercise to demonstrate that. You can do it sitting in profile in front of a mirror, if you like.

1. Sit down with your knees comfortably together and let your arms hang down so your elbows are just in front of your rib cage.

2. Now bend your right elbow and rest your right hand just outside and a little behind your right knee, holding your hand as if you were holding the reins (as described on pages 201–202).

3. Bring your left forearm across your chest so your fingers are pointing at your right elbow (see the photo on page 312).

4. Now *bend* your right elbow and bring it back at the same time, so your right thumb comes up to your left fingers. Be sure your wrist is a little higher than your thumb joint. Notice that your hand comes *up* and back to pull.

The reins and arms form a straight line from elbow to bit. Note the horse's light but solid contact with the bit, and the firm and forward stride of his hind legs.

5. *Straighten* your elbow and bring it forward, so your right hand returns to its place beside your right knee. Your hand goes *down* and forward to release.

Practice this frequently, with either hand, so the motion becomes natural for you. Then add a "shorter" rein. (Later on in the chapter we will see how and why this second exercise applies.)

1. Start with step 1 as in the previous exercise, and bring your left forearm across as in step 2 to mark the position of your elbow.

2. Now reach out with your right hand, allowing your elbow to straighten until your arm is fully but not stiffly extended and your hand is beside your knee. This is the position your hand would be in after you shortened the rein.

3. Bring your right hand up and back by bending your elbow, as in step 3, but only until your elbow reaches its original position just in front of your rib cage.

4. Straighten the arm as before. Practice with both hands.

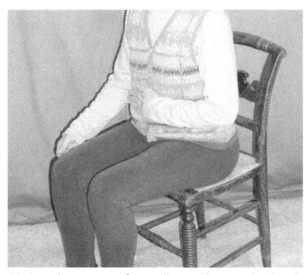

Marking the position of your elbow with your other hand.

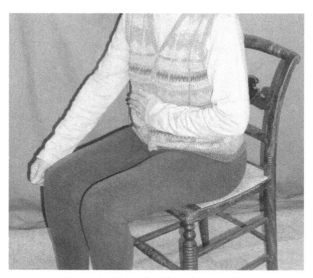

Preparing to pull with a shorter rein;
this is also the release position.

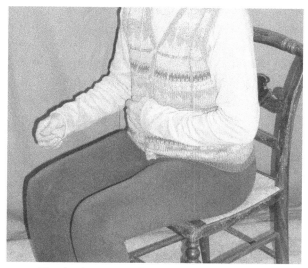

The final position of your hand when you are pulling on the rein. If you were using an active hand, your hand position would go from the position in the previous photo to this position and back again— or at least along the same upward line.

In addition to the importance of the direction of the pull, it is equally important for the rider to *raise* her hands when the horse raises his head to follow it up, and to *lower* her hands when the horse lowers his head to follow it down and keep the bit in the correct position. When the horse turns his head, the rider's hands follow laterally as well. However, while the hand on the side toward which the head is placed can be moved away from the horse's body as much as necessary, the opposite hand only moves toward the horse until there is a straight line to where the rein presses against the neck. For all practical purposes the hands *never cross* the horse's neck.

The most common problem in using the reins is the tendency to pull them in a way that creates tension in the rider's body, and thus in the horse as well. Therefore, you need to learn how to apply pressure to the reins and still remain relaxed.

To avoid this problem, some instructors teach that you never pull the reins with your arm at all, but activate them by closing and opening your fingers. While activating the fingers does have a function in helping some horses to relax their jaws, this idea leads to the rider trying to use only her hands to increase pressure on the reins. If she needs to use more than a very small amount of pressure, the result is a tense hand, rather than the soft one that is our goal.

If, instead, the rider uses her whole body, transmitting the rein pressure through herself into her seat or stirrup (which you have learned to do with the neck strap), the result is a soft feel with no tension, which completes a circle of communication with the horse's entire body. But the only way to make this understandable is for you to try the ground exercises that follow. If you can find an interested participant to work with you, you will get an even better feel for the reins, especially from the horse's point of view.

Pulling in Half Seat

For the first exercise, which is done standing, you will need either a pair of reins or something similar, and something to fasten them around, such as a heavy table leg, at a level that simulates the position of the horse's mouth relative to yourself when you are seated on the horse. A full-length mirror so you can watch yourself from the side would be helpful. You can also stand facing the edge of an open door, holding the door knobs in each hand instead of reins. (You can use this variation to sneak in some practice at the office!)

1. Fasten the reins around whatever support you are using for standing work. Stand far enough away from the support that it doesn't interfere with your body movement. Run through the first five of the Seven Steps.

2. Now take your half seat position, holding the reins one in each hand with your hands almost flat, as though you were holding the neck strap.

3. **To pull correctly, your reins must be short enough before you begin so that when you pull and your hands move back, your elbow never gets behind your shoulder.** Therefore, the first step is to shorten your reins without tightening them or leaning forward, so your arms are somewhat straight, giving you room to pull and still keep your arms in the correct place. Think in terms of moving your hands forward rather than making your reins tighter. (This is the purpose behind the exercise on page 311.)

4. Use pressure on the reins exactly as you did on the neck strap when you were working on half seat (page 243). **In the same way, you must check for tension—places where the pull gets "stuck"—and release it so that the pull travels evenly through your body all the way through your feet into the ground.** Be sure to adjust the length of the reins as you pull, if necessary, so that your elbows don't get behind your shoulders. Your upper arm should hang a little forward of the vertical.

Preparing to pull in half seat with the reins
shortened. My arms are nearly straight.

Pulling the reins so that they ground you.

5. The difference between pulling against the neck strap and pulling on the reins is only in the hand position, but this is a very significant point. Turn your hands now so that instead of being almost flat, they are almost vertical (see Chapter 10). Pull on the reins again and observe that the pull, which is against the fingers that the reins pass under as they come from the bit, is now affecting your wrist, so the thumb is higher than the wrist and the back of your hand may be outside your wrist as well.

This is how the pull on the reins affects your hand position.

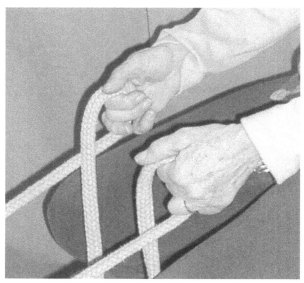

Pulling from under the forearm keeps the hands
in the correct position.

> ### *Tidbits & Supplements*
>
> A concept that may be helpful in keeping your hand in the correct position is to place your hand in position, then imagine you have a plaster cast around your hand and wrist, extending as far as your thumb. Thus your fingers can stay flexible while your wrist is fixed in place without being tense.

6. Ease the pressure on the reins for a moment, to allow you to adjust your hands. Turn them until they are in the position you learned in Chapter 10. As long as there is no pressure on the reins, it is easy to maintain this correct position. Now start to pull gradually, watching your hands and not allowing them to change position. You will find that to do this, you must pull mostly from the *underside* of your forearm, bending your elbow and lifting your wrists a little at the same time, to offset the pull of the reins against the underside of your fingers. Think of the pull as starting at your little and ring fingers, going up the *underside* of your forearm, crossing your elbow, running up the *front* of your arm, crossing your shoulder, running *down your back*, crossing your hip, running down the *front* of your thigh, crossing your knee, running down the *back* of your calf, and finally crossing your ankles to the *top* of your foot and into your toes.

7. Notice that wherever a joint is flexed, the pull crosses over, as in the elbow, while if the joint is held straight, as in the wrist, the pull stays on the same side. **Also especially notice that you are pulling yourself firmly down onto your heels, helping to stabilize you against the forward pull.**

8. Now bend your hands up from the wrists so that your thumbs, instead of pointing down toward the bit, are pointing almost straight up. Pull on the reins again. This time you will feel that the pull starts from the top of your hand and forearm instead of the bottom. Then it goes along the top of your forearm, the *back* of your upper arm, down the *front* of your torso, the *back* of your thighs, the *front* of your calf and the *bottom* of your foot—that is, just the opposite of the way it ran before. This combination of pulls makes your wrist lock, your elbow straighten so you pull down rather than up, your stomach muscles tense so you tend to tip forward, and your leg and foot muscles act to lift your heels and throw your weight on your toes. **You've lost your balance forward!**

9. Return to the hand position of step 6 and practice it, occasionally throwing in a step 8 position so that you clearly feel the difference and learn how to correct it by lifting your wrists, letting your hands fall and move forward and your shoulders come back. **Notice that you have to ease the pressure on the reins momentarily to regain your position.**

Reversing the pull at the hands prevents you from grounding. Compare with the photos on page 315. You really have to try this to realize how startling a difference this little change makes.

10. Now try increasing the amount of pull. To avoid tension, you must increase the pull throughout your entire pulling system. What you should *feel* is stronger pressure on your hands where the reins come in, stronger pressure on your feet where they contact the ground, and very little else. You will find that you can take quite a strong feel with almost no tension, which can come in handy in some advanced situations.

Practice increasing and decreasing the tension. **You can only put as much pressure on the reins as you can pull without creating tension in your own body.** Anything more is self-defeating, since it creates tension and thus resistance in the horse. Also, you must put *equal* pressure on both reins. Most people have a tendency to pull harder on one rein than the other. Be sure you have equal pressure on both feet as well.

Also, try *not* shortening your reins before starting the pull, just to see what it feels like. That is, begin with light contact and your upper arm vertical.

Tidbits & Supplements

If you can find a piece of surgical tubing or a wide exercise band, substitute it for the reins. Notice the soft, elastic feel you get when you pull. The contact is firm, but there is a life to it that you don't get with the regular reins attached to a table leg. This elastic feel is what you want the horse to give you. If you don't feel it, there is tension somewhere that needs to be attended to. This *doesn't* mean you should ride with elastic reins; it means **you and the horse both must keep an elastic feeling through your bodies by eliminating tension whenever it arises**. Without this elasticity, neither of you can maintain a grounded connection through the reins while you are moving.

Notice how, as you pull, your elbows go behind your shoulders and you find yourself tipping forward badly (see the photo on page 318). This is a very common mistake, and is the reason you have to practice shortening the reins until you can do so easily and correctly without thinking about it (see Chapter 10). **Shortening your reins must become an automatic action any time you are preparing to pull on them.**

Pulling in Full Seat

For the next exercise, which is done seated, if possible have both an ordinary straight chair and a chair with wheels, such as an office chair. Work on a floor with a hard surface.

1. Fasten the reins around a support, such as the leg of an upholstered chair. Sit in a straight chair a comfortable distance away. Sit toward the front of the chair and bring your feet back so they are under you with only your toes touching the ground. This will prevent you from bracing with your feet against the pull. Run through the first five of the Seven Steps. Take your reins and hold them as in step 6 in the previous exercise.

2. Now experiment with pulling on the reins, as in the previous exercise. Notice that now when you pull correctly, the pull goes into your seatbones just as it did into your feet when you were standing up. If you pull incorrectly, you get pulled forward from the hip, collapsing the hip joint. Be careful not to let your lower back either round up or hollow out.

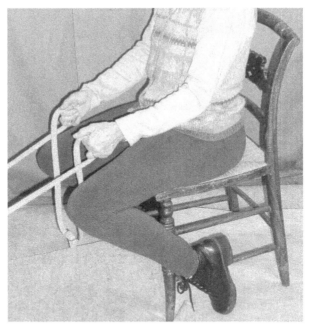

Pulling correctly in full seat. The chair stays firmly grounded.

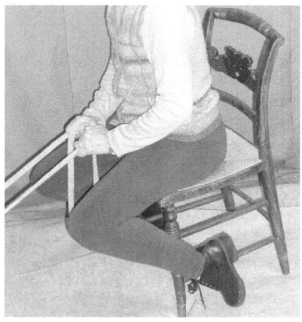

Pulling with the incorrect hand position. This is another one you need to try for yourself. It's difficult to keep from tipping the chair over!

3. Now sit in the wheeled chair. Place it as far from the support as you can while still holding the reins correctly. Then pull on the reins and see how, when you hold your body correctly, the chair rolls easily toward the support. If you bend forward at the hip it tends to "nail the chair down" so it moves less easily. This demonstrates how the weight and rein aids can work together.

LEARNING REIN SKILLS: RELEASING

When you first learned how to hold the reins (Chapter 10), you also learned how to release them when the horse pulls suddenly against the reins, to keep from being pulled forward. However, releasing the reins is also an integral part of communication. The release can tell the horse he has made the right move. It can also encourage him to rebalance himself, and it can head off resistance before it begins.

The Active Release

An active release is a combination of a positive movement and a feel. Since the horse is able to shorten and lengthen his neck, thus bringing the bit closer to or farther from your hands, you have to feel what is *actually happening in terms of pressure on the reins* to determine whether there has been a release. For instance, if you release the reins and the horse lengthens his neck at the same time, the rein pressure will stay the same. So you will have *lengthened* the reins but not *released* them.

The next exercise is best practiced on the ground with a helper holding the reins and taking the part of the horse, but you can do some of it using a support for the reins, as in the rein-pulling exercises you just did. If you are using a helper, she should be sitting in a chair if you stand, or on the floor if you are seated.

1. Take your position either seated or standing and establish a correct pull on the reins. Since the shortest distance between two points is a straight line, the quickest and most effective way to release is on a straight line toward the bit. *Maintaining the steady pull with your right hand,* extend your left hand *forward and down* toward the "bit" by straightening your elbow as in the photo on page 312. Be sure to keep your hand in the same position relative to your wrist. As you move your left hand forward and down, the left rein will become slack— that is, a *release* (of pressure) has occurred.

Releasing the rein. My left hand has moved exactly parallel with the right rein, that is, directly toward the bit.

2. Next, reestablish contact on the left rein. Smoothly bend your elbow and bring your hand and rein back up the line of your elbow to the "bit" until you feel contact, again being careful not to change your hand or wrist position. See how subtly you can establish pressure, so that the change from no contact to contact is hardly noticeable.

3. Practice releasing and taking up contact several times, using first one hand, then the other. **The release should always be quick, the take-up should be slow and smooth.** As you release with one hand, try to maintain steady contact with the other. Be sure to keep your wrists and hands in the same relative position and only move your arm and elbow.

4. Try the same exercises with the surgical tubing or elastic band, if you have it. The elasticity makes the feel of the release more subtle, but the take-up smoother.

5. Have a friend face you holding the other end of the reins, and as you release, have her pull so the reins stay tight. She should move her arms, but not her feet. Continue releasing, if necessary letting the reins slide through your fingers, until *she can no longer pull* and slack appears in the reins. This is the

equivalent of the horse who has been going on a tight feel with his neck short-ened; as you release, he lengthens his neck so the reins do not become any looser. If you want a full release, you must continue to release until the horse is forced to release as well. Provided the reins are longer than his neck, at some point you can let out more rein than he can take up. This is why it is impor-tant to have reins that are long enough!

The Passive Release

If you *allow* him to do so, the horse can also create a release. Try this exercise sitting down, resting your hands on your thighs but keeping a soft hold on the reins. Your friend should sit on the floor facing you.

1. Have your friend first establish a firm hold on the reins, then ease the pressure. If you keep your hand exactly where it is, the reins will go soft. Resting your hand on your thigh helps keep your hand from springing back. Ask your friend to see how subtly she can release, then close your eyes and try to feel the first softening of the reins. Say something like "now" when you feel the release begin.

2. Then try the same exercise standing in "half seat," so your hands are not stabilized, and see if you can feel the release and allow it to happen. Your instinct will be to take up the slack when it occurs, which would be wrong in this case.

3. Take a turn playing the part of the horse, to see how it feels to him.

Tidbits & Supplements

A way of using the hands that I have mentioned before is opening and closing the fingers, squeezing and releasing as it were. This is usually done with alternating hands and creates lateral movement in the bit in the horse's mouth *without pulling*. This is a way of encouraging a horse to relax his jaw and poll, and can be very useful in some circumstances. However, you have to be careful that it doesn't become sawing, in which the bit is worked strongly back and forth, causing the horse to swing his head from side to side. A trainer friend described that as the horse say-ing, "No, no, no!"

LEARNING REIN SKILLS: THE FOLLOWING HAND

The passive or following hand is the hand you use most of the time. It could also be called the neutral hand. **The following hand means continuously keeping an absolutely steady amount of contact on the bit**. It can be likened to keeping a telephone line open between yourself and another person, but not saying anything. The line of communication is there and available, but no commands are being given. The amount of contact in the following hand can be just the weight of the reins—that is, moderately loose—or it can be fairly firm, depending on what the horse needs at a given moment, but it is constant without being rigid. **To maintain this constant contact, your hand must follow every move the horse's head makes**.

As you saw in the game of horsie (explained in Chapter 7), it is only when you move with the horse that you can stay still, that is, keep a constant relationship to his body. This ability to move with the horse's body enables you to find the contact between your hand and his head comparatively easily, because the movements of the horse's head are a direct outcome of the movements of the rest of his body. Therefore, if you can allow your body to follow his with the following seat, free from tension, your hands will naturally follow the movements of his head *as long as you do not need them to maintain your balance*.

For the preparatory exercise you will need another person, preferably someone close to your size, since what you are learning involves movement. Other than that, you need a pair of lead ropes or the equivalent, and a decent size space to walk around in. Some good marching music might also be helpful.

1. Begin with both you and your friend going through the first five of the Seven Steps. Then have your friend take the snap ends of the ropes, hold one in each hand and stand well grounded with her back to you. Her arms should be hanging by her sides and she should hold each rope so the end is between her thumb and forefinger and the rope itself trails out from her little fingers and hangs behind her.

2. Stand behind your friend facing the same direction, a couple of feet away. Pick up the reins but hold them the same way as she is. The ends of the reins will fall down behind you, from your little finger.

3. Starting with one hand, have your friend swing her arm gently forward and back to the vertical. Let your whole arm be absolutely slack, beginning where the shoulder blade joins the spine. As she swings her arm forward, your arm should follow effortlessly, then fall back as she releases and gravity takes over. Ask her to feed back to you if she feels any resistance other than just the weight of your arm. Be sure you maintain your longitudinal balance. The pressure on your feet should remain constant; don't allow yourself to rock back and forth from your toe to your heel.

4. Experiment with tensing your fist, your elbow, and your shoulder, one at a time, and have your friend tell you what she feels.

5. Change places and have your friend be the rider. Try the same exercises and see how they feel from the horse's point of view.

6. Practice these exercises with each arm until your whole arm structure is really loose and relaxed.

Now you and your friend are going to try following the total movement, not just the reins.

1. By yourselves, not connected by the ropes, walk briskly around. Try to be fluid, and nicely centered and grounded. Let your arms hang loosely. Notice how your arms swing themselves without any conscious effort on your part.

2. Now position yourself holding the ropes behind your friend as before. Leave the ropes fairly loose at first. Begin walking and stay exactly in step with her. This is the equivalent of riding with following seat, since your movement coincides with hers. At first you will find your arms do very little, since the ropes are distracting (which tells you something about how horses respond to the reins at first).

3. Think about letting your arms swing normally, and gradually increase the contact on the ropes until you have a steady, light contact. Your goal is for both of you to move normally and maintain a steady contact with one another through the ropes. You will notice that when you turn, your outside arms make a longer swing. Practice turns and transitions, using voice commands, to practice keeping the steady contact. Be sure to walk directly in your friend's tracks at all times.

4. Experiment with tensing different parts of your body: neck, shoulders, arms, pelvis. Notice how this affects your ability to follow and thus affects the horse as well. Ask for feedback. Have your friend also tense her body so you can feel how that affects you.

5. Change positions and play the part of the horse as you go through the previous steps.

6. Finally, have your friend hold the reins as before while you take the reins in your hands as though you were riding. Practice walking with turns and transitions. Ask for feedback on whether the reins feel just as soft with your hands in this position.

Tidbits & Supplements

"Even rein pressure" has a dual meaning. It means the pressure on the reins should be constant at whatever pressure you have decided to use, whether it is half an ounce or half a pound. It also means the pressure on each rein is the same. This second point is essential if you want the horse to be grounding equally with both hind legs.

Before you go on to the hand effects in Chapter 18, spend some more time on the exercises in this chapter. Try things such as being deliberately tense or using uneven pressure to see how this feels to the horse.

These three actions—pulling the rein, releasing the rein, and following the horse's movement—are the methods by which all communications with the reins are created.

18

Overcoming Rein Resistance
Simple Hand and Rein Effects That Work

Several times on e-mail lists I have found myself in a discussion about riding a horse "in contact," that is, keeping a steady, passive feel on the reins all the time. There is a large group who believe this cannot be done and still have the horse be comfortable. They think either the horse will feel pain all the time or he will become desensitized. This is the same group that thinks the bit works by causing the horse pain, but as we saw in the preceding chapter, this should not be so.

To clarify this thought a bit more, think of walking along holding hands with someone. Both of you have relaxed arms and hands, and you are chatting away and looking at the scenery without distraction, except you have this nice little communication that exists passively between you. There is no interference with movement or any active signaling taking place. Then one of you sees something off to one side that she wants the other person to stop and look at, so she gives a tiny little tug with her hand to attract his attention. After you both look at whatever it was you go on, still holding hands. That's what riding in contact is supposed to be. Nobody ever really gets desensitized. You may let go for a while, but when you pick up again you are just as sensitive as before. You have a constant, open line of communication, which is the first thing passive reins do.

Now let's carry it a step further. Suppose the she in this story happens to be wearing high heels and the footing is rather rough and rocky (romantic, isn't it?). Now there are going to be moments in their walk when, for her, holding someone's hand is going to feel very supportive and helpful. But—the gentleman's hand has to be just right! It would be all wrong if the hand she was holding on to constantly dragged on hers so she couldn't walk along comfortably, or if it frequently gave little meaningless tugs, or if it was wearing sharp jewelry that was painful against her hand. If her partner pulled or let go at the wrong moment, she might seriously lose her balance, or he could lose his own balance and fall down, pulling her with him. All these are ways people use contact in a negative way that *does* disturb the horse and make him either fussy or desensitized. But they are all *incorrect*!

However, if the gentleman can offer just the amount of support the lady needs, which is by no means as difficult as it sounds, she will be able to move much more safely and effectively. And this is the second thing that passive reins do.

∾

HAND EFFECTS

As we said in the preceding chapter, hand effects are the result of combining pulls, releases, and steady contact on the reins. They are what you actually *do* with your hands to communicate with the horse. They are also the way you prevent the horse from resisting. By understanding the hand effects, you can use your reins in a way that doesn't interfere with the horse, giving him no physical reason to resist. You can also use the reins in ways he cannot resist effectively, yet without causing him pain, so you can control a willful horse without frightening him into becoming more stubborn.

The generally recognized hand effects are the active hand, the passive hand, and the fixed hand, to which I have added two more: the holding hand and the taking hand. I also include an action called combing the reins, which is a cross between passive and active hands.

The active hand is the most important, but the least used and least understood of the hand effects. The fixed hand is the most difficult for the rider to learn. The taking hand is more of a learned (by the horse) aid than the others. The passive hand and holding hand are similar in function, and require more experience on the part of the rider than the active hand. However, because you need to understand the passive hand to understand the others, we will begin there.

The Passive Hand

In the previous chapter you practiced following the movements of another person's arms with your own. Now you are ready to try it on the horse. Riding in contact with a curb bit is only for experts, so the horse should be wearing a comfortable English snaffle. If it's at all feasible, instead of using a bit, use either a mild hackamore, a sidepull or a standard halter with the reins attached to the side rings. Be sure the nose piece is comfortably padded. This way, your mistakes will not be as uncomfortable for the horse.

On the Horse

When you first try riding a horse using the passive hand, have the horse well warmed up so he is moving forward fluidly. If you have a choice of horses, pick one with a big, swingy walk. Work in an area without obstacles or other horses. If the horse is quiet about it, having someone on the ground to keep the horse going for you, perhaps on the longe, will make your task easier,

Tidbits & Supplements

Do not begin work on the passive hand on the horse until your position is very secure and correct at the gait you wish to use. The Seven Steps must be so embedded in your muscle memory that you don't have to think about them at all.

because then you don't have to think about control at all. Another good way to do this exercise is while walking home from a trail ride, assuming your horse does this without excitement.

Think of this exercise as an extension of the work on giving up control found in Chapter 9.

1. During the first part of the exercise, if your reins are long enough, hang them over the pommel or horn; otherwise, hold the buckle in one hand and concentrate on the other hand. Go through the Seven Steps, focusing particularly on centering and the following seat.

2. Now, with your horse walking actively but not tensely, allow your hands to drop to your sides. Think about having very loose arms and shoulders, without allowing yourself to slump. Notice that your arms begin to swing rhythmically all by themselves, albeit only slightly. If they don't, try singing or talking to someone or whatever you can think of to take your mind off what you're doing. The harder you try to let your arms move, the tenser you will get and the less effective it will be. I realize this is like being told to try not to think about elephants for 30 seconds, but it can be done!

3. Pick up just one rein. Usually the left rein is the easiest for the horse, but you can experiment to see which one seems the best. Begin by holding the rein between your thumb and forefinger—called a "driving rein" because it is used when you drive a horse and wagon—as in the initial ground work in the previous chapter, taking as firm a hold as you can without disturbing the horse or making yourself tense. Then just allow the horse to walk around while you think about keeping a constant amount of feel on the rein. Don't think about moving your hand, just think about keeping your arm relaxed and having a little spring attached to the back of your elbow. The horse may start to walk in a circle, but that is okay. If he does, you can change direction so the rein you're holding becomes the outside rein, and the rail will keep him from turning.

Holding the rein like a driving rein is an easier way to keep your wrist relaxed when you're working on passive hand. The "spring" behind your elbow brings your arm back into position after the horse's motion pulls it forward.

4. After a few minutes, and sooner if the horse begins to seem uncomfortable, change to the other hand, changing direction if necessary. Change back and forth a few times, observing how your hands and arms feel and how the horse responds.

5. Now take both reins, one in each hand, still between your thumb and forefinger. You may observe that the horse doesn't want to take as much feel on one rein as the other. Be sure you keep an even feel on both reins, even if this makes him go in a circle. Remember, at this point you are trying to be completely passive, that is, not give any directional commands at all with the reins. All you're asking the horse to do is ground equally with both hind legs against the even rein pressure, and many horses don't do this naturally. Again, you can place him so that the rail prevents him from turning.

6. Finally, hold your reins in the normal way and allow your hands and body to follow the horse's movement as above. Be sure to keep your wrists as soft and straight as they were in the other hand position.

When you are working on the passive hand, keep the picture in your mind of allowing the rein pressure to go through your body into your seat or stirrups without tension. At the same time, try to picture the horse doing exactly the same thing with his body—allowing the rein pressure to go through his head, neck, back, and legs and into the ground. **This use of the reins to help the horse ground himself is your goal.** If it is necessary to keep him going, at first try to use your center with voice or stick rather than leg, to maintain your grounding more easily.

Horse and rider comfortably grounded with a soft passive rein. Colette is using all of the rein to lengthen and round her top line, and I've had to drop my hands down to maintain the elbow-to-bit line. My left hand is a bit too flat.

Wherever possible, practice the passive hand in conditions under which the horse will go forward willingly—which is why the trail is a good place. It is all too easy for the novice to get the horse shortened up by degrees without being aware of it. Signs of discomfort will include head tossing or hanging heavily on the bit and short, "proppy" strides. It is easiest to practice at the trot, providing you can stay balanced and grounded, since the horse moves his head very little at that gait. Practice periods should be limited to a maximum of five minutes at a time, and less if the horse seems distressed.

The passive hand is the one you use most of the time. **If your horse is well trained and balanced at the work you are currently doing, the reins may be slack but the pressure, or in this case lack of pressure, must still be constant to be passive.** You will sometimes see a rider whose reins, though loose, are constantly changing tension because the rider's hands aren't following. This rider would probably be very surprised if you told her she was bothering the horse with her hands!

The passive hand is the direct result of the correct basic position you have been learning via the Seven Steps and the seven seats. Therefore, as your skill in these areas improves, your passive hand will improve as well.

The Holding Hand

The holding hand is a variation on the passive hand, used when the horse goes behind the bit, that is, breaks his connection to you and the ground by making the reins loose. It is used especially when the problem occurs laterally, that is, the horse bends his head around to one side and bulges the opposite shoulder.

Wills has dropped behind my left hand and the rein has gone slack.

I take a firmer hold on the left rein and ease the right rein. After a minute, Wills takes the left rein again and starts to walk forward. My next step is to make the reins even and passive.

Ground Work

Before we begin with the holding hand, you must first learn the underlying philosophy. You will need a moderately heavy object, such as a pail of water, not so full that you can't carry it reasonably easily in one hand. Wear gloves if necessary so the handle feels comfortable in your hand.

1. With the pail beside you, pick it up with the nearest hand, just enough so it is off the ground. You will be bent over to that side.

2. Walk around in this position for a little while. You will find it quite tiring!

3. Now straighten up so you are leaning a little *away* from the pail.

4. Walk around again. Ahhh, that's a lot better!

5. Take up the scrunched position again and have someone pull down on your other hand in an attempt to straighten you up. Chances are it will just scrunch you even worse!

What happened? We balance with our hands, and when you picked up the pail in one hand, it unbalanced you. At first you allowed your body to scrunch up in response to the pressure, but this was very awkward and uncomfortable. (Children learning to carry heavy things will often do this.) When you stretched up and *away* from the pressure, it enabled you to move more freely and balance better.

The horse balances with his head. When he meets with pressure on just one side, his first response may be to scrunch up, referred to as "going behind the bit" or perhaps "popping a shoulder." But given the opportunity and the right kind of rein pressure, he will find that lifting the pail up, that is, pulling against the rein just enough to balance himself, will enable him to straighten up and go forward in balance.

Now fill the pail of water so that it is very full. If you are strong, add a few rocks to make it really heavy (don't hurt yourself!). Try the exercise again. The bucket will probably be so heavy that you *can't* straighten up and balance yourself. You have to stay scrunched up. This is what happens to the horse who is ridden with a heavier feel on the bit than he can deal with. With work, the horse may get stronger, but who wants to have to work that hard?

Now empty out the pail so it is the same weight as in the first exercise and find a piece of string or baling wire. It has to be strong enough not to break under the weight of the pail. Use it to replace the handle and take off your gloves. Try the exercise again. Now you will find that pulling against the bucket to get your balance hurts your hand! Owwww! This is what happens to the horse who has a severe bit such as twisted wire in his mouth.

You can try these exercises using two buckets, one in each hand, to see how the horse needs to deal with pressure on both reins.

By now you should be getting the picture that there are times when you *want* the horse to take a firmer hold on the bit; when **you want the horse to pull on the rein, not to resist you but to balance and ground himself better.**

On the Horse

Begin just as you did with the passive hand work, getting yourself loose and swingy.

1. Put the horse on the rail going left around and pick up just the outside (right) rein. Let the other rein drop, as long as it isn't dangerous, and rest that hand on your thigh or the saddle. Sit squarely on the horse and establish a firm, steady contact with the rein, but as light as you can manage. Hold the hand a bit on the low side, so you break the line of elbow to bit somewhat downward.

2. At first the horse may curl his head way around toward the rein (scrunching up!), but try to keep the contact steady. Be prepared to move your hand out to the side so you don't break the elbow-to-bit line inward. Soft eyes, breathing, and following seat will help.

3. Look for the least little effort on the part of the horse to straighten his neck. Watch his head and also feel what's happening in your hand.

4. At the *first* sign of straightening—that is, taking the rein—release and allow it. This can be very subtle, so you have to really pay attention. Allow the horse to rest, then repeat with the same hand a few times before trying the other hand in the other direction.

Do not confuse the holding hand with the horse hanging on your hands or actively resisting. The holding hand is quite a different feeling, with the horse remaining elastic and responsive. When you smoothly release a holding rein, the horse remains light and balanced and does not thrust his head immediately downward, which would indicate he was trying to release tension resulting from restriction.

Troubleshooting

Horses tend to fall into two categories in this work: those who don't want to take the bit and those who don't want to give it up. If you are dealing with a determined member of the first group, try the following.

● Use different amounts of rein pressure, both more and less. The important thing is for the pressure to be steady, not bouncy. Give each method a solid try to see if it makes the horse better, the same or worse. He may be worse in the beginning, especially with the heavier feel, but the tighter the knot he ties himself in, the more he is going to *want* to straighten out.

● If it is the left rein the horse won't accept, try adding a little passive pressure on the right rein, being careful always to have *less* pressure than you are using on the left rein.

● Using the original pressure, add some active seat and leg on the opposite side to encourage him to step up against the rein with his opposite hind leg. If he is very crooked, especially to the right, try using your right leg back to move his hindquarters over and straighten him out. Sometimes a horse gets himself into such a knot that he can't get out of it without some help.

● Ride for a few minutes with moderate pressure, then release for a few steps to show the horse that you will let him go. Praise him when he stretches, then try again. But instead of releasing completely, just lighten the feel and see if he will take it.

● Check to be sure you aren't breaking the elbow-to-bit line inward. Also be sure your hand is a little on the *low* side.

● Try riding in the opposite direction using the other rein. A very scrunched-up horse will usually find the right rein easier, but a not-so-scrunched horse may do better with the left.

● Try a milder bit or a halter with reins.

● Try it on the trail coming home, if the horse is quiet.

If none of these works, either you or the horse may not be ready yet.

For the horse who wants to grab the bit immediately, the solution is very easy. All you have to do is to release every time he tries to grab it. Many people would tell you that you are rewarding him for disobedience, but I don't agree. For him to "win," there would have to have been a battle, and you never get into that. As soon as he says, "I want the rein," you say, "That's fine." And then you go back and do it again.

The truth of the matter is that most horses who grab the reins do so not to get their own way, but to get their balance and freedom of movement back. As soon as you start saying to the horse, "I'll give you your head whenever you need it for balance and movement," 99 percent of the "resistance" goes away!

Once the horse will take the single rein softly and easily when you apply quiet pressure, you can use the same technique with both reins when he curls his head to his chest—always keeping in mind that the "buckets" mustn't get too heavy. You need to keep your hands *very* low as well.

Besides grounding the horse, the holding hand helps in straightening him and is often used in ring work where the horse has gotten into the habit of sucking back on one or both reins because he is insecure. **When used correctly,** the holding hand results in the horse taking a steady, soft feel on the bit, directly correlating to the amount of pressure being applied. Your hands can then become passive and the horse will ground himself.

The Active Hand

The passive and holding hands described in the previous sections both act to balance the horse and encourage him to take contact on the bit and ground against it. As you gain experience, you will see the value of having the horse "accept the bit," which is one name for this response.

However, the more common problem many riders meet with, especially inexperienced riders, is the horse leaning or hanging on the bit. The horse pulls against it stiffly rather than responding by slowing or changing direction. We got a little clue of how to deal with this in the Troubleshooting section above, but let's look at the problem in more depth.

Ground Work

For these exercises you need a friend to play the part of horse and two ropes or a pair of reins. If your friend is a bit stronger than you, so much the better. The "horse" may only hold the reins or ropes by the ends, she may not shorten or adjust them. She may not bring the reins farther back than her sides, which represents the horse's head fully extended. Neither of you may move your feet.

1. Your friend (the "horse") stands, or, if she is taller than you, sits in a straight chair with her hands by her sides, holding the reins by the bit ends. You (the "rider") face the horse from several feet away, depending on the length of the reins. Hold the reins in your hands correctly, about six inches from the buckle with the reins very slightly loose.

2. Now the horse brings her hands up in front of her. This represents the horse holding his head in normal position. Adjust your reins until you have light contact with her hands.

3. The horse now starts to pull on the reins, bringing her hands down to her sides (like the horse pulling his head down). Her goal is to pull you out of balance. She should pull as hard as she can, but not jerk the way she did in the exercise on page 203.

4. When she pulls so hard that you can no longer balance and you start to lose your grounding, release the reins, first by extending your arms (though not to the point of stiffness), then by letting the reins feed through your hands.

5. Repeat, changing places.

No matter how hard the horse tries, as long as the rider is able to release the reins, the horse cannot pull her out of balance or get a hold on the reins. Again, you can see why it is essential that the reins are long enough to allow the horse to fully stretch his neck without pulling the rider out of position.

For the next exercise you still need your friend to play the part of the horse. You also need an open space with safe footing and no obstacles.

1. Face each other with your arms extended but not stiff. Place your palms against your partner's palms as if you were playing patty-cake. Your friend may not change her arm position.

2. Start walking around, keeping a comfortable, steady pressure on one another's hands. You will be walking backward and your friend will be walking forward. (Your friend should not try to walk you backward faster than you can go—in theory, you are sitting on her back.)

3. Now your friend should start pushing harder with her hands and arms. At first, and as long as you are comfortable, you can respond with equal pressure. Notice that to do this without tension, you will have to let the pressure go through to the ground and have a stronger pressure on the ground.

4. Now your friend should start leaning heavily into you, putting a lot of weight on her—and your—hands.

5. You respond by releasing suddenly—jerking your hands back quickly so your friend can no longer push against them.

The "horse" now has a choice: She can fall on her face or she can shift her weight quickly backward, "off the bit." Most horses will choose the latter, but there are times when a sudden release from heavy pressure like this, sometimes called dropping the horse, will cause the horse to lose his balance so badly that he *does* fall. It is particularly dangerous just in front of a jump. Therefore, it is important to release *before* the horse gets really heavily out of balance.

Go back and do the exercise again, but this time keep adjusting your arms so your friend can never really lean on you; at the same time, try to offer her a comfortable support. Have your friend experiment between pushing evenly throughout her whole body with grounded feet and pushing mostly with her arms, similar to the horse tensing his neck. Try to feel the difference. Pushing from the ground without tension is how the horse uses the bit for extended gaits, to maintain his balance and increase his thrust. Pushing with his neck is what the horse does only when he feels restricted or unbalanced.

> ### *Tidbits & Supplements*
>
> Let's take a quick look at what makes horses pull about 90 percent of the time. Clasp your hands behind your back and start walking or running briskly around your open space. Then stumble on purpose so you start to fall. If you stumble badly you will *have to* unclasp your hands to regain your balance. If you don't want to risk a fall, just experiment with stumbling first with your hands clasped and then with them free. You will find it *much* easier to regain your balance with your hands free, of course.
>
> When you ride, if the horse loses his balance and you keep the reins restrictively tight, the compression on his neck and shoulders makes it difficult for him to use his front legs (his "hands") to regain his balance, so he instinctively pulls to get his head, and thus his neck and shoulders, free. If you happen to be going fast at the time, you may think he is trying to run away, and start pulling even harder. And that's the way bad habits are born! Rein pressure should *not* interfere with the horse's balance in a way that frightens him.

Change places and try the exercises again, this time with you playing the part of the horse.

From this exercise we begin to see that by judiciously releasing and steadying the rein, we can help and encourage the horse to ground and balance himself, rather than trying to lean on the rider's hands or drag her around.

Now take the reins again. This time you're going to walk one behind the other, with your friend (the horse) in front.

1. Walk around for a few minutes getting comfortable with the reins and each other.

2. Using only one rein, when your right hand swings forward, swing it a little extra so the rein goes loose.

3. Then, when your right hand starts to swing back, carry it out to the side a little and smoothly pull a little harder. If your timing is right, your friend's right foot will be in the air and she will step in the direction of the pull.

4. As she starts the step, release the pull to allow her to step. Then repeat steps 3 and 4.

5. Now try pulling when your right hand should be swinging forward and your friend's right foot is on the ground. You will get resistance because she can't move the foot. (Incidentally, if you are following well, you will find this quite difficult to do!)

6. Try it with each rein. If your timing is right, your friend will turn to one side. If your timing is off, she may either cross the other foot over or resist the turn altogether. If you release too soon, she will just swing her arm to the side but her foot won't come along.

7. Try this exercise as the horse so you can feel how the pull on the rein leads you to the side or unbalances you, depending on the timing.

On the Horse

It is particularly important in this exercise to use the mildest bit or hackamore so you cannot *force* the horse by accident, which would teach you nothing. Whatever you use must be a direct pull device—that is, the rein should fasten at the horse's mouth or nose, not at the end of a shank. Ride in a space with no other horses or obstacles. Use the hand that is away from the rail.

1. Begin with a passive hand, or take one rein and focus on getting that hand moving with the horse's shoulder on that side to get the timing. If you are riding with two reins, the other one must stay passive throughout, becoming neither tighter *nor looser*, so if you aren't too good at that, stick with one rein.

2. *Without moving your body,* reach forward and downward with your hand to create a release; then, bending your elbow as you do so, pull smoothly up toward your shoulder until one of three things happens:

● The horse takes a step with his front foot in the direction of your pull; oh, goody, you did it! As soon as he starts the step, release and praise. If your pull happens to occur when his foot is on the ground, he will probably start to slow down or stop instead. That is an equally correct response.

● The horse bends his head around but continues in the same direction at the same speed; lead your hand farther out to the side so it is directly behind his nose, lower it a little and pull fairly firmly and steadily (holding hand) until he takes a step in that direction or slows down. Then release as above.

● The horse turns his head away and pulls the rein; quickly release and try again, bringing your hand higher and more forward. If the horse continues to resist and you think your timing is right, he's simply telling you that side of him is quite stiff and not ready to give, so try the other side for a while.

Like everything else, learning the active hand takes a bit of practice, but the following seat will help you with the timing. **Put simply, you can pull as long as you aren't feeling any resistance from the horse. As soon as you feel resistance, you must release until the horse lets go.** Notice that we begin the active hand with a release. It is essential that the pull be very smooth and gradual, while the release is quite sudden. The comparison I usually use is that of braking a car on a slippery surface: You apply the brake smoothly until you feel the wheels begin to lock, then *quickly release* the brake and *smoothly* apply it again.

So, when using the active hand, what you are doing is *actively* releasing and pulling on the rein in time with the horse's movement. **The active hand is generally only used with one rein at a time, since the horse can only respond with one foot or diagonal at a time. When used correctly, the horse yields (gives) to an active hand.**

Combing the Reins

Combing the reins is a cross between the active and passive hands, and is particularly useful with a horse who is unwilling to accept even the briefest of steady contact on the reins. Rather than holding the reins firmly, the hands continuously slide along them.

1. Hold both reins together in one hand with your palm down, your two middle fingers between the reins and the index and little fingers outside them. Establish a light contact with the bit. Your arm should be extended but not rigid.

2. Draw your hand toward you, allowing it to slide smoothly up the rein and maintaining the same contact with the bit.

3. As your elbow approaches your side, reach out with the other hand and place it on the reins the same way. Begin to draw with that hand so the contact is not lost or changed. If the horse stretches his neck, simply allow the reins to run through your hands as much as necessary to keep the same contact.

4. Continue changing hands, combing the reins first with one hand, then with the other. Gradually you should feel the horse becoming less tense, more accepting of the contact and more willing to either ground or give to the reins.

If you wish to turn, you can comb only one rein, which requires you to cross one hand over, and you can also do so if the horse is more resistant on one side. You can apply more pressure on one or both reins without creating resistance if the horse is one who tends to go from being behind the bridle to leaning on it.

Combing the reins. My left hand slides
softly up the rein toward me . . .

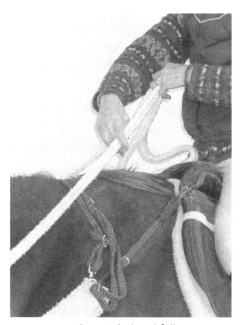

. . . and my right hand follows.

This is also a good exercise for riders who tend to hang on the reins, especially when they're frightened. It helps them discover that the horse will respond better when they *don't* have a death grip on the reins!

The Fixed Hand and the Taking Hand

The fixed hand is a very subtle rein effect in which you hold the rein steady without following, and allow the horse's motion to create a release. Parelli has a very good way of teaching it: He has you take hold of the rein while the horse is standing still by combing the rein toward the bit using the thumb and index finger, to establish a gentle contact. Then you place the rest of your fingers around the rein, one at a time. If you do it right, the horse will soften in his pull a little and accept the pressure without resistance. It does take a fair amount of experience to recognize the right "feel," though, and I have found the active hand much easier for the novice to use when she wants the horse to yield.

The taking hand is a continuation of the fixed hand. Although this is the hand effect most riders are taught to use, it is by far the most difficult to do correctly, for both rider and horse. I put it in the book because many readers probably already use it, but I do not advocate its use except in special circumstances.

From the horse's point of view, the taking hand feels similar to the holding hand, except that when the horse takes, the rider *doesn't* release. The horse has to *figure out* that he must, in essence, "bend *toward* the bucket" (page 334) to get a release. So it is not an aid that creates the correct response automatically, and in the sense of *helping* the horse to perform the desired action, I do not consider it an aid at all. **It is important for the horse's training that he first learn to respond correctly to the holding hand before he is exposed to the taking hand.** If not, it will be difficult for him to learn to accept the bit properly—and thus be able to use it to ground if he gets in trouble.

1. On the horse, take one rein as you did for the active hand.

2. Without releasing, bring your hand *upward on a line toward a point just outside your shoulder* until you have a moderately firm pull on the rein. One of three things will happen:

   • The horse will give and turn his head toward the rein; immediately release and praise.

   • The horse will take the rein and turn his head away; maintain the same or slightly more pressure. If the horse continues to pull, release slightly and briefly to break up the resistance, then pull again. Also try raising your hand so you pull on a more upward angle. When the horse gives, immediately release and praise.

   • The horse will neither resist nor give; increase the pressure gradually and move your hand upward more. As before, when he gives, immediately release and praise.

Notice that the direction your hand is moving is different than for the holding hand—upward rather than downward. We will discuss this further when we talk about rein effects.

The taking hand is used to create the "disengagement of the hindquarters" or the "one rein stop"—two phrases you may have seen elsewhere. It is like the first exercise you did with the bucket. As we discovered, when you bend *toward* the steady pressure of the bucket, you can no longer move forward freely. This is not something the horse does very easily or willingly once he finds out what's happening, so it becomes more of a learned aid. To give to an unyielding pull, the horse must step sideways under himself with his hind leg, which also is not stepping as far forward as normal. If used constantly by a novice rider, this action can lead to hock damage and lameness.

Balancing the Reins

The amount of pressure on the two reins *relative* to one another is an important factor in the effect of the hand. **Whichever rein is softer is the one the horse will tend to give to; whichever one is firmer is the one the horse will tend to take.** This is just another aspect of the bucket concept (see the photos on page 333).

REIN EFFECTS

While hand effects are the different *ways* you can pull the reins, rein effects are the different *directions* in which the reins can be pulled. Each direction has a different effect on the horse's body, and thus produces a different result. Using different hand effects will change the way your horse responds to a particular rein effect, and vice versa.

There are a number of rein effects, but as a starting-out or starting-over rider you need not concern yourself with all of them. You just want to be able to do simple steering and stopping without interfering with the horse's balance. That means you want to use the reins in a way that allows the horse to keep his feet underneath him.

We will start with the turning aids, since those are the easiest for both you and the horse to do correctly. The term "opposition," as we will be using it, refers to pulling back on the reins in the *opposite* direction from which the horse is moving.

The Leading Rein

If you lead the horse around as described in Chapter 5, you will get what is called normal tracking. Walk briskly forward, making sure you stay in front of the horse so the reins are *leading* the horse—that is, if you give a little tug, it will pull *forward* on the horse's head. Don't drag on the horse, but make some nice free turns allowing the horse to follow your hand (see the photos on page 88). You will observe that as he turns, the horse's body and legs follow the track of his nose just like a train going down a track. Allowing for natural crookedness, which will be discussed in the next chapter, each hind foot will follow in the track of the forefoot on the same side. It should also step well forward, at least into the track of the forefoot and probably in front of it, especially if you are walking briskly. This is the pattern that occurs when the horse is relaxed and going forward, and this is what you are after. When you are leading the horse, there is no opposition. **You lead his nose and his feet follow and balance him without difficulty.**

Now get a little behind the horse's head and start him walking again. (If you've trained him properly, you'll have to use a little encouragement to get him to walk in front of you.) Once he is walking fairly well, ask him to turn by pulling *back* on the reins. You are pulling *in opposition*. Don't pull so hard that you make him stop or pull against you, and keep moving yourself. Keep him turning and watch what he does with his feet. Instead of tracking well underneath so that his hind foot track lands in front of the front foot track, his hind foot will come down well behind it. It also may land to the outside of the front foot. When the hind foot is in this position on a turn, hanging back and to the outside, it forces the horse to use his front leg for balance, and we say the horse goes on his forehand. Since this makes him more likely to fall and therefore more tense, we want to avoid this. So we want to try not to use opposition in the inside rein when turning, and to use it carefully when we do use it. **When you use opposition to turn his nose, his feet cannot easily follow and balance him.**

It's easy enough not to use opposition when you're on the ground leading; all you have to do is make sure you stay in front of the horse's head so the reins are *leading* him. But when you're sitting on his back, you can't get the reins out in front of him. There is a way, though, to use the reins with virtually no opposition, and that's by raising your hand and bringing it forward so it makes an angle of 45 degrees or less with the horse's head, then leading it *slightly* in the direction you want the horse to turn his head—out to the side. The horse's head is set on his neck in such a way that when you do this, there is virtually no opposition. This is the closest you can get to a *leading* rein from the horse's back. And, as on the ground, this is the easiest rein effect for the horse to yield to and follow with his head.

The leading rein begins with a release. The rein is then lifted upward and used with an active hand so the horse can yield his head and still keep his hind leg engaged.

Preparing to use the opening rein. When Wills lifts his left front foot, the direction of pull on my left rein—out to the left, away from his shoulder—will bring his foot in that direction, without necessarily turning his head. Compare the direction of pull to the photo above.

Tidbits & Supplements

Most authorities consider the opening and leading reins to be the same thing—an outward pull. The leading rein as I have defined it is quite different. For the opening rein, you do lead your hand out to the side, more or less on a line with the withers, and this is supposed to lead the horse's head around. However, because the hand is at a 90- rather than a 45-degree angle to the horse's head, it becomes a rein of opposition, thus interfering with the hind leg engagement, so the horse finds it difficult to yield to it by turning his head.

The leading rein is only used with a device where the reins attach to a ring fastened directly to the mouthpiece or nosepiece, not a device with a shank. This is usually an English snaffle, but can be a flat halter, a sidepull or a jumping hackamore, with the ring on the side of the nosepiece that hangs in the same place relative to the horse's jaw. When you pull on the reins, the pull travels through the mouth or nosepiece to the far side of the horse's face, where it presses. The horse moves his head *away* from the pressure, *toward* the rein that is being pulled.

The neck rein is very similar in effect to the leading rein. It is used at the same upward forward angle as the leading rein, but instead of carrying your hand *away* from the horse's head, you bring your hand in *toward* the horse's midline, so the rein presses against the side of his neck. The neck rein is most effective when used with a device with some sort of shank, such as a curb or a mechanical hackamore. The pull on the rein tips the bottom of the shank away from the horse's face, so the top of the shank presses in against his face. As well as yielding to the pressure on his neck, he yields to the pressure on his face by turning his head *to the opposite side* from the rein that is being used.

So we can say that to get the horse to turn his head in a particular direction, the correct rein effect is either a leading or a neck rein. They can also be judiciously combined by an experienced rider. **And if we get the nose going in the right direction and we don't interfere with the horse's balance, we have the beginning of a turn.**

A more experienced rider, especially one who is showing, might say, "I can't carry my hands up in the air like that every time I want to turn!" Years ago, I was watching Nuno Oliveira at a clinic riding someone's young and very unbalanced horse. He carried his hands in all sorts of different ways as he worked with the horse. At one point he said, "Of course, I don't have my hands in the 'correct' position, but when you're training a horse, first you have to *show*

This picture shows the direction of pull of the neck rein.
Again, there is virtually no opposition.

Tidbits & Supplements

Western riders use the neck rein and English riders use the leading rein because of the types of bits used by the different disciplines. Western riders traditionally use a bit where the rein is attached at the end of the shank. English riders usually use a bit where the rein attaches directly at the horse's mouth.

him what to do!" We're back to that concept—that the aids are supposed to *help* the horse. In the next chapter we'll learn a little more about how the horse will progress to less obvious aids.

The Direct Rein of Opposition

The direct rein of opposition is the other rein effect you will be using. It simply means pulling *straight* back, rather than pulling back and to one side (which would be either the opening rein or the indirect rein of opposition). The problem with using opposition is that if it is used incorrectly, it cramps the horse so he can't use his legs properly. He then loses his balance, and one way or another you are in trouble.

Direct opposition can be used in two desirable ways, depending on the associated hand effect and the position of the horse's body at the start. If you use it with an active hand, the horse will either slow down, turn or shift his weight back, or some combination of these. If you use it with a passive or holding hand, the horse will take the bit and ground with the hind leg opposite to the working hand. However, if you use opposition with a *taking* hand any way except very briefly, the horse will compress and become rigid, which is not desirable. The horse is unable to respond, and everyone gets angry and frustrated.

Compression is at the root of most of the control problems people have with the reins. Here are a couple of little exercises you can try on your own to gain an understanding of the effect of compression on the horse's body.

1. On the ground, begin by running through the first five of the Seven Steps, and include the swan neck exercise (page 144) so your body is long and free.

2. Now walk around, letting yourself be loose and swingy, and see how athletic and coordinated you feel.

I'm using two direct reins of opposition with a softly holding hand, and some active leg to keep Wills coming forward. We have a more active walk and a more balanced carriage, but Wills is still light and grounded.

3. While you're walking, draw your neck into your shoulders as though someone had put a weight on top of your head. Notice how your whole gait shortens and stiffens, and how you can feel the compression all the way down your back.

4. Standing still with your neck long again, use your arms as though you were swimming the crawl, seeing how long you can make the strokes—that is, reach well up over your head.

5. Again draw your neck in. You can hardly move your arms above your shoulders!

The pattycake exercise found on page 338 also helps you understand the concepts of opposition and compression. Work in a fairly large space (the barn aisle is good). With another person, walk around experimenting with different degrees of pressure, trying to discover how much opposition (pressure from the other person) you can deal with without tension. Keep your arms straight but not stiff and *don't* allow tension to build up in the rest of your body. All the pressure should go from your hands *through* your body into your feet, and if the other person lets go, you should be able to easily rock back and rebalance. You will find that you can take longer, stronger steps against a stronger pressure.

Also try using too much pressure, so you can feel how it restricts and tenses your whole body. You can also feel how it forces you to hang on the other person's hands, just as a horse hangs on too heavy a feel on the bit.

Knowing how extremely important it is for the horse to be able to move freely in front, both for balance and to allow free movement behind, you can easily understand that opposition has to be handled very carefully. When you feel resistance to the reins, it is nearly always because opposition has been used in a way that restricts the horse. **The rule about using opposition when riding is never to use more than the horse can comfortably accept.**

Next, let's find out how the hind legs and the reins pair up. I did this exercise against a windowsill, but you could use a heavy table. It just shouldn't move, and should be about waist height.

1. Stand with your feet a couple of feet away from the table and place the heels of your hands against it as if you were going to try to push it, but don't push yet. Feel the pressure of your feet on the floor.

2. Still pressing against the table, lift your right hand and right foot up and push with just your left hand and left foot. Then put your right foot down and lift your left foot up and push again (right foot against left hand).

You will find it much easier to keep your balance when the push goes diagonally through your body, left to right or right to left. You can also push much more firmly. So when you take a steady hold with your left hand, the horse pushes against it by engaging his right hind leg, *provided your right rein is soft enough to allow it.*

While opposition can help the horse to ground, too much opposition blocks the movement of his legs so that he loses his balance. If you think about movement, you can see that to be effective, each foot must ground—get a good grip on the riding surface—and then immediately lift again. Think of walking briskly and catching one foot on something so you can't bring it forward. Unless the foot comes loose, you will fall. So the rein can be pulling and the horse can be grounding against it, but then the rein must allow the foot to come off the ground again. When the rider's hand is following the movement, this occurs naturally. But when the rider is asking, say, for a downward transition, some release must occur for the foot to step forward as freely as necessary.

How much of a release must occur depends on a number of variables, none of which need really concern you. What does concern you is how the horse is reacting—how he feels on the other end of the reins. Simply put, if the horse starts to resist your holding rein, you must release it enough, and long enough—usually just for a step—for him to find his feet again, and then reapply it. If your timing is just right, you should never feel any real resistance at all.

> ## Tidbits & Supplements
>
> Many riders use indirect reins without knowing it, especially the right rein, because of lateral imbalance. If you tend to sit to the left, your whole right side will be tense and you will tend to draw your right hand toward your navel when you pull, in an effort to keep your balance.

One more caveat about reins of opposition. Until you get quite advanced, it is very important to avoid using them *indirectly*, that is, in toward the horse's neck. Indirect reins of opposition, unless used absolutely correctly, will compress all but the most advanced horse, with the result being resistance, or if used consistently, lameness.

High and Low Reins

So far we have talked about pulling by moving the hand forward (leading rein) and back (rein of opposition) and a little bit about moving the hands to one side; away from the horse (opening) and toward the horse (indirect). The third dimension, which must also be considered, is up and down. Because of the horse's conformation, the more upward the direction of pull relative to his mouth, the more the horse will tend to give, while the more downward, the more he will tend to take.

So if we combine what we have learned about hand effects and rein effects, we have two simple rules for using the reins. **If you want the horse to give to the rein, you use your hand high and/or actively. If you want the horse to take the rein, you use your hand low and/or holding.** In the next chapter we'll see how these rules are applied.

19

Putting the Aids to Work
Go, Turn, Stop, and Back

Some years ago my husband and I spent two weeks vacationing in England. We soon discovered that you could rent quite nice horses and go for an escorted trail ride, so we made that a theme of our trip. Most of the people from whom we rented horses were very pleasant and welcoming. However, there was one man who seemed to want to prove to us, especially me, that we were just ignorant Yankees.

We started out on our ride across the countryside. After about half an hour of walking and trotting, we reached a large field. With a little smirk our escort said to me, "Your horse always runs away across this field. But don't worry, there's a gate on the other side where she always stops." He didn't say how *fast* she stopped—or what he hoped would happen to me when she did.

He then swung his horse around and took off at a gallop across the field. My mare took off after him, trying to pull the reins out of my hands. So I let the reins slide through my fingers a ways, then started using some gentle active hand. By the time we were halfway across the field, the mare was galloping nicely in hand, though fully extended. Meanwhile the owner, who was about 50 yards ahead of me, reached the gate, stopped and turned to watch. When I got about 20 yards from him, I used my active hand again and brought the mare quietly back to the trot, jogged up to him, and stopped. His face fell. He looked very confused. He wasn't going to ask me how I did it, and I sure wasn't going to tell him. But I'll bet he thought about it a lot in the next few days!

Once you truly understand how the aids affect the horse, applying them is just a matter of a little experimenting. There aren't that many ways the horse can resist, and you soon learn what to do in each situation. Rather than learning how to ride a particular horse, you learn what aids to use when *any* horse tries to evade you in a particular way. That's why I was able to get a horse I hardly knew to be so responsive.

Tidbits & Supplements

There is one big difference between riding horses and building bookcases (well, perhaps more than one): The bookcase isn't going to help you build it. But if you do things the right way when you're working with the horse, he can become part of the solution rather than a problem to be solved. One of the most significant things my trainer taught me is that **the reason a correct action the horse performs is called "correct" is because that is the easiest, most comfortable, most efficient way for the horse to do it.** That's the beauty of correct riding. You don't have to *make* the horse do it that way—he *wants* to do it that way because it's easier for him, so he looks for ways to help you.

When you ask your horse to do something and don't get the response you want or expect, the first thing to check is whether you are sitting correctly and using your aids appropriately. Your aids can be thought of as the tools with which you communicate—just as a carpenter's hammer, drill, and saw are the tools with which he builds things. By now you should have a pretty good idea of how to use your tools. But, just as a carpenter has to actually use his tools to build things to really know how to use them properly, you have to try doing different things with your aids to understand them better and become skilled in their use. So, it's time to "build a bookcase!"

To build your bookcase well, it helps to understand not only the tools but also the material you will be working with—in this case, the horse. Up to now we have talked almost entirely about the rider; now let's talk about some of the not-always-understood physical characteristics of the horse.

THE ETERNAL TRIANGLE

To begin with, to get the horse to respond to your aids, it is essential to have some understanding of what *forward* really means; the underlying concept of how a horse should be if he is to respond to the aids at all.

The concept of "forward" in riding is probably one of the least understood. Many people think it refers to the rider's position, as in "forward seat." Others relate it to speed—the faster the horse is going, the more forward he is. But neither of these is correct. Forward in the broad sense, from the rider's point of view, can be best described as the feeling that everything is right. The horse responds easily and fluidly to every command, his gaits are comfortable, and the first time it happens you find yourself saying, "*Now* I understand what riding is all about!"

The classic description of the correct horse is "calm, forward, straight." I believe one of the big sources of confusion about the *concept* of forward has been the use of the *word* "forward" in this formula. In the formula, "forward" refers to impulsion (power, delivered principally from the thrust of the hind legs, the horse's "engine") and energy (the horse's ability to produce impulsion easily when asked). But having power and energy alone is *not* "going forward" in the full meaning of the phrase. A horse who is running away is showing plenty of power and energy, but is not forward in the sense we mean. Therefore, I think using a different term might make the whole concept a bit clearer. Since the word "impulsiveness" has a totally different meaning, I settled on "energetic/powerful." So the description of the correct horse is "calm, energetic/powerful, straight." It is by no means perfect, but perhaps it will make the concept of forward a little easier to comprehend.

The easiest way for the novice to understand the total concept of forward is to think about automobiles. Calm relates to the mechanical condition of the car. Energetic/powerful is the fuel and the engine. Straight refers to the car's wheels and frame.

Calm

For the car to do what you want it to do, every mechanical part must function correctly. Consider a car that is not "relaxed." If the electrical system has a short or the fuel line is dirty or the transmission is falling apart, the car won't respond when you step on the gas. If the brake drums are worn, the car won't stop when you apply the brake. Similarly, if the horse is stiff and sore or tenses his neck against the bit from fear or is soft and out of condition, he won't be able to respond correctly to your commands. He may rush off out of balance and control, he may buck or otherwise actively resist, or he may simply ignore the command and continue on his sluggish way.

Tidbits & Supplements

Many horse owners like to think of their horse as spirited, because he seems to be very energetic under tack. Horses are, by nature, pretty peaceful animals. If you watch them in the field, they are usually just grazing quietly or sleeping, and even most of their games don't involve a great output of energy. If a horse is quiet in the field and his stall and "spirited" under tack, he probably is *really* just plain tense, and you need to look for the cause and fix it.

Energetic/Powerful

Just as with the car, warming up the horse is essential for his engine to function with maximum efficiency. During the car's warm-up, you may rev up the engine a little to get it running better. Similarly, you might ask the horse for a little extra energy/power to help loosen him up. But just as racing a cold engine will be bad for it because it is not yet ready to handle the speed, so asking for too much energy/power from a cold or insufficiently relaxed horse will cause problems both physical and mental, because the horse's body will not be able to handle it.

When the horse (or car) is warmed up, you can successfully ask for more energy/power without creating tension (mechanical problems).

Cars differ, and so do horses. You wouldn't expect the family sedan to handle with the responsiveness of a highly tuned race car. The amount of time spent tuning up either the car or the horse, as well as their basic potential, will affect the results.

Straight

A well-balanced horse will go forward on loose reins, but if the horse is inexperienced or the work becomes more demanding, the horse needs to go forward into the bit, so the rider can help him control his body by helping him balance and ground himself. For this mutual assistance to work, the horse must be willing to push (generate impulsion) against both reins with both hind legs equally, without resisting by either stiffening or overflexing his body. A car with one wheel on ice would not thrust forward evenly; instead, it would skid out of control, whether starting up or stopping. A horse pushing against only one rein will also slide out of control—dangerously so if he is jumping or galloping downhill.

Virtually all horses are crooked one way or the other, especially when they are tense or compressed. Therefore, if your horse is not warmed up and you put even pressure on both reins, the horse will probably end up going in a circle, since he won't thrust evenly against them. To go back to the car analogy, a horse who is not straight is like a car with a soft front tire or bad wheel alignment. You have to fix the tire or have the wheels aligned—you don't just try to cope by dragging on the steering wheel.

Completing the analogy, for the horse to be a pleasant ride (or for a car to be in the best driving condition,) the trainer (mechanic) must know a lot about horses (cars), how they work and how to fix whatever goes wrong. The rider (driver) must know how to ride (drive) to get the most out of the horse (car). She also must understand the horse (car) so that she doesn't undo the trainer's (mechanic's) work. Functioning as a team, they can create a useful horse (car) that will be a pleasure to ride (drive).

Tidbits & Supplements

When you are checking out the horse, *how* you listen is also very important. You must pay attention to what your horse is *actually* doing—not what you *think* he might or should be doing—and respond accordingly. Any time you see an unusual discrepancy of behavior (loss of calmness) in the horse, *don't continue*, but look for an external cause—*not* a training or "attitude" problem.

    Putting the same paragraph entirely into equestrian terms, for the horse to be consistently responsive to the aids, he must be going forward—that is, he must be calm, powerful/energetic, and straight. The trainer must understand how to maintain these qualities, and the rider must know how to enable the horse to use himself in the best possible way, so that his training is not interfered with. Together, trainer and rider can bring the horse to his maximum potential at any given time.

    The more the horse possesses of these three attributes—calmness, energy/power, and straightness—the better he will be able to respond to your aids and desires.

    When you meet with a problem, *after* you have checked your own tools you should check the horse against the standard of calm, energetic/powerful, straight. I think I can safely say that 100 percent of the time, you will find the problem is in one place or the other, or a combination of the two.

BENDING AND FLEXION

This is an area that is rarely touched upon but that can cause significant problems in control. The horse's body, as we know, is flexible both laterally (bending) and longitudinally (flexion), and this can be confusing to the rider who is trying to perceive what is happening at any given moment. First think about how a car responds to the controls. As long as it is moving and the ground is not slippery, if you turn the wheels left the car will go left. If you step on the accelerator the car will go faster; step on the brake and the car will stop.

    Now think about a Slinky spring. If you lay it down on a carpet and pull one end, it will *stretch* out for a while before the whole thing *moves*. If you pull it along on a smooth floor in a stretched out position and then stop pulling, it will *compress* together before it *stops*. You can *bend* it around in a C shape with both hands, but it won't *turn* unless you pull the front of it around. That is, the fact that you stretch it out or pull it together or bend it doesn't necessarily mean that the whole Slinky actually *goes* anywhere.

The horse's body works in somewhat the same way as the Slinky. So you must learn to be aware of whether the horse is responding to your aids with just bending/flexion like the Slinky, or with go/turn/stop as well, like the car.

Bending/Straightening vs. Direction

Let's begin with bending, straightening, and direction, because they are a little easier to understand. *Bend* is the lateral shape the horse's body takes. Usually, but not always, the horse's body bends in the same shape as the curved path he is on. *Straightening*, obviously, is the reverse of bending. *Direction* is just that: the direction in which the horse's feet are moving. So for an ordinary right turn, the horse would be bent to the right and his feet would be moving in a curved path to the right.

The difficulty arises when the horse *bends* but does not *go* in the desired direction. The inexperienced rider then asks for more bend, which, rather than making the horse *turn*, cramps the horse so that movement in the desired direction is blocked. The horse very often then goes in the wrong direction. The horse is quite capable, like the Slinky, of having his body bent in one direction while he moves in a straight line or even in the opposite direction, and in fact will often choose, when loose, to move counter to the way he is bending.

The rider can also be confused when she asks the horse to bend and he doesn't, but does start to *move* in the desired direction, unobserved by the rider. She keeps demanding bend, which in essence tells the horse that she isn't interested in direction. It helps to understand that for all practical purposes **a change in direction occurs when the horse's front leg on that side begins to move in that direction.**

Flexion/Extension vs. Speed

Flexion, extension, and speed (called by some trainers "miles per hour") are somewhat less obvious, but the principal is the same. As the horse extends his body he takes longer steps, so he may go faster (that is, cover more miles per hour) or he may slow his rhythm at the same time and so maintain the same miles per hour or even slow down. Or he may stretch out just his neck without lengthening his stride. He can also increase his miles per hour without lengthening or taking longer steps, just by moving his feet faster.

However, where this usually confuses the rider is when she is trying to slow down and perhaps pulls the reins too hard and cramps the horse, so he pulls back to get his head free. He pulls the reins out of her hands and extends his neck to release the cramp. The rider mistakes this *extension* for an increase in *speed* and pulls the reins harder, making the horse even more uncomfortable and thus more resistant. He then may speed up, either because his balance is affected or because the discomfort makes him want to escape.

The horse can also shorten in his neck without slowing down. In fact, because the shortening of his neck interferes with the use of his "front brakes," shortening his neck can actually *prevent* him from slowing down. The rider sees his neck shortening and thinks she is slowing him down, which is not happening. This is particularly likely to happen when the horse is unbalanced. In this situation you must get the horse to *extend* his neck before you can *slow* his speed.

Observing all these different phenomena, perhaps with the aid of a ground person or by watching other riders, will help considerably in your understanding of the "controls."

Now that you know quite a lot more about the material you have to work with, let's get a little more specific about getting the horse to do what you want. I originally titled this chapter "Stop, Go, and Turn," mostly because it sounded good; but in thinking about it I realized that in order of difficulty, *go* is by far the easiest, then *turn*, and *stop* is by far the hardest. Therefore we will discuss them in that order. So we'll start with getting him to move a little faster.

GO

In the great scheme of nature, the horse is prey. That is, if he isn't careful all the time, some lion is going to have him for lunch! Luckily, horses are faster and have more endurance than lions, so usually they can get away. The only two ways a lion can catch a horse are if he doesn't run soon enough or if he falls down. Because of this need to be able to get away in a hurry, the easiest movement for the horse to make is straight forward; that is, **it is easier for him to go than to do anything else.**

In Chapter 8 we learned what makes horses, who should find going forward very easy, become "sticky" or "lazy." Essentially, this is caused by the rider interfering with the horse either with the reins, or with her center and weight by leaning or rocking forward. The correct aids for *go* are pretty simple. It's avoiding the mistakes that *prevent* the horse from going that are difficult. Here's how to approach the problem.

To ask your horse to increase pace:

1. Keep your upper body *still* relative to the horse, that is, don't shift your upper body forward and especially don't rock back and forth, either of which will affect his balance. Your seat and thighs should be soft and your reins even and passive.

2. Keep your center slightly behind his, but directed forward (page 178) *until you have reached the speed you want.* Do not try to use your seat muscles as a driving aid.

3. Apply the active leg (page 298), assisted by the voice (page 49) and stick (page 158), if necessary. The driving aids must be applied with sufficient pause in between—usually about three seconds—to give the horse a chance to respond before being asked again. If the leg aid, especially, is used continuously, as many riders do with "sluggish" horses, it becomes like white noise that the horse soon learns to ignore. Don't use any driving aid so strongly that it causes pain and thus tension.

Another way many people get in trouble is if the horse, for whatever reason, instead of moving straight forward moves off to the side. The rider's response is usually to get busy with the reins, in the process interfering with the horse's ability to go. She may also lose some of her centering. This is most likely to occur in the ring, moving from halt to walk or walk to trot.

Upward transition, halt to walk.

Tidbits & Supplements

By using the lightest possible aid first, then giving the horse a chance to respond before moving to the next level, you teach the horse to listen to the light aid, but he also learns that if he chooses to ignore you, the aid will gradually escalate to discomfort (though never to the point of causing real pain). Parelli calls this "levels of pressure." However, you are treating him very fairly by giving him the choice, each time, of responding to the light aid. If you find yourself always having to escalate to the strongest aid, you need to look for reasons, first in your own technique, then in the horse's physical condition, as well as possible previous abuse.

A simple rule, and a classic one, is: **When your legs are active, your reins should be passive, and vice versa.** So if you are having trouble with upward transitions, stop worrying about the *direction* of the transition until the transition itself is occurring easily. Generally, once that happens the direction will take care of itself. When the horse starts to go forward, he will become straight.

Tidbits & Supplements

Many riders find the concept of a box easy to visualize. Imagine you have drawn a rectangle around your horse. The front of the rectangle is formed by pressure from the reins of oppositon. The sides of the rectangle are formed by a combination of reins, center, and leg. The back of the rectangle is formed by your legs and weight. If you want the horse to go forward, you open the front of the box while keeping the back of the box closed. If you want the horse to turn, you open the side of the box. The reins on the sides work like folding doors; if you slide your hand forward, you slide the door open and the horse can go out; if you bring the hand back, the door closes and keeps the horse in. When you want him to stop you close the front of the box. If he tries to push through the box in any direction, you simply move the box just enough so he can't get past it. By thinking of the box as moving along with the horse, you can keep the horse going and direct him without restricting him.

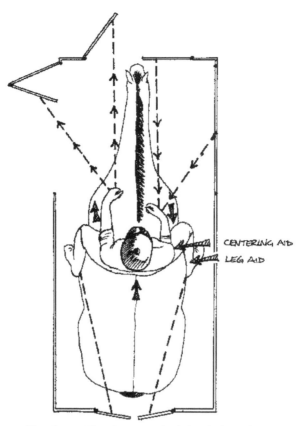

CENTERING AID

LEG AID

The "box." The doors on the left side have been
opened by the releasing left hand, while the right hand
keeps the right doors closed, with the support of the
right center and leg. The weight and legs are keeping
the rear doors closed.

TURNING

When we think about turning, it helps to go back to the analogy of driving the
car. A small child playing with the wheel of the car will turn it back and forth
in great sweeps, imagining herself guiding the car down the street. The experienced driver knows it doesn't happen that way. Steering—and keeping the car
going straight, which is a part of steering—consists of making a number of
small adjustments, depending on what is happening at any given moment. We
constantly monitor our speed and the feel of the car under our hands, correct-
ing as necessary. The same technique is used in steering the horse.

Earlier on, we said that if the horse is going forward, where his nose goes his body will follow. So the simplest turn involves getting the horse's nose to go in the direction we want his body to go. Even though this is written below as steps—"push button 1, then turn handle 2"—it doesn't really work that way. The horse may overbend and have to be straightened, or raise his head and stop going forward. Remember, you have to listen to what is actually happening at the time!

1. Begin with a centering aid. That is, for a left turn move your center slightly right. This tells your horse which way to go and frees up his legs on that side. Be careful that your longitudinal center doesn't get ahead of the horse.

2. Soften your inside rein pressure and increase the pressure on your outside rein to create a direct holding rein on the side away from the turn. Your horse should stretch his outside up against the holding rein, bringing his nose to the inside and beginning the turn. As his nose comes around, make the pressure on the two reins even.

3. Use enough leg and longitudinal weight (page 178) to keep him going against the rein pressure, timing it so that both legs press as your inside seat drops. Place your legs so that they help to curve the horse's body, using one leg more actively and adding some active seat if he feels stiffer on one side. The seat may be the better aid, especially if the horse tends to get a bit fast, but be sure not to move your lateral center accidentally.

4. If necessary, use an active leading rein to lead the horse's head in the direction you want. Be careful not to move your lateral center over until the horse begins to turn.

5. If you're circling, use your lateral center to make the circle smaller or larger, then adjust the horse's bend as needed. Listen to the horse's rhythm so you know whether the circle is getting so cramped that the horse cannot bend easily around it. The rhythm will slow noticeably if the horse finds the circle too small.

The most common problem with turning is that the horse refuses to turn his head. If this happens early in the ride, it usually means the horse is not sufficiently warmed up, so he just doesn't bend that way. He needs more stretching before bending becomes easy. Think of the Slinky again: When it is stretched out, it bends easily in any direction; when compressed, it doesn't bend at all. The bending to the left is particularly difficult for most horses, and often has to be avoided until the end of the lesson or even for some time.

Asking for a right turn. Eyes are to the right, center slightly left, the left leg is behind the girth. The left rein is holding, the right rein is releasing, ready to lead if needed.

Asking for a left turn correctly. From this side you can see the active inside leg.

Horses may also resist the leading rein because they expect to be hung on or pulled out of balance. This becomes a matter of the rider's self-control more than anything. It is *so* tempting to pull harder and drag the horse's head around to get the turn! And indeed you may get the turn that way; but you won't get it in a way that is easy for the horse, since his hind leg will not be in position to balance him. So the next time, you will get just as much resistance, or even more. Or, if the horse is noncombative, you'll get a horse who goes lame before his time.

When you are asking the horse to bend and go forward, the inside rein should *always* be softer and lighter than the outside rein. Only then can the horse step evenly forward with his inside legs and balance correctly without strain. Unless you are using the inside rein very loosely, always begin by establishing contact on the outside rein *before* you add any activity on the inside rein. **Once the horse has reached the degree of bend you want, the reins should be even in pressure.** If the horse begins to overbend to the inside, then the inside rein becomes firm and the outside rein soft. It's the same routine of listening to what is happening and adjusting your aids accordingly. **In all your turns, look for a flowing feeling and a lack of tension.**

Rider error has created resistance. My weight slid a little to the outside, causing my left leg and hand to tense up. This blocked Colette's left hind leg (her left hind cannon is not parallel to her right forearm, as it should be).

You should also understand that if the horse is giving you the *direction* you want and seems balanced, it is not necessary to insist on the bend, especially if either of you is a novice. This often happens when turning left until the horse is fairly advanced.

Horses can fool you. Most horses tend to cut in, but I worked with one horse who really liked to stay out on the rail. It took me a while to figure out that he hated to turn so much that he would never turn until he absolutely had to! Another horse showed an unusual willingness to turn away from the gate when crossing the ring, until I realized he only did it when the gate was on his left, because he found left turns so difficult in the arena.

Riding Straight Lines

Straight lines are a function of turning, in the sense that the horse tends to wander off the straight line for a variety of reasons and the rider has to continually correct and *steer* to keep him straight. The box concept on pages 361–362 is very helpful here.

Intent is very important for straight lines, which means your eyes must be looking ahead to tell the horse where you want to go. This is especially true if you are approaching the end of an arena, because many horses are concerned about running into the wall, so you have to tell them ahead of time which way you plan to turn. Soft eyes looking ahead are also essential to help you notice the *start* of a fluctuation in direction.

Another important element is your lateral center, which should be ready to shift to block any unwanted lateral movement. When you approach the end of your straight line, your lateral center and eyes will prepare the horse for the turn at the end.

The third element is enough impulsion. This does not mean speed; just enough energy and lack of tension for the horse to keep moving forward. Think of how a bicycle gets wobbly and difficult to keep straight if you ride too slowly.

The fourth element is even pressure on the reins, so the horse pushes off evenly with both hind legs. If the horse does not keep his body straight with even pressure on the reins, then he needs to be helped to correct it. If the horse keeps making one rein loose, ride him in a circle in that direction, using an inside active hand a little at first to ask him for a bit *more* bend than he offers, so that the outside (stiff side) is asked to stretch and loosen. After a short time he will ask to straighten out by taking up on the formerly loose rein.

Straight lines are much more difficult for the horse than most people realize, which is one reason cutting in in the arena is such an ongoing problem, especially for beginners. The unbalanced rider makes it almost impossible for the horse to go a straight line, and the unbalanced horse feels he would rather fall *away* from the wall!

Once you recognize the soft feeling you get from the horse when you are using correct steering aids and know how to adjust your aids as necessary to get that feeling, you will find that circles, serpentines, figure-8s, and straight lines are very simple and effortless for both of you.

STOPPING AND OTHER DOWNWARD TRANSITIONS

If there were an absolute, guaranteed, foolproof mechanical way for *anyone* to stop *any* horse safely, someone would have figured it out sometime in the last 5,000 years. The word would have spread and we would all use that technique. The fact that there are a million bits around, that plenty of good riders *do* get bolted with, and that there are a thousand techniques being taught at any given time is indication that this foolproof technique does not exist. There is *no* bit or training technique that will safely stop a horse whose mind is blown.

Getting the horse to go and to turn are comparatively easy, the first because it is his instinct to move whenever he doesn't know what else to do, and the second because his lateral axis is short, so it is easy to shift his weight in such a way that stepping to one side is his natural response. Stopping is something else again. Probably the most meaningful insight came from the late Dr. Reiner Klimke, who said, "Upward transitions come from the seat and leg, downward transitions come from God."

I think perhaps we can narrow this down a little. Loose horses who feel secure both physically and emotionally will always either stand still or, if grazing, move very little. Horses who feel insecure will virtually never stand still, since their instinct is to run from danger. Therefore, the simple downward transition begins with having a horse who feels secure (for which we can read "balanced physically and unthreatened emotionally"—in other words, calm), and then simply allowing him to do the natural thing.

> ### *Tidbits & Supplements*
>
> There *are* two sure ways to stop a horse, but they're not very safe. One is the running-W, a special harness the rider can use to throw the horse down. The other is a lead-butted crop to hit him between the ears and knock him out. The first one is used by rough-and-ready trainers when they know in advance that the horse will bolt, so they have the equipment rigged. The second was used by a friend of my husband on a horse who was bolting toward a 50-foot cliff!

Thus, if you are trotting and you become passive, the horse will come to a walk on his own. In the same way, you can get him from canter to drop into trot. A transition from gallop to a slower gait may be more difficult, because gallop is a stimulating gait; but a calm horse who has been galloping for a while is quite willing to slow down.

Walk to halt is often the most difficult transition, for two reasons. The first is that the walk is a difficult gait in which to maintain correctness and impulsion, so as the rider starts using aids to stop the horse, she can easily make him insecure instead. The second reason is that riders tend to have higher expectations of this transition, and quickly get annoyed and frustrated if the horse doesn't stop immediately.

I have often used the following exercise with riders who are either novices or new to my teaching. At the end of the lesson, when both horse and rider are relaxed and working well together, I ask the rider to simply allow her whole body to become passive so that she is no longer telling the horse to keep going. Sure enough, within a few steps the horse stops and the rider says, "Wow, that was so simple." But very often when she tries it again, she now has an expectation that the horse will stop, and when he doesn't stop immediately she becomes frustrated, so the horse picks up on her tension and keeps walking.

The same sort of thing happens when the rider uses the rein aids. Due to lack of skill, her timing may be a little off, interfering with the horse's response. When he doesn't stop immediately, she starts using stronger aids and becomes more tense. Depending on the horse's training he may speed up or he may perform an incorrect halt. This does not make him feel either comfortable or secure, so his downward transitions do not improve.

Many horses learn to cope with all this by performing incorrect but usable downward transitions. These horses often become either school horses or

Tidbits & Supplements

Some trainers make a practice of teaching the horse to maintain a gait without any supporting aids until he is given a command to change it. I consider this unnatural and also unsafe. You certainly wouldn't want a bicycle that wouldn't stop if you stopped pedaling! If the horse is in trouble, he should feel that he can stop and fix it if necessary. Horses who are not allowed to do so often develop such habits as bucking or bolting when things go wrong, because the natural solution is denied them. And of course, the passive downward transition is no longer available to the horse or the rider.

A-show amateur horses, depending on their conformation and way of going. Because their hind legs are not engaged correctly in their downward transitions, the horses usually end up unsound sooner than they should. Many more horses do *not* learn to cope, and these are the ones who end up with severe bits, or are sold with the description "for advanced rider only."

Learning to *stop* a horse correctly is one of the ways you start to learn the meaning of *forward*. A horse who is not going forward always has trouble stopping because he is tense and therefore not grounded. To understand the nature of stopping a little more clearly, run rapidly across a smooth, level, open space, then stop. Try stopping both quickly and gradually. In both cases, observe that in order to stop, you have to get your *feet* out in front of your *center* to brake yourself. This is how the horse stops if he is properly balanced.

If your *center* gets too far ahead of your *feet*, you can't stop unless you can catch yourself with your hands on some support. This is the equivalent of the horse stopping primarily by propping himself with his front legs—stopping on his forehand. If you can't use your hands, you have to try to fling yourself back over your feet, which is very painful to your back. When you see a horse stopping with his mouth open and his head in the air, it is that kind of stop, and you can imagine how painful it must be. If all of those methods fail, the only way to stop is to fall, which will certainly stop you, and a horse, but is not very desirable!

For the horse to keep his center over his feet, he first needs to be loose enough in his back and hindquarters and confident enough in his mind to take long steps with his hind feet so that they come up under his center. This is called tracking up. He can also use his front feet to help him push his center back, just as you would use your hands if you stumbled, but to do so he must be able to reach out in front of himself with his front legs. When he moves his center back toward his hind feet, it is called self-carriage, which is necessary for easy downward transitions. Unless the horse is fairly advanced in his training, he only holds this self-carriage during the transition itself.

As we've discovered in Chapter 18 on rein effects, when you start to use opposition in the reins, the tendency is to shorten and compress the horse, forcing him to take shorter steps. Think about that Slinky again. If you push on both ends, you bring them closer together for a while, but there comes a point where the Slinky won't compress anymore, the ends are still separated and the whole thing is rigid. *Bending it around vertically brings the ends together without losing flexibility.* This is the picture you want to have in your mind as you ask your horse to slow down: helping him keep his body long and flexible throughout, and bringing both ends together from underneath. A flowing feeling and evenness of rhythm are once again your guidelines.

The Aids for Stopping

Aids that you use on a horse who is out of control will be discussed a little later. For now we are simply concerned with getting a calm, nicely schooled horse to stop while still keeping him relaxed and comfortable. Consider how you learned to stop the horse when you were leading him (Chapter 5). You found that if you just locked up against the rein, the horse had trouble stopping easily. What worked was to give the horse a *signal* to stop by using the lead in opposition, and then allowing the horse to make the stop himself. You also found that it worked better if *you* kept moving until the horse stopped, keeping you both from locking up.

1. Begin by becoming passive with all your aids, especially your leg aids, and allowing your body to slow its rhythm a little. Use your longitudinal center and weight aid to keep the horse balanced and going just enough so that he keeps his feet under him as he slows down. If the horse drops immediately into a clunky downward transition, reapply leg aids to keep him going and grounded.

2. If you're trotting, do not go from a posting or half seat position to a full seat position *at the same time* as you ask for a downward transition from the trot to the walk. The horse has to adjust his back for the change and cannot deal with the transition as well. If you wish to be in full seat, either go to it first, allow the horse to adjust, then ask for the transition, or wait until the transition is nearly complete before sitting.

3. Allow your weight to come back a little, but not so much that it starts to redirect and send the horse on again.

4. Using two direct reins of opposition, start using one rein passively or lightly holding and the other rein actively. Whichever rein feels heavy should be used actively, and the other passively. If the horse starts to slow down by himself, both reins can become passive or lightly holding.

5. If you are already sitting, allow your following seat to work softly to keep the rhythm of the gait going and the horse's back soft. If you are posting, allow your posting to slow a little and become smaller.

6. Gradually slow the horse down using the rein/hand aids as necessary, until you reach the pace you want. Keep being very aware of how the reins feel at all times, changing from active to passive, or vice versa, when needed.

To clarify a bit, the *hand effect* for stopping is active with one hand and passive with the other. Thus, one set of legs is always free to move. This is because the horse can only stop with one leg at a time. If you run and stop, you will see how one leg comes forward and braces to slow you down, then the next leg does

Asking for a transition from walk to halt. I'm encouraging Wills to keep coming forward from behind with my center, my left hand is holding and my right hand is working actively in opposition.

Here Wills is just about to halt. I've allowed him to lengthen his neck so he can use his "front brakes."

the same thing. If you try to stop both legs simultaneously, you end up stamping your feet into the ground. Looks stupid, and hurts a bit besides!

The *rein effect* is direct rein of opposition. So you will maintain steady, passive contact with one rein while you use the other one actively, the direction of both hands being about the same, except the passive hand will tend to be low and the active hand higher. You will **always use an active rein on the horse's stiff side and a passive or holding rein on the soft side.**

Sometimes, if you or the horse is having a lot of trouble with the stop, you will find that you need to switch hands as your hand effects begin to work, and the horse takes on the holding hand and gives to the active one, switching sides, as it were. Again, what needs practice here is feeling the two reins, mentally looking at first one and then the other, and creating the feel that *you* want by softening or taking more.

If the horse's steps become short and choppy, indicating that he is compressing rather than rounding, you should become passive with your hands and *ease* him forward with weight and legs until he smoothes out, then start again. Do the same sort of thing if his head and neck come up and become tense or very shortened.

A problem that often occurs when the rider uses her reins in opposition is that she locks her back and hips so that she braces against the rein, rather than letting the pull flow through her body. Locking causes the horse to become rigid

Reins in opposition for a downward transition. The left
rein is low and holding, the right rein is high and active.
At this point the right hand is releasing.

Tidbits & Supplements

Here's a Centered Riding trick. If you can get access to one of those little trampolines, about three feet (1 m) in diameter, you can practice your following seat into the halt. Stand in the center of the trampoline and start to jog in place. The trampoline will, of course, move with you. Now stop jogging. The trampoline will keep vibrating for quite a while. Start jogging again, and this time slow your jog gradually, staying with the trampoline, until you stop together. This is the feeling you want on the horse. You can also attach a pair of reins to a nearby object and practice applying pressure to the reins without losing your softness and following.

---

as well. Therefore, you need to be very conscious of your following seat during downward transitions.

When you first start working with halts, many horses as they try to stop will begin to turn, usually to the right. If you make a fuss about this, you will often scare the horse about stopping—and the more tense he is, the more difficult he will find it to stop, and the more crooked he will tend to be. As in your upward transitions, work on getting the transition first. Once it is easy, you can begin to make it straight.

The other thing that happens with inexperienced riders and horses is that the horse can't keep his center and hind feet vertically aligned all the way into the halt. He starts to lose his balance forward and can't quite stop. So the last step or two he needs to use his front legs as front brakes to get the stop. In order to do this, he needs his head. When you get to what feels like the last step or two, without changing anything else, just ease the reins a little, which will allow the horse to use his front brakes, and you'll get the stop (see the bottom photo on page 371). Often the rider feels the horse taking the reins at that moment in the transition. He's just trying to get his balance and use those front brakes, but she thinks he's trying to break away, so she pulls harder—exactly the wrong thing to do! Again, as the horse advances in strength and training, he won't need to do this (but it's a pretty advanced level, and he may never get there).

EMERGENCY STOPS

Emergency stops are just that—aids to be used only in emergencies, because they work by breaking up the horse's ability to use his legs normally to run. This means his feet hit the ground in a way that is very destructive to the horse's joints. Therefore, if you use them all the time, your horse will quickly develop unsoundness. Also, the horse can learn to anticipate them and set up resistances that you *cannot* overcome, so you lose the advantage.

Pulley Rein

The first emergency stop is called a pulley rein, and is used mostly by English riders. It uses the rider's center as a stopping aid, as well as the reins, and is one of the few instances where the rider's center is used in *front* of the horse's center. You can practice the moves gently at the standstill, and maybe perform one stop during a session, but unless your horse was being very aggressive, apologize to him afterward for being rough!

1. From the half-seat position, holding the reins one in each hand with both reins even and fairly snug, place your left fist, knuckles down, on the horse's neck in the hollow just in front of the withers. Shorten the left rein if necessary so that it is snug.

2. Place the right rein in the slot between your left thumb and forefinger and slacken it until it is slightly looser than the left.

3. Throw your weight forward onto your left hand, and at the same time pull sharply up on the right rein through the slot. The rein effect will be somewhat indirect, that is, toward your opposite shoulder.

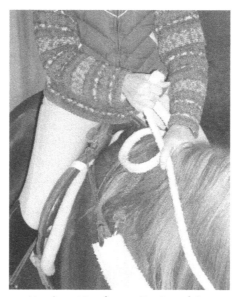

Hand position for application of the
pulley rein.

The big trick in the pulley rein is in the timing. You would, of course, probably only use it at the gallop, and you must use it just as the horse starts to come up in front of you and his outside hind leg is coming forward. If you get it right, the horse will stop dead in his tracks.

One-Rein Stop

The second emergency stop is called a one-rein stop. Until recently this was used mostly by western riders and it is comparatively new to me. However, I have studied it very carefully and used it effectively with my students. The horse must first be trained on the ground, or be well schooled in both yielding laterally to the leg and in the taking hand.

Ground Work

1. Standing by the horse's right shoulder, use the taking, direct rein until his head is bent well around toward you but not pulled in toward his shoulder.

2. Now open the rein slightly, using it passively or taking as necessary to keep his head in place. At the same time, use your other hand against his side to ask the horse to step to the left with his hindquarters. As soon as you get a step, ease the rein and praise.

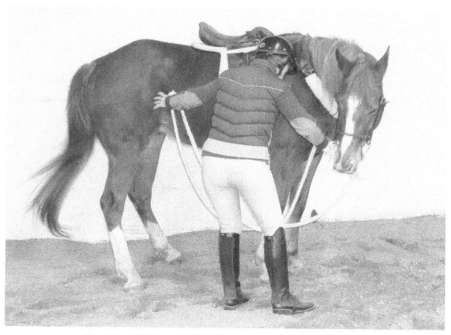

Teaching Wills to yield his hindquarters on the ground.

3. When the horse performs the exercise easily at the standstill, ask him to perform it at the walk. Do not work at it for more than five minutes, and use much encouragement and praise.

Plan to work on this exercise on the ground over several sessions before you try to use it mounted.

On the Horse

1. With the reins even and snug and your weight well back, use the taking, direct rein on the right side until the horse's head is well around. If you get resistance you can make the rein effect higher and more indirect until the head is where you want it.

2. With the horse's head swung around, open the rein slightly, keeping his head in place, and use your right leg back as your left seat drops (left hind in the air) until you feel the horse step over to the left with his hindquarters.

3. *Ease the aid for a step*, then reapply as necessary until the horse stops.

This technique breaks up the horse's longitudinal resistance, then allows him to go forward for a step. If the horse is merely tense and not aggressive, he will often settle down within a step or two and give himself to normal aids. If he is being aggressive, you can keep doing this forever, until he finally gives up.

The pulley rein is usually used on a horse who is already running, but the one-rein stop is very effective on a horse who is *trying* to run, since it prevents him from setting up against you, and as long as you keep releasing each time he gives in, it is not threatening.

Notice that both the pulley rein and the one rein stop/disengagement are done with the right hand. This is because virtually all horses bend more easily to the right. Since they are for emergency use only, there is usually no real need to practice them to the left. However, if you expect to use the disengagement exercise in a sustained way, as with a horse who is very uncontrollable on the trail, it should be taught on both sides. Of course, what you should really be working on is the horse's calmness on the trail!

BACKING

The novice should only attempt backing on a horse who backs easily, because it is easy to compress and scare him. I have found backing to be one of the areas where horses often have to be started all over again because they have so many hang-ups.

Disengaging the hindquarters for a one-rein stop. I'm using two reins, rather than one, but I'm trying to keep Wills comfortable. As you see, he does not look happy.

1. Sit with your hip angle a little closed, so your center is slightly forward and the direction of your weight is pressing the horse back. As the horse moves, adjust your center either to keep him moving or to allow him to stop.

2. Use the same combination of hand and rein effects for backing that you used for stopping. The direct reins of opposition, with one hand active and the other passive, help the horse shift his weight back while still allowing him to use one front leg at a time for balance.

3. You can also add leg and seat aids, if appropriate—leg aids if he is not moving and seat aids if his movement seems stiff. However, many horses find leg aids for backing confusing, so they may not help.

When you apply the rein pressure, observe whether the horse resists or overbends in the neck. In the first instance, make the reins more active; in the second, more holding. Be sure you release the reins and praise *when the horse shifts his weight back,* not merely if he yields in the neck. (This is an example of flexion and speed, although backward.) Using the reins in this way, only ask for one step at a time at first. As with the transitions, don't worry about direction until the backing comes easily.

PROMPTNESS

Getting quick responses begins with the horse developing (through practice) the strength, confidence, and coordination to respond easily to the commands. After that, it is as much a trick as anything else. Effusive praise when the horse responds quickly results in far better transitions than the use of sharp aids, which cause tension and can actually slow the horse's reaction time.

If you want a horse to be highly schooled in his responses, you or someone else is going to have to spend time—lots of it—to get those results. I will always remember the words of a world-famous veterinarian at a Professional Horsemen's meeting. Someone in the audience asked him, "What's wrong with our horses that they seem to go lame so much?" The veterinarian replied without a pause, "There is nothing wrong with your horses; it's the way you ride them!" Shortcut methods may produce results in a hurry, but they also produce unsoundness.

You will probably spend quite a long time working through the techniques in this chapter, but as you work with them, you will see how they fit together. Try to work with them in a situation where the horse is neutral, that is, he does not have an agenda that affects his responses. A horse who is actively trying to get back to the barn is likely to be trying to figure out how to evade you, not cooperate.

In any case, when you do finally put the puzzle together, you will be astounded at how rarely control becomes an issue. Horses will go where you want and do what you want with very little apparent effort on your part. And that's how you'll know that you're riding the horse the way he wants!

Conclusion

Build Self-Confidence in Yourself and Your Horse

Be the Perfect Student

My late husband spent the years just before World War II in Middleburg, Virginia, training field hunters and polo ponies. At that time, some of the finest horsemen in the country worked and rode there and were generous with their help and advice to a dedicated young man. Eventually, he informed me proudly, he was told by the best of the best that he was one of the better riders in Virginia. An accolade not at all easy to earn, so he was justly proud.

What I remember about him most on a horse was his supreme confidence. But as I look back, what also stands out is that I don't ever recall seeing a horse he was riding appear upset or disobedient. No matter how a horse might behave with others, when my husband rode him he never bucked or ran or spooked, and if anything happened that might startle him, something in my husband's presence seemed to soothe the horse and restore his confidence immediately. Every horse he rode always seemed to be enjoying himself.

When I originally wrote this book, my intention was to try to help the many riders who experience fear every time they ride. It was only much later that I finally realized that only if the horse is happy and confident can the rider be happy and confident, as well. Now, thinking about my husband's riding has made me understand that, as he was fond of saying, "It's a two-way street." That is, confidence in *either one* helps to build confidence in the other.

At this stage in your riding, however, your principal concern is to build your own confidence first. So let's define a confident rider. First of all, a confident rider is not the same as an aggressive rider. A confident rider has no need to bully a horse, because she is confident that she can get the best out of the horse without resorting to force. Confidence results from knowing at every level that you are safe: safe physically because you can deal with the unexpected even if it occurs too suddenly for conscious thought; safe mentally because you know what to do and how to plan for safe riding; and, finally, safe emotionally because you are secure enough in your skills and self-confidence to give your horse emotional support if he needs it.

Reaching this level of confidence is not going to happen in an afternoon. It results from hard work on a lot of different aspects of riding and related areas. But the results are beyond wonderful. I guess "soul-satisfying" is the closest I can come to describing the feeling. I think perhaps it is the real meaning behind the old, old saying (dating back at least to the early 19th century): "There is something about the outside of a horse that is good for the inside of a man."

But, as I said, it is neither quick nor easy to achieve. James started lessons with me full of enthusiasm. He had plenty of money, a good build, and he was fearless. But he had a busy schedule and missed more lessons than he attended. After he had been riding irregularly for about a year, he was very discontented with his progress. I pointed out that he missed a lot of lessons, but he shrugged it off. He had always found sports easy and saw no reason why riding should be any different. One day he said to me, "I've been riding with you almost a year. I met Mr. Smith [a well-known local trainer] at a cocktail party last week and he told me that if I came and rode with him every day for 90 days he could make a pretty good rider out of me." I looked at him and burst out laughing. "James," I replied, "so could I!"

Sometimes even the most intelligent person fails to realize the truth of the old adage, "You get out of something only what you put into it." Learning to ride even moderately well takes a lot of effort. The best instructor and the best information, while they are certainly important, cannot replace the student's desire to learn and improve by her own efforts.

Another thing people like James rarely discover is the immense satisfaction that comes from working really hard at something and seeing the positive results accumulate over the years. Things that come easily are never as satisfying. Most professionals have met with at least one rider who was able to win in competition solely because she or her parents were able to afford the expensive horse who could do the job. The blue ribbon is far less rewarding to this rider than the second or even lesser place won by the rider who has spent many hours reschooling an abused horse.

How does this apply to building confidence? Confidence comes from knowing you can deal with whatever happens. The rider who reschooled the horse is going to have far more confidence—and self-confidence—than the one who is being packed around by a superb horse, regardless of her own abilities.

This book has been about building confidence by learning how to deal with just about whatever happens. You have learned how a combination of a good relationship with the horse, a good position, and good communication skills will give you that confidence. Having those skills also gives your horse confidence, which helps him to respond better to training. The result is that riding becomes easier and more fun for both of you than you ever dreamed.

So what now? What else can *you* put into the equation? First, some suggestions. The more nonthreatening miles you can get—riding quiet horses in safe situations—the quicker you will progress. Listen to what your body and your horse are telling you. If it isn't working, why not? Your greatest enemy may be yourself, setting standards that you can't meet, often based on what you perceive as others' opinions of your riding. As long as you are learning and trying to improve, there is no such thing as failure. At worst, you may be going in the wrong direction and have to retrace your steps, but even that will increase your awareness and knowledge.

Besides studying riding through clinics, books and tapes, look at alternative areas of study to improve yourself physically, mentally, and emotionally. You may want to explore chiropractic, massage or acupuncture to improve your body. Yoga, tai chi, and other similar disciplines will also help your body, and your mind and emotional balance as well. Think about diet, not just to lose weight but to control tension and general health. Especially in America, we are so accustomed to eating poorly that many people accept exhaustion and irritability as a normal part of life. It's hard for either you or your horse to enjoy a ride when you're tired and cranky.

If you want to get away for a bit and still help your riding, skiing uses the same principles of biomechanics and physics, and is a sport where good position and confidence go hand in hand. Centered skiing, following the same basic principles as Centered Riding, is taught at many ski resorts.

Sailing, especially in small boats, develops your awareness of response to hand aids. The tiller of a boat requires the same light, sensitive, aware feel that you need on the reins to get the best performance.

Ballroom dancing and ice dancing both improve your ability to follow the movements of another individual. They also teach the importance of grounding and the way each partner assists the other to ground through hand contact, just as rider and horse help one another to ground through rein contact.

But perhaps the best advice I can give you is taken from an article by my friend and well-known author and instructor Dr. Jessica Jahiel. In the magazine of the American Riding Instructors Association, Jessica describes her ideal, the

Perfect Student. I have chosen those points that I think apply to learning from this book. Dr. Jahiel writes:

In an ideal world, I would teach only those students who

1. Truly want to learn

2. Are willing to work

3. Understand that the best progress is slow and steady

4. Have a genuine affection for horses and take genuine joy in riding

5. Want to learn horsemanship, not just riding skills

6. Aren't afraid to ask a question—any question

7. Think about their lessons and their riding at other times

8. Show love for their horses by the way they care for them, handle and ride them

9. In and out of competition, always put horsemanship and sportsmanship first

10. Are always interested in learning something new

So I would advise you to take all the help you can get, but also be willing to take responsibility for your own progress. This includes not only the willingness to work, but also the willingness to accept cheerfully the limitations your life puts upon you. You do your best, but if you don't learn it today, there's always next week. The most important thing about any learning experience is that the journey should always be fun. Enjoy your trip, and see that your horse enjoys his, too!

Gincy Self Bucklin
Narragansett, Rhode Island
www.whatyourhorsewants.com

Appendix A

Making and Fitting a Neck Strap

Partly because of the unbelievers, neck straps cannot be bought as such in your local tack shop. You have to make your own. There are a number of different ways to do this, depending on the materials you have available and your needs, but whichever way you decide to make a neck strap, you must first consider the horse's comfort. If the neck strap interferes with his functioning, it will cause problems for both of you.

SIMPLE LOOPS

You can make a simple neck strap using a fairly thick, soft cotton rope. Not so thick that it is awkward to hold, but as thick as possible. You can make a non-slip knot by tying an overhand knot in the end of the rope and another one along the rope as far as you need to get the length you want. Leave the second knot loose and put the first one through it, then tighten. To adjust the length, move the second knot. Tie off the loose end around the neck rope so it doesn't dangle around the horse's legs. You can also use an ordinary horse leg bandage in the same way, but the knots are more likely to jam.

You can use a long English stirrup leather, or two buckled together if the horse's neck is heavy. This is much easier to adjust if different people ride the horse or if you frequently go from riding bareback to riding in the saddle. A fuzzy tube placed around the bottom half will make it more comfortable for the horse.

Using either of the above devices, you have to be careful that the loop doesn't slide down the horse's neck if he drops his head, especially to graze, when he could put his foot through it. A cord that fastens the neck strap to the saddle or surcingle is a good safety precaution.

If you ride with a martingale, the yoke (the loop that goes around the horse's neck) can be used as a neck strap for short periods, but it is too narrow to use constantly because it would cut into the horse's neck.

The problem with using a simple loop device is that all the pressure is on the horse's neck and shoulders. I prefer to use a neck strap that also attaches to the girth, so some of the pull is concentrated there and it doesn't interfere with the horse at all.

MODIFIED BREASTPLATES

If you ride with a hunting breastplate, you can turn it into a neck strap by adding an extra strap across the withers. The strap should be adjustable in some way. You can adapt the breastplate to bareback by making extenders to the straps that fasten to the D-rings of the saddle so that they will reach around the bareback surcingle. You also need to put nice, thick fuzzies around the long straps that run down the horse's shoulder, or they will cut into him.

The chest strap, which runs down to the girth, must be adjusted short enough so that it takes the pressure off the horse's gullet. For some reason this strap is nearly always very long, so it may need extra holes or even professional shortening.

The difficulty with using a hunting breastplate is that even with padding it is rather narrow on the horse's shoulders. More important, the part that goes across the top of the horse's neck usually sits quite close to his withers, which means it tends to be under your hands when you are in half seat, rather than out in front of them. This makes it harder for you to balance, because your hands are in the wrong place.

My personal preference, which I used in my school for many years, is a neck strap made with a padded nylon Western breastplate. A Western breastplate is Y-shaped, with a short branch going to each side of the shoulders and one to the girth. It needs some adapting to make it usable with either an English saddle or a bareback pad. You can either do the adapting yourself or have a tack shop do it for you. Each branch of the Y consists of a thick, padded piece with an adjustable strap at the end for attaching to the saddle. All the adjustable straps are too short for English or bareback tack and need to be replaced with longer ones. In addition, you need two pieces to go over the top of the horse's neck: one to hold the breastplate in place so it doesn't slip down over the horse's shoulder points, and one that is the actual neck strap to hold on to.

If you like making your own equipment, you can buy long braided nylon reins and conway buckles and use them to make a very serviceable neck strap out of a Western breastplate, as I've just described. It will not win any beauty contests, but it will be comfortable for the horse and a great comfort to you as you learn.

You can also use an English jumping breastplate, adding a chest strap made of nylon and conway buckles, and over-neck straps as previously described (see the photo on page 68).

FITTING THE NECK STRAP

Whatever the type of neck strap you choose, correct fit and adjustment to both horse and rider are essential if it is to do its job. You must be careful that the neck strap doesn't fall so low that it gets in the way of the horse's shoulder points, nor so high that it presses against his windpipe. If you notice a change in his way of going when you're using the neck strap, check the fit first.

From the rider's point of view, the neck strap should be adjusted so that whether you are sitting or standing, when your hands are pulling lightly on the neck strap your elbows hang just slightly in front of your shoulders. For bareback work this means the hand part of the strap will come about to the center of the withers, while if you will be standing in the stirrups it will be forward of the withers. A long-armed person standing up on a short-necked horse is always going to have something of a problem positioning the strap far enough forward, and may end up having to use the mane.

Appendix B

Plateaus
Charting Your Progress

The Plateaus are a way for you to keep track of your progress. If you check off each skill and date it, you can look back and see what you were working on six months or two years ago. It helps you to realize that you really *are* doing more things better.

Once you have learned a skill, you may consider that you have reached the Plateau for that skill. Ideally, however, you should stay with it, continuing to practice it until you *really know* it; that is, until it is in your muscle memory to such a degree that you don't really have to think about it. Only when you *know* each skill in a group can you really say you are finished with that Plateau.

It's not a competition, and there won't be any medals or prizes—only the satisfaction of knowing that you have completed a task and completed it well. But you're welcome to write to me and tell me about it!

PLATEAU I: GROUND WORK

- The first five steps of the Seven Steps and grounding on foot (Chapter 2).

- Greet an unfamiliar horse (Chapter 3).

- Move all the way around the horse safely and correctly (Chapter 3).

- Demonstrate correct grooming positions (Chapter 3).

- Move the horse a step to the side, front, and rear (Chapter 3).

- Hold a quiet horse in a controlled situation (Chapter 3).

- Halter, put the horse on crossties if appropriate, and attach a lead line (Chapter 4).

• Groom the horse, except his feet, using voice commands where appropriate (Chapter 4).

• Work with the stick on the ground and introduce the horse to the stick (Chapter 5).

• Lead a quiet horse in a controlled situation with the halter and lead rope and with reins (Chapter 5).

• Tack with a bareback pad, neck strap, and hackamore (Chapter 4).

PLATEAU I: ON THE HORSE

All Plateau I riding is either bareback or without stirrups in a controlled situation.

• Mount bareback from a mounting block (or mount into the saddle from a mounting block, with assistance, if you are not riding bareback) (Chapter 6).

• Do the Seven Steps and ground on a bareback pad or a saddle without stirrups (Chapter 7).

• Hold the stick correctly, switch from one hand to the other and mount holding the stick (Chapter 8).

• Apply the stick, using the four levels of pressure, to get a halt to walk transition (Chapter 8).

• Use the active seat bilaterally and unilaterally (Chapter 8).

• Use your center actively and passively to ask for turns and downward transitions (Chapter 8).

• Use your weight for upward transitions and to maintain gait (Chapter 8).

• Use your eyes to indicate intent of direction or distance (Chapter 8).

• Ride without reins in a controlled situation on a quiet horse (Chapter 9).

• Ride the slow sitting trot, bareback or without stirrups (Chapter 9).

• Pick up and hold the reins correctly (Chapter 10).

• Demonstrate releasing, lengthening, and shortening the reins (Chapter 10).

- Hold the reins in a half bridge (Chapter 10).

- Hold the reins, neck strap, and stick (Chapter 10).

- Use a soft leg at the walk to ask for halt to walk transitions, combining it with the stick and voice aids as necessary (Chapters 16 and 19).

PLATEAU II: GROUND WORK

- Clean the horse's feet (Chapter 4).

- Tack with the saddle and a bridle with a bit (Chapter 4).

- Give another rider a leg on (Chapter 4).

PLATEAU II: ON THE HORSE

- Mount into the saddle from the ground or a low mounting block, depending on the size of horse (Chapter 6).

- Ride at the walk, demonstrating loose and fixed leg, bareback or in the saddle (Chapter 11).

- Ride at the walk with stirrups, demonstrating correct leg and foot position in full seat ∩ position, full seat Λ position, full seat forward, and half seat (Chapter 12).

- Ride at the trot, demonstrating correct position in half seat open position and half seat closed position (Chapter 13).

- Demonstrate using the reins separate from the neck strap. Demonstrate using the stick separate from the reins and neck strap, changing the stick from one hand to the other and reversing the stick (Chapter 10).

- Ride at the walk, demonstrating combing the reins (Chapter 18).

- Ride at the walk, demonstrating a passive hand in moderate contact (Chapter 18).

- Demonstrate correct balance and position at the posting trot, changing diagonals as needed (Chapter 14).

- Perform turns and transitions from the walk using the appropriate aids (Chapters 8 and 16 through 19).

Appendix C

The Flowchart

Where Can You Go from Here?

The purpose of the flowchart is to give you some choices and some variety in your lessons and practice sessions, since nobody wants to do the same thing over and over. It's boring for you and tiring for the horse. On the other hand, you don't want to try things you're not ready for, for two reasons. One is that you will undo the good work you have already done in building your foundation, and the other is that it is very unfair to your horse to try things you really aren't ready to do. He finds it hard enough to deal with your mistakes as you work on the things you *are* ready for! And he may well tell you in an unpleasant way if he thinks you've gone too far.

Generally, you should try to stick to the activities in one box of the flowchart, at least until you're pretty comfortable with everything in that box. Then you can start picking items out of the next box. Try not to get overeager and skip two or three boxes just because something looks like fun.

Another thing to be careful of: Very often, the first time you try something that's a little difficult for you, it goes pretty well. That's because your body doesn't know what to expect. But if it's a bit *too* difficult, you'll find that when you try it again, instead of getting better, you're getting worse. That's a sure sign that you have overextended yourself and should go back to where you were for a while and try that difficult skill again sometime later. Remember, your goal is to ride correctly, safely, and with confidence, and to keep your horse comfortable.

- The first five steps of the Seven Steps and grounding on foot (Chapter 2).
- Greeting an unfamiliar horse (Chapter 3).
- Moving around the horse (Chapter 3).
- Correct grooming positions (Chapter 3).
- Moving the horse a step to the side, front, and rear (Chapter 3).
- Grooming the horse, except his feet (Chapter 4).
- Mounting bareback from a mounting block (Chapter 6).
- Mounting into the saddle (Chapter 6).
- The Seven Steps and grounding on a bareback pad or a saddle without stirrups (Chapter 7).

- Haltering, putting the horse on crossties and attaching the lead line (Chapter 4).
- Working with the stick on the ground and introducing the horse to the stick (Chapter 5).
- Holding the stick (Chapter 8).
- Applying the stick (Chapter 8).
- Picking up and holding the reins correctly (Chapter 10).
- Leading a quiet horse (Chapter 5).
- Releasing, lengthening, and shortening the reins (Chapter 10).
- Holding the reins, neck strap, and stick (Chapter 10).
- Tacking with a bareback pad, neck strap, and hackamore (Chapter 4).

- Cleaning the horse's feet (Chapter 4).
- Tacking with a saddle, bridling with a bit (Chapter 4).
- Active seat (Chapter 8).
- Active and passive center (Chapter 8).
- Using the weight aids for upward gait transitions and to maintain gait (Chapter 8).
- Using your eyes (Chapter 8).
- Changing the reins from two hands to one (half-bridge) (Chapter 10).
- Working with the reins, stick, and neck strap (Chapter 10).

- Riding without the reins (Chapter 9).
- Sitting the slow trot, bareback or without stir-rups (Chapter 9).
- Soft leg at the walk (Chapters 16 and 19).
- Fixed leg, bareback or in the saddle (Chapter 11).
- Full seat in ∩ position, full seat in Λ position, full seat forward, and half seat (Chapter 12).

• Half seat open position and half seat closed position at the trot (Chapter 13).

• Combing the reins at the walk (Chapter 17).

• Passive hand in moderate contact at the walk (Chapter 17).

• Posting trot (Chapter 14).

• Changing diagonals (Chapter 14).

• Turns and transitions from the walk (Chapters 8 and 16 through 19).

Appendix D

Resources

EDUCATIONAL GROUPS

American Riding Instructors' Association
www.ridinginstructor.com
aria@riding-instructor.com
28801 Trenton Court
Bonita Springs, FL 34134-3337
(239) 948-3232
Find a certified riding instructor in your discipline and your area

Centered Riding Inc.
www.centeredriding.org
P.O. Box 12377
Philadelphia, PA 19119
(215) 438-1286
Nonthreatening riding skills for all disciplines, and qualified instructors
Centered Riding, by Sally Swift, St. Martin's Press, 1985
Centered Riding 2: Further Exploration, by Sally Swift, Trafalgar Square, 2002
Videos are also available

http://groups.yahoo.com/group/ridingwithconfidence
A support group especially for riders and owners with fear problems, moderated by Gincy Self Bucklin.

www.whatyourhorsewants.com
Essays, photos, books, help for readers.

www.egroups.com
All kinds of equine discussion groups.

RELATIONSHIP TRAINING

Clicker Training

Web sites, e-groups, and contacts
www.theclickercenter.com
kurlanda@crisny.org
49 River Street, Suite 3
Waltham, MA 02453

www.clickertraining.com
(800) 47-CLICK
Clickryder@onelist.com

Introductory books and videos
Don't Shoot the Dog, by Karen Pryor, Bantam Doubleday Dell, revised edition, 1999
Clicker Training for Your Horse, by Alexandra Kurland, Ringpress Books, 2001
Clicking with Your Horse, by Alexandra Kurland, Sunshine Books, 2003
The Click That Teaches (video series), by Alexandra Kurland, Sunshine Books

Parelli Natural Horse-Man-Ship

Web sites, e-groups, and contacts
www.parelli.com
pnhusa@parelli.com
Parelli Natural Horse-Man-Ship
56 Talisman Drive, Suite 6
Pagosa Springs, CO 81147
(970) 731-9400

Introductory books and videos
Natural Horse-Man-Ship, by Pat Parelli, Lyons Press, 2003
There are numerous videos and other learning tools available. Call or visit the Parelli web site.

Round Pen Training
Web sites, e-groups, and contacts
www.johnlyons.com
generalinfo@johnlyons.com
John Lyons Symposiums
P.O. Box 479
Parachute, CO 81635
(970) 285-9797

Introductory books and videos
Lyons on Horses, by John Lyons, Doubleday, 1991
Many videos are available at tack stores and through the Lyons web site.

TTeam: Tellington-Jones Equine Awareness Method
Web sites, e-groups, and contacts
www.animalambassadors.com
info@tteam-ttouch.com
TTeam
P.O. Box 3793
Santa Fe, NM 87506
(800) 854-8326

Introductory books and videos
The Tellington-Jones Equine Awareness Method, by Linda Tellington-Jones and Ursula Bruns, Breakthrough Publications, 1988
TTouch of Magic (video), Linda Tellington-Jones, Animal Ambassadors

Index